P. C. Chang
and the
Universal Declaration
of Human Rights

PENNSYLVANIA STUDIES IN HUMAN RIGHTS

Bert B. Lockwood, Series Editor

A complete list of books in the series
is available from the publisher

P. C. Chang
and the Universal Declaration of Human Rights

Hans Ingvar Roth

PENN

UNIVERSITY OF PENNSYLVANIA PRESS

PHILADELPHIA

Copyright © 2016 Hans Ingvar Roth and Dialogos förlag.
Published originally in Swedish under the title:
*När Konfucius kom till FN: Peng Chun Chang och FN:s
förklaring om de mänskliga rättigheterna.*

English translation copyright © 2018
University of Pennsylvania Press

All rights reserved. Except for brief quotations used
for purposes of review or scholarly citation, none of this
book may be reproduced in any form by any means without
written permission from the publisher.

Published by
University of Pennsylvania Press
Philadelphia, Pennsylvania 19104-4112
www.pennpress.org

Printed in the United States of America
on acid-free paper

1 3 5 7 9 10 8 6 4 2

Library of Congress Cataloging-in-Publication Data
LC record available at https://lccn.loc.gov/2018007661

Hardcover ISBN: 9780812250565
Paperback ISBN: 9781512825541
Ebook ISBN: 9780812295474

For my children, Julia and William

CONTENTS

Preface ix

Introduction 1

PART I. LIFE AND TIMES

Chapter 1. Peng Chun Chang's Early Life in China
and Studies in the United States 9

Chapter 2. Raising a Family, Theatrical Activities,
University and Diplomatic Careers 45

Chapter 3. New York and the United Nations 82

Chapter 4. Chang's Multifaceted and Intense Life 100

PART II. THE IDEAS BEHIND THE UN DECLARATION

Chapter 5. Peng Chun Chang and
the UN Declaration on Human Rights 115

Chapter 6. Chang's Ideas About Ethics and Human Rights 141

Chapter 7. Chang, Malik, and Cassin 174

Chapter 8. Chang's Intercultural Ethics and the UN Declaration 188

Chapter 9. Chang's Triumphs, Defeats, and "Blind Spots" 225

Conclusion 239

Appendix 253

Notes 257

Bibliography 275

Index 285

Gallery follows page 144

PREFACE

A very special artwork adorns the platform walls of the subway station at Stockholm University. Look carefully and you will find in it all thirty articles of the United Nations Declaration of Human Rights. Strikingly, all are reproduced in uniform capitals and without spaces between words or periods at the end of the sentences. They include the right to life, liberty, and security of person; the right not to be held in slavery or subjected to torture; the right to freedom of thought, conscience, and religion; as well as the right to an adequate standard of living (Articles 3, 4, 5, 18, 25). The artwork also illustrates the central idea behind this important statement of rights. It is, above all, a matter of a whole, or an assembly, of human rights, none of which can be separated from each other. Each of its articles plays an important role in contributing to that unity which might be described as the declaration's overarching function: to promote respect for the inviolable dignity of every human being.

The artwork has its origins in an art project by the French-Belgian artist Françoise Schein titled *To Write the Human Rights*, or, alternatively, *TO INSCRIBE the Human Rights*. There is an equivalent mural in the Paris Metro station of Concorde. Realized by the organization INSCRIRE, this global art project is just one of many instances that illustrate the fact that the UN Declaration is one of the most widely disseminated and best-known documents in the world today. (I will use the expressions the UN Declaration, the Universal Declaration of Human Rights and the UDHR as equivalent in the following text.)

As a student, I used occasionally to stop and look at the articles, wondering about their meaning. Later on, I was fortunate enough to be able to work as a researcher and teacher with a specialist interest in human rights. Initially, I did not think about the individuals involved in drafting the declaration, with the exception of Eleanor Roosevelt, the distinguished chair of the Commission on Human Rights. My interest in this aspect has deepened over the years, however, with my attention becoming increasingly drawn toward the principal authors of this document. While the drafters of the founding documents of the United States are very well known persons all around the world, the drafters of the Universal Declaration of Human Rights are not so famous (with the exception of Eleanor Roosevelt).

One person has emerged as particularly fascinating with respect to the core elements of the Universal Declaration: the Chinese philosopher, pedagogue, and diplomat Peng Chun Chang. When I began this writing project several years ago, I discovered to my surprise that very little had been written about Peng Chun Chang and his contribution to the UN Declaration. Despite the appearance in recent years of growing numbers of articles on Chang and his involvement as coauthor of the declaration, the scholarship on him remains relatively slight and includes no critical study or biography dedicated to Chang specifically. The present book is an attempt to fill that gap.

A number of people have provided me with inspiration, information, and valuable input during the writing process. I wish to offer special thanks to Stanley (Yuan Feng), son of Peng Chun Chang, without whose kind assistance this book would not have been possible. I should also like to acknowledge the generosity of Habib Malik, Willard J. Peterson, Harald Runblom, Göran Möller, Sven Hartman, Göran Collste, Mary Ann Glendon, Torgny Wadensjö, Torbjörn Lodén, Ove Bring, Jenny White, Pierre Etienne Will, Yi-Ting Chen, Magnus von Platen, Hans Ruin, Alex Trotter, and Gunnar and Hongbin Henriksson. My thanks go also to the participants at the research seminars at CASS (Chinese Academy of Social Sciences), Peking University, Tsinghua University, and Nankai University, which I joined during a visit to China in March 2017, as well as to my audience at the Norwegian Centre for Human Rights in February 2017. I am also grateful for helpful discussions on the philosophy of human rights with James Griffin, David Miller, and John Tasioulas through the years. For granting me research leave I am grateful to Paul Levin and Stockholm University's Institute for Turkish Studies. I am also indebted to Lily R. Palladino, my editor at Penn Press who did an excellent job with my manuscript. Last but not least, a big thank you to Birgit och Sven Håkan Ohlssons Foundation for a translation subsidy, and to my translator, Stephen Donovan. To one and all, my deepest thanks!

Introduction

The significance of some historical figures becomes increasingly apparent with the passing of time. This book is about one such person: the Chinese diplomat and philosopher Peng Chun Chang (or Zhang Peng Chun) (1892–1957), who for many years remained largely unknown to the general public.[1]

Why write a book about a virtually unknown Chinese philosopher and diplomat who died, disappointed, in a small town outside New York City? By the time he came to spend his twilight years in modest circumstances in Nutley, New Jersey, Peng Chun Chang had seen many of his dreams and visions come to nothing. His life story, whose finest hour was a key role in determining the shape of one of history's most important documents, the Universal Declaration of Human Rights, ended in bitterness, frustration, and hardship.[2]

Peng Chun Chang lived his final years in the shadow of the Cold War and Senator Joseph McCarthy's vicious campaign against communists, supposed as well as actual. Toward the end of his life, Chang drifted out of view from the world, eventually dying disappointed and alone. A diary kept by his colleague Charles Malik, a Lebanese philosopher on the UN Commission on Human Rights, records that during a lunch in autumn 1949 Chang expressed particular bitterness toward the US, complaining about its almighty dollar, its business culture, and its materialism. It was, he declared, a country utterly lacking in morals.[3] Interestingly, Chang had expressed a similar attitude while an undergraduate in the United States, something which reveals that certain ideals were a more or less constant presence in his life. In one of his early articles, titled "Shakespeare in China" (1915), Chang observed: "I come from the East—from the land of the Religion of Responsibility. But the lands of the Religion of Greed are fast encroaching upon us."[4] In these remarks Chang referred to what he called the commercial lands of twentieth-century Europe and America. In an article from 1931 Chang also claimed: "A common task is facing all people of the world today. In the seething cauldron of greedy contentions, we must attempt to build, and build together, a paradise for poets out of the paradise for profiteers."[5]

By way of answer to the question of why we should care about Chang's life, the following study will start from the fact that he was the coauthor of one of the most important documents in history. His particular contribution to that document has also taken on a special relevance for the present moment as a consequence of China's current situation and probably future direction. Not least, a study of Chang's life and work promises to deepen our understanding of the contents and significance of the UN Declaration of Human Rights, a document in whose drafting he played so decisive a role.

Almost seventy-five years have passed since the declaration was adopted, and sixty since Peng Chun Chang's death. With the disappearance of the last generation to have lived through the Second World War, the Holocaust, and the aggression unleashed by the Axis powers, it has never been more important to keep our historical consciousness alive. The drafting of the UN Declaration of Human Rights was one of the earliest and most forceful global reactions to the Holocaust, fascism, and the horrors of the Second World War. In the space of just a few years—years that were characterized by growing ideological polarization—a group of individuals who had themselves experienced the cruelty of war succeeded in hammering out a broad bill of rights.

The issues on which Chang focused have also moved to center stage in recent public debate and world politics. When certain issues become increasingly urgent, politically and ethically, the result can be that particular ideas and responses take on an even greater significance than when they were first formulated. Multiculturalism, intercultural dialogue, globalization, the religious neutrality of states, and the boundaries of religious tolerance—all are claiming an ever more central role in contemporary public and academic debate. And Chang was intensely engaged with these questions. Indeed, pluralistic tolerance was one of his guiding concepts, especially in connection with his writing of the UN Declaration. He also emphasized that human rights are important not only for the regulation of the relationship between the state and its citizens, they are also important for interpersonal relations in social settings such as the family, the school, and the local neighborhood. This view has also become more widespread in recent ethical debates.[6] Further, Chang stressed the limits of law and the limits of coercion, complaints, and punishment in fulfilling the respect for human rights more generally. He also wanted to include positive measures, such as educational efforts. In other words, it is hardly an exaggeration to say that in political-theoretical debates, Chang has once again become our contemporary.

Closer examination of Chang's ideological interventions in connection with the drafting of the UN Declaration reveals that his focus was on the key issues, including the declaration's function and nature, its justification and realization, and its principal articles, notably Article 1. Chang was one of the authors who bore perhaps the greatest responsibility for what we now consider the most significant characteristics of the declaration, especially when the latter is compared with earlier bills of rights. These include the declaration's claims to religious neutrality and universalism as well as its focus on the individual and its ambition to be an instrument for the advancement of humanity's moral maturity or stature. The British writer and diplomat Brian Urquhart has aptly claimed that Chang was the one among the key drafters who gave the strongest sense of universalism to the work with the Universal Declaration.[7] The Universal Declaration has been criticized (according to some, unfairly) for its Western orientation. However, Chang did much to make the document all-inclusive and, hence, contributed to its global legitimacy.[8] Pivotal in this process was Chang's intercultural perspective on ethics, his emphasis on religious neutrality, and his ability to reach constructive compromises.

The Chinese philosopher Confucius (551–479 BC), who interested Chang greatly, is currently enjoying a renaissance in China, where his philosophy is often invoked in support of the political order. Chang, however, tried to reconcile and support human rights thinking through references to Confucian thought, such as the individual's duties to one's society, welfare rights, the emphasis on moral education, and the concept of sympathy for others. Chang also interpreted Confucius as a philosopher who did not engage in metaphysical queries. According to Chang, Confucius was more interested in the concrete world that we live in and in ethical questions that concern with our daily challenges. Chang also stated that Confucius taught that an ideal government was founded not on laws primarily but on ideals of personal conduct.[9] This principle of government by "prestige," or virtue, would later be an important theme in Chang's writings and statements in the UN context. Several themes that were pivotal for Confucian ethics would also influence the UN Declaration of Human Rights through the work of P. C. Chang. One could, for example, mention the strong emphasis upon education for the fulfilment of central moral principles, such as human rights, and the creed to act in a spirit of brotherhood. Chang also stated that stress should be laid upon the human aspect of human rights. A human being had to be constantly conscious of other men in whose society he lived.

Now an ever-growing superpower that has endorsed globalization, China also suffers from human rights failings and restrictions to fundamental freedoms such as freedom of speech. As one of China's first pioneers in human rights on the world stage, the importance of Peng Chun Chang will undoubtedly become more widely acknowledged, not least in Chinese history books. In the Chinese context too, then, Chang has once again become our contemporary.

Chang's life was fascinating and dramatic. A true cosmopolitan, he was at home in several cultures. He experienced firsthand some of the tensest and most violent phases of twentieth-century world history, including the Second World War, even as China itself underwent major social transformation, civil war, and political revolution.

That Chang was an anxious globetrotter will be emphasized in this study. He shuttled between continents and countries, seeking to understand their cultural similarities and differences. Chang also saw it as his mission to disseminate not only knowledge of China to the rest of the world but also ideas from the West to China. During his lifetime he devoted himself to a startling range of activities. Before beginning his career as a diplomat in China, Chile, Turkey, and at the UN, he worked variously as teacher, school principal, professor, playwright, and theater director. Toward the end of his UN career, he became a "diplomatic maverick," acting with a high degree of independence when his regime in China was on the brink of ruin, an attitude that became even more pronounced when the regime relocated to Formosa (Taiwan).

A study of Chang and his contributions to the UN Declaration is especially timely at a moment that is witnessing the rise of brutality on an almost unprecedented scale. With ideological polarization, religious and ethnic discrimination and crass power politics on the rise, there is a particular urgency in turning the spotlight back onto that engaged and talented group of individuals who assumed primary responsibility for the UN Declaration and who fought stubbornly to ensure that the brutality of fascism and the Second World War would never be repeated. The principal members were Eleanor Roosevelt, René Cassin, Charles Malik, John Humphrey, Hernán Santa Cruz, Hansa Mehta, and—a central figure in the group—Peng Chun Chang.

A colleague of Chang's in the writing group, the Lebanese philosopher Charles Malik, once remarked that it would be an interesting project to identify all of the fundamental positions that underpinned Chang's comments on the UN Declaration. Chang was not a communist, according to Malik, and at the time the UN Declaration was being drafted, Mao Zedong had not yet assumed supreme control of China. Malik hypothesized that Chang's ideas instead originated primarily in classical Chinese traditions which were independent of Western Marxism.[10]

Another of Peng Chun Chang's colleagues, John Humphrey, a Canadian law professor and the secretary of the writing group, made the following statement about Chang during a long-haul flight from Chile to Panama in March 1951: "I sat next to P. C. Chang on the plane. He told me the story of his life and also of the life of his elder brother, who died in China about a month ago. It is a fascinating story indeed and will someday, I hope, be the subject of a book."[11] I offer the following study as fulfillment of Humphrey's wish, sixty-five years after he and Chang took that flight from Chile to Panama.

A number of themes running through Chang's life culminated very visibly in his work on the UN Declaration. Information provided by his son Stanley has allowed me to shed new light on Chang's interactions with several of his coauthors as well as on his position within both the UN and the Chinese delegation. What is more, Stanley's accounts of his father's complicated and dramatic life, political engagements, and wide range of interests have made possible a new understanding of Peng Chun Chang's life and work and his unique contribution to the UN Declaration.

While in several respects distinctly nationalistic, Chang was deeply cosmopolitan, a trait that emerges very clearly in his son's recollections. For all his emphasis upon universalism and pluralism during the writing of the UN Declaration, he was also clearly keen that the document be influenced by Chinese philosophical traditions. This approach evidently created tensions with other delegates in the writing group. The way that Chang prepared for and conducted himself in UN debates likewise followed a pattern that was discernable in many other aspects of his life, such as his habit of drawing up systematic and near-comprehensive inventories of possible opinions and counterarguments before sitting down to formulate his own view. His repeated references in UN discussions to humanity's dual nature—part benign and empathetic, part brutal, malign, and destructive—can perhaps even be seen as a reflection of his own existential doubts, which are amply documented in Stanley's account of his father. Chang's fondness for metaphors and figurative language was also a recurrent feature of his writing and commentaries.

Biographers of human rights advocates from the past are often guilty of a tendency toward hagiography. In the literature on the UN Declaration, this tendency is further reinforced by the tacit assumption that so perfect a document must have been authored by almost perfect individuals. Such is the case with several of the more distinguished monographs about the authors of the UN Declaration, such as Mary Ann Glendon's *A World Made New*, which mainly focuses on Eleanor Roosevelt's and Charles Malik's importance for the declaration, or Jay Winters and Antoine Prost's biography of René Cassin, *René Cassin and Human Rights*.[12] My hope is that the following study can offer the most truthful and nuanced account possible of an extraordinarily fascinating life without indulging in embellishment or undue faultfinding.

PART I

LIFE AND TIMES

CHAPTER 1

Peng Chun Chang's Early Life in China and Studies in the United States

Peng Chun Chang (1892–1957), or Zhong-Shu as he often called himself, grew up during a dramatic era of China's history. He was part of a special generation that experienced the rule of the last emperor, the foundation of the new republic in 1912, and, starting in 1949, Communist rule under Mao Zedong. Other members of his generational cohort included Chiang Kai-shek (1887–1975), long-time president of the Republic of China, and Mao Zedong (1893–1976) himself, the first leader of the People's Republic of China. Another famous member of this special generation was the philosopher and diplomat Hu Shi (1891–1962), who was an advocate of Chinese liberalism and language reform. Both Chang and Shi belonged to an exceptional generation of men who were schooled both in Confucian/Asian and Western traditions. As the historian Diana Lary has stated, they were multilingual, often bicultural. Many of them were committed both to China's land and culture and to "Western" scientific method and liberal traditions.[1]

This generation experienced many dramatic events, including the Boxer Rebellion (1898–1901) and the brutal reprisals that it provoked from Japan and the Western states concerned. Unlike the earlier Taiping Rebellion (1850–1864), the Boxer Rebellion was not directed against the imperial dynasty; indeed, in its final phases, it enjoyed the support of the regime. Instead, its aggression was aimed at foreign interests, whether commercial, military, or religious in nature. The rebellion, which originated in the disaster-hit Shandong Province, was led by a secret society called the Fists of Righteous Harmony, which believed that practice of a particular martial art could make one invulnerable to bullets.[2] Other dramatic developments included the republican Xinhai Revolution of 1911, the First World War, wars with Japan during the 1930s and 1940s, the Second World War, and the civil war that followed the end of the Second World War. Collectively, these factors meant that the lives of the members of this generation were profoundly shaped by war, conflict, and radical political change. During their lives, Chinese society also underwent modernization, urbanization, steady population growth, social reform, and cultural transition.[3]

Chang and his peers lived in an era of political upheaval during which the masses increasingly sought to challenge the old imperial order. Calls to introduce a republic and modernize China, not least its educational system, were heard increasingly loudly, especially after the country suffered a series of military defeats and interventions by foreign powers. The Manchu Qing dynasty, which had held power in China since 1644, had been visibly weakened by the two Opium Wars, the first in 1839–1843 and the second in 1856–1860. Defeated twice, China was forced to accept the opium trade and to grant special trade privileges to France and Britain. China's defeat in the Sino-Japanese War of 1894–1895 also contributed to a sense of vulnerability and an urge to modernize the country. The powers interested in dominating China—especially Japan, Great Britain, France, and Russia—also introduced the idea of spheres of influence in 1898 in order to make a partition of the whole country.

The Qing Dynasty and Its Education System

During the first hundred years of the Qing dynasty, China developed into a rich country that was greatly admired in the rest of the world, particularly Europe. And yet, for the remainder of the nineteenth century it became a welcome El Dorado for merchants and missionaries, mostly from Europe and the United States. China also came to be viewed in many quarters as "the sick man of Asia." The European colonial powers arrogated to themselves so-called extraterritorial rights (rights and laws of their own that had judicial force beyond their own borders) that curtailed the authority of the Chinese state and its control of several key ports. The First Sino-Japanese War of 1894–1895 also resulted in a major loss of prestige for the Qing dynasty. The superannuated Chinese army showed itself in combat to be inferior to the modernized Japanese army. The status of Manchuria was to become a highly fraught issue for China and Japan, particularly following the 1905 Convention of Peking, by which China was forced to accept that Russia would cede authority over Manchuria to Japan. The convention also resulted in Japan acquiring control over Guangdong Province, Korea, and Taiwan.[4] The Meiji Restoration in Japan, which began in 1868, had radically increased the political and economic strength of Japan through industrialization, modernization, educational reform, and centralization of the state.[5]

The state of political crisis in China at the turn of the twentieth century prompted educationalists and politicians to scrutinize the Chinese education system of the imperial period, a system that had consisted primarily of recitation of classical works of Chinese literature under the supervision of a teacher. The civil service's meritocratic recruitment system likewise was centered on the knowledge of ancient Chinese texts, such as the writings of Confucius. Numerous observers argued that the secondary and tertiary education systems needed to be reformed in order to meet the economic, military, and cultural challenges of a new era. This was especially true of China's military expertise, which had shown itself to be quite inadequate in confrontations with Japan and the Western powers. The fact that university-level study was focused on law and civil administration was also deemed problematic in view of the pressing need for scientific and technological proficiency.

Many in China also regarded several of the overarching aims of primary and secondary schooling as obsolete. During the final years of the imperial system, the goals of school instruction had been described as loyalty to the emperor, respect for Confucius, public spirit or patriotism, martial courage, and a practical and technical disposition. When the republic was declared in 1912, these objectives were replaced with moral training, technical skills, instruction in "military citizenship," and aesthetic orientation. In 1918, the goal of inculcating a spirit of popular democracy was added to the list.[6] At the same time, no change was made to the nationalist framework, according to which school was regarded as an important instrument for the creation of a national identity. The American Scout movement subsequently became a highly valued "import" and inspiration for civics instruction in society at large.

By the end of the nineteenth century, however, even the imperial regime had begun to try to develop a more socially relevant education system that was oriented toward the needs of the army and navy, an educational ambition that grew after the turn of the century to include other areas. Greater resources were dedicated to subjects such as science, agronomy, and engineering. Before its abolition in 1905, the imperial civil service examination system also began to place greater emphasis on science than had been the case in the previous century, when it had principally focused on the humanities and classical education.[7]

Looking back on these developments in the 1950s, Peng Chun Chang reflected that the old teaching forms of the imperial system, namely recitation of classical texts, were not entirely without merit. The overarching aim of this system of education had been to develop the ability to memorize and absorb Chinese wisdom and knowledge by using both voice and hearing. Recollection of a text became, as it were, incorporated into one's own sound-memory bank. When someone schooled in the old way tried to recall a passage from a work of Chinese philosophy, Chang claimed, an observer would first hear them make a faint humming sound before beginning to recite the text. Their recall was also often perfect.[8]

Childhood and Early Education

What were Chang's early years like? Peng Chun Chang (or Chung Shu / Zhong Shu) was born in 1892 in Tianjin (formerly Tientsin), an important coastal town in northeast China. He had one brother and three sisters. However, only one of the sisters, Zhuchun, survived, and so Chang grew up with an older brother and an older sister. His sister went on to marry the famous revolutionary and educator Ma Qianli, who worked closely with Chang's older brother, Poling, in his Nankai school.[9] Stanley Chang was unable to say what happened to the sister and where she lived in China: "My father's sister was called 'Third Aunt' by those of us in the family, so she was older than the two brothers. I don't know what happened to her in the later years of her life because I left China in 1940."

Chang's family came originally from Shandong Province, which had also been Confucius's home province. They supported themselves by trading on the large canal that connected Hangzhou and Beijing from south to north, gradually becoming wealthy and moving to the city of Tientsin. Chang's grandfather had a passionate interest in literature and, despite his financial success, regarded his business career as a compromise in life. Chang's father, Jiu-an Zhang Yun Zao, 1834–1909), loved music, especially the flute, riding, and archery and spent much of the family fortune on his leisure interests. Jiu-an was forty-nine years old when Chang was born, a fact reflected in the child's nickname, Number Nine. (In China, birthdays ending in nine, such as forty-nine or fifty-nine, are often celebrated in place of an even anniversary, the concern being that the person in question might not live for another year.) In the United States, Peng Chun Chang would often be called P. C. by his friends.

Because Jiu-an deeply regretted his life choices, he imposed strict discipline upon his children and impressed upon them the value of study. Having himself failed to pass the imperial examination, he was insistent that his own children would be educationally successful. In this respect, it can be said that the imperial examination system contributed in different ways to disseminating a culture of learning in China: partly by selecting those who would go on to enter the civil service, partly by imparting knowledge about the system and a passion for it further afield, including among those who had themselves not passed the examination.[10]

Chang's older brother, Poling (Shouchun), born 1876, was subjected to corporal discipline by his father as a spur to study. By the time Chang was born, however, Jiu-an had moderated his approach to parenting, with the result that the younger son was given very different treatment than his brother. One important legacy that Chang received from his father was music. As a child, he accompanied his father to several opera performances. Chang's mother (Yang Shi, 1850–1922) is an invisible figure in his "history writing." Stanley Chang remembered Peng Chun Chang talking on some occasions about his father but never about his mother. The fact that Chang never discussed his mother's life with his own son is very striking and raised questions about his childhood. Instead, the most important figure for Chang was Poling, a powerful personality who dominated Chang's life virtually from cradle to grave. Poling's nickname was Number Five, because he was considered the fifth child. According to Stanley, Poling was also a nickname that his uncle had been given. In Chinese tradition, children are customarily given two nicknames.[11]

Poling was sixteen years Chang's senior and thus became a kind of a father figure to him after the death of their father in 1909. Poling had evidently inherited his father's severe attitude toward child-raising and began regularly thrashing Chang, something that was to affect his life profoundly. Despite his severe parenting style and the large age difference, Poling influenced Chang's life in several regards, positive as well as negative, and inspired him in his studies and choice of career. According to Stanley Chang, it seemed as though his father perpetually sought his brother's approval and in certain situations was highly dependent upon his brother's advice on different matters. The problematic nature of Chang's relationship with his brother was to express itself in different ways, among them Chang's continual traveling.

Chang's deep and lifelong interest in art, theater, literature, music, philosophy, diplomacy, and politics may even have been a way for him to break loose from his older brother, rather than merely emulating Poling's interests in school, sport, and education in a wider sense. Involvement in his many other activities was likely a way for Chang to dispel any suspicions that he might be clinging to his elder brother's coattails.[12] However, it is obvious that Chang had a genuine interest in many fields and activities in which he also excelled.

The Nankai Schools

Poling's interest in educational issues was to affect Chang visibly throughout his life. In 1904, Chang entered the Nankai School, which his brother had been involved in establishing and subsequently administered. After a while there were several Nankai schools. In addition to the school in Tientsin there was also a school in Chunking. After 1919 it was also the Nankai University in Tientsin. Among his classmates was Mei Yiqi (1889–1962), who later became a famous educator in China. (He became the president of Tsinghua University in 1931, and during the years of the Second Sino-Japanese War, he was president of South West United University in Kunming.) Chang concluded his school years in China at Zhili (Chihli) provincial college in 1910.

Together with the educationalist Yan Xin, Poling had founded Nankai School in 1904 with the help of donations during a climate of rising discontent with China's old educational system and the political situation.[13] The original cohort of students consisted primarily of the children of friends, neighbors, and relatives. The school was located on the south side of Tientsin in an area known as Nan-Kai ("the open space in the south"). Thereafter it expanded in its number of buildings, students, and levels, and in 1919, as was mentioned before, a university under Poling's direction was established.[14] In 2017, Nankai University consists of two campuses—the older one in the city of Tianjin (Tientsin) and a newer one in a suburb. In a speech given in 1956, Chang recalled his early experiences of the school:

> The school (which started in 1904) began with an enrolment of 73 students. It carried on its work in the courtyard of a private resi-

dence and had at its disposal only three large rooms for classrooms, one small room for the use of teachers, and a hall for schools assemblies. It would be natural to ask how so humble an establishment could have been the starting place for any story worth relating. Yet the growth of this institution in the first twenty-five years of its life is perhaps one of the most phenomenal chapters in educational history anywhere. By the beginning of the second year, the school enrolment had swelled to burst the confines of the old courtyard. Something had to be done, and quickly, to find new quarters. After persistent searching and pleading, a piece of land was located; and it was donated to the school. It was situated to the south of the city of Tientsin in an area called "Nan-Kai," meaning "South Open-Space." New buildings were speedily erected. And we moved into our new compound in 1907. The name of the school was changed to "Private Nankai Middle School." From that day on, the name "Nankai" became increasingly famous, eventually reaching far and wide.[15]

In addition to their emphasis on sport, art, and theater, the Nankai Schools were permeated by the creed of strict discipline, healthy living, and a strong spirit of nationalism. Poling had served in the navy, where he had been trained by English officers. His experiences there had led him to become increasingly involved in the struggle for Chinese independence.

In the late 1800s, Poling witnessed an event in the port of Weihaiwei that acquired a profoundly symbolic importance for him. He watched as the Japanese flag was lowered to signal the transfer of authority over the port to China. The Chinese flag was raised, but only for a moment before the British flag was raised—and left flying. After this painful and humiliating experience, Poling resigned his commission in the navy and at the age of twenty-three dedicated his life to sport and teaching.[16]

A characteristic saying of Poling's was that a good teacher must also be a good athlete. As he saw it, the dire state of affairs that the schools needed to remedy comprised: (1) physical weakness and poor health; (2) superstition and ignorance; (3) economic poverty; (4) insufficient community spirit; and (5) egoism. When it came to childrearing, Poling's watchwords were "ability" and "social responsibility."[17]

Poling was also a driving force with regard to China's participation at an early stage in the Olympic Games. Poling's efforts to promote sport in China in the 1900s were publicly acknowledged when China hosted the Olympics in 2008. In a book published to coincide with the games, Poling was described as the father of Chinese Olympic sport by Jacques Rogge, then president of the International Olympic Committee. Poling's contributions to sport have also greatly enhanced the prestige of the Chang family name in China today.[18] While Poling is fairly well known in those circles in Chinese society who are familiar with Nankai, his younger brother Peng Chun is not. The same is clearly also true in the Chinese university world.

Although the old school system was not entirely without merits—such as the forms for reciting the classics mentioned by Chang—it became increasingly apparent with the passage of time that a more modern educational system was required. It was in the shadow of these circumstances that Poling became involved in creating a new educational model. Initially influenced by the Japanese educational system, he became increasingly inspired by American educational ideas after making a study visit in 1908–1909 to the United States, where he visited seats of learning such as Princeton and Harvard Universities and Wellesley College. Phillips Academy in Andover, Massachusetts, proved a particularly strong source of inspiration by virtue of its emphasis upon the notion that students and the entire staff should collectively form a kind of educational family.

The Nankai School system was on several accounts a runaway success during the republic, with Chang's brother playing a decisive role. According to Chang, the rapid expansion of this school system was probably one of the most astonishing occurrences ever to take place in the history of secondary education in China. From this point on, Chang himself became highly involved in helping his brother to expand and run the Nankai Schools. As mentioned earlier, further expansion resulted in the creation of a university—Nankai University—which in 1919 opened its doors to both female and male students. At first, the university was situated near the Nankai Schools, but with time it became necessary to find new premises. Land was purchased twenty kilometers south of Nankai in an area known as Pai-Li-Tai, and the university relocated there in 1922. The university nevertheless retained the old name Nankai since it had become nationally famous.[19] On Peng Chun Chang's advice, another school was founded in Chungking in 1935, something we will return to later. After Poling demonstrated his loyalty toward Chiang Kai-shek, the leader of the republic, during the war, Nankai University was upgraded to the status of a nationally supported university in 1945. Poling served as its chancellor from 1919 to 1948.

Pupils and students from the Nankai Schools and University went on to develop a strong identity, forming, among other things, alumni associations in different cities around the world. Stanley recalled that when he and his siblings had visited events arranged by the Nankai Association in California, they had been treated almost as royalty by virtue of their belonging to the Chang family. Stanley Chang told the following story as an illustration: "When my sister Ruth went to China in the mid-1980s, she was warmly embraced, almost as a sister, by Mrs Zhou Enlai (Deng Yingchao), who showed her around. Zhou Enlai had attended the Nankai School when my father taught there, and people assumed that he had been a pupil of my father's. According to my father, however, Zhou Enlai had never been one of his pupils or students but had merely occasionally listened to some of his lectures." However, Zhou assisted Peng Chun Chang in his drama program at Nankai and was influenced by Chang's introduction of Western plays in China.[20] The above story from Stanley provides revealing glimpses of how Peng Chun Chang and his family were regarded in certain Communist circles in China in the 1980s. Although Chang had represented the republic and voiced his support for political ideals far removed from those of the Communist regime, there was nonetheless a positive aura around the Chang family in consequence of their creation of the Nankai Schools and Nankai University. This reputation was undoubtedly helped by the fact that the beloved politician Zhou Enlai (1898–1976) attended them both the Nankai school and the university. Today, Nankai University is also one of China's most reputable, according to Stanley Chang. Advertising for the university also makes much of its having been Zhou's alma mater. Another famous alumnus of Nankai is Sun Yu (1900–1990), one of China's most famous film directors. Wen Jiaboa, the prime minister from 2000 to 2012, also attended the Nankai School.[21]

Since the founding of the Centre for the Study of Human Rights Studies at Nankai University in 2005, Peng Chun Chang's name has become more recognized in the university, which commissioned a statue of him. The unveiling ceremony of the statue took place during the summer of 2017 (8 June) at the new campus of the Nankai University (Jinnan). Stanley Chang's account contains the fascinating detail that Nankai University was one of a rather small number of universities permitted to keep its name after Mao Zedong took power; another was Sun Yat-sen University, founded in Canton in the early 1920s.[22] Stanley's theory is that Nankai University was allowed to keep its name because Zhou Enlai was a former student. According to

Stanley, Nankai University was the national, with a capital *N*, university when it was founded, something that Zhou Enlai would no doubt have relayed to Mao if the latter was not already aware of it.

Chang's daughter Ruth recalls that Zhou Enlai acted as a so-called student secretary to her father, together with two other students, who would also go on to have brilliant careers: Zheng Taoru and Duan Maolan.²³ Another of Zhou Enlai's college friends was K. C. Wu, who became mayor of Shanghai in the 1940s. Zhou Enlai was also very active in the Nankai School's theater group, Chang's pet interest. In 1917, Zhou Enlai graduated with distinction from the Nankai School.

Zhou Enlai was for several decades Mao Zedong's right-hand man. He is widely regarded as a deeply educated and diplomatic man who exerted a moderating influence on Mao. Trained in classical Chinese philosophy, he studied in Tientsin and at the Nankai School between 1913 and 1917 and at Nankai University as well as spending time at schools and universities in Japan and France. Zhou Enlai participated in Nankai extracurricular dramatic and debating activities and was inspired by Poling's motto for the school—the principles of *gong*, the commitment to sacrifice oneself for public interests, and *neng*, the ability to fulfil this commitment. When Peng Chun Chang returned to Nankai in 1916 after his studies at Clark University, Zhou assisted him in directing both Chinese and Western plays.²⁴ After the Communist take-over at the beginning of the 1950s, Zhou protected Poling because Poling was closely associated with the Kuomintang regime. When Chang Poling died in 1951, Zhou Enlai flew to Tientsin to pay his respects. In China, Poling was viewed as an important figure, as evinced by the way that both nationalists and, at times, Communists sought to claim him as one of their own.²⁵

For Chang and his family, Nankai was also a crucial shaping force in their lives. It says much about how Chang viewed the Nankai Schools that as late as 1956, a year before his death, he gave a lecture on their origins at an alumni meeting hosted by New York's China Institute.²⁶ In the lecture, Chang also underscored his brother's very great importance for Nankai. In nostalgic but also insightful fashion, Chang described his student years in the first Nankai School as a period that fostered self-confidence and faith in the future.²⁷ As Stanley Chang explained:

> Nankai and my father were very closely intertwined. When in the 1920s my father returned to China from his studies in the United

States in order to begin teaching, he wanted to break away from his brother Poling and Nankai. He therefore accepted a new job as dean at a rival university—Tsinghua. That's what he told me, at least. But in the end, we still wound up at the Nankai campus in Tientsin in 1927, so clearly he had chosen to return to his alma mater to teach. On the subject of building the Nankai School in Chungking (Chongqing), my father said that he had persuaded Uncle Poling to open a new school in the city. The reason he gave was that he expected China to go to war with Japan imminently and so the best option was to open a school far inland. Later, he was proud of having predicted correctly. Uncle Poling also happened to be in Chungking, away from Tientsin, during the Japanese bombing raids of 1937, leaving my father as his representative at Nankai University. For this reason my father found himself in grave danger and, when the Japanese invaded, he was forced to flee from Tientsin in the middle of the night dressed as a woman.

The Boxer Indemnity Reparation Fund and Chang's First Period of Study in the United States

After the Boxer Rebellion ended in 1901, the European powers and Japan demanded economic compensation from China on the grounds that their property and interests in China had been specially targeted. The United States instead chose to request that compensation take the form of a grant-giving foundation for talented Chinese students who wished to study at American universities, something that would help promote the United States' reputation in China.[28] The fund that gave scholarships between 1909 and 1929 included more than 1300 students from China. Chang passed the selection test and received a scholarship from the American Boxer Indemnity Reparation Fund and a place at Clark University, a renowned university located in Worcester, Massachusetts. In 1913, after three years' study, Chang received his bachelor's degree in pedagogy and philosophy.

Founded in 1887, Clark University was one of the first graduate colleges in the United States to offer master's degrees in pedagogy and psychology. In 1900, the university also started to confer doctoral degrees on both men and women. The university's first president, G. Stanley Hall, was also a distinguished professor of psychology and pedagogy who established the American Psychological Association. Sigmund Freud's only lecture series in the United States, at which he introduced psychoanalysis to the American public, was given at Clark University in 1909. The university was well known for having an ethnically diverse student body, including many students from Japan, as well as for its socially progressive profile.

That Chang formed part of an extraordinary cohort of Chinese scholarship students was to become clear in hindsight. Perhaps the most famous of his pals in the group was Hu Shi. After completing his studies, Hu Shi went on to become one of China's most liberal philosophers and literary historians; like Chang, he was powerfully inspired by the ideas of the American philosopher and educationalist John Dewey. A graduate of Cornell and Columbia, Hu Shi emerged as a leading spokesperson for China's New Culture Movement, which sought in various ways to liberalize Chinese society and institute language reform.[29] Hu Shi and Peng Chun Chang were holders of scholarships from the Boxer Indemnity Scholarship Programme, and they came to the United States on the same ship as young students. Both of them endorsed the proposal from the New Culture Movement to replace the difficult classical language (*guwen*) with a written form of the oral vernacular language (*baihua*).[30]

Other members of Chang's cohort, which arrived in the United States in 1910 (on the second boat), were Zhu Kezhen, subsequently a Harvard-educated meteorologist, and Zhao Yuanren (Y. R. Chao), also a future Harvard alumnus. Y. R. Chao (1892–1982) was a pioneering linguist whose textbooks are still used in university courses today. He went on to become a professor of oriental languages at the University of California, Berkeley. Chao also composed music that became widely known in China. He became Chang's best friend and was the only outsider to regularly visit him and his family during the last years of Chang's life. According to Stanley, his father described Chao as a genius. (Stanley also said that Chao once surprised his audience during a lecture by speaking English backward without a "flaw.") On the ranking list for scholarships to the United States, Chao was number two, and Chang, number ten. The scholarship program included many excellent scholars who went on to have successful careers, such as the Nobel laureate in physics Chen Ning Yang, the educator Kuo Ping-Wen, and the rocket scientist Tsien Hsue-shen. The educator Chen Heqin, who studied at Teachers College, Columbia University, through the Boxer Indemnity Fund between 1917 and 1918 would later be the first modern Chinese theoretician of early childhood education.³¹

Chang was, as was said before, part of a unique cohort that had been schooled in both the old Confucian ways and the educational traditions of the West. Several members of this cohort became multilingual and viewed the preservation of the core defining features of Chinese culture as an urgent task even as they sought to convey valuable insights gleaned from their experiences in the West, especially the achievements of modern science and the liberal political worldview.³² This cohort formed a network in which most of the scholarship recipients were acquainted with each other.

During his time at Clark University, Chang wrote prolifically, including for its newspaper the *Chinese Student Monthly*. There he published essays on Chinese nationalism and the effects of colonialism on the international legal system and China, essays that show him to have been deeply engaged with international politics and the political problems in China from an early stage.³³ These early works also reveal his close involvement in the problems of politics and national-identity formation in his native country. Later writings from Chang would show a pattern of connecting with important political problems of the day that specifically affected China and its identity in a volatile world.³⁴

In "National Ideals," Chang's first published essay, which won second prize in a lecture competition in Williamstown, Massachusetts, he discussed what he understood by real patriotism and the prerequisites for a democratic republic. The essay was undoubtedly inspired by political events in China, which included the overthrow of the imperial order and the creation of a new republic in 1912. In the essay, Chang set out his national ideals and his vision of a "healthy republic" in terms of patriotism, an unswerving and productive life, and a public morality capable of counteracting the selfishness and political conflicts of society. As regards patriotism, Chang did not consider citizenship of the world—or a world state—as realistic options; the focus must instead be on a nationalism capable both of counteracting narrow local interests in China and of utilizing the Chinese people's shared frames of cultural reference. A democratic republic, Chang argued, also presupposed an educated citizenry, a condition that was essential for being able to claim that the republic was government *by*, *of*, and *for* the people.³⁵ It is worth noting that by this point Chang was already meditating upon the meaning, potential, and desirability of a kind of global organization and global citizenship. As noted above, later in life Chang would play a part in defining the shape and direction of the UN and, with it, a way of thinking specific to citizens of the world.

In another article by Chang from 1912, titled "China's Real Situation" and also published in the *Chinese Student Monthly*, he reflected upon what he called the external and the internal problems of China. On the one hand, the Chinese Republic faced the challenge of confronting the colonial powers (Japan, France, Great Britain, Russia, Germany) and their ambitions to curtail China's independence and freedom. According to Chang, China was bound by protocols, conventions, treaties, and contracts that had annulled her powers as a free agent. On the other hand, the internal problems consisted of severe poverty in many provinces. In addition to these internal problems, China also had to confront serious problems such as famine and flood. Chang also stressed that the Manchu dynasty had not left a well-organized department of administration. For example, there had not been any definite, uniform system of taxation in China. A common currency and a well-functioning educational system were also lacking, as well as a developed railroad system. Additionally, the country had no dialect in common, and its written language was so hard to learn that the common people were unable to read an ordinary newspaper. A simplification of the written language was urgently needed. At the end of the article, Chang stressed that the group to which he belonged—the chosen few who had been privileged to receive a university education overseas—had an important duty to help the self-sacrificing populace at home to modernize China and fulfill the goal of making China an independent, prosperous, and free country.[36] He was to follow this precedent himself when, after completing his studies in the United States, he returned to China and worked intensively to modernize Chinese society through education.

In another early essay, published in 1913, "A Brief Survey of Extraterritoriality, or Consular Jurisdiction in Non-Christian Lands," Chang discussed the phenomenon of having different laws for foreign citizens and natives. In this article, Chang presented a historical overview of how individual-based law emerged as an entity distinct from simple territorial legislation, focusing in particular on conditions in China and in Muslim countries. In the latter, such as Ottoman Turkey, extraterritoriality was based on custom and early treaties. These traditions, treaties, and practices would later on serve as "role models" for the treaties and extraterritorial laws that were established in the Far East.[37] Chang's hope in this essay was that the advent of the new Chinese republic in 1912 would steadily eliminate the rights and influence of foreign powers in China. In the case of states in which religion and legislation were closely intertwined, as with Muslim states, Chang argued that there were grounds—from both perspectives—for having separate legislative codes.[38] From the perspective of the Western countries, there was also the concern that the citizens of their countries would not be treated in courts in a safe and fair manner according to their legal principles if no extraterritorial laws existed.[39]

Chang was very active in various student organizations during his time at Clark, including associations for Christian Chinese students and the Congregational Church of China. This kind of engagement in the college environment was typical for many of the students in the Boxer Indemnity Scholarship Programme. Chang also attended Christian student conferences during his tenure as secretary of the Chinese Students' Christian Association, even giving an address to the conference of the association, a large convention held in Missouri in 1914. He organized bible classes at various American universities.[40] The Christian circles in which he moved at this time were evangelical and heavily involved in missionary work overseas, particularly in China. During this time, Chang also published three confessional essays on Christianity.[41]

Where did this Christian involvement spring from? Poling had become a Christian a few years previously as a result of his contact with the YMCA and other organizations. In seeking to account for Chang's own interest in religion, it is easy to speculate about his brother's influence. In 1908, Poling visited the United States and Britain for the first time and pursued studies at several educational institutions. During these visits he also came into contact with a number of Christian networks and, upon returning home to China in 1909, chose to be baptized; he was then thirty-three years old.

The Americans had hoped that their scholarship program, among other things, would result in the Chinese students becoming drawn into the Christian culture of the United States. In the 1920s, '30s, and '40s, however, and in contrast to his brother, Chang's interest in Christianity appears to have flagged, something we will return to in due course. Poling's Christian faith seems not to have affected the character or image of his schools, which were established with the intention of being a nonconfessional alternative to the Chinese mission schools. In the 1910s, P. C. Chang's intellectual environment in the 1910s was deeply influenced by the efforts of Christian missionaries to allow Christianity to take root in China on the country's own terms and by means of the Chinese themselves.[42]

In the republic's early years, religious freedom also increased in China, with thousands of missionaries from different societies travelling around the country. Chang's view was that only by taking indigenous traditions as its starting point could Christianity acquire real momentum and influence in Chinese society. He opposed the notion that Christianity was, as a religion, alien to China. The Good News should be spread, in other words, by utilizing what was best in the Chinese traditions. In this way, Christianity would realize, rather than destroy, China's distinct identity. At this time Chang was convinced that spreading Christianity throughout Chinese society could remedy many of the fundamental problems with which China was wrestling, including widespread egoism and an inadequate sense of social community.[43]

This question of how best to achieve a reasonable balance between a culture's unique characteristics and cultural influences from without was to become a continual theme of Chang's writing. Chang addressed this subject in the contexts of religion, ethics, social life, politics, science, technology, theater, and art more generally. He engaged with the issue at an early stage, as can be seen from the essays that he published in student newspapers during his time in the United States. In an early article titled "China's Desire to Retain the Best in Her Own Tradition" and published in 1914, Chang identified the great challenge facing China as one of how to steer between the Scylla of narrow-minded self-sufficiency, and the Charybdis of superficial copying of other traditions and neglect of that in Chinese traditions which deserved preservation.

When describing this kind of hasty cultural emulation, Chang was fond of using the metaphor of bad digestion that resulted from trying to ingest as much as possible of a foreign diet.[44] This metaphor was to recur repeatedly in later life when he reflected on and criticized different cultural influences. Japan's use of technology and science, for example, seemed to Chang a sign of how cultural imports from the West could become degenerate. Chang argued that Japan's rapid but superficial absorption of modern technology and science could well be described as a nightmare caused by bad digestion, especially with reference to the use of technology in the military sphere. Chang and others in his generational cohort maintained an attitude about the West that was sometimes characterized by an ambivalence toward what was culturally indigenous vis-à-vis what would need to be imported.

As well as being highly active in Christian student groups at Clark University, Chang was also the head of the debate club at the university. This club took home victories in various competitions on the American university circuit and provided Chang with valuable training in rhetorical and argumentative techniques, skills that he would later put to good use in his career, particularly in various UN contexts. According to his son Stanley, Chang was very proud of his argumentative prowess. Stanley relates that his father knew the best way to prepare for a highly charged debate. Having thoroughly prepared himself on a particular subject, read up on and made an inventory of possible arguments and counterarguments, and, finally, participated in the debate itself, he would move quickly to studying a new subject area. Chang was ever impatient to satisfy his boundless curiosity for unresearched fields.

Chang often took great pains to identify conceptual distinctions and clarifying principles, regardless of the subject he was occupied with. Whether writing confessional articles, scientific papers, essays on poetry, theater, or art, or political opinions, Chang sought, usually successfully, to adhere to his ideals of clarity, simplicity, thoroughness, and cogency. According to Stanley, he brought this same attitude and basic strategy to an array of projects. Be it for an academic article, a political opinion, an artistic project, or a hobby (such as his record collecting), Chang attacked issues as if he were writing a doctoral dissertation. His colleague on the UN Commission on Human Rights, the Canadian law professor John P. Humphrey, recorded the following observation about Chang's interest in music and record collecting in his diary entry for 1 November 1950: "I took P.C. Chang for lunch in a Chinese restaurant in Great Neck. He talked about music and the theatre; says he now has a collection of about a hundred long-playing records chosen as a result of study over nearly three years."[45] Stanley Chang also remarked upon his father's record collecting and love of music:

> He collected LPs in a way that resembled a systematic study of music appreciation in general. His collection contained everything from Gregorian chants to twentieth-century music. It seemed to me that the more unlistenable the music, the more he wanted to listen to it. He started with Beethoven's Fifth and worked his way back in time to just before Bach and then forwards again up to the strangeness of twelve tone. When he played his records, I usually locked myself in my room. He wasn't looking for particular composers but rather

investigating different musical forms. He bought his records mainly at Sam Goody's in New York City. Being a regular customer he obtained special treatment. He could buy any record and return it if he did not wish to keep it. Sometimes we sat together and listened to the records he had brought home.

Chang's time at Clark University was evidently very important for him. During these years he sought to immerse himself in Western cultural traditions and developed interests that he was to sustain for the rest of his life—with the exception of his religious involvement, which dwindled thereafter. Chang graduated from Clark University with a bachelor of arts in 1913, three years after matriculating. He then moved to New York, where he continued his studies at Columbia University, where he took two master's degrees, one in comparative literature and one in pedagogy, in 1915. Columbia was well known for its large Chinese student groups, and it would later on be closely connected to the China Institute, which was founded 1926 in New York City. Several distinguished Chinese graduate students at Columbia such as Wellington Koo and T. V. Soong would later on make successful careers in the Chinese Foreign Office.[46]

Chang's Theatrical Interests

During his time as a student in New York, Chang's interest in theater became increasingly manifest, including in his writing of articles for various student newspapers.[47] These articles show Chang as eager to criticize what he felt were common misunderstandings about Chinese themes and characteristics in Western plays about China. In a 1914 article titled "Chinese Themes on the Stage—A Comment on 'Mr. Wu,'" Chang wrote:

> If we believe that struggle of the human will is the central support of the structure of the drama, as it is, then perhaps, there is no other country where this struggle in the political and social realm is so marked and inevitable as in China today. She is undergoing a great transition . . . and dramas of all descriptions are being acted out in real life every day. That this is a ready and prolific field for dramatic themes, every student of the history of the drama can easily discern.

But it is a sad fact that so far, on the western stage, these legitimate and truly dramatic stories have scarcely been touched.[48]

Chang emphasized that there needed to be more plays that did not reiterate common misconceptions about the Chinese people and prejudice about their characteristics, such as deviousness in business (a theme of the play *Mr. Wu*). Chang cited Aristotle's dictum that "a work of art must be full of beauty, agreeable, desirable, and morally worthy." According to Chang, no prejudice, however cleverly dramatized, could ever form the substance of a work of art, "for it is neither beautiful, nor agreeable, nor desirable—the present war ought to convince us of this. And certainly not morally worthy if we believe in any Golden rule other than the Golden rule that the only Golden rule is that there is no Golden rule" (Chang apologized for the reiteration!).[49] Chang here touched upon issues that would later form the focus of the "Orientalism debate" initiated by the Palestinian scholar Edward W. Said in his famous book *Orientalism* (1978), which examines misperceptions and misrepresentations of Asia by the Europeans, particularly European scholars.

In his early years in New York, Chang also wrote plays—*The Intruder*, *The Man in Grey*, and *The Awakening*—that reflected topical political and social problems in China, where some of these problems had been caused by the conflicts with Japan and the deep divisions in the country.[50] All three plays were subsequently staged at the Nankai School in both Chinese and English. *The Intruder* was also performed in New York in 1915. *The Awakening* proved very popular in China, where it was the first English-language play to premiere before a Chinese audience. Since Chang's political involvement often overlapped with his artistic endeavors, the plots of his plays warrant brief summaries here.

The Intruder takes as its theme the significance of social virtues, such as family togetherness, diligence, courage, and the importance of contributing to the common good. The play centers upon the threat posed to a family by greedy creditors in a hardening social atmosphere. The family has fallen into debt because several of the sons have borrowed money from an unscrupulous creditor, with devastating consequences for the family. The play ends, however, with the situation being partly resolved by the return of the hardworking and conscientious son. He keeps the loan shark at bay and, with his sister's help, saves the family from shame and ruin.

The Man in Grey is a tale of war and peace whose main protagonists are evoked allegorically as "the red man" (war), "the white man" (peace), "the yellow woman" (love), and "the grey man" (the people). The play takes the form of a dialogue in which peace and love try to convince the people to love their neighbor. Love, the yellow woman, appeals to the people (the grey man) to cooperate with their neighbors instead of waging war against them as the red man (war) has been urging. Only through cooperation can the barriers to making life more acceptable be removed. According to love, these barriers comprise poverty, ignorance, selfishness, prejudice, injustice, and hypocrisy. The struggle against these negative qualities was also to be a guiding principle of Chang's political project within the framework of the UN.

The Awakening is about a scholarship student who has just returned to China from his studies in the United States and is now looking for work. He meets an old friend and his sister. They discuss the societal problems of the day, including the rise in selfishness and short-sightedness. The trio also discuss how the returning student ought to approach his native land in light of his experiences overseas, an issue with which Chang himself wrestled intensely after his own return from studying in the United States. In the play, the student's friend is investigating a sprawling network of corruption in the railways, and the drama ends with him falling victim to one of the subjects of his investigation.[51] After his friend is murdered, the scholarship student promises the sister of the friend that he will try to help to realize the ideals articulated by his deceased friend in their conversations. Chang makes a thinly concealed gesture toward his brother Poling's Nankai School by having his protagonist harbor the ambition of opening a small school that might help create a new social order free from corruption and greed.

Chang also wrote another play in 1915, *The New Order Cometh*, which deals with the tension between loyalty to the old family traditions in China and the "new values" that the Chinese students encountered in the US in the form of individual freedom. The play was staged in New Haven and New York and had a cast of Chinese students from Yale and Columbia. The play was reviewed in very positive terms in the newspapers. It grappled with the theme of romantic love as the foundation of marriage. Two students fall in love during their time of study in the US. The boy tries to end his previous engagement with a Chinese girl in China. Her father, who represents "the old order," refuses to accept the break up because the engagement has been decided by both the boy's and the girl's families. According to the girl's father, because the boy's father no longer lives, the engagement should continue, unless the boy can bring his father back to life again and ask him for permission to disengage. However, the girl in China solves the stalemate, and, with a surprising act of generosity, she accepts the breakup. As a "reward," at the end of the play she meets another man with whom she falls in love.[52]

China in the 1910s

During Chang's early years of study in the US, China underwent dramatic political changes. Between 1907 and 1911, disaffection with Qing dynasty rule became increasingly apparent, resulting in riots in several cities across China. By 1911, the situation for certain religious groups, among them Christians, was becoming precarious as a consequence of the mid-nineteenth-century Taiping Rebellion, which the imperial regime regarded as a religious uprising. Following the revolution, the Republic of China was created in 1912, forcing the abdication of the last of the Qing dynasty emperors, six-year-old Puyi. This marked the end of more than two thousand years of imperial rule.[53] China became a nation-state with leaders by election instead of being an imperial state having leaders by inheritance. Following the dissolution of the empire, the situation for religious groups was also improved by greater religious freedom. Many Christian missionaries from the West came to China in these years, with intense and successful missions from a number of churches during the 1920s in particular.[54]

In 1912, Sun Yat-sen (1866–1925), an intellectual anti-Manchu leader who was also a converted Christian, became the first president of the republic. That year also saw the founding of the Kuomintang (KMT), the Chinese nationalist party. Sun Yat-sen's first term of office was cut short, however, when a general from the late Qing dynasty, Yuan Shikai, seized power. Sun Yat-sen was driven into exile in Japan, while his challenger sought to restore the monarchy and appointed generals as administrative commanders of China's provinces. (In July 1913, seven of those provinces rose up against Shikai's rule.) In 1915, during Shikai's rule, China became a signatory to the Twenty-One Demands, which resulted in Japan gaining considerable jurisdiction over Manchuria and the Shandong Province as well as special protectorate-like rights. These concessions led, four years later, to protests in the form of the May Fourth Movement.

After Yuan Shikai's death in 1916, China became fragmented as a national entity, with local warlords assuming control of the provinces.[55] The period directly following the revolution of 1911 was thus a great disappointment for all who had hoped that it would usher in a new, modernized, and unified China. Nonetheless, the one great consequence of the revolution was that the empire was dissolved and the ideological debate over China's future social development became more intense.

In 1917, Sun Yat-sen returned to a fragmented country that had become the object of foreign control in several key aspects, such as the extraterritorial laws that stipulated separate judicial codes for Chinese and foreign citizens. The customs system was also divided. Sun Yat-sen waged a propaganda campaign with three principal objectives for the new republic: (1) national independence; (2) constitutional democracy; and (3) economic freedom and self-sufficiency. The creation of national unity was, of course, a central objective. Sun Yat-sen's principles were adopted by his successor Chiang Kai-shek in the late 1920s. For both Sun Yat-sen and Chiang Kai-shek, it was essential to remove foreign influence in China and to put a stop to the fragmentation that had defined the warlord period.

The so-called warlord period refers specifically to the years 1916–1928, when warlords mobilized private armies in order to take control of different territorial areas. Some of these warlords were supported by foreign powers and engaged in a series of wars and minor conflicts with each other, many of which had their origins in ideological disagreements. Some warlords, such as Zhang Xun, were deeply conservative and wanted to restore the empire, whereas others, such as Yan Xishan, advocated what for its time was a highly progressive social policy in Shanxi Province. Opinions are divided as to how to understand this period. Although some commentators have characterized it as an early attempt at substantive modernization and the balancing of power, the majority of Chinese tend to view it as a period of confusion and internal struggle.[56]

Brief Return to China and the May Fourth Movement

In 1916, at the age of twenty-four and after almost six years in the United States, Chang returned to China to teach in his brother's Nankai School, where he also became vice principal and director of the school's new theater group. The plays mentioned earlier were performed at the school after Chang's return and served to establish him as the school's artistic leading light. During his early years as a teacher and school administrator in China,

Chang also evinced a deep interest in subjects far removed from theater and literature. For example, he became involved in the struggle to retain agricultural and forestry programs at Gingling University, Nanking. The following year, 1917, Chang stepped in as a temporary replacement for his brother Poling as school principal. He was to serve in that position for the two years that Poling studied at Teachers College, Columbia University, under the supervision of John Dewey. When the school was hit by major flooding in autumn 1917, Chang helped to save several pupils from the floodwaters and even managed to maintain the teaching schedule despite extensive damage to the school buildings. In summer 1918, the school moved back into its old premises.

After the school had got under way properly, Chang put on a new play, *Xin Cun Zheng* (*The New Village Head*), in which he introduced modern, Western directorial methods. For Chang, this meant that everyone involved in a dramatic production should follow an agreed-upon script and that the director should play a central role in rehearsals. In so doing, he broke with the improvisation-based theatrical tradition in China, which was largely centered on so-called star performers. Chang instead advocated a system in which every actor had a principal part under the director's strict guidance. Chang admired the theater traditions in the Western countries, which had their origin in ancient Greece, and he was eager to introduce these traditions to China. He thought that many people in the Western countries saw theater not mainly as "entertainment," as in China, but as something unique and important on its own, so-called pure theater. In Chinese theater, there was a combination of speech, singing, dancing, and pantomime to different extents. Theater and theater actors also had a higher social status in Western countries than in China, according to Chang.

The play *The New Village Head* would in time come to be seen as an early intellectual forerunner of the May Fourth Movement, which emerged in 1919 against the backdrop of Japan's expanding geopolitical ambitions in China. What exactly did the May Fourth Movement stand for, and what was its origin? The movement was a protest against the fact that Japan's demand to assume control of Shandong Province had been largely accepted by the delegates at the Versailles Peace Conference of 1919. In contrast to the new states of Estonia, Latvia, and Lithuania, China as a whole was not accorded any real independence. Most Chinese had hoped that China's participation on the French and British side against Germany during the First World War—in the form of 200,000 relief workers at the front—would result in the return to China of German-occupied territories such as Shandong Province. Instead, these territories were placed under Japan's control. In so doing, the Versailles Peace Treaty left deep wounds in China that were to form the basis for the May Fourth Movement. Allied with that movement were various modernization campaigns between 1915 and 1921 that emphasized the value of science, simplification of the language, greater democracy, and less hierarchical family norms. Their rallying cries were "Mr. Science" and "Mr. Democracy."[57] Key figures in this New Culture Movement included Lu Xun, the author of "A Madman's Diary" (a short story written in vernacular Chinese), and Chen Duxiu, a dean at Peking University and editor of the *New Youth Magazine*. Other well-known members were the linguist Qian Xuantong and the politician Li Dazhao. These persons were pivotal in creating the Communist Party (CCP) 1921 in Shanghai. As mentioned earlier, the philosopher Hu Shi, a key member of the May Fourth Movement, also worked intensely to replace Classical Chinese with Vernacular Chinese as the standard written language. This language reform was effected in the 1920s. The new literary style was based upon the syntax of the national dialect "kuo yu." The classical style was, according to Chang, very condensed and abstract and full of literary allusions that concealed the meaning of the words for the layman.[58]

On 4 May 1919, three thousand students from a number of universities, including Peking University, began processing toward Tiananmen Square and the entrance to the Imperial Palace, where the foreign legations were situated. After being driven away from this area, the students instead marched toward the residence of the communications minister, Cao Rulin, which they set on fire. Cao Rulin's house was singled out because Rulin had previously negotiated a very large loan from Japan, which protestors regarded as excessively compromising.[59] Cao Rulin (1877–1966), a politician friendly toward Japan, had also been a signatory to the infamous Twenty-One Demands of 1915, drafted during the brief regime of Yuan Shikai, which gave Japan greater influence over China. Rulin had also been a delegate to the Paris Peace Conference in 1919, at which German-occupied areas of China were ceded to Japan. Following clashes with police, thirty-two students were arrested and one died in the hospital. The demonstrations spread to other cities in China, including Shanghai. The overall purpose of the May Fourth Movement was to struggle for China's national sovereignty and fight against the people who were regarded as traitors at home. Throughout June, popular involvement grew, with demonstrations attracting not only students but also businessmen and workers, and a boycott of Japanese goods was called for. It should be noted that, according to official histories, even Zhou Enlai was active in the May Fourth Movement.

Chang paid close attention to the student activities within both the May Fourth Movement and more generally the New Culture Movement during his time as a graduate student in the US. He gave a lecture that dealt explicitly with the origin and main purpose of the May Fourth Movement at the Third World's Christian Citizenship Conference in November 1919 in Pittsburgh. This lecture was later published as an article—"The Rising Consciousness of Civic Responsibility Among the Students of China."[60]

In his article, Chang praised the students' mobilization against the Shantung Settlement in Paris 1919. He regarded these students—from universities, colleges, and secondary schools in China—as an avant-garde group that inspired other groups in society, such as the merchants, the gentry, and trade guilds, to fight against the unjust settlement. Because learning had always been highly respected in China, the influence of students could be strongly felt in all spheres of society, according to Chang. Many of the present students had also acquired a new socially relevant education after the fall of the old empire. In other words, the students were vitally interested in the real problems of their environment, and they had cultivated a civic responsibility that took into account the concerns of several interest groups in society. They had also allied themselves with liberal movements the world over who endorsed freedom, justice, and peace. The students quickly organized themselves into a student's national union with headquarters in Shanghai. They called for strikes from 4 May to 12 June and managed to effect the resignation of the three "traitors" from the Peking government (Cao Rulin, Zhang Zongxiang, and Lu Zongyu).

According to Chang, what was remarkable about the student mobilization was that the students rose to fight not for Shantung alone, and not only for China, but also for democracy and democratic principles in the world as a whole. Chang said:

> The far-sighted all over the world are aware of the fact that if a militaristic nation should be allowed ultimately to dominate China—the largest, yet undeveloped, field of natural resources and of manpower in the world—thee will develop the greatest military power that has existed on earth; and that the world will have a far more powerful and dangerous Prussia to face in the next world war. While fighting for

an independent, democratic China, the students believed that even as a policy—not to mention the supreme justice of the case—the safest course for the world, and particularly for the security and development of democratic institutions, is a free, peaceful China.[61]

Chang revealed in this article that he had a very clear idea about the dangers that the Japanese militarists presented for China and the rest of the world. The main danger consisted in using China as a tool for a war on democracy on a global scale. Unfortunately, he was right in his pessimistic prediction of a new world war and the destructive role Japan would play in that forthcoming war during the 1940s.

In his article Chang expressed his beliefs in the national importance of the educational efforts that had taken place in China after the establishment of the republic in 1912. Chang was an advocate of a multifaceted education that had relevance for solving urgent problems in society. According to his friend the educator Tao Xingzhi (T'ao Hsing-chih), who also had studied at Columbia University, Chang was critical of "the book worm"—a person who emphasized book reading as the main path to real knowledge. Chang coined the term "scholar ghost" to designate this kind of personality.[62] Chang stressed in a later article published in 1933—"Redirecting Educational Effort in China"—that:

> In the old days the wisdom of the race could be garnered from books and a faith in the written word was to that extent justifiable. This old regard for books and book knowledge as carried over by the "scholar-ideology" is making for sad results among the students in the modern schools. Although the subjects they study are nominally modern, the extent to which they trust the written word is sometimes piteous. Instead of memorizing classics, many students today are memorizing school texts—sometimes even texts in geometry and in chemistry. This form of mental exercise obviously does not fit one to face concrete problems. It is also often noted that students are apt to consider a thing accomplished as soon as it is written on paper and announced. "A ghost from the past" threatens calamity for the present and the future![63]

Chang hoped that "the New Student . . . will not be bookish, as he will have contact with, and control of, the material changes in his environment.

He will have moral self-reliance; he will not need to crowd 'the gates of the powerful and the rich' in order to eke out a livelihood. He will be able to increase the wealth of the community. And, not the least important, he will be in close sympathy and understanding with the toiling masses. That is the type of educated leadership that the China in transformation urgently calls for."⁶⁴ Hence, for Chang it was important to emphasize practical skills among the students and also vocational training. According to him there was no innate obstacle to the development of technology in China. The Chinese mind has never been blighted by any thoroughgoing mysticism, and in the making of material things, the Chinese have not been deficient in skill and inventiveness.⁶⁵ One could guess that Chang had (in addition to the student mobilization in the May Fourth Movement) his own Nankai School in mind as a role model for ideal educational efforts as Nankai mixed activities in workshops with activities in the classrooms for the pupils.⁶⁶ The Confucian ideal of learning also stressed that one should strive for a comprehensive learning that included social understanding and moral education and, hence, not only book reading.⁶⁷

In 1921, Chang also wrote a commentary on the student protests that had sought to prevent the ceding of Shandong Province to Japan. China, he claimed, had gained greater respect, not least in the eyes of the United States, by withholding its approval of the Japanese takeover. According to Chang, the lesson to be learned from the Shandong affair was that the eyes of the Chinese people had been opened. Although ancient Chinese cultural traditions had made many of its citizens into gentlemen, these traditions clearly had another aspect: they had failed to inculcate in its population an ability to counter the threat of war from without. During the most recent war, the Chinese people had been sleeping on a beautiful golden bed covered with fine promises of peace. The Shandong affair had thus been a wake-up call for greater knowledge and realism; it was, he wrote, the antidote to a debilitating dose of morphine.⁶⁸

Nationalist sentiments found expression in further riots on 30 May 1925 in Shanghai, which resembled the demonstrations organized in 1919 by the May Fourth Movement. These protesting students and workers were to become known as the May Thirtieth Movement. Their protests had been sparked by the shooting of striking workers by police officers under foreign control. The political rhetoric of the May Thirtieth Movement subsequently became highly influential within the domestic debate in China. For the May Thirtieth Movement, the frog became a symbol for everything that a good

Chinese ought to avoid, namely dutifully adapting him- or herself to be an American, a Japanese, and a consumer of foreign products, as the context dictated. The movement's activities also strengthened the position of Sun Yat-sen's Nationalist Party.[69]

While Chang was not directly involved in either the May Fourth Movement or the May Thirtieth Movement, he was nonetheless active in other organizational contexts.[70] In the 1920s, he had contacts with the Crescent Moon Society (Xinyue), a Chinese cultural organization created in 1923 by the poet Xu Zhimo (1897–1931). The society, which lasted until 1931, published a culture magazine that commented on the cultural and political situation in China. The magazine took its name from a poem by the Indian Nobel Prize–winner Rabindranath Tagore. Zhimo was a pioneering advocate of modern Chinese poetry and had himself been strongly inspired by the English poets John Keats and Percy Bysshe Shelley. He had also studied at the same universities as Chang—Clark and Columbia. The famous Chinese intellectual Hu Shi was also a member of the society, which later became part of the larger New Culture Movement.[71]

Second Period of Study in the United States— Doctoral Studies and Marriage

Chang's stay in China became rather brief as he decided to continue his graduate studies in New York. In 1919, Chang returned to the United States to complete his doctoral studies at Columbia, during which period he gave lectures as a way to support himself financially. In 1920, he and several other educationalists also made a study trip to several American universities, including Vassar College, which had invited him to give an address. Titled "The Problems of the Pacific," his lecture had an obvious political content. When Chang visited Vassar, he was received by a female Chinese student named Ts'a Sieu-Tsu (Sieu-Tsu Ts'a). Since Chang was from northern China and Ts'a from the south, they did not understand each other's mother tongue; Chang spoke Mandarin and she spoke Cantonese and "Shanghai" Chinese. As a result, they had to speak English with each other. During his visit to Vassar, Chang and Ts'a fell in love; they were married on 24 May 1921 at Union Theological Seminary in New York. Stanley said the following about his parents' ways of communicating with each other: "My mother spoke 'Shanghai' Chinese or Wu which was used in 'the half—way south' or Shanghai region. My mother and father spoke English to each other until they returned to China and then my mother learned Mandarin. I myself can partially understand 'Shanghai' Chinese from hearing her speaking to her friend Mrs Chiang (who was from the same region and who lived in New York at the same time as my family)."

Ts'a was born in Soochow (now Suzhou) in January 1898, the third of nine children (six girls and three boys). Her father, Shi-Zhi, encouraged her in her studies, in which she showed tremendous potential from an early age. She was sent to Haygood School for Girls before she had turned six, and, like Chang, after graduating in China was given the opportunity to go to the United States with support from the Boxer Rebellion Indemnity Reparation Fund. She placed first in the fund's scholarship examination (as already mentioned, Peng was number seven) and arrived in the United States by boat in 1916. While Peng arrived with the second boatload of fifty students in 1910, Ts'a came on the last boat in 1916. She spent a year at Delaware College before moving to Vassar College in 1917, where she took her bachelor's degree in 1920 with the highest grade in every subject but one (in which she got the second-highest grade). As magna cum laude, she was able to continue her studies at Columbia University, where she completed a master's degree in chemistry in one year. A recurrent motif in Stanley's recollections of his mother is his deep admiration for her prodigious talents. She managed to keep the family together under dramatic circumstances while their father was away traveling for long periods. She also devoted a great deal of time to the children's upbringing and education and was an expert manager of the family's finances. Despite her obvious intelligence and considerable scientific abilities, she was often overshadowed by her husband, as Stanley recalled. He related the following about his mother's dramatic upbringing:

> My mother's father was a Methodist pastor. She told us that the family had to hide from the authorities during the Republican revolution against the Qing dynasty. For a while during the 1911 revolution they lived on a boat in very straitened circumstances. Christian groups were viewed with suspicion at that time as a result of the mid-nineteenth-century Taiping Rebellion. She was the third of six daughters and also had three brothers. Because boys are especially valued in China and the family had three, they gave away their youngest boy to another family. I only learned of his existence after my mother died in 1986 and I was sending out notices of her death to all the

people in her address book. His surname was Cheng, not my mother's maiden name Tsai, and he lived in Houston, Texas. This was thirty years ago.

Mu Lan, Public Lectures, and PhD Studies

In the same year as he got married, Chang tried to raise money for famine victims in China by writing a play, *Mu Lan*, which was based on a sixth-century Chinese folktale. The play was staged at the Cort Theater on Broadway, where it was directed by Hung Shen.[72] The play was about a Chinese Joan of Arc who saved China from a Hun invasion. The heroine, a young woman named Mu Lan, dressed up as a male soldier in order to save her ailing father from being drafted into the Chinese army. The play was very warmly reviewed by the *Christian Science Monitor* and the *New York Times*.[73] In 1998, the story of Mu Lan was adapted as the blockbuster animated Disney film *Mulan*.

In 1921, Chang was also active in educational policy circles, representing his home town of Tientsin at a conference in Washington DC. He gave several public lectures during his time in the United States, alternating politically oriented lectures with talks on art, poetry, literature, and theater at a range of venues across the country. These lectures were well received as the following review revealed: "Mr Chang has a charming personality, a fine delivery, and held his audience from the moment he started to speak until he had finished the last word."[74] At the Poetry Foundation's annual dinner at New York's Hotel Astor in 1922, for example, he appeared on a panel of speakers that included Amy Lowell and Carl Sandburg. Chang spoke about poetry's potential to counteract the mechanizing tendencies of modern industrial society and its capacity to make people see what is essential in their world rather than slavishly seeking material gain. To illustrate his thoughts on the importance of poetry, he declared: "Poetry is like the sound of the rhythm in the void, is like the color in phenomena, is like the moon in the water, the image in the mirror. There is an end in words but the meaning will waft on forever."[75]

A year after his marriage to Ts'a Sieu-Tsu, Chang completed his doctoral degree at Columbia University. His dissertation was titled "Education for Modernization in China" and was published as a book the following year.[76] The overarching aim of Chang's monograph was to analyze educational reforms in the particular context of China's modernization. In his view, this modernization should be premised on the need to preserve the inner core of China's traditional culture. Chang's wide-ranging analysis of Chinese civilization focused on the factors that had enabled the West to achieve a much higher degree of technological development and material growth than China during the previous two centuries. Science, individuality, and democracy have been the authentic voices of the modern age, according to Chang. The sudden and extensive expansion of the European peoples following the discovery of America conditioned the striking progress of modern Europe. Curiosity, imagination, exploration, and the will to make comparison were encouraged during these times of expansion. In a so-called frontier society equality, community and individual initiatives were also encouraged.[77]

Chang argued that only by means of modernization's *processes*, not its products, could the special character of a national culture be revitalized and adapted to entirely new circumstances. His analysis also examined what he regarded as the dark sides of economic and technological growth in the West. His dissertation criticized the spirit of competition and the materialism in Western societies, which had resulted in crassness, insensitivity, and cruelty. Chang was concerned that a powerful desire for modernization would lead China to develop into just one more superficial, materialistic nation. His own study urged students to remain always mindful of those intrinsic human values that can counter the impulse to imitate Western trends blindly.

It is interesting that Chang's dissertation contained normative statements about the potentials and limitations of cultural change. Chang's view of knowledge evidently allowed for an academic study to contain more than simply empirical descriptions, explanations, interpretations, and logical analyses. For him, an academic study could also contain arguments about normative issues relating to what we might call adequate civic education and constructive cultural exchange. This was not an uncommon perspective at the time: many academic monographs in the humanities and social sciences shared the same theoretical premises regarding knowledge.

It is interesting, too, to note that this motif—attending to what is central in Chinese culture as it encounters other cultures—is also present in Chang's earlier writings on how a Christian mission ought to profile itself with regard to Chinese traditions. The same rhetorical figures also recur in Chang's later writings on politics, art, and cultural change.[78] For Chang, the central elements of the Chinese philosophical tradition seem to have constituted the historical core, which he believed should be respected. These elements, he repeatedly underscored, were humanistic traditions that took into consideration the needs and dignity of individuals and their responsibilities toward their fellow human beings. In later writings, Chang also emphasized that the spirit in Chinese philosophy was surprisingly humanistic and "modern" even two thousand years ago.[79] (The focus upon the human being was something that Confucian thought shared with "the philosophy of the UN Declaration.")

Chang's dissertation received uniformly positive reviews. One reviewer saw it as an ingenious application to China's situation of the ideas of John Dewey.[80] Another reviewer described it as an interesting illustration of how members of a traditional civilization could incorporate an educational program that had been created in a context shaped by quite different social, economic, and philosophical traditions. The issues addressed by Chang in his dissertation, including the school as a forum for fostering democracy and the role of education in social modernization, still have great relevance to Chinese society. (Chang also stressed in the context of his work on the Universal Declaration later on that schools were very important arenas for fulfilling human rights in society.[81]) Yet the reviewer also emphasized that Chang's warnings about the dangers of modern industrial society, such as consumerist materialism and the spirit of consumption, needed to be weighed against the ignorance, poverty, and economic inefficiency of traditional society. If China chose the path of modernization, its citizens would have to be prepared for things like individual competition and materialism to become evident in society.[82] These observations are thought-provoking insofar as they problematize Chang's ideas about reconciling modernization from "without" and the traditional forms of Chinese culture.

Peng Chun Chang and John Dewey

Chang's thesis was strongly inspired by the educator John Dewey (1859–1952). Both men underscored the importance of knowledge, individuality, individual rights and freedoms, and democratic processes when seeking to resolve the common problems of society. These lines of reasoning were to establish a frame of reference for Chang in his later writing of the UN Declaration. Chang shared Dewey's view that education is the decisive method for achieving constructive societal change. Although Dewey evidently played a major role in Chang's intellectual development, Chang's son Stanley recalled that he later in life only seldom spoke about Dewey and his writings. Chang's friend and former fellow student Hu Shi recalled Chang being clearly surprised at Shi having sufficient peace of mind to listen to a lecture on Dewey's logic at Columbia's Philosophical Club in 1937.[83] By this Chang seems to have meant that abstract philosophical thinking about logic was hardly an urgent priority at a time when China was experiencing dramatic historic events during its war with Japan. But more broadly, Chang's political views and philosophy harmonized well with Dewey's ideas.

Having studied pedagogy as a master's student at Columbia University, Chang had been naturally drawn to Dewey. Yet Chang seems not to have been personally supervised by Dewey to any significant degree, perhaps largely because Dewey was traveling for much of the time while Chang wrote his dissertation.[84] Dewey began a sabbatical at roughly the same time as Chang began his doctoral studies, making several trips overseas, including to China. In his dissertation, Chang makes acknowledgement to Dewey but also to William Heard Kilpatrick, Paul Monroe, and Isaac Kandel from Columbia, who had been involved in supervising him. All were famous educationalists, nationally and internationally.

Paul Monroe had a particular interest in China, which he visited several times during the 1920s and 1930s. He was also active in the China Institute of New York, one of whose purposes was to enable cultural contacts between the United States and China. The institute had ties to the Boxer Indemnity Scholarship Program, partly through financing and partly through visits to the institute by program scholars. Meng Chih, the institute's head from 1930 to 1967, was also a Nankai School alumnus and had contacts with Chang's brother Poling. For his part, Isaac Kandel was well known in the field for his research on comparative international pedagogy. William Heard Kilpatrick (1871–1965) and Helen Parkhurst (1887–1959) were both actively engaged in the pedagogical implementation of Dewey's more abstract pedagogical-philosophical ideas. They would later become highly influential in American educational debates. Kilpatrick was also an active liberal who went on to move in liberal political circles that included Eleanor Roosevelt, while Parkhurst's Dalton School was a pioneering institution that sought to find a balance between the individual needs of its pupils and the interests of society.

From the 1920s, debates in China over education were increasingly influenced by the work of John Dewey. Considerable numbers of teachers and school principals in China had read the writings of a thinker who had become a kind of apostle for the new American ideas about educational policy, which had begun to reach countries undergoing radical social transformation. One of the most well-known educators during the period of the Chinese republic was Tao Xingzhi (1891–1946), who had also studied under John Dewey. Tao Xingzhi developed an original pedagogical method for rural teacher education, and he rewrote Dewey's dictum "Education is not preparation for life, education is life itself" as "Life is education." In the 1920s, Dewey travelled to a range of countries, including Turkey, Mexico, and the Soviet Union and made study trips to China and Japan in 1919–1921, during which he was especially struck by China's special forms of social community.[85] Several other leading intellectuals from the West also visited China in this period. One of the most prominent was the English philosopher Bertrand Russell, whose writings Chang was subsequently to find extremely useful. Russell's translator during his visit to China in 1920 was Chang's good friend Y. R. Chao. Chang cited with approval Russell's assertion that Western civilization's particular contribution to the world had been the scientific method, while China's had been insights as to the purpose and value of life.[86]

Chang's brother, Poling, had been similarly impressed by Dewey's ideas when organizing his system of Nankai Schools. Dewey and the educational progressives emphasized the value not only of theoretical studies but also the value of aesthetic and practical attainments and of inculcating democratic thinking. These precepts were to become guiding principles for teaching in the Nankai Schools.[87]

How exactly was Chang affected by Dewey's ideas? For Chang, like Dewey, it was important to recreate the circumstances and factors that had resulted in the pioneering spirit and delight in discovery that had been defining features of the "frontier mentality" of American society and the journeys of discovery by previous generations, something we touched upon earlier. These journeys had led to the clear technological, cultural, and material development of "the West." The purpose of a school was thus not only to create a challenging environment—one that encouraged a combination of thought and action, discipline, and responsibility toward matters of common concern—but also to foster a spirit of eager, critical discovery.

At the Nankai School, Chang had also introduced a school council with representatives from the school's sports clubs and musical associations in order to promote democratic participation in the running of the school.

Chang shared Dewey's opinion that it was vital to preserve the valuable elements of the old culture while seeking to implement new and creative curricular reforms. In this Chang parted company with several members of the New Culture Movement, who wanted more radical changes in Chinese customs, language, and habits of thought.[88] Chang seems to have been unwilling to tone down the Confucian legacy, which was to become increasingly pronounced for him with the passage of time. In the 1920s, China's growing economy led to the emergence of major urban centers, such as Shanghai, whose increasingly Westernized cultures were being criticized by intellectuals, Chang among them, for being materialistic and fashion-obsessed.[89]

There are other striking similarities between John Dewey's pragmatist philosophy and Chang's anti-metaphysical view of human rights: both emphasized the importance of finding agreement on practical ethical questions and of not becoming embroiled in abstract philosophical considerations that lacked practical relevance.[90] Ideals and precepts must be "lived" by the students in order for them to gain knowledge.

Chang and Dewey also shared the view that Communism represented a too-hurried and too-radical strategy for societal transformation. The path to modernization of China should instead be gradual and focused upon educational means.[91] There is, then, a direct line from Chang's doctoral dissertation to his activities as an author of the UN Declaration. Chang's dissertation makes clear that he had thought deeply about the rights and freedoms of the individual, a theme to which he would return several times in his later writings. Several of the issues on which Chang focused in his dissertation—the importance of a basic education for all, the value of consuming and producing culture, respect for the individual's particular needs and conditions—would once again come to the fore in his work on the UN Declaration. Chang also shared Dewey's and Kilpatrick's rejection of authoritarianism in schools (as well as their rejection of political theories of authoritarianism). Even though Dewey did not talk much in terms of human rights he was a strong supporter of academic freedom and free speech.[92] Dewey as well as Chang was also eager to emphasize community values. In other words, Dewey did not accept a "self-centered individualism" but endorsed instead a "social liberalism."[93]

Both Chang and Dewey were profoundly influenced by the dramatic societal changes that their respective countries were undergoing. Dewey grew up in a nineteenth-century agricultural society that by the turn of the last century had rapidly transformed into an increasingly urbanized industrial society. While not experiencing the same rapid pace of change as the United States, China in the first decades of the twentieth century was nonetheless characterized by increasingly rapid industrialization and urbanization. According to Chang, China was also experiencing growing emancipation and individualization among its citizens, particularly after the breakthrough of modernism and urbanism, with the result that its citizens were increasingly acting in accordance with their own conscience and following laws that they themselves had played a part in creating.

Dewey and Chang also shared a broadly congruent conception of democracy. According to Dewey, democracy should be understood as "communicated experience." What a democratic society should strive for, he argued, was for its citizens to be able to freely share their experiences on the principle of freedom of thought and expression, without the restrictions imposed by cartel-like formations.[94] While this democratization process might entail a liberalization of and liberation from oppressive customs, Chang argued, these wide-ranging social changes nonetheless contained the seeds of egoism and a failure of social community.[95] In this emphasis upon the individual's duties toward the rest of society, the Confucian legacy in Chang's thinking revealed itself most clearly.

CHAPTER 2

Raising a Family, Theatrical Activities, University and Diplomatic Careers

For Chang, much of the 1920s and 1930s were taken up with raising a family, pursuing a career, and continued involvement in the dramatic arts. He began traveling between the United States and China with greater frequency. In addition to becoming a professor at the newly founded Nankai University at the end of the 1920s, he was a guest professor at various universities around the world and was also intensely active in matters of educational policy. In the mid-1930s, he also became increasingly involved in foreign policy issues, due in part to the serious conflicts that erupted between China and Japan. Because Nankai University wielded considerable political influence in China and was strongly engaged with issues at a national level, Chang and his brother Poling found themselves drawn into these political conflicts. Thanks to his successful campaigns in Europe and the United States to argue China's case with regard to Japan, Chang had by the early 1940s qualified himself for diplomatic postings in Turkey and Chile.

Raising a Family, Return to China and Tsinghua University

In June 1922, Chang and his wife had their first child, Ming-Ming. On the invitation of the Chinese Education Advancement Organization, Chang made a trip home to China that summer. He had been studying the educational systems of an array of countries, including Britain, France, Germany, Russia, and Denmark. His journey home from New York to Tianjin (Tientsin) took him through Europe and the Indian Ocean, via the Suez Canal, and lasted several months. Chang's wife Ts'a was seasick for much of the journey, leaving her unable to look after her newborn daughter. When they arrived in China, one of her sisters remarked, "This child is not well." During the long journey, Ming-Ming had contracted meningitis, which damaged the left half of her brain. The consequent disability left her with considerable learning difficulties that resulted in her being unable to look after herself or be fully independent for the rest of her life. She finished school to the sixth grade, showing an ability for elementary mathematics, and she learned English from watching television. According to Stanley, she was well aware of her limitations, including in logical thought, but despite these challenges showed great patience.

It has already been mentioned that P. C. Chang tried in a number of ways to shake off the influence of his elder brother Poling and to find sources of income other than the Nankai School. In September 1923, Chang accordingly began working as vice-dean at the Tsinghua School, an institution that was supported by the US Boxer Rebellion Indemnity Fund. Before Chang's engagement in Tsinghua, his mother, Yang Shi, passed away in January. During his short engagement at this school, he reorganized it into a college and reformed its curriculum with more liberal education. One of his aims in doing so was to enable students from Tsinghua School to move directly after graduation to a graduate college in the United States. The older teachers at the school opposed this idea, however, and Chang encountered major difficulties in realizing the project. During his years at Tsinghua, Chang also kept a diary (*Richeng cao'an*) in which he made notes on school "politics" and his own desire after studying in the United States to reconnect with the classical Chinese tradition. Indeed, he explicitly stated in his diary that his understanding of classical Chinese philosophy was greatly inferior to that of his colleagues. One of them whom Chang admired in this respect was the literary scholar and educator Wu Mi, who had also studied in the US almost at the same time as Chang.[1] During the end of his graduate studies there, Chang had also showed a keener interest in Chinese philosophy; for example, he gave a lecture titled "The Teachings of Confucius" at the Albany Institute and Historical and Art Society in 1921.[2]

In November 1923, another daughter was born: Hsin-Yueh (Ruth), whose name means "new moon." Ruth was to follow in her mother's footsteps and become a chemist. She studied chemistry at Vassar College, her mother's alma mater, before taking a doctoral degree in the same subject at the University of Wisconsin. At around the time of Ruth's birth, Chang had become active in the Crescent Moon Society, a literary group whose number included

Hu Shi and which shared the same name as Chang's second daughter. As was mentioned earlier, the name Crescent Moon Society came from a poem by Tagore. Xu Zhimo, the founder of the society, helped Chang in 1929 to buy poems and scripts for the library at Nankai University. Xu Zhimo and Huiyn Lin (1904–1955) served as guides and translators for Tagore when he visited Tsinghua and Beijing in 1925 upon Chang's invitation. In his lectures in China, Tagore warned against importing materialistic values from the West into Chinese society.[3] Huyin Lin would later become a famous architect and poet in China. After a brief love affair with Xu Zhimo, she married Sicheng Liang (1901–1972), who would also become a famous architect in China. Sicheng Liang was the son of Qichao Liang (1873–1929), whom Chang also invited to Tsinghua.[4] Sicheng Liang was a famous journalist and reformist who was involved in the Hundred Days Reform, a modernization reform from 1898. He was the mentor of Xu Zhimo. Later on, Huiyin Lin and her husband helped Chang with stage design in 1934 when Chang staged the play *The New Village Head*, with the famous actor Cao Yu.

It is a remarkable fact that Chang was so well connected with some of the most distinguished people in the cultural life of China during the 1920s. All these people also knew each other in different ways. These kinds of networks would later be a constant presence in Chang's life in addition to the networks that Chang developed through his Nankai connections and the Boxer Indemnity Scholarship Fund. In other words, it is fascinating to see how Chang's life interleaved with those of numerous other Chinese intellectuals, particularly during his years as a student in the United States and through the Boxer Indemnity Scholarship Program. The network that he acquired during his student years in America were to prove decisive in a number of ways, including for his activities in the worlds of literature and the arts and in politics and diplomacy.

Because of the resistance to his changes that Chang encountered from some teachers and administrators at Tsinghua College, he resigned from the college in 1926 and returned to the Nankai School where he was made principal. He also began teaching at Nankai University and served as a professor of philosophy from 1926 to 1937. He remained passionately interested in theater and continued to stage plays by various foreign dramatists. Perhaps the Western dramatist whom Chang most admired was the Norwegian playwright Henrik Ibsen. Chang was strongly inspired by Ibsen, not least because of his plays' sociopolitical themes and his dramatic technique. Chang subsequently sought to write plays of his own in the same vein. In 1927 he staged *An Enemy of the People* and the following year he directed the Nankai School's new drama group in *A Doll's House* as part of the school's anniversary celebrations. Ibsen's play *An Enemy of the People* gave voice to a special form of individualism, according to Chang, and it later transpired that the title of the play had prompted the city's military authorities to seek to prevent it being performed. After the second act, Chang received a phone call from the authorities in which he was instructed to bring the play to a halt. The following spring in 1928, Chang nonetheless staged the play again; this time it bore the title *The Stubborn Doctor* and there were no difficulties with the authorities.[5] The reason for restaging the play was to celebrate Ibsen's one-hundredth birthday.

Between 1926 and 1929, Chang translated several Western plays with sociopolitical themes that he adapted to the situation in China. In an article written in 1933, Chang mentioned that he had personally collected and read dramas by over forty different authors, including Shakespeare, Molière, Goethe, Schiller, Sheridan, Ibsen, Strindberg, Hauptmann, Wilde, Shaw, Galsworthy, Rostand, Brieux, Tolstoy, Chekov, Andreyev, Lunacharsky, and Pirandello. The names on his list are impressive and attest to Chang's passion and methodicalness once he had embarked upon a project—here, introducing foreign drama to China. Chang seems to have abandoned collecting books in a systematic fashion later in life, according to Stanley, unlike his good friend Y. R. Chao. When I asked Stanley about his father's library in the family home in Nutley, he replied that his father did not have a particularly large collection. One of the books from his father's collection that Stanley later read was Arnold Toynbee's study of Western civilization, *A Study of History*. Like his son, Chang had a very good memory and did not need to consult books once he had read them. (Chang had, however, a large collection of records that the two sons divided between themselves after his death.)

During his drama training, Chang had been considerably impressed by several directors from the West, including the German director Max Reinhardt and the English director Gordon Craig. Chang also visited Russia twice and got to know the director and theorist Konstantin Stanislavski. Moreover, when Chang had come to the United States as a student, the Little Theatre Movement had begun to make itself felt in theatrical circles across the country, above all in its hometown through Chicago's Little Theatre. This theatrical form, which had also been inspired by Max Reinhardt, advocated small-scale productions and intimacy between the stage and auditorium and aimed to stage plays of major social relevance.[6]

In his capacity as director of Nankai's new drama group, Chang developed a close collaboration with actor Cao Yu, who in 1928 played the lead role in Chang's production of *A Doll's House*. The figure of Nora in *A Doll's House* became an important role model for many Chinese women in their efforts to achieve emancipation, with Chang's advocacy of Ibsen's plays undoubtedly playing a major part. In traditional Chinese theater, female roles had regularly been played by men, but from the 1930s, it became increasingly common for women to perform women's roles in theatrical productions. In 1929, Chang staged John Galsworthy's play *Strife*, which was the first occasion when female actors performed alongside males. Chang also directed the play *Lady Windermere's Fan* by Oscar Wilde.

Toward the end of the 1920s, Chang's life, in addition to theatrical activities, was characterized by administration, teaching, and educational development work. For example, he and his brother met with Chinese political leaders and foreign guests from American universities in order to discuss potential ways to reform China's educational system. Chang's family also continued to grow. A son, Chen Chung, was born in October 1927, and another son, Yuan-Feng (today, Stanley) in October 1928. Both of them went on to become academics. Chen Chung became a professor of mathematics at the University of California, achieving fame in the fields of logic and model theory (his PhD supervisor was the famous logician Alfred Tarski); Yuan-Feng became a professor of applied physics, holding posts at a number of institutions, including the University of Nebraska, Lincoln.

The Twentieth Century's Second Chinese Revolution and Chiang Kai-shek

How was China developing politically during the 1920s and 1930s? The Chinese leader Sun Yat-sen died of cancer in spring 1925 and thus did not live to see the temporary union of an array of different provinces under the so-called Northern Expedition, a coalition between Sun Yat-sen's nationalist Kuomintang party and the Communists. In 1926–1927, this Soviet-trained army forced the divided regions, including the Shanghai region, to accept national rule. Peking was captured by the National Revolutionary Army in June 1928. During the fighting, one soldier distinguished himself, "Generalissimo" Chiang Kai-shek, who subsequently turned on his Communist former allies, killing several of them once Shanghai had fallen. The new regime was thus initiated in 1927 with a domestic bloodbath in Shanghai. The Kuomintang and the Communists would henceforth be mortal enemies.[7]

Chiang Kai-shek succeeded Sun Yat-sen after the latter's death, ushering in a period of Chinese history known as the Nanking period (1928–1937). In 1928, a new Chinese government was announced in Nanking, which lent its name to what has come to be called China's second revolution of the twentieth century (the first being the revolution of 1911 against the emperor, and the third being the Communist revolution of 1949).

Nanking thus became the country's new capital and there began a period of attempted modernization, including educational reforms, industrial investments, and new infrastructure. The position of women was improved during this period. In 1934, Chiang Kai-shek also began promoting the New Life Movement as an ideological alternative to communism.

Chiang Kai-shek converted to Christianity in 1931 partly because of the influence of his wife at the time, Soong May Ling. His new philosophy was an attempt to modernize China by emphasizing Confucian norms such as diligence, loyalty, and a modest, healthy way of life.[8] This philosophy had minimal impact in the Chinese republic, to judge from the rising levels of materialism and corruption. At the same time, Chiang Kai-shek strove to underscore the importance of science and modern technology for the development of society, and he fought against a variety of superstitions. He stressed the importance of the family and harmony and order in society, and he was completely against the Communist creed of class warfare.

Despite their ideological differences, the Kuomintang and the Communists had a number of points in common. Both parties stressed the value of frugality, and they wanted to unite China and liberate it from foreign influence.[9] They also sought to implement modernization and liberation from traditional mythologies and religious attitudes. The Kuomintang's supporters and the Communists also shared the Leninist perspective of the party as the primary political entity in society. A national collectivism and solidarity was also emphasized. During the Nanking period, however, the Japanese encroached upon China in a growing number of ways, and the Kuomintang regime became increasingly drawn into conflicts with the various Communist groups. The end result was an undermining of the republic's capacity to create the modern and unified China that had been Sun Yat-sen's great vision. Chiang Kai-shek shared this vision, too, and wanted to unite China with the Kuomintang as its ruling party. Chiang's attitude toward the Communists found expression in his famous aphorism that the Japanese were a disease of the skin but the Communists, a disease of the heart.[10]

Opinions on Chiang Kai-shek have changed throughout history. What stands out are his authoritarian tendencies as well as his inability to prevent the spread of corruption during the final years of the republic. He was also accused of having been capitalism's errand boy. This latter accusation is debatable, however, given that Chiang Kai-shek initiated state industrial projects, in the spirit of Roosevelt's New Deal, during the global depression that prevailed throughout the 1930s. What is more, he also worked closely with the League of Nations to counteract and mitigate the effects of natural disasters, such as that which resulted from the Yangtze River's flooding in 1931.[11] His famous retort was also uttered in the context of his failure to prevent the Communist seizure of power in 1949. At the same time, a number of commentators regard the failings of his early career as having been partly compensated for by his subsequent career as the co-creator of the modern and economically successful republic of Taiwan following the Communist seizure of power on the mainland.[12]

How did Peng Chun Chang view Chiang Kai-shek and the political changes that took place during the first decades of the twentieth century? Stanley Chang relates the following:

> My father had a lot to say about the political upheavals in China. He characterized the political changes in China as being like a child experiencing a succession of diseases of childhood: mumps, chicken pox, etc. The original toppling of the Qing dynasty in 1911 took place when my father was at Clark University, so he was not involved in it. Sun Yat-sen became leader of the new republic. He died shortly after in 1925. In the power struggle after his death, General Chiang Kai-shek assumed the leadership role. His wife Soong May Ling (Song Meiling) had been educated at Wellesley College in the United States, so my father knew her well. However, my father had an extremely low opinion of the General, as emerged from various asides which he made in my presence.

Stanley Chang's recollections are illuminating, not least in light of his father's poor relations with the Chinese delegation to the United Nations at the end of the 1940s. That Chang did not rate Chiang Kai-shek highly undoubtedly proved to be a handicap for him later in life, even if it was perhaps cushioned by Chang's friendship with Chiang's wife and by the fact that Chiang held his brother Poling in high esteem. In official settings during his time as representative of the Chinese government, however, Chang clearly articulated a loyalty to the regime for a long time and, above all, Chiang Kai-shek.[13] He was positive about certain things that Chiang Kai-shek did during the 1930s. In an article published in 1938, Chang said the following about the political leader:

> At the end of 1935, General Chiang Kai-shek went to Nanking and assumed the Premiership; he formed his Cabinet containing intellectuals and experienced businessmen, as well as party members. Now that was a widening of the basis of the government; it began to assume something of a true national character. He started, first of all, the currency reform—at the end of 1935. That is very significant. Before that time the currency was not uniform; after that time currency all over the country become to be uniform.... Through 1935, various constructive efforts took place, the increase of trade, the improvement of the international situation, the building of the railroads.[14]

The fact that Chang managed to secure prominent posts in the 1930s and 1940s was a good indication that Chiang and his closest circle viewed Chang approvingly for at least part of his professional life.

It should be mentioned that Chiang Kai-shek did not enjoy broad popular support among liberally inclined circles in China, because of, among other things, the widespread corruption in society and the unsatisfactory progress of the campaigns against Japan and the Communists. As a leader he also showed strong intolerance for people who disagreed with him.[15] The alternatives were few, however. In the 1930s, one could either join the Communists, who were practically a guerrilla group that had no substantial territories under their control, or Japan, which was unthinkable for most people. The liberal-democratic discussions that were conducted in liberal circles similarly lacked any politically powerful mouthpiece.[16]

Chang and Mei Lanfang

Despite Chang's many commitments to family and university life, his aesthetic interests did not slacken. As we have seen, he was not only interested in introducing Western plays to Chinese audiences, he was also eager to introduce Chinese culture to American and European audiences. In 1930, Chang met the famous Chinese opera singer Mei Lanfang (1894–1961) at the Chinese Embassy while on a trip to Washington DC for the purposes of fundraising for Nankai University. Mei Lanfang, who was the most famous performing artist in China for many years during the twentieth century, played female roles (the *dan* roles) in the performances, and he took the Peking Opera outside China and made it famous for the first time.[17] Chang then accompanied Mei Lanfang on his six-month tour of the United States, during which Chang was invited to act as master of ceremonies. Chang had told Mei not to try to change his performance style for Western audiences but to act on stage just as he had in China. He also advised Mei on which dramas were particularly well suited for performance before a Western audience, such as *Slaying the Tiger*, the story of which was easily comprehensible even to those with no knowledge of Chinese. An opera that also was performed was *The Fisherman's Revenge*. Chang was eager to initiate a press campaign before Mei performed on Broadway. He urged him to hire a professional producer who knew the American theatre and opera world (F. C. Kapakas). Before Mei Lanfang started his performances in the US Chang had given lectures on Chinese culture in various clubs in New York to prepare the visit.[18] Chang even managed to see to it that the University of California conferred an honorary doctorate upon Mei Lanfang in connection with the tour.

At the award ceremony, Mei Lanfang read out a thank you message that Chang had penned:

> We are here to exert what little strength we have to promote peace, which is eagerly hoped for by civilized people. History shows that real peace cannot be obtained by force. People hope to obtain peace but not quietness after turbulence. Real peace should promote people's development and growth—mentally, rationally, and materially. To maintain real peace in the world, people need to learn to know, to understand, and to show sympathy for each other, instead of fighting each other. The peace in the hearts of these two great peoples, the Chinese and the American, accords with the norms of international trust and sincerity. To reach this goal, all peoples should conduct active research in the arts and the sciences so as to understand each other's ways of life, historical background, and problems and difficulties.[19]

Chang's declaration has clear relevance for the work he would later do for the United Nations as the latter sought to formulate a way to articulate the conditions for sustainable peace. Chang's wife and his daughter Ruth also accompanied him on the tour. It was a triumph for Mei Lanfang, who played to sold-out houses in New York and other cities, and his performances received generally very positive reviews.[20] At first, Chang was clearly surprised that Chinese opera and Mei Lanfang received such a rapturous reception in view of how greatly its musical form differed from Western opera.

Chang also contributed to the writing of a short book about Mei Lanfang, which was published in 1935. Titled *Mei Lanfang in America: Reviews and Criticism*, it contained a foreword by Chang.[21] During his American tour, Mei Lanfang met a number of celebrities, including Charlie Chaplin, Mary Pickford, and Douglas Fairbanks. Mei Lanfang went on to become a global superstar, the most recognized face of Chinese opera in the rest of the world. Many people around the world were evidently impressed by his special falsetto singing style, body language, and costumes.

Like other Chinese opera stars before him, Mei played women's roles. In 1935, touring took him and Peng Chun Chang to the Soviet Union, where they met notable stage personalities such as Konstantin Stanislavski, Vladimir Nemirovich-Danchenko, Alexander Tairov, and Vsevolod Meyerhold. Bertolt Brecht happened to be in Moscow at the same time and was deeply impressed by Mei Lanfang's appearances.[22] Gordon Craig also met Mei Lanfang in Moscow during his tour in 1935.[23]

Several commentators have argued that Brecht's notion of a "distancing" or "alienation" effect in the audience originated in his observation of Mei Lanfang's performances. That effect describes when listeners or spectators cease to identify with what is taking place on stage and instead begin to reflect upon the events being portrayed.

Mei Lanfang had also greatly impressed the Japanese during his performances in Japan, and they were keen for him to perform during the Japanese occupation of China. Mei Lanfang refused to comply, however, and instead lived in obscurity and poverty until Japan's capitulation in 1945. After Mao Zedong seized power in 1949, Mei Lanfang resumed his career and played to similarly enthusiastic audiences in Communist China.

Chang was involved in Chinese theater and opera for much of his life, an involvement which expressed itself in a number of ways. His son Stanley has a peculiar memory of a particular opera performance at the China Institute in New York. Stanley's father had been presented with tickets to this opera because it was his sixtieth birthday. As already noted, all Chinese opera is sung in falsetto. Midway through the performance, one of the girls lost control of her voice and began to sing in a normal tonal range. Chang immediately stood up and shouted "Disaster!" which Stanley found very amusing. Such attentiveness to Chinese etiquette and the proper forms of expression was clearly something that permeated Chang's life in several ways. Stanley also remarked that the family went to the China Institute very rarely. One occasion when Peng visited the institute was when his brother Poling came to New York in 1946. Toward the end of the 1920s, however, Chang seems to have had more contact with the institute, which served as a meeting place for Chinese students at Columbia University and scholars, as well as for Americans with an interest in China.

Chicago, Honolulu, and Nankai

In 1931, after touring with Mei Lanfang in the United States, Chang was invited to take up a guest professorship at the University of Chicago, and during the year he taught philosophy and art history both there and at the Chicago Art Institute. That same year, he also taught at Columbia University, touring Europe in the summer and spending the autumn at the University of Chicago. During his tenure as a guest professor in Chicago, Chang's two sons and his daughter Ming-Ming stayed behind on the Nankai campus in China, as they had while he toured with Mei Lanfang.

In the early 1930s, Chang was also active on the American lecture circuit, speaking about China and topical problems in cities such as St Louis and New York. In a talk given to a women's society in Scarsdale, New York, in autumn 1931, he warned about a scenario in which China would be forced to go down a military path in response to Japan's aggressive colonial policy in Manchuria. Chang argued that ever since the founding of the republic, China had sought to follow the path of modernization by learning all it could from modern science and technology. While China was not yet a modern society, noted Chang, its enormous efforts to attain this goal should not be underestimated. He also argued that China was a more modern society than Japan in one vital respect: it had long abandoned the notions that the emperor was divine and that the army and navy should be under feudal control. "China may be slow in her adjustments," said Chang, "but at least she long ago discarded these absurd beliefs that properly belong in the museum."[24]

In late 1931, Peng Chun Chang was offered a tenured professor position at the University of Chicago. He declined, however, because of the grave political situation in China, which had worsened after dramatic events near the city of Mukden. On 18 September 1931, a bomb had exploded near the city on a railway line controlled by Japan. Japan accused Chinese groups of responsibility for the attack, which it took as a pretext for invading Manchuria. After the invasion, Japan created a new tributary, Manchukuo in Manchuria, and installed the last Qing emperor, Puyi, on the throne even as it retained actual control itself. Manchukuo remained in existence from 1932 to 1945. The only state to acknowledge Japan's tributary (apart from Japan itself) was El Salvador.[25] Chang said that the Japanese invasion caused a wildfire that spread to other parts of the world. After Manchuria followed Abyssinia, Austria, Czechoslovakia, Memel, Albania, and Poland.

Japan had been a signatory to the Nine-Power Treaty of 1922. This treaty was intended to guarantee China's territorial integrity, which had now been violated by Japan. Unlike other colonial powers such as France and Britain, who were more interested in trade and control of the ports—as well as certain major cities, such as Shanghai—Japan had clear geopolitical interests and wanted to have complete control over large swaths of China, including Manchuria.

In its summary of a speech that Chang gave in Chicago to the Convention of the League of Women Voters, the *Milwaukee Journal* described Chang's understanding of the situation in China.[26] According to Chang, the grave situation in Manchuria—or in the three northeastern provinces—was the fault of the Japanese military, a military that was responsible to none but the emperor. Chang urged the League of Nations to do something to rectify the critical situation. He argued that although Japan was invoking its right to the southern Manchurian railway because it fought with Russia over it, the Japanese were bandits in this instance in exactly the same way as the Russians had been before them.

The Kellogg-Briand Pact (after the secretary of state Frank Kellogg and the French foreign secretary Aristide Briand) had also stressed that aggressive war and the conquest of territory was no longer acceptable as a national policy for a country. It emphasized instead the peaceful settlements of conflicts and disputes. The multilateral pact had been signed by Japan and many other countries in August 1928 in Paris and was an attempt to eliminate war. Hence, several countries, including the US, did not recognize the Japanese conquest in 1931. The Lytton Report of 1932 recommended that the League of Nations seek to compel Japan to return Manchuria to China. Japan refused, however, and the following year it quit the League of Nations.[27]

The Chinese republic was deeply engaged with the League of Nations during this period. China was anxious to sign several of the league's conventions and also sought to use the organization for various political purposes, above all, counteracting Japan's colonial policy. And yet, as the Lytton Report well illustrated, the League of Nations showed itself to be incapable of bringing to an end the conflicts between China and Japan.[28]

In early 1932, Chang returned to China with some members of his family. They traveled by ship from Vancouver since at that time it was not possible to make the journey from Los Angeles. They reached Tientsin only after nearly two months of grueling traveling; the train connection from Shanghai had been interrupted once the city became a war zone. The Japanese presence meant that there was widespread fear in northern China of new attacks. Chang therefore advised his brother Poling to send out feelers to investigate the possibility of building a new Nankai School in the city of Chungking in Szechwan Province, in western China.

The domestic political situation and the state of war with Japan nonetheless did not deter Chang from his usual professional activities. In summer 1933, he represented China at the International Conference of Pacific Nations in Banff, Canada. During the next few years, far from easing up on travel, he embarked on even longer journeys, including to Hawaii (a research and teaching visit) and Russia (a tour with Mei Lanfang).[29]

In 1933 and 1934, Chang was a guest professor at the University of Hawaii, where he taught Chinese art, philosophy, and literature. This was the first American university to offer regular courses in Chinese philosophy. Chang also took part in teaching at the Summer School of Pacific and Oriental Affairs in Honolulu. The purpose of this school was to study the cultures of countries bordering the Pacific Ocean. During his time in Hawaii, Chang also wrote a textbook on Chinese history, *China: Whence and Whither?*, which he later expanded into a history book, *China at the Crossroads*, intended for a wider audience.[30] Chang's wife and two sons eventually joined him in Hawaii.

The Chinese author and philosopher Hu Shi, who had been on the same boat to the United States as Chang and the other scholarship students, met up with him again while Chang was in Hawaii. In October 1933, he wrote to his girlfriend, Clifford Williams, about his meeting with Chang: "P. C. Chang is now teaching at the University of Hawaii, his wife and children have not yet joined him there. His family life has not been quite happy, it seems that he feels more at home in foreign academic centres than in China. . . . P. C. gave me a copy of H. G. Wells's *The Shape of Things to Come*, which fits in the picture of the gloomy world as I see it from the ship."[31] The contents of Hu Shi's letter accord well with Stanley Chang's reflections upon his father's many trips and even his radical changes in occupation. The latter—his involvement in very different activities—can also be accounted for by Peng Chung Chang's being driven by impatience and curiosity, something mentioned earlier by his son Stanley. Once his father had immersed himself in an activity and excelled at it, it was time for the next challenge. Nonetheless, he remained faithful to some of these activities as far as possible. He strove to sustain his deep interest in theater and opera for much of the 1930s despite intensifying his foreign policy activities, as he did for his wide involvement in teaching and research. Stanley recalled:

> Like all brilliant people, my father was a profoundly multifaceted person with several different areas of expertise. My guess is that he travelled so much because he wanted to get away from my uncle Poling. Because of their sixteen-year age difference, the brothers' relationship was more like that of a parent and child. Uncle Poling physically beat my father in order to make him study. It always seemed to me as though my father was looking for approval from uncle Poling. During the short period of time when we lived in Chungking on the Nankai campus, I once got into a quarrel with one of my uncle's grandchildren. It was just an ordinary quarrel between two children (I was eleven years old). My father's reaction surprised me. He immediately went to uncle Poling and apologized. What was there to apologize for?!

That Chang was highly valued as a lecturer was doubtless also a contributing factor to his journeying from one university to another. His tenure as a guest professor at the University of Hawaii in 1933 and 1934 was warmly appreciated, and students were clearly deeply affected by his lectures.[32] Additionally, as was his habit, Chang gave several public lectures while at

Hawaii. Reviewing one such lecture, Norman C. Schenck had the following to say about Chang's performance: "There is something magnetic about this great man from China. He is tall and powerful. His appearance instils confidence. His speech and gestures are charming. He seems to be entirely at home with the English language . . . a voice with beautiful intonation, one that by turns can sound like a powerful organ and a gentle flute."[33] In another article published in the newspaper *KA Leo o Hawaii*, the writer expresses the following impressions of Chang: "Dr Peng-Chun Chang, noted Chinese educator who was visiting professor here last year, was honoured last Friday at a tea party in the Honolulu Academy of Arts by the Oriental Institute. He stopped for one day in Honolulu on his way from China to England where he is to lecture at leading colleges. Dr Chang is remembered here for his brilliant lectures on Chinese art, philosophy and history which he delivered at the University last year. His feminine admirers still speak about his "gentle and graceful hands and just perfect diction."[34]

That Chang felt at home and ease in different university towns is revealed in a poem ("New Year in Princeton") that he wrote after visiting Princeton when he was a graduate student in the US. Chang wrote:

Princeton, all beauty and repose!
Why hurry? What's the care?
Ah Monster City that sucks human blood and brain!
Here is life self-knowing, leisure inviolate.

The Tower—the Gothic Tower—
In sunlight, in moonlight,
And in dark and cloudy night
Watch it at a distance, it draws you near . . .
Its firm upward lines dart with this mystic power.
You aspire higher and higher at hither your wavering steps . . .
And when close by, your hope penetrates heaven![35]

For Chang, 1935 was another year defined by theater and opera. He accompanied Mei Lanfang on a tour of the Soviet Union, as was mentioned before, and found time to stage Molière's *L'Avare* (*The Miser*) in China, giving the play a topical spin by making its focus the widespread corruption in Chinese society. One purpose of the play was to collect money for needy children.[36]

Research and Lectures in England

In 1936, Chang was given an opportunity to go to Cambridge University on a one-year visiting professorship. During his time in England, he finished writing his book *China at the Crossroads*.[37]

While Chang's doctoral dissertation had introduced Western educational concepts to a Chinese context, this book aimed to do the opposite: to introduce China to Western readers in order to give them as accurate a picture as possible of the country's history and social development. In this book, Chang examined in detail how China had historically been regarded by the West. He also highlighted all of the ways in which China had contributed materially to the West, such as the manufacture of paper, porcelain, the compass, gunpowder, and the sedan chair. Silk had existed in China several thousand years before Christ. Printing was also invented in China, five hundred years before it came to Europe. Chang emphasized the intellectual inspiration given by China to Europe and its political consequences, such as the struggle against feudalism and absolute monarchy. These latter notions of "political cultural exchange" were to recur in Chang's reflections on the history of human rights and how Western philosophers during the Enlightenment had drawn inspiration from Chinese traditions.

The West's negative perception of China, which had deepened during the nineteenth century, ultimately derived from the fact that China during that century had fallen behind in the fields of scientific discovery and industrial innovation. The Chinese army's inability to hold its own against Western armies, Chang argued, served to further confirm the impression that China was an underdeveloped country. Nor was it a coincidence that these negative assessments became more entrenched in tandem with Europe's creeping expansion eastward.

In his book, Chang sought to situate these negative conceptions of China within a corrective historical framework by highlighting the ways in which the situation had been radically different prior to the nineteenth century. In this period, China and Chinese traditions were the object of widespread admiration in Europe and the West, with Chinese culture making an especially powerful impression.[38] During its three- to four-thousand-year history, Chang contended, China had developed a humanistically oriented philosophy that emphasized the importance of prosperity for every member of society. It had been commonly understood in China that emperors and political leaders were authorized to rule only if they treated their peoples well. This notion accorded closely to the social ideals espoused by the classical Chinese philosopher Mencius (Meng Tse) (372–289 BC).[39] (Similar ideas would later be included in the preamble of the UN Declaration: "Whereas it is essential, if man is not to be compelled to have recourse as a last resort, to rebellion against tyranny and oppression, that human rights should be protected by the rule of law.") According to Chang, it was also striking that China had never been a *military* feudal state for over two thousand years.[40] However, Japan had the experience of being this for a long time.

Chang was eager to analyze the historical relationship between China and Japan in order to understand the actual conflicts between the two countries. Chang laid out the historical circumstances in the following way in the article "Civilization and Social Philosophies," which he published for the American journal *Progressive Education* in 1938:

> Japan, a smaller country with a centralized control, also had the readiness to learn foreign things quicker (than China). Japan's modernization has proved quicker. China's larger, more loosely knit organization, and also China's stupid attitude of having itself achieved a valuable civilization made the process of modernization slower. You have heard that the cultural relation between China and Japan is often said to be about the same cultural relationship as between Greece and Rome. You have heard that, but I don't think you can say it is true. For one thing, Rome took over things from Greece, and then after that, creativeness in Greece died. Another thing: Rome overran Greece. In this respect, Japan learned from China, and the Chinese culture continued and Japan continued to learn from China—from roughly speaking, around the fifth or sixth centuries—and then new movements reached Japan from China even down to the eighteenth century. You should trace it in art, philosophy, court matters, and in literature. Furthermore, Japan never overran China. So it is not at all the same type of relationship; it is rather a matter of relative speed in modernization. That is one reason for the conflict today—it is the speed of modernization. Another reason is the nineteenth century attitude toward expansion in that area. Gradually all the people who have interests in the Pacific are giving up that attitude, and I hope gradually, even suddenly, our neighbour will give up the idea that China cannot modernize herself.[41]

In a speech at the Royal Albert Memorial Museum in Exeter in 1936, Chang noted that there was a general impression abroad that Chinese civilization and culture were not merely ancient but also static and backward. In the seventeenth and eighteenth centuries, perceptions had been very different. The French philosopher Voltaire, for example, regarded the Chinese social and political organizations as humanistic in comparison with its European counterparts, which had been founded on religious thought. Chinese culture was not in fact spiritual, despite there being a common misapprehension that Eastern culture was spiritual and Western materialistic. That view, Chang argued, was wrong. It was indisputable that the Chinese had been more worldly than Westerners because religion in China had never grown into a significant force. Right up to the nineteenth century, China had continued to provide the world with material things. Tea, ceramics, paper, printing, and gunpowder—all originated in China. The country, it was true, still lagged behind as regards the production of railways, motorcars, and manufactured goods as well as in its capital accumulation. However, Chang argued, there were no intrinsic obstacles to modernization. The real difficulty came from the impatient and persistent pressure from the territories that happened to have already modernized. In the past ten years, and particularly during the past four, there had emerged in China a new movement, one which could be characterized as a critical adjustment, according to Chang. No longer would there be a blind imitation of cultural trends and political institutions, but, instead, Chang hoped, from this movement would emerge something that would make real improvements possible.[42]

Chang's assertions about China's past and the positive appreciation of China from European scholars are nonetheless vulnerable to the charge of being overly idealizing and generalized. There were also Enlightenment philosophers in Europe during the eighteenth century who were more critical of China's political system and traditions. Baron de Montesquieu, for example, regarded the government of China as a despotic system that created a social and political order through repression and fear.[43] Some Enlightenment philosophers in Europe may also have idealized Chinese history and culture for political reasons. They were eager to criticize the role of the state churches in their countries, and they looked favorably upon the more secular character of Confucian ethics.[44]

Chang's talk of China and its millennia-long history in his writings was also a modified version of the facts. In an interview I conducted with the sinologist Willard Peterson in 2015, he noted that, while the term "Middle

Kingdom"—*Chung-kuo*, or *Zhongguo*—is more than two thousand years old, the idea of a homogenous Chinese nation is a relatively late invention. When scholars and politicians refer to a Chinese history that stretches back three to four thousand years, they do not have in mind a Chinese nation-state as part of an international system. This notion of the nation-state only took hold at the time of the establishment of the republic in 1912, being further consolidated with the founding of the new People's Republic in 1949. Chinese history prior to this point had been a succession of different political entities, often called dynasties, and a dominant social group, the Han people. Yet these entities did not collectively form a nation-state in the current sense of the word. To describe China as having a three-thousand-year history is thus to project a modern, twentieth-century notion backward onto the past. For Chang's ideas about China's millennia-long history to have validity, it is therefore important to acknowledge that the word "China" denotes a long line of dynasties that emerged as a nation-state only in the twentieth century. It should also be noted that Chang subsequently qualified his account of China's long history precisely by referring to the separate histories of those territories that today compose the state of China. At the end of the nineteenth century and the beginning of the twentieth, China was no longer seen by many citizens as an empire, representing a world civilization. It was perceived more as a state among other states in an international system.[45]

Chang's book *China at the Crossroads* was nevertheless well received, and the reviewers were evidently surprised by the amount of factual information and reflections that he had managed to compress into a work of under 200 pages.[46] It was often remarked that Chang had a particular talent for condensing texts and finding more concise formulations. This ability would serve him well during his work on the UN Declaration, when he would distinguish himself by presenting alternative formulations for the articles that were short and elucidative.

During his time in England, Chang was also in demand as a speaker on political and cultural issues in a range of settings. Chinese culture such as fine art or horticulture, Chang argued, was relatively accessible for those from a Western cultural setting. Philosophy and poetry had also become available thanks to translations. By contrast, Chang noted, Western audiences still found it extremely difficult to understand and appreciate Chinese music, although the enthusiastic reception of Mei Lanfang in the West had shown that this was changing.[47]

Chang also wrote an article during his time in England that compared the different university systems in the UK and in China.[48] In this article, Chang spoke favorably about the tutorial system at Oxford and Cambridge. This system created a personal relationship between the tutor and the student, according to Chang. It also encouraged the students to be humble and creative in their pursuit of knowledge through critical engagement with the opposing views of the tutor. In the Chinese universities, teaching was based more on lectures, which was a less costly system than the tutorial system but more "mechanical" in nature. The Chinese universities suffered also from a lack of a critical and personal/communal atmosphere in the academic environment. Chang pointed out critically, however, that the Oxbridge system had a close connection to the state church, a connection that curtailed freedom of religion for the students who did not belong to this church.

Chang emphasized in his article that the Chinese university education should not be involved in the "lazy" enterprise of copying Western universities. One should instead utilize one's own experiences and look carefully at what the most crucial problems are at the moment. This was a well-known theme from the educational philosophy of John Dewey. Similar thoughts about the problems of an uncritical imitation would also appear later in Chang's work on the Universal Declaration. Chang meant in this context that the declaration should not be an imitation of earlier rights documents.[49]

The Second Chinese-Japanese War, Escape, and the Family Divided

What had been happening in China during Chang's visit to Britain? The years 1935 and 1936 witnessed dramatic events in China, above all in the form of the Communists' Long March. After Chiang Kai-shek's troops surrounded the Communists in Jiangxi Province in 1934, the Communists tried to break through their lines and find a safe haven. They were forced to make a long march to Shanxi Province in the northwest.

Of the eighty thousand who set out, only four thousand reached their "final destination." Thereafter, fortune favored the Communists, who, with the help of Manchuria's military leader, Zhang Xueliang, succeeded in kidnapping Chiang Kai-shek, in the so-called Xi'an Incident of December 1936. Zhang opposed the idea of fighting the Communists before defeating the Japanese. The condition for Chiang's release was therefore that the Communists and the Kuomintang would begin to collaborate again in order to present a united front against Japan. During this period, Mao Zedong increasingly emerged as the self-evident leader of the Communists, a charismatic revolutionary who wanted to transform Chinese society, starting with its peasant farmer class.[50]

The economic and political problems faced by Chiang Kai-shek's republic in the 1930s and 1940s, which resulted in the Communists seizing power, are customarily explained in relation to two phenomena.[51] One key reason why the republic had encountered such difficulties in its attempts at modernization was that it had focused on the populations of the major cities and failed to recognize that peasant farmers constituted China's real core. These latter were to become Mao Zedong's primary focus. The second principal reason for the weakening of the republic was the Second Chinese-Japanese War, which lasted from 1937 to 1945, in which the Kuomintang and the Communists' Eighth Route Army fought against the Japanese invasion. This was triggered by the Marco Polo Bridge Incident of 7 July 1937. A Japanese soldier was assumed to have deserted to the fortress city of Wanping, southwest of Peking. The Japanese army asked for permission to enter Wanping in order to arrest the soldier. When the Chinese refused, the Japanese attacked, taking control of the Marco Polo Bridge (Lugou Bridge). Although they were at first driven back by the Chinese army, the incident became a prelude to Japan's escalating assault on China.

After the bombing of the Marco Polo Bridge and, that same month, Nankai University and the city of Tientsin, many members of the Chang family fled from the Nankai campus in order to avoid further Japanese attacks. Nankai University and the Nankai School were regarded as hostile to Japan because of their nationalistic stance and because of criticisms of Japan's presence in China by its teachers and students.

The Polish-Jewish-Chinese journalist Israel Epstein recalled in his memoirs the dramatic events of July 1937:

> The invaders were dive bombing Nankai University, particularly concentrating on its library: books, along with patriotic students seemed the main object of their hate. I long kept the record I made of a press conference at the Japanese headquarters. We foreign newsmen asked, "Why bomb the university?" "Because, gentlemen, the outrageous Chinese are keeping troops there." The "outrageous Chinese" was the official stereotype used by Japanese spokesmen to designate, in

English, all Chinese opposed to them. "I saw no troops there," said one correspondent. "But the buildings are very strong. The Chinese would use them." "How do you know?" "If I were the Chinese commander, I would use them." Is this any reason to bomb a world famous educational institution?" "Gentlemen, Nankai University is an anti-Japanese base. We must destroy all anti-Japanese bases. Nankai students are anti-Japanese and Communist. Always making trouble for us."[52]

Peng Chun Chang also found himself in the firing line by virtue of his high profile at the university as well as by his criticisms of Japan in his plays and speeches. Several of the university's buildings were destroyed in the Japanese attacks. After the bombings, Chiang Kai-shek made the following remark to Poling Chang: "Nankai has been sacrificed for China but so long as China exists, so will Nankai."[53] The statement reflects the exceptional standing of Nankai University and the Nankai Schools in the Chinese national consciousness. After the Japanese attacks, Poling himself declared: "Nankai has the honour of being the first and the most severely devastated university in China." Chang Poling suffered a further catastrophe shortly after the destruction of Nankai University by the Japanese. His beloved son Xihu, a pilot, was killed in a flying accident when his plane crashed in the Kiangsi Mountains.[54]

Stanley Chang remembers the bombing of Nankai clearly, having himself been in the vicinity of the university. He describes his recollections of the dramatic events and the events after as follows:

> My education was delayed partly because of a hospital admission (TB in my legs) and partly because of the war between China and Japan. The Japanese bombed the Marco Polo Bridge in 1937. That month, they also bombed Nankai University, where my father was teaching. The University was an obvious target for the Japanese because it was famous for its credo of self-reliance, self-esteem, and nationalism. Teachers and students at the University had long expressed fiercely anti-colonial and anti-Japanese sentiments. For these reasons, the Japanese attacked the University and the city of Tientsin, and sought out prominent lecturers.[55] My father, who was one of the most voluble and well-known faculty members and who was serving as university chancellor—because Uncle Poling was in Chungking—was forced

to flee in the night. My mother helped him to disguise himself as a woman, after which he fled to the harbour and managed to get on board a boat. He escaped from Tientsin to another harbour, Wei Hai Wei, on the Shandong peninsula, and from there to the capital city of Nanking. There he was commissioned by the government to relate the facts of Japan's attacks on China to the West. He therefore travelled to Europe and the United States after his escape from Nankai, giving lectures and organizing events to raise funds for the Chinese government and its resistance to Japan's attacks. My father was absent from China for more than three years.

After the Japanese attack on Nankai, my mother and the rest of our family fled to the British zone, where we lived in a compound for several months. During this time, my Uncle Poling continued to pay out my father's salary so that my mother was more or less provided for while on the run. Prior to the attacks on Tientsin, Uncle Poling had moved all his family to Chungking, where a new Nankai school [Nankai Middle School] had been established. After a while, it became clear that my mother and our family would also head inland in order to avoid the Japanese attacks as best they could. In early 1938, she took the whole family by ship, all the way around China, via Hong Kong, to Haiphon and Hanoi in Vietnam. The first stage of the journey was to Shanghai, where we visited mother's brothers and sisters. During the boat journey we shared two and a half hammocks, in which we were fortunate, seeing as how most people had to sleep in the deck. I often slept beside my mother in a hammock. My sisters slept together and my elder brother Chen had to share a hammock with a stranger.

While we were in Vietnam, my mother was robbed of all her money in Haiphon by a pursesnatcher. She was a very short woman, barely 152 cm tall. (My father was 180 cm tall.) Somehow she managed to borrow money in order to continue to the city of Kunming (she met passengers on the boat who knew of the Nankai Schools and were willing to lend her money). After reaching Vietnam by boat, we continued by train for another three days, travelling north through the mountains to Kunming, which lies three hundred miles south of Chungking, the country's temporary capital since the attacks on Nanking. At night, we slept in boxes because the trains did not run at night. My mother was travelling with a nine-year-old boy, a ten-year-old boy, a fourteen-year-old girl, and a brain-damaged fifteen-year-old girl. Kunming was a temporary haven for Nankai University, which had joined with several other universities to form the Southwest Associated University. The weather in Kunming was often cloudy, which meant that the Japanese could not bomb it easily as they had the city of Chungking; even so, Kunming suffered many bombings. After we arrived in Kunming, my sister Ruth travelled on to Uncle Poling's school in Chungking. My mother was far too proud to go with her and live on the Nankai campus in Chungking.

Instead, my mother rented three rooms in Kunming, cooking food on a tiny charcoal stove on the ground. I shared a room with her, and my brother and Ming-Ming slept in the room opposite. We slept on thin mattresses laid on wooden boards. Flies and lice were our constant companions. The toilet was a deep hole in a room to the side of the house. It was emptied once a week. When the man came to collect the latrine bucket, the smell was appalling.

One night my mother did not come home. When I woke up in the middle of the night, I went to my brother and told him that our mother had not come home. He said that I should go back to bed. In the morning, to my enormous relief my mother came back. She never said what had happened and I never asked. (A similar incident occurred many years later. One day, in the summer of 1948, my mother disappeared. At that time we were living in Peter Cooper Village in New York—my father, me, my brother, and Ming-Ming. Ruth had gone to graduate school in Wisconsin. I had taken over the kitchen duties. After several weeks, Ruth wrote to us to say that our mother was in New York City, to judge from the stamp on the letter which she had sent to Ruth. After a few more weeks, my mother came back, to my father's great joy. On that occasion, too, I did not ask where she had been or why she had disappeared.)

When words reached us that my father would be coming to Chungking in April 1940, we travelled by car from Kunming to Chungking. It was a new car that needed to be driven to Chungking from Vietnam and so the driver was earning a little extra cash by taking some passengers from Kunming. I sat in the front passenger seat, while my mother, brother and sister sat in the back. How my mother survived those three years without my father continues to amaze me.

In this moving account, Stanley relates the hardships that the family had to endure in the 1930s. His mother revealed her tremendous strength of personality in bringing the family safely from Tientsin to Kunming and Chungking. The sacrifices that she had to make for the family can only be glimpsed between the lines. The entire story would serve as the basis for a dramatic film. Stanley's brother Chen Chung also developed asthma in the damp tunnel shelters that were used when the Japanese attacked Chungking; he would be afflicted by this asthma for the rest of his life. Stanley's account of his mother's escape with her children also highlights how distant Peng Chun Chang was from his family for several years. In many respects, they lived parallel lives. While Chang moved in the world of high politics, his wife was fighting to keep their family together and to enable them to survive in war-torn China.

After attacking Tientsin, the Japanese turned their attention to Nanking, which was devastated with great brutality between December 1937 and January 1938. According to Chinese sources, more than three hundred thousand Chinese died during the Japanese attacks. In addition, more than twenty thousand Chinese women were raped by Japanese soldiers while parts of the city were being destroyed. The Nanking (Nani-jing) Massacre is one of the most fraught events in modern Chinese history and continues to be a major obstacle to Japanese-Chinese relations.[56] Chiang Kai-shek's army was cut in half by the Japanese attacks, thereby becoming discredited in the popular view. Wuhan, the new capital, was also attacked in autumn 1938, and a new capital accordingly established in western China: Chungking.

Chang's "Propaganda Trips"

P. C. Chang was thus traveling as an official representative of China's Department of Foreign Affairs in the wake of the Japanese attacks in 1937. The purpose of his trips was to inform the world about Japan's brutal military assault on China and to secure aid and sanctions against Japan. P. C. Chang remembers his journey in the following way:

> I left China ... in September after personally witnessing the destruction of my own university by bombing and bombarding and burning. That took place the end of July. After that I went to Nanking, the capital of the country at that time. While in Nanking I witnessed the

air raids there, what took place, the calmness of the people, the resolution on the part of those in responsible positions. Then I left China by air from Hankow, the present seat of the government, thence to Hong Kong, from Hong Kong to Singapore, then through Siam, Burma, India, Iraq, Palestine, northern Egypt, Greece, finally reaching Europe—all the way by air. After reaching Europe I had the opportunity of jumping around quite a little from place to place, visiting the different centers of interest, especially from the point of view of the strained conditions in the world today. For instance, in chronological order, I visited Geneva (to meet the Chinese delegation), Paris, London, Brussels, Rome, Berlin, Moscow then back to London and . . . New York.[57]

In 1938, Chang also visited Washington DC, London, and Geneva, returning the following year to London and Washington in the capacity of government representative—all with a view to alerting the world to Japan's brutality in China.

He clearly had good contacts in China, not least in government circles, which enabled him to secure this commission. Like Chang, a number of those who went on to have stellar careers in the university world, the civil service, and other influential spheres had studied in the United States as Boxer Rebellion Indemnity Fund scholars. According to Stanley, most of the scholars knew each other. In effect, they formed a "community," an influential network. At this point Chang was also a member of the People's Political Council, a body comprising two hundred members intended to represent China's various regions and professional groups. Chang was a member of the Council from 1938 to 1940.

One of the most prominent protest meetings in which Chang took part was held by the *Liberal Magazine* in London's Royal Albert Hall on 5 October 1937. The headline for the meeting was "Japan's Attack Against Civilians."[58] In tandem with the meeting, a campaign was launched to impose an embargo on the import of Japanese products. The eight thousand people who filed into the Royal Albert Hall were shown a film titled *Bombs on China*, which was screened, to the surprise of those present, using the hall's technologically sophisticated system of loudspeakers. The speakers list included several famous names, including Peng Chun Chang, who gave a gripping account of how his university had been bombed to smithereens by the Japanese. In addition to Chang, the speakers list at the meeting included the

Archbishop of Canterbury Cosmo Lang, Dorothea Lady Hosie, and Professor Harold Laski.[59] Laski saw Japan's politics as possibly a turning point for evil in history of civilization and a "deliberate effort on the part of a militarist autocracy to stifle a nascent Chinese democracy."[60] A message from Madam Chiang Kai-shek was also read. The overarching goal of the meeting was to inform and mobilize British public opinion against Japan's brutal attack on the Chinese civilian population as well as to stimulate the British government impose economic sanctions on Japan. After the meeting, Chang met with Clement Attlee, leader of the British Labour Party. Later on Chang also gave a speech at Columbia University in July 13, 1938. In this speech Chang said the following things about the crisis in the Far East:

> The undeclared war in the Far East has been going on for a year. Millions have already died and tens of millions are now in great suffering. Aside from the natural feeling of horror in the face of such colossal calamity, we are especially concerned about the tragic outlook of continued and expanding threats to peace and prosperity not only in the Far East, but also in other parts of the world. Will the struggle and suffering continue for years to come? Can peace in other parts of the world avoid being disrupted by the spreading effect of the conflict?[61]

Unfortunately Chang was correct concerning his worries and the war in the Far East was a prelude to what would soon occur in the rest of the world.

Chang stayed for only a short while in China after his awareness-raising tour of Europe and the United States. During this tour he strived to make the world pay attention to "the Rape of Nanking."[62] Hence, in 1939, he returned again to the United States in order to seek funding to finance China's war against Japan. On this trip he managed to convince the US Congress to impose economic sanctions on Japan. This was clearly an important task as the US furnished 48.5 percent of all machinery purchased by Japan and used in the war against China.[63] But his visit to the United States was not solely taken up with work commitments for the Chinese government. In June, Chang was given an honorary doctorate by his alma mater, Clark University. In July, he traveled to England, where he wrote an essay titled "Universities and National Reconstruction in China" as well as continued his lobbying work against Japan's policies of aggression.[64] In 1939, Chang also published another essay, "The Second Phase of China's Struggles."[65] This essay was based on a lecture he had given at London's Chatham House, a distinguished venue for debates on international politics.

Both essays addressed the grave problems facing China in the context of its war with Japan. In his essay on universities in China, Chang took up the challenges that the university system was enduring as a result of the Japanese military campaign. Fifty-four of China's 114 institutes of higher education had been either completely destroyed or seriously damaged. His own Nankai University, he went on, had been bombed on 29 and 30 July 1937, mere hours after its students, personnel, and their families had fled the campus area. According to Chang, the consequences of the grave military situation faced by universities in China were not all negative. As things had turned out, there were also a number of unanticipated, more-or-less positive effects. Several universities had been evacuated to western provinces of China where previously there had been no universities. These universities had also begun to collaborate with each other in an entirely new way. Students and teachers had also approached educational issues with a clearer focus and a greater willingness to prioritize socially relevant areas of knowledge. Chang also praised the firm commitments among the students to re-establish the educational institutions in the inland provinces. Chang said: "The marching of hundreds of students over a distance of a thousand miles from Changsha to Kunming in Yunnan Province has been appraised as a demonstration of epic significance on the part of the present generation of youths in China."[66]

In Chang's essay "The Second Phase of China's Struggle," he referred to what he called the second phase of the war with Japan, which is to say Japan's attempts since 1937 to quickly destroy China's army. The first phase had involved testing China's military forces in order to see if they were capable of resistance. However, Chang claimed that Japan had utterly failed in its goal of rapidly eliminating China's army, whose fighting spirit remained strong. Three factors in particular, he argued, had helped the Chinese military in its war with Japan. China comprised a huge land mass and it was difficult for the Japanese army to control territories on this scale. The further the Japanese army penetrated inland, the harder it became to extract itself. Moreover, China's cities did not exert control over the countryside, because the majority of the population still lived on the land. Several of the cities were also not modernized. According to Chang, the fact that China as a country was defending itself against an external foe at the same time as it was involved in a nation-building project was yet another powerful incentive for its army to stand up to Japan.[67]

The essay "The Second Phase of China's Struggle," which Chang presented to the seminar at Chatham House, was primarily intended to emphasize China's capacity to repulse the Japanese attack, and to underscore that the coalition between the Kuomintang and the Communists was working. In the essay, Chang also stressed that Japan had benefited from the great economic depression that had struck in the 1930s, intervening in Manchuria at precisely the moment when the rest of the world was preoccupied with the grave economic situation. Chang emphasized in his essay the need for a more global solidarity in order to stop the destructive war and this terrible phenomenon in human history. Chang said that "it is not a matter that can be settled in one corner of the earth alone, because it is inextricably bound up with affairs in other parts of the world as well."[68]

Here, as in other of his essays, Chang made reference to classical Chinese philosophers and quotations in order to illustrate the problem at hand. In this particular context, he quoted from the philosophy of Lao-Tzu, whom several commentators had identified as pacifist, a perspective that Chang did not share. As he saw it, Lao-Tzu had proposed that the softer side always defeats the harder because the latter is inflexible and therefore more fragile. It was a matter of fighting with fist and glue. Glue would envelop one's opponents and make it hard for them to get out.[69]

Chang was also eager to emphasize the role of careful analysis in international affairs. When Chang dwelled upon the war between China and Japan in 1938 he made the following remark: "The challenge to statesmanship today seems to lie in widening the margin between war and inaction and to fill it in with concrete and practical step-by-step procedure. All of us have an important part to play in clarifying the complex situation and in preparing public understanding so that statesmanlike action may be taken at this late date."[70]

Diplomatic Postings in Turkey and Chile

In April 1940, Chang returned to the republic's temporary capital, Chungking. After his visits to the United States and Britain for the purpose of building support for China's struggle against Japan, he was amply qualified for a diplomatic posting to Turkey. During his time in Chunking, he also directed Moliere's *The Miser* once again. He was sent to the embassy at Ankara with the diplomatic rank of minister, just below that of ambassador, and effectively became the head of China's diplomatic personnel overseas between 1940 and 1942. In connection with his appointment, Chang said in an interview in Chunking that he had always admired the great struggle of the Turkish people for national regeneration and the results and spirit of national reconstruction in Turkey, which has been transformed into a modern state. Turkey is not only a great power in the Eastern Mediterranean, Chang said, but is also one of the most important links in international relations. He added that he would strive to improve the mutual understanding in all fields between the Chinese and Turkish peoples.[71] These aspirations were also something that Chang fulfilled as he engaged himself in intercultural understanding during his time in Turkey.

For this period of almost two years, Chang's family was split up, with only his wife and two sons accompanying him to Turkey. After long and intense discussions, Chang and his wife decided that only the boys would join them in Turkey; their two daughters were instead to spend almost six years with an aunt in Shanghai's French zone.[72] After Japan's attack on Pearl Harbor in 1941, this territory was subjected to Japanese occupation, during which their daughters, Ming-Ming and Ruth, suffered from malnutrition and dental problems, Ruth even contracting TB of the kidneys.

Stanley Chang can remember the day Japan attacked Pearl Harbor: 7 December 1941. His father had been sitting all day listening to the BBC on shortwave radio, and Stanley remembers him saying: "Now they (Japan) have made a mistake." Stanley does not remember that his father ever referred to Japan again. His assumption is that the subject was too painful for him. After suffering the first of several heart attacks while in Santiago, Chile, in 1943, Chang would also exert himself to keep a check on his temper.

The journey to Turkey involved first flying across Japanese territory to Hong Kong. From there, the family continued by ship to Basra in Iraq and then by train through Baghdad to Ankara. Stanley Chang's memories of his father's time as a diplomat in Turkey and Chile are understandably fragmentary. Stanley was between eleven and thirteen during these years and did not have any insight of his own into his father's professional life. Even so, he related some personal memories from their time in Turkey:

> I remember that when we were in Turkey my father told me that Chinese law gave him the right to kill me if I misbehaved. I took this with the utmost seriousness and thereafter tried always to obey him. In our second year in Turkey, my brother and I were sent to the British

High School for Boys. After our stay in Turkey, I was able to speak several languages, including Chinese, English, and Turkish. Our father also tried to impress Confucian rules upon me and my brother while we were in Turkey, such as that every person must bear the responsibility that comes with their particular station in life. But he gave up after only a month.

Stanley remembers a number of the meetings that his father had with various diplomats in Ankara: "Turkey was a neutral country during World War Two and so my father was able to talk to the German ambassador, Franz von Papen. He told me that von Papen was an intelligent man, unlike certain other diplomats who were merely superficial businessmen. After Pearl Harbor, however, my dad and von Papen were no longer able to talk to each other." Franz von Papen had been part of the Reichspräsident Paul von Hindenburg's closest circle and after the war was accused of having helped Hitler to seize power. At the Nuremburg Trials, however, he was found not guilty of war crimes. Von Papen served as ambassador to Turkey until 1944, when diplomatic relations between Turkey and Germany were suspended.

During his time in Turkey, Chang was also involved in negotiating a pact with Iraq—the Mutual Friendship Treaty of 1942—and a treaty with Saudi Arabia. That same year, on 6 and 11 March, Chang gave two lectures at King Faisal II's palace in Baghdad.[73] In both, Chang emphasized the historical relations between Iraq and the Arab world, and China, as well as their common struggle against enemy Japan and the other Axis powers, whose military aggression constituted a grave threat to human freedom and dignity. It may be of interest in the present context to review some of the key points in Chang's lectures since they very clearly reflect his conception of which historical facts had particular relevance for those who would understand China in the present moment.

In his first lecture, Chang devoted special attention to the contacts between China and the rest of the world throughout history, particularly the Arab and Muslim worlds. Starting with journeys undertaken by Marco Polo and the Arab explorer Ibn Battuta, Chang painted a picture of China's cultural contacts across the centuries. China had influenced the West not only from a material point of view but also intellectually through political ideas that, among other things, had called feudalism into question. The Arab world had been a source of inspiration for China in the fields of geography, mathematics, and medicine. Muslim missionaries also came to China at an early stage, and in 1942 there were more than fifty million Muslims in China. The Great Mosque in Canton attested to the historical presence of Islam in Chinese society.

In his second lecture, Chang expounded at length on the significance of scholarship and science in China in the three thousand years that had passed since Confucius. The lecture was peppered with a succession of quotations from Confucius, such as "To study and not think is a waste. To think and not study is dangerous." Chang quoted approvingly the American scholar and educator Arthur N. Holcombe's description of China's political and social structure. Throughout history, China had been neither aristocracy, oligarchy, autocracy, nor democracy but rather a "democracy of merit" in which the educated have always had a high standing among the majority of the population. (In his book *The Chinese Revolution* the historian Arthur N. Holcombe called China "The Scholastic Empire" as the scholar held an almost sacred position in Chinese political and social life.[74]) In the second lecture in Baghdad, Chang also underscored the importance of a spirit of discovery for promoting a scientific attitude toward one's environment. China and other countries had much to learn from the scientific development that had taken place in the West during the great age of discovery, which had begun in the sixteenth century when critical, comparative studies became possible through the steady discovery and opening up of other areas of the world.

Chang's two lectures in Baghdad were compelling in their broad grasp of cultural questions. His lectures not only ranged across literature, philosophy, and religion but also encompassed economic, scientific, and technological issues. The first lecture contained reflections that Chang had already formulated in connection with the writing of his textbook *China at the Crossroads*, while the second lecture contained themes that had figured earlier in Chang's dissertation, *Education for Modernization in China*.

Both of his Baghdad lectures also addressed a key question on which Chang had long focused, namely the attitude that China ought to adopt toward external cultural influences in order to avoid either stagnation or the risk of selling its soul. When I asked Stanley Chang if, after the lectures in Baghdad, his father had shown any further interest in Islam and the Arab world during the rest of the 1940s and 1950s, he replied in the negative: "My father's interest in Turkey and Muslims did not extend further than his professional duties. He also had a strong tendency to prepare thoroughly on a subject and take pains with his argument, something he had learned during his time as a member of the Clark University debate team." Stanley Chang's statement should nonetheless be qualified by the fact of his father's unwavering fascination with China and its cultural development and relations across the centuries. Chang was a highly educated person with a wide range of interests. While he may not have dwelt at any length on questions relating to Turkey and Islam in his subsequent writings and public activities, they intersected with a number of areas in which he was later to become interested.

Peng Chun Chang's time in Turkey was to be short, however, and in May 1942 he was appointed to the ambassadorship in Santiago, Chile, where he worked from 1942 until 1945. Since both Turkey and Chile were neutral countries during his period of diplomatic service, he and his family did not experience World War II in any particularly dramatic fashion. Indeed, it was a period of calm for some in the family. By contrast, Chang's daughters, Ming-Ming and Ruth, who had stayed behind in China while Chang was posted in neutral countries overseas, had to endure the Japanese occupation.

Chang traveled with his wife and two sons to Chile from Turkey via Egypt. Stanley recalled the trip as follows:

> We travelled from Ankara to Cairo by train over night. We stayed in Cairo for a few days while the Germans were knocking on the door in Alexandria because of the miles of British canons facing them. My parents left my brother and I alone in a hotel in Cairo for one day. So we walked over to a big pyramid. My brother talked to a guide in English. I asked my brother "What did he say?" in Turkish. My brother answered in Turkish, "He wants too much." We were in the habit of talking to each other in Turkish to avoid our parents listening in. When the guide overheard us, he walked up and offered to take us for one third of the price. So we climbed the big pyramid all the way to the top and also went deep inside. The guide took us all the way to the inside tomb and showed us the ventilation opening in the wall of the tomb. When we came out, the guide wanted us to go and see the Sphinx, but we were too tired to go. We then travelled by military planes from Cairo—including the famous PBY around Africa to Dakar. We flew across the ocean to Natal in a famous Pam-Am flying boat. We flew down the east coast of South America in a small 8-passenger airplane to Rio. We stayed in Rio for a month while my mother recovered from the malaria she caught in Africa.

> We flew down to Argentina in a DC-3, and then across to Santiago. But it took three tries to get across the Andes mountains, so the DC-3 had to return to Argentina for the night and it made it across the Andes in less than three hours the next morning. That is a the story of our trip from Turkey to Chile in 1942.

As mentioned earlier, Stanley Chang does not remember much of his father's working life in Chile. His father did, however, have a heart attack, which his son recalled clearly:

> My father had his first heart attack in Chile in 1943 after challenging me and my brother to a race down the long driveway leading to our house. He collapsed and fought to get into the house. [According to a chronology written by Stanley's sister Ruth in 1995, their father had a heart attack in Santiago in autumn 1942. However, Ruth had not come with the family to Chile.] He had a second heart attack in 1952 in New York City. It was then that he told me the pain was so severe that he felt as if he was dying. He was sent to the Harkness Pavillion, at the Columbia University Presbyterian Medical Center. For the entire month that my father was at the hospital I went to see him everyday after work. I was trying to be a good son in spite of our distance. His third heart attack, which he did not survive, came in 1957 in Nutley, New Jersey. After his first heart attack in Chile, he stopped smoking and ate less salt, and he was forced to keep reminding himself not to get angry. Even so, there were occasions when he was unable to stay calm, like the day when he was on a bus in New York City and got so angry with the driver that he burst out: "Don't you know who I am?" On that occasion, my brother and I wanted nothing more than to disappear. I think it must have been 1947 or 1948. However, for the most part he managed to remain calm. My father would sometimes exclaim "Don't you know who I am?," in public as well as in private, when he felt that he was not being treated with enough respect.

In her chronology of their father's life, Stanley's sister Ruth also mentions that Chang had a further heart attack in February 1951 while attending a UN summit in Santiago. This statement is contradicted by Stanley Chang's recollection. P. C. Chang's colleague John Humphrey's diary notes from the same period likewise make no mention of a heart attack but instead relate that Chang was having stomach problems, which Humphrey's wife was trying to help him with.[75]

Chang was evidently deeply engaged in political conditions in South America during his time at the Chinese embassy in Santiago. In one memoir, he relates that during his time as a diplomat in Chile he traveled around studying industrial projects not only in Chile but also Brazil, Colombia, and Peru. He reflected upon the vulnerability that existed in countries that placed their trust in the export of a single primary product. For a country to achieve greater national independence and economic development, it needed to be able to refine the primary product itself and also invest in raising the educational level of its people—an idea that also has particular relevance in the present moment.[76] Meanwhile, a letter from the British delegation indicates that Chang and his wife were greatly appreciated in the diplomatic colony in Santiago: "Dr Chang has been very successful in fostering sympathy for China in Chile and both he and his wife are popular. Both speak good English and are Christian."[77] This statement is also interesting for the way it mentions that Chang and his wife were regarded as Christian by people from the British embassy. According to Stanley, his father was never involved in any religious activities during the time they lived together. By contrast, his mother and her family were Methodists, which presumably left its mark on family life. This situation may perhaps explain why both were described as Christian in the British delegation letter. Stanley also related that in China the family celebrated Christmas—he was five at the time—in the traditional way. But Stanley emphasized that both his father and mother were never involved in any religious activities during the time that he lived with them. They never went to church for example.[78]

Stanley Chang's memoir also highlights that Peng Chun Chang had close contacts with elements of the political establishment in China during his time in Chile: "When we lived in Chile, Madam Chiang Kai-shek was invited to speak to the US Congress. My father sent her a telegram giving advice on how she should address Congress on 18 February 1943. At the time I thought it was presumptuous of him to do so. But afterwards I learned that he knew her personally because she had studied at Wellesley at the same time as my father was studying at Clark University."

The speech, which was an appeal for help from the United States to China in its struggle against Japan, was in any event a triumph for Mrs. Chiang Kai Shek, who thereby became the first woman to address both chambers of the American legislature. Madam Chiang Kai-shek, or Soong May-ling

(1898–2003), was an international celebrity at this time who helped ensure that China received substantial support from the Allies at the start of World War II, particularly during the period when Japan was attacking China. Following her speech to Congress, she appeared on the cover of *Time* on 1 March 1943. She often accompanied her husband on trips, including to the top summit of Allied leaders in Cairo in 1943, where she acted as interpreter for her husband. She came from a distinguished and wealthy family in China. Her father, Charlie Soong (1863–1918), was a Methodist missionary and a successful businessman who had studied in the US. He had played an active political role during the first years of the Republic of China and was initially in Sun Yat-sen's inner circle. Her sister Ching Ling had been married to the founder of the republic, Sun Yat-sen, while her sister Ai-ling married H. H. Kung, a wealthy banker and businessman who also became minister of finance in the Nanking government during the 1930s. After her husband's death in 1975, Madam Chiang Kai-shek moved to the United States, where she died in 2003.[79]

The Chang family's time in Chile was, like their stay in Turkey, relatively short. The first step in bidding farewell came when both their sons traveled to New York in summer 1944. As Stanley related:

> My father put me and my brother on a Liberty ship, *Knute Rockne*, from Chile to New York in July 1944. The person who met me and my brother at the ship pier in New York on September 1 was Yen Jen Ying. He was the grandchild of the person who let Uncle Poling use his household to start the first Nankai school. It was he who talked the immigration officials out of sending us to Ellis Island. He took us to his tiny room at the YMCA where we spent the first night in the US. The next day he delivered us to my mother's best friend from Vassar College, Mrs Todd M. Miller, who took us to a boarding school in Windsor, Connecticut, the Loomis School. We thought we would spend Christmas with Mrs Miller. Later that autumn, we were instructed, to our surprise, to go to an apartment in New York City on the corner of Broadway and 100th Street. Our parents had come to New York by plane just before Christmas. They told us that my father had given up his job in Chile. I knew nothing about how he spent his working hours and only several years later learned that he had participated in the formation of the United Nations. He rarely spoke to me about his professional affairs in Turkey and Chile. In early sum-

mer 1947 I also remained unaware of what he was actually doing until he asked me to come with him to the United Nations meeting at the Sperry Gyroscope plant on Long Island when he started work on the UN declaration.

Some of Peng Chun Chang's colleagues at the embassy in Santiago were also clearly surprised by the family's abrupt departure to the United States. Stanley continued:

When my father was sent to Turkey as Minister, there was no first secretary. There were only second, third, and fourth secretaries. After a year, the Chinese government sent a first secretary with the surname Yuan, a very calm and intelligent person. So when we left Turkey for Chile in 1942, Mr Yuan became responsible for the embassy until the government sent a new head. This took about two years. When my brother and I were sent to the United States at the end of July 1944, we thought that our father and mother would stay in Chile for a few more years. As I say, it came as a complete surprise to us that we were to go to New York City, to the corner of Broadway and 100th Street, to meet our parents there at the end of 1944. The only condition for my father to be allowed to resign his ambassadorship in Chile was that a replacement could be found quickly. Mr Yuan had admired my father so much during our time in Turkey that he had specially requested to be moved to Chile in order to serve under him again. But now my father was once again leaving his post, and Mr Yuan was left behind in Santiago. I have sometimes wondered sadly about Mr Yuan and thought that it was a pity for him to have been twice left in the lurch by my father.

Stanley's narrative conveys the abruptness of foreign service life for his father during World War II, with one new assignment after another and continually improvised solutions. His story also reflects the dominant impression given by Chang's professional activities, regardless of the subject, namely that, time and again, he elicited the profound admiration of his colleagues and those he came into contact with through his work and public speaking.

CHAPTER 3

New York and the United Nations

After relatively short diplomatic postings to Turkey and Chile, Chang's life took a new and unexpected turn. When the Second World War ended, a new international organization—the United Nations—was created with the primary task of working for world peace. Chang was invited to represent the Republic of China in the new organization, and following the first General Assembly meeting in London in 1946, he was given the opportunity to help write the UN Declaration on Human Rights. At this time, an intense civil war was raging in China, and successive Communist victories against the republic in the late 1940s made Chang's position within the UN increasingly untenable. Following Mao's seizure of power in 1949, Communist states questioned Chang's presence in the UN and made attempts to exclude him at several of its meetings. In certain circles, Chang came to be regarded as a kind of diplomatic "outlaw" who persisted in staying at the UN even though his regime, after losing the civil war in China, had fled to Formosa.

UN Work Begins

In 1944, Chang and his family returned to New York, where he took part in an official meeting in October. After the meeting, he resigned his diplomatic post in Chile. He then briefly taught again at Columbia University before becoming involved with the embryonic UN organization. He was also asked by the government in China to go to San Francisco in 1945 to be present at the founding of the UN as an international organization. The leader of the Chinese delegation to San Francisco was T. V. Soong—a famous diplomat and businessman from China—who belonged to the rich and influential Soong family. One of his sisters was Soong May Ling, whom Chang knew from his undergraduate days in the US. T. V. Soong had also done his postgraduate studies at Columbia at almost the same time as Chang. Since they moved in similar social circles, it is a reasonable conjecture that Soong and Chang had met early in their postgraduate studies. Chang wrote a letter to T. V. Soong at the Foreign Office in Chunking when he was in New York during the fall. Soong was the minister of foreign affairs between 1942 and 1945. In the letter, Chang wrote that he was deeply grateful for being able to take sick leave. Heart trouble did not permit him to return to Chile and he asked Soong to kindly relieve him of the post in Santiago. Chang wrote in the letter that his postwar efforts would be in educational work. Chang also emphasized that if he could be of any service in the contacts with intellectual circles in the United States, he was at Soong's command and awaited his Excellency's instructions.[1]

After Japan capitulated in August 1945, Chang traveled to China. One purpose of his trip was to spend a few months helping his brother Poling reclaim property belonging to the Nankai Schools and Nankai University in Tientsin. Another was to collect instructions from his government regarding his upcoming UN work. He also rearranged Ibsen's *A Doll House* while he was in Chongqing (Chungking).

In 1946, Chang went to London, where he helped to organize the United Nations. He was one of four delegates from China. As part of the summit, he was made resident chief delegate (with the rank of ambassador) in the Economic and Social Council of the United Nations, and subsequently also vice chairman of its Human Rights Commission, which was later to be tasked with writing the UN Declaration on Human Rights. After the end of the Second World War, the victorious Allies sought to bring into being a new international organization that would work for peace in the world. The lessons learned from the earlier failures of the League of Nations would be incorporated into the foundation process.

As part of his involvement in the London summit, Chang gave a number of speeches in which he expressed his hopes for the new international organization and, more specifically, its Economic and Social Council. Among other things, he underscored the importance of combating global epidemics and of developing the economies of countries whose business activities were insufficiently diversified. Since epidemics did not respect national boundaries, Chang argued, they also represented a problem that required a global response. He thus strove to encourage the UN to create an organization that would check the spread of global epidemics.[2]

As in his other speeches, Chang quoted from Chinese philosophers in order to lend weight to his observations. In his opening address at the launch of the UN's Economic and Social Council in 1946, Chang invoked Mencius when describing the purpose of the new organization: "Subdue people with goodness; people can never be subdued. Nourish people with goodness and the whole world will be subdued" (Mencius IV.B.16). Chang argued that the aim of the council was to promote human prosperity and to facilitate humanity's joint efforts to resolve grave global problems. This demanded a new form of loyalty.

In his description of ideal social relations, Chang also referred to Confucius in one of his statements. For Confucius, the ideal social order will, when "the great way dominates," take the form of people caring about each other regardless of whether they are related by blood. Those holding office will be chosen on the basis of competence and virtue. Provisions will be made for the physically disabled, orphans, and the old. Those who are young and strong will be given education and work. Wealth will not be squandered. Intrigues will be resisted, crime will disappear, with the result that no one will need to bolt their doors at night. In this address, Chang drew on Confucius in order to articulate a line of thinking that could well have been formulated by postwar political thinkers such as the American philosopher Michael Walzer. Walzer articulated a theory of complex justice in which a fair, equitable division is realized when different goods, such as merit-based higher education or needs-based health care, are allocated on the basis of different criteria for distribution.[3]

Chang's speech at the London summit makes clear his deep engagement in social policy and welfare issues, doubtless in large part as a result of the profound social problems with which his own country was wrestling. After returning from the London summit to New York, he became a driving force in the creation of the World Health Organization (WHO). As Stanley Chang explained:

> My father had an office in the Empire State Building in around 1945 (room 6301). Opposite his office was another office with a golden sign reading W.H.O. (World Health Organization). My father was also involved in the creation of this body. My father's office was on the 63rd floor. His office was part of a suite of offices. There was a main door to the suite, which was what he used to get to his office. However, his room had a side door that opened onto the outside corridor. It was

for escaping from potentially unwanted visitors. One day I was inside his room discussing something about a planned family trip. Suddenly the secretary announced a very important visitor. My father made me use the secret door because he did not want that visitor to know that I was there. One foggy morning—it was Saturday 28th of July 1945—an AB25 bomber flew straight into the North wall of the Empire state building right at the 78th floor and 14 people died. My father had tried to go to his office on the 63d floor in the morning. But of course he had to give up and come home.

In an article from 1948 titled "My View of the United Nations," Chang claimed that the UN is a complicated organization tasked with a heavy and complex workload.[4] Chang stressed in the article that this fact should not, however, create pessimism about the organization. According to Chang, the shared goal of creating global peace and order is an important common denominator for the participating countries, a common denominator that provides a reason for being optimistic about reaching reasonable compromises in spite of long discussions and polarized debates. The following is a representative statement of Chang's worldview and opinion about the UN:

> The author of this article is the representative of China to the Economic and Social Council. The council's duty is to solve real social and economic problems in the world. The discussions regarding these issues demand practical understanding, careful analysis, cautious planning and wisdom from experts. Newspaper reports regarding these discussions are, of course, not as lively as the ones about the sessions held at the Security Council. However, let's not forget that dealing with these problems is a step-by-step, down-to-earth work. The social problems in various parts of the world are extremely complex and wide ranging. To solve these problems it is obvious that many organizations need to act in concert. So, over the past year, the greatest task of the Economic and Social Council has been to build and organize these institutions in a way that all aspects of their work can be put into action in a co-ordinated fashion. We think that the Economic and Social Council has been successful in this respect. Today there are already nine specialized agencies working with the Council to establish a division of labor, for example, the International Labor Organization, the Food and Agriculture Organization of the United

Nations, the United Nations Educational, Scientific and Cultural Organization, the World Health Organization, the International Bank for Reconstruction and Development, and the International Monetary Fund. These specialized agencies have their own specific responsibility to solve each aspect of their problems.[5]

This article in interesting on several counts since it expresses Chang's pragmatism and his emphasis upon the importance of reaching compromises and intermediary positions even at heated political moments, something that characterized all his work for the Human Rights Commission.

Chang was also convinced that it was possible to reach agreement about overarching values or objectives in international politics. In his capacity as chief of the Chinese Delegation to the U.N. Conference on Freedom of Information in Geneva in March 1948 Chang stressed that "freedom of information ... is one of the keystones, if not the keystone, to better understanding between nations and therefore, the maintenance of peace throughout the world. We submit that the differences which exist among ourselves lie not so much in the objective to be obtained as in the approach by which this objective can be obtained."[6]

Change's involvement in high politics did not prevent him from becoming increasingly engaged in private and cultural questions. In October 1946, he helped to arrange a conference in honour of his brother Poling, which was followed by an anthology, *There Is Another China*, published in 1948. In it, contributors examine Poling's life and pedagogical achievements during the Nankai Schools' fifty years of existence.[7] Several Nankai alumni participated in the conference.

Chang's arrangement of this conference and publication of the anthology were symptomatic of his relationship with his elder brother. Even though Chang helped in realizing the entire project, he did not want to be acknowledged in connection with the event. The spotlight was to be on his brother alone. The 1946 conference coincided with other important events in Poling's life. He underwent a successful prostate operation in New York, and during his stay there, he also received an honorary doctorate from Columbia University.[8] While in New York, Poling also visited the Silver Bay resort with Peng and his family.[9] Peng Chun Chang would presumably never again see his brother Poling, who spent his final years on the mainland under the Communist regime. Poling, despite his personal relationship with Zhou Enlai, was also far too closely associated with Chiang Kai-shek to be able to have any real influence on educational issues in Mao's China. In 1948, Poling was nominated chair of the Chinese state's Examinations Division, where he was responsible for entrance testing for all branches of the civil service.[10]

Soon after moving to New York in the mid-1940s, Peng Chung Chang reunited his family, which occupied a series of different residences in and just outside the city. What were the residences of the family Chang in New York? Stanley recalled:

> Regarding our houses in New York, I can tell you the following. First we had a small apartment on the corner of Broadway and 100th. We rented it for one year. Thereafter we rented an apartment on 110 Morningside Drive. Then a rented house on 61st Street in Garden City on Long Island (as part of my father's work on the UN Declaration). After Garden City we moved to an apartment on the 14th floor at 531 East 20th Street in Peter Cooper Village in New York and finally to a house in the town of Nutley, New Jersey at 142 Rutgers Place. The house that my father bought was a small two-storey house with three bedrooms and a bath on the second floor. The living room, dining room and kitchen were on the first floor with a breakfast nook in a corner of the kitchen. The house had a full basement and behind the dining room there was a back porch which had been walled in. There was a beautiful small dog wood tree just to the left of the front door. It looked like a gingerbread house.

Stanley and his brother nonetheless continued to attend Windsor boarding school in Connecticut, seeing their parents mostly at the weekends. At times Stanley found boarding very difficult:

> My father did something that was very good for me. I was unhappy at boarding school and things were not going well. In 1945, my father came to visit me at school and gave me a present of piano lessons. This gave me an outlet for my emotions and by the summer of 1951 I had managed to learn Beethoven's *Páthetique* sonata. This enabled me to get a place at Harvard. Happily, my piano teacher agreed to put up a security of 5,000 dollars which the university required. I was quite certain that I did not want to ask my father for help in this particular matter.

A running theme in Stanley Chang's memoirs of his relationship with his father is how for long periods of time he experienced anxiety and a sense of distance. Stanley relates that he was often afraid of his father but without quite being able to explain why. Chang was evidently a highly demanding father, even administering corporal punishment to Stanley on several occasions during his early childhood. Unlike their mother, Chang was not particularly involved in his children's upbringing and schooling. Stanley recalls how, as a teenager, he was at times so desperately unhappy about his relationship with his father that he tried to run away from home, only to return on each occasion at the last moment. For much of his life, Stanley hated his father, but after Chang's death he was able to reconcile himself with his father's memory and learn to appreciate his positive qualities. While Stanley was growing up, Chang knew that his son was often unsure of himself and extremely unhappy, yet he made no real effort to try to help him. On the contrary, Stanley recalled that his father exploited the situation and criticized his son whenever he showed the slightest indication of fear or anxiety. Nevertheless, Chang appreciated explicit honesty and sincerity, according to Stanley. When Stanley was completely open about certain failures or shortcomings, such as some of his study results, his father praised him for that.

When asked about what he considered his father's positive treatment of him—aside from the piano lessons that gave him the window to music, operas, and ballets—Stanley gave the following reply:

> As we recall my brother and I arrived in New York on a foggy morning on the first of September 1944 on the liberty ship Knute Rockne. My father had obtained student visas to the United States for us when we left Chile that year. My brother married an American girl in 1951, so he was automatically given an American passport. I was forced to get a special permit from the US Congress in order to be able to stay in the country as a legal permanent resident. Practically speaking, I was an "illegal" immigrant in the United States from 1950 to 1958. My father managed to get me into Purdue University because he had a friend there. My father later influenced me to change the direction of my studies, from aviation technology to electrical engineering, because I would have been unable to find a job in the aircraft industry without a valid residency permit. My father also gave me carpentry lessons in Chile, which led me to all things working with my hands.

> When I was studying at the Grange school for boys in Santiago my father also helped me with one important thing. In the British system the boys were ranked according to their grades. So the top student sit in the first chair by the door followed by the second, third, and so forth. I was doing very poorly and was ranked dead last in my class. My father went to have a talk with the headmaster and had the school give me math lessons beyond my class. The following quarter, I went all the way from the bottom to the fifth chair.

It was typical of Chang that he made a handful of limited one-off interventions that he probably regarded as completely decisive for Stanley's life. The summer of 1951 was also special because Chang and Stanley were given the chance to meet Frank Lloyd Wright, one of the most famous architects in the world:

> In the summer of 1951, my father rented a house from a professor at the University of Wisconsin–Madison. There was a large piano in the house with which I was able to learn the *Pathétique* sonata. That summer we visited Frank Lloyd Wright, the famous architect, in Taliesin, Spring Green. I was shocked when Wright remarked deprecatingly that "philosophers are useless in our society," but my father only smiled at Wright's words. He did not want to contradict the famous architect, which made me ashamed of him. My father had a formidable capacity for argumentation and could easily have rebutted Wright's prejudices, but he chose not to. For many years, he had also impressed upon me the importance of studying Confucius and other Chinese philosophers.

Chang came into contact with a huge number of famous people in his lifetime as a consequence of his studies, his theater work, his dramatic political activities, and his diplomatic missions. The fame of the Nankai Schools in China also meant that Chang and his brother were well-known figures in China, regularly meeting with politicians and cultural luminaries. It is also safe to assume that Chang moved freely in domestic political circles in China, thanks in part to his acquaintance with Madame Kai-shek from his student days in the United States and because of his friends from the Boxer Indemnity Scholarship Fund. During his time in America, Chang had got to know intellectuals such as the famous philosopher Hu Shi, with whom he likely remained in periodical contact throughout his life, at least until the mid-1940s, when Hu Shi contributed to the anthology published in honor of Chang's brother Poling.[11] During their years as graduate students in New York it seems that Hu Shi and Peng Chun Chang met each other quite often and attended plays and dinners together.[12] Hu Shi had been ambassador for China to the United States from 1938 to 1942, and he went on to become chancellor of National Peking University from 1946 to 1948.

During Chang's time as a representative for China's State Department, he was to meet Lord Ernest Bevin and Anthony Eden in England. His passion for the theater meant that he was frequently introduced to famous actors, opera stars, and directors from various countries. He also tried to keep in touch with the university world to some extent. He met, for example, the famous historian Charles A. Beard in Beard's home in 1946.[13] Yet he rarely spoke to his son Stanley of his meetings with these famous individuals. Stanley's understanding was that his father simply thought it not worth discussing such meetings with his son. But Stanley did recall one peculiar meeting that his father had with an extraordinary individual: "My father once met Helen Keller, who was both blind and deaf. Nonetheless, her brain worked fine and it was possible to communicate with her using hand-signals on her hand, that is to say, signing letters. My father said that it was also possible to communicate with her in another way entirely. She had taken hold of his face and felt it as he spoke the words. He said that it was extremely unpleasant to be touched in that way." Helen Keller (1880–1968) was an American author and human rights activist. She was the first deaf and blind person to obtain a university degree. The story of her life, including how her teacher Anne Sullivan managed to break her isolation, is portrayed in the play and film *The Miracle Worker*.[14]

Civil War in China

How had the situation in China been developing during Chang's time in Turkey and Chile as well as his first years in New York and at the UN? The collaboration between the Kuomintang army and the Communists had long been creaking at the joints. Major defeats for Chiang Kai-shek, including the loss of Wuhan in 1938, and a succession of victories for the Communists led to acute tensions within the coalition. An especially dramatic incident occurred in eastern central China at the start of 1941, when the Communists' new Fourth Army was surrounded and nine thousand of its soldiers were killed by the Kuomintang army. The incident compromised the Kuomintang army in the eyes of the public and increased the popularity of Mao Zedong and the Communists' army among the general population. The Communists' popularity was further enhanced by their growing successes against the Japanese.

Despite the series of conflicts within the union, the collaboration continued, in large part because of pressure from the Allies, particularly after the Soviet Union entered the war in June 1941, followed by the United States in December that same year. Stalin even tried to persuade the Communists to work with the Kuomintang regime.[15] As noted previously, the Kuomintang regime and the Communists had a number of significant points in common. Both wanted an integrated China with a strong centralized power, and both supported a vigorous modernization of Chinese society.[16] In retrospect, the Chinese resistance to Japan also seems to have been successful. Unlike other invasions in Chinese history—such as the Moguls during the Middle Ages—the Japanese never conquered China and were never able to fully dominate its enormous territory. China succeeded in defending its sovereignty in a number of key respects, despite the loss of Nanjing and Peking. However, after the Americans defeated Japan in 1945, the tensions between the Kuomintang and the Communists in China escalated, and the civil war between them intensified. The Communist army gradually began to receive help from the Soviet Union, while the Kuomintang regime found it increasingly difficult to rely on support from the general population, particularly in the northern regions. Even the support of the United States steadily slackened off. The Kuomintang had its power base in the south and the major cities, while the Communists could count primarily on the north and the countryside, where the majority of the population lived. Mao's promise of land reform also increased his support among the rural population.

Corruption and runaway inflation further deepened popular disillusion with the Kuomintang establishment, while the more Spartan lifestyle of the Communists appealed to the general population. Those in the Kuomintang camp who showed signs of wanting to cross over to the other side were also encouraged to do so by the Communists and were met, at least initially, with positive acceptance.[17] When hopes for greater democracy were dashed at the end of the war, as China became increasingly autocratic, disaffection spread to groups within the Kuomintang's heartland, that is, the cities. This gave people yet another incentive to go over to the Communists. During the 1930s and '40s, the Kuomintang government's aim to achieve rural and other reforms was hampered by its inability to gather tax revenue.[18]

Despite initially enjoying the support of the United States, the Kuomintang regime thus lost its military and political advantage over the Communists, an advantage that had previously been quite substantial, taking the form of a far larger army and control of many more regions. In military terms, it was also a serious disadvantage for the Kuomintang regime that the bulk of its forces were situated in the western parts of the country. Mao Zedong's forces, which had previously been engaging in guerrilla warfare, also began waging a more conventional military campaign whose strategy consisted of luring enemy forces far inland, then surrounding them and cutting off their lines of retreat—a strategy that had previously been used against the Japanese army and that can be traced back to the principles of the "war philosopher" Sun Tzu (544–496 BC).[19]

How did the situation in China affect Chang's work in the UN? On 4 December 1948, just before the Universal Declaration of Human Rights (UDHR) was due to be voted on in the General Assembly, Chang's colleague John Humphrey recorded in his journal some impressions of Chang's state of mind regarding the civil war in China. The Republic of China was at this point losing the civil war against the Communists. All of Manchuria had fallen to the Communists in November 1948, and in early December Mao's forces marched to just south of the capital Nanking, having already surrounded Peking in the north.[20] "P. C. Chang was less helpful than usual. His emotional outbursts became more frequent and he has made some personal enemies. I am told, however, that he has not been well and he must be disturbed by events in China. In intellectual stature he towers above any other member of the committee. I also like his philosophy."[21] It is interesting that Humphrey should have made these particular observations about his colleague. His journal notes record the fact that he was deeply appreciative of Chang and sought to rationalize his deficient attention. Chang had rapidly distinguished himself as one of the most driven and acute delegates in the UN's Commission on Human Rights, and his work on the UN Declaration was generally much appreciated, particularly by Humphrey and Roosevelt. At that moment, however, Chang found himself in an unenviable situation.

He represented a regime that was slowly but surely losing the civil war, and we can speculate about how this affected the way he regarded his political legitimacy and position in the UN.

After the end of World War II, the Communist army had initially given up territory and evacuated Yan'an in Shaanxi Province in northern China. From 1947, however, the newly renamed People's Liberation Army (PLA) began to win back territory, entering Peking on 1 January 1949. On 1 October 1949, Mao was able to stand and look out over Tiananmen Square and declare the birth of the new People's Republic.[22]

After Mao Zedong assumed power in China and the Kuomintang government fled to Formosa, Chang's position in the UN became increasingly precarious and called into question, particularly by the Soviet Union. Stanley Chang explained:

> The Russians were behind many attempts to remove my father from the UN, and they had a legal point since Kuomintang (KMT) had moved to Formosa. The KMT government tried to maintain appearances and make all of the regional representatives permanent members of its legislative body because regional elections were not possible on the mainland. My father told me these things, and it was one of the reasons why he resigned his position.
>
> He also had problems with the head of the Chinese delegation and did not receive his monthly salary consistently. When, in 1952, he found that he no longer represented China but an island off its coast, he resigned. My mother, who was so extraordinarily talented, managed the family's finances. Many years later after my father's time at the UN, she told me that he had not received a proper salary while at the UN but instead been paid *per diem*. I was shocked to hear this. I cannot understand how she managed to make ends meet. When the "Chinese" government escaped into Formosa Island it took "everything" with it. The whole democratic process, i.e., the entire legislative branch, was moved. So all the provincial representatives were transported. The idea was that the whole government could claim to be "democratic" as all the provinces were represented. Afterward, there could be no elections to continue the "democratic" process. If and when a representative died, a new one was handpicked from among his/her staff, who had lived in that province.

My father explained these facts to me. It was the only time he actually talked to me one-on-one, which he never did before or after. He even pointed out to me how the "democracy" was fake as there could not be provincial elections. He then stated his difficulty in being able to make statements in the United Nations, that he represented "China." The whole of China and not just an offshore island. My father did not tell me he had resigned. But it was clear to me that he must have resigned for the reason stated above. It violated his sense of democracy. This important decision made by my father clearly showed his character, and sense of value and principle. His final years were bitter years when he isolated himself from the false Chinese government. And that brings up the point of why he so violently refused to attend my planned wedding in Washington D.C. He would have to meet the then Chinese ambassador who would have been invited to my wedding.

Chang also did not have good relations with the leadership of the Chinese delegation to the UN, Tsiang Tingfu (Jiang Tingfu) (1895–1965). They had disliked each other for several years. Both had taught at Nankai University, and Tsiang Tingfu had resented the fact that Chang had been allowed to stand in as acting university chancellor for his brother Poling. In a memoir titled "My Five Incursions into Diplomacy and Some Personal Reminiscences," the veteran diplomat Hsia Chin Lin remarked on the friction between Chang and Tsiang as follows:

> They (Chang and Tsiang) were professors at Nankai University in Tientsin. When the president of Nankai University, Poling Chang, took a long period of leave of absence, he appointed his younger brother Peng Chun Chang as acting president. There was a faction of professors who objected to this appointment, and the leader of this faction of professors was Mr Tsiang. The result of this was that Mr Tsiang resigned and went and taught at Tsinghua University.

In an article the event was described in the following way:

> Peng Chun Chang tended to be his own master, on the other hand Tsiang Tingfu had a narrow capacity for tolerance and liked to cause small harassments. Mr Tsiang treated his "subordinate" in the UN,

Peng Chun Chang, in a deliberately harassing manner, which created in Mr Chang a feeling of what another colleague, Hsia Chia Lin, called "prickles down the back." Partly because of this bad feeling, Peng Chun Chang retired from the diplomatic service in 1952.[23]

Stanley recalled some encounters between his family and Tsiang's family:

> Tsiang's wife was from Southern China, as was my mother, so they were friends from way back, when their husbands were both at Nankai. At the time, around 1948 or '49, we were living in Peter Cooper Village around 24th Street. Mrs Tsiang often came to visit my mother, because she was in desperate need of human support: her husband of more than twenty-five years had gone to Mexico to get a divorce from her. (Why could he not get a divorce in USA?) He then married some young lady. That was quite a scandal, and for a long time Mrs Tsiang would go to all the official functions and demand to be treated as the legal wife. I could understand less than half of the words spoken between the two ladies, as I do not know the Southern Chinese dialect well.

The fiction that the state of Taiwan covered all of China was maintained for several years after Mao's victory in 1949 by the General Assembly in Taipei having representatives from every province on the mainland. As the years passed, these representatives got older and older. Hope of recovering the mainland faded with the steady consolidation of Mao's rule.[24] After Mao took power, more than two million Kuomintang followers had fled to Formosa from the mainland with the help of the United States, with the result that military personnel made up a not inconsiderable proportion of its civil service. Other Chinese chose to flee to Hong Kong, Australia, and Canada. The years immediately following the move to Formosa were dramatic because the Kuomintang regime and the Communists each feared an invasion by the other. However, the Korean War, which was fought between 1950 and 1953, brought Taiwan increased economic support from the United States, and the country's economy and education system began to develop in a positive direction, not least thanks to the already well-developed infrastructure and industrial base left by the Japanese.[25] As Mao's regime increasingly focused its attention on the Korean War, Taiwan and the Kuomintang regime found themselves on the periphery of Communist interests. In 1971, China finally took over Taiwan's seat in the United Nations, and in 1992 Taiwan abandoned plans to draw the mainland into the republic. Between 1949 and 1987 Taiwan had martial law and experienced an authoritarian rule. Since 1947 ("February 28 Incident") there were crackdowns on protesters who opposed the Kuomintang party's rule over Taiwan. During the period called "the White Terror" that lasted for several years thousands of people were killed and imprisoned.[26]

Chang's final years in the UN were marked by Soviet attempts to have him excluded. Eleanor Roosevelt, who had tried to help Chang in various ways during this time, defended his presence in the UN in the face of Russian criticism. His friend and colleague John Humphrey describes in his journal how Chang was received by a UN delegation from the Eastern bloc at a UN meeting on 9 January 1950 in Great Neck on Long Island:

> There were some fireworks when (V.I.) Formashev (U.S.S.R) objected to P. C. Chang's presence. He was way off the mark, however, because Chang is sitting in his own personal capacity and not as the representative of Nationalist China. Unlike most U. N. bodies, members of the sub-commissions of the Human Rights Commission were not appointed to represent their countries but rather because of their individual qualifications. These were the first sessions of the U.N. after Mao Zedong's victory in the Chinese civil war and the Soviets refused to participate in any activity where Nationalist Chinese delegates were present.[27]

Another incident that also took place in Great Neck earlier in 1949 was recalled by Humphrey as follows: "In the course of the debate this afternoon, Pavlov (the Russian delegate) accused P. C. Chang of hiding behind Mrs. Roosevelt's skirts. I again admired Chang's restraint under great provocation."[28]

Humphrey additionally recounted another revealing incident that occured in February 1951 in Santiago, Chile, where the UN's Economic and Social Council had begun its spring session: "The council began to work in the afternoon. There was of course the usual incident about representation of China. (The Polish representative) Katz-Suchy attacked Chang bitterly. The latter was dignified but emotionally upset."[29]

As already noted, Stanley Chang recalled that his father tried to restrain himself following his first heart attack during his diplomatic posting to Chile. Evidently he succeeded in this on several occasions, including during those tense meetings in Chile.

Chang's Attitude Toward the Chinese Civil War and Communism

The Chinese Civil War thus affected Chang powerfully during his time at the UN and steadily undermined his position within the Economic and Social Council. How did Chang view the civil war in China, and why did he choose to remain in the US? Stanley recalled:

> As for the question of how my father viewed the civil war in China during the 1940s and how he came to take the decision to stay in the US, I can say the following. My guess is that he felt that he still had something to contribute to the UN's work.[30] My father also thought that the Communists would not last particularly long in China. Indeed, my father talked about the political changes in China as being like a child passing through the various diseases of infancy: mumps, chickenpox, etc. He also hoped that China would emerge from its communist phase in the same way as one gets over a disease of infancy. But the more time that passed, the clearer it became that Mao & Company were here to stay, so my father chose the "simple" path of resigning his commission in the UN in 1952 and then staying on in the US. He only visited Formosa once in September 1951 for consultations with the "Chinese" government.

This is a highly illuminating piece of information that has never before been mentioned in the literature on Chang. A number of commentators have asked the question why Chang chose to stay in the US.[31] Before Chang resigned from the UN, there was a certain amount of speculation within the organization about whether or not Chang was holding the door open for the Communists. John Humphrey recorded in his diary:

> I had lunch with P. C. Chang. He said that he considered it possible to bring the communists around to a reasonable point of view, that there is a middle way between communism and capitalism. I have never heard him talk this way before. I also note that he has abstained lately on many of the issues dividing East and West. Does this mean that he is preparing himself mentally for a personal compromise with the Chinese communists? He made quite a point of the fact that the leader of the Chinese communists has never been in Moscow. But not

so many months ago he told me that all the Chinese communists were "dyed with the Russian brush."[32]

In the months immediately following, Humphrey continued to speculate about Chang's attitude toward communism. In his diary entry for Geneva, Wednesday, 10 August 1949, Humphrey wrote: "Took P. C. Chang to dinner at the Perle du Lac. We went for a walk afterwards and talked about China. He is optimistic about the future but whether he hopes for a revival of the nationalist cause or the modification of communist policies is not at all clear." However, in an entry made just over six months later, on 24 February 1950, in Great Neck on Long Island, Humphrey wrote the following about Chang's possible attraction to communism: "Had lunch with P. C. Chang. We talked about philosophy and music. I think that the rumours about him selling out to the communists are pure slander."[33]

* * *

Stanley Chang related that his father harbored no particular sympathy for communism as an ideology but that he nonetheless was not entirely dismissive of the Communist regime, for several reasons: "Because Zhou Enlai was a former Nankai student and also a member of the Communist government, I think that my father was not entirely opposed to the Communist regime. As I say, he regarded communism more as a serious disease of infancy." Other colleagues, such as Charles Malik, also stated that Chang was no communist. Malik argued that time would show Chang's positions to have been based primarily upon elements from classical Chinese culture.[34] At the same time, Chang was not ideologically close to Chiang Kai-shek and the Kuomintang establishment, so a move to Formosa was hardly an attractive alternative either. Malik's commentary is very reasonable given how important the classical Chinese philosophers were for Chang's thinking for long periods of his life.

In some remarks in his 1936 book, *China at the Crossroads*, Chang issued a warning that China might go down either the militarist or the communist path if the country did not receive sufficient international encouragement in its attempts at modernization and its struggle against Japanese colonialist policy.[35] The statement reveals Chang's negative view of communism in the 1930s—at least in a public setting. On a number of other occasions, he had also declared that Chinese culture was capable of absorbing most interventions or ideas from without. The Mongols had invaded but after a while they had become absorbed and, after several hundred years, "completely Chinese." The same had happened with the Manchu people. It is easy to imagine Chang similarly believing that there would be a China after communism.

Given his notions of creative and sustainable cultural adjustments and recalibrations, and his ideas about not trying to achieve an "equilibrium" by resorting to coercion, it is very possible that Chang regarded communism as an inordinately rapid, hectic, and radical change, immature and excessive but also something that perhaps had to be experienced and overcome in order to achieve a better social order—as with all diseases of infancy. In contrast to a more pragmatic perspective that emphasized a more gradual and partial change, the communist idea of society advocated radical revolutionary methods and coercive measures that would apply to society as a whole.

Chang often used the diseases-of-infancy metaphor when describing societal changes in China. His topics of discussion included what it would take for the state to develop in a healthy direction and what was needed in order to achieve equilibrium. In other words, in political discussions, he was keen on using metaphors that expressed various stages in human development, such as childhood and maturity. Moving further afield, it can be noted that medical metaphors have played a prominent role in descriptions of societal and national changes, not least in contemporary debates. It can be discerned, for instance, in the idiom of national healing that is now invoked in relation to traumatic conflicts of the past. This figure of speech permeated all of Chang's political activities during the major portion of his life.

CHAPTER 4

Chang's Multifaceted and Intense Life

Peng Chun Chang's life was intensive, multifaceted, and dramatic in several ways. He became a globetrotter who shuttled between his homeland, China, and an array of countries in Europe, Asia, and South America. Problems and challenges of the day, not least the Sino-Japanese War and the Second World War, resulted in his being given important missions by his government in a series of locations around the world. His work at the UN also entailed a great deal of travel between Europe, the United States, and South America. His passionate involvement with cultural activities such as theater and opera, like his abiding interest in educational issues, provided yet another reason for journeying to different destinations around the world.

China's social transformation after the collapse of the imperial dynasty, particularly a growing emphasis upon educational and research questions, meant that Chang and his brother Poling acquired prominent roles in Chinese society, not least as a consequence of their establishment of the Nankai Schools and Nankai University. Chang's involvement in research and teaching meant that he naturally sought out the university milieus of other countries, where he also fostered contacts with other Chinese Boxer Indemnity Fund scholars. The brothers' Nankai Schools and the contacts that Chang established through this scholarship program to the US clearly had a formative influence on Chang throughout his life.

Chang's life coincided to a considerable extent with that of the Republic of China. It was to a republic that he initially pinned his hopes, as can be seen in his early writings, particularly those prior to the early 1940s. In them, he described the final years of the Qing dynasty as decadent and as blighted by corruption.[1] In contrast to the earlier Ming dynasty, which had its origins locally, the Qing dynasty had begun as a foreign conquering force, something that may well have been a factor in exacerbating Chang's negative opinion. His desire was that the republican experiment would produce a modernization of China, on its own terms and with respect for its native traditions. During the last years of the republic on the mainland, however, Chang became increasingly alienated from the Kuomintang and its leader, Chiang Kai-shek, as well as from Communism. In effect, the two main ideological alternatives in China were, for Chang, non-alternatives.

During its time on the mainland in the twentieth century, the republic was, as noted earlier, marked by conflict and it never succeeded in extending its rule to all of China. Chang and his family experienced in dramatic fashion all of the social convulsions and tensions that characterized the republic's relatively short history on the mainland. Even so, there were occasional oases of peace and constructive social development, as well as a desire for innovation that also created a basis for the expansion of the Nankai Schools. In his lectures, Chang frequently returned to China's past, foregrounding its unity, wealth, and humanistic traditions, which he regarded as the true foundations of the republic. When the republic began to disintegrate, Chang instead found himself part of the creation of a basis for a system of international law and a document that was to emerge as the cornerstone of a global ethics and societal identity for "the world citizen."

Chang's personal experiences were on several counts important factors in his work on the UN Declaration. The Chinese tradition, above all its classical philosophers such as Confucius and Mencius, were a vital source of inspiration for Chang during debates over the various articles of the declaration. China's political experiences—particularly of war and its various conflicts with Japan—were likewise a key point of departure for Chang in his UN work. The social and economic problems endured by China in the 1940s were also unquestionably of importance for Chang's own focus on social and economic rights.

Chang's periods of study at American universities had also played an important part in broadening his horizons as regards the West's political traditions. His acquaintance with the influential educationalist John Dewey had a decisive impact on his thinking. Chang's involvement and interest in pedagogical issues also left a strong impression upon the drafting of the UN Declaration, a document that Chang believed should be easily understandable and logically organized. He also took a strong interest in the right to education and managed to formulate Article 26 so as to also include the right to a basic adult education.² Chang's interest in cultural and research issues more generally were reflected in his engagement in those articles of the declaration that focused on culture, religion, the arts, and science.

In Chapter 2, I made reference to the possibility that Chang's involvement for much of his life in so many different activities and fields stemmed from a desire to escape from the shadow of his elder brother Poling. This likelihood has been further confirmed by Chang's son, Stanley. Stanley also emphasized that his father was always seeking approval from his older brother. Nonetheless, it should not be forgotten that Chang was a brilliant individual with a broad range of areas of interest and expertise who was driven to immerse himself in whatever issue he happened to be devoting himself to at that particular moment. Right up to his diplomatic postings in the early 1940s, he sought to combine several of his areas of interest, namely politics, theater, opera, music, teaching, research, and writing. In his last years, following his achievements at the UN, Chang tried to reconnect with literature, music, and philosophy, albeit this time more as a consumer of culture.

From the 1940s, however, when Chang was on diplomatic postings in Turkey and Chile and working in the UN, these other interests had to give way almost entirely to his duties as a representative for China. Toward the end of the 1940s, Chang also suffered from health problems, which affected his work. It is possible to speculate about how his time in Turkey and Chile affected his political thinking. Turkey had become a secular republic in the 1920s, and when Chang lived there, the country was in the midst of a radical program of secularization and modernization. In Chile, as in other South American countries, socioeconomic issues were high on the agenda, too. Chang was also involved in current political issues in Chile and elsewhere, and he followed political debates in the daily press, particularly social questions. Chang would later articulate a desire that the UDHR should be a religiously neutral, or "secular," document that also included socioeconomic rights in addition to civil and political rights.

For Chang's family, the breadth of his activities and frequent travels, particularly during the 1930s and 1940s, clearly posed tremendous challenges. While overseas, he was at times apart from his family for several years. It is also striking just how often he shuttled between China and the United States and Europe, especially during the 1920s and 1930s, in light of the great distances involved and the limitations of the communication networks at that time. Even so, it was a hallmark of the era of the republic that many Chinese, regardless of profession, traveled to different parts of the world thanks to the spread of the steamboat network.

Chang's political engagement in China's war against Japan during the 1930s in particular also made traveling to and from China a necessity for his political mission. Chang took some of his children with him for some of these trips, and others at different times, but rarely all together. After a long absence, he might suddenly appear and surprise the family. All of his traveling involved a disruption to the continuity of family life. Like many other Chinese families at this time, the Changs were separated for long periods as a result of the war with Japan, but they were also separated because of Chang's many interests and professional commitments. Stanley's older sister Ruth described their father's relationship to his family as follows:

> Father loved his family. Although he traveled repeatedly to foreign lands, his heart always stayed with the family. He always inquired about his children—their health and their schooling. I remember those days in New York when I stayed home. The two of us often visited the Metropolitan Opera together. He did similar things with the other children. Mother had a hard life! As Father was absent so much, all the fatherly duties fell on her. When my sister was growing up, she showed retardation and difficulties in her schooling. Mother was the one to face the problems. Then my younger brother was found to have tuberculosis in his leg bone. He was bed-ridden with a cast for a long time. Mother had to attend him like a nurse. During the war with Japan, Mother took care of all four children by herself while traveling from place to place under trying circumstances. It took a strong person to do that. Finally, she accompanied Father after he received diplomatic positions. In each new place, she had to deal with servants in local languages and customs. They had only the boys with them and she worried about the girls who were cut off from them in Shanghai.[3]

In short, the family paid a high price because of the global situation and Chang's continual traveling. For many years, Chang's wife's extraordinary ability to deal with very trying circumstances in her husband's absence proved decisive for the family's survival. Stanley Chang has made no secret of his deep admiration for his mother and has declared that behind every great man there stands a strong woman. His mother, he emphasized, was one such impressive individual. Stanley described the splitting up of the family as follows:

> The following can be said of my father's various trips. When he was a guest professor in Chicago in 1931, my mother and my sister Ruth went with him. My brother was only seventeen months old and I was only five months. This may explain why my brother and I remained so very close during our upbringing and even later in life. (I did become more distant to my brother, however, after he divorced his American wife Marjorie, whom I am very fond of.) When my parents returned to China from the United States, there was a period of time when I refused to accept my mother. During my father's visit to Hawaii in 1933, I and my brother were eventually reconciled with my mother. When we left China in 1940, travelling by ship from Hong Kong to Turkey, via Basra in Iraq, my parents left my sisters Ruth and Ming-Ming with one of my aunts in Shanghai—my mother's next younger sister for almost six years (a city that was occupied by the Japanese, the British and the French.) My parents thought that being in a big city, even when it was occupied, would be a rather safe option for my sisters. They thought that my sisters would be safer in Japanese occupied Shanghai than in the constantly bombed capital of China. My sister Ruth was very bitter about this arrangement to stay in China (she was at that time in her late teens). Ruth and Ming-Ming were then brought back to the United States in 1946 after my father came back to China to fetch them and my aunt. My aunt was paid by my mother somehow for taking care of my sisters in Shanghai. Hence, during my father's postings in Turkey and Chile, only I and my mother and brother accompanied him.

Peng Chun Chang's Final Years

Peng Chun Chang's final years differed markedly from how he had lived prior to his retirement from the UN in 1952. Until that point, Chang had criss-crossed the world while maintaining an intensive social life across all of his various professional circles, as is amply attested to by the journal entries made by his colleague John Humphrey in New York, Paris, Geneva,

Montevideo, Santiago, and elsewhere. By contrast, his final years were marked by a sedentary life with few social contacts in the little town of Nutley, New Jersey. On a few occasions, Chang gave lectures on music, theater, and literature to various societies. In 1955, for instance, he gave a talk entitled "Chinese Theatre: Development and Technique" at the China Institute in New York as part of a lecture series in which the philosopher Hu Shi also participated. The circle thus seems to have been in some sense closed for Chang. Hu Shi, the same person who, like Chang, had been a Boxer Indemnity Fund scholar and, again like Chang, had studied under John Dewey and then been a lecturer at the University of Hawaii, was a speaker in a lecture series that included what was to be one of Chang's last public appearances. In February 1956, Chang also wrote an essay on the history of the Nankai School in order to memorialize his brother Poling's eightieth birthday.[4]

Chang also addressed his former teacher and supervisor at Columbia University—William Heard Kilpatrick—on his eighty-fifth birthday, 20 November 1956. The birthday was celebrated at Horace Mann Auditorium, Teacher College, Columbia University. Chang addressed Kilpatrick with a quotation from *The Analects of Confucius*: "The teacher, by orderly method, skilfully lures one on. He has broadened me with learning and restrained me with considerations for others. Even if I wanted to stop, I could not. Just when I feel that I have exhausted my ability, something seems to rise up before me sharp and clear. Though I long to follow it, I can find no way of getting to it."[5] Through these remarks, Chang revealed his continuing interest in educational matters and in the philosophy of Confucius. The years as a graduate student had clearly been formative in Chang's life. His teachers—Kilpatrick and Dewey—had influenced him, not at least through their ideas about democracy and non-authoritarianism in schools.[6]

Yet Chang's interest in concrete political issues seems to have dried up almost entirely at the end of his life, at least regarding lecturing and article writing. Stanley Chang recalled his father as having not much contact with either Taiwan or mainland China during the last years of his life. His children had grown up and were scattered across the United States. The United States of the 1950s was also characterized by forces that Chang may safely be assumed to have found deeply problematic. The Cold War between the United States and the Soviet Union had intensified. Senator Joseph McCarthy's militant campaigns were creating deep unease in American society. The policy of economic growth in the US was also connected to a pervasive culture of consumption centered on materialism and the white middle and upper classes. The struggle against racial segregation and discrimination was also beginning to be felt more and more as it increasingly took the form of civil mobilization. During his time at the UN, Chang was active in condemning racism and colonialism, and one can assume that he was very critical of the pervasive racism in American society.

What was this final period of Peng Chun Chang's life like? Stanley recalled:

> In the summer of 1957 (July 19), my father died, a bitter man, of a heart attack shortly after his sixty-fifth birthday. He had resigned from his position at the UN five years earlier because he thought it idiotic to claim to represent China when his government was actually in exile on an island off the coast of China. He did not believe that his work on the UN Declaration of Human Rights would have any meaning for anyone, and he was dismayed at having received no recognition for all the work he had put into the text of the Declaration. My father was a remarkable man, but he died a very unhappy man. He felt unappreciated by everybody and ignored by the world. He was also a very lonely man in his last days. I was living at home while working in New York City for the two years before I applied to Harvard in 1953. My father spent almost all his time studying classical music and the philosophy of the Tao; he also played the Chinese game Solitaire with tiles. He was not studying the Tao scripts for any religious purpose. Rather, he wanted to analyze the Tao maxims and search for hidden meanings. For him, the Chinese philosophers were not religious figures. He taught me to try to understand them in order to teach people to do the right thing according to their station in life.[7]

Stanley continued his story about the last years of his father's life:

> He was really bored during his final years. Between 1952 and 1957 his frustration was very apparent. My parents did not have a large social acquaintance, either. They simply weren't the social type, something that became very clear in New York in the 1940s. Few friends came to visit them in Nutley, New Jersey. During our time in New York and Nutley, it was mostly my father's best friend, Y. R. Chao, who visited us, along with my mother's younger sister—who had

taken care of my sisters Ruth and Ming-Ming in Shanghai from 1940 to 1946 while my parents, my brother Chen Chung, and I were living in Turkey and Chile. My parents had bought a house in Nutley because a friend of theirs, Mei, who was principal of a Chinese university, also lived there. Mei also gave my father a modest amount of money in order to help him out.

My mother had bought a small apartment in New York City in order to be able to look for clerical work in an office. But my father absolutely refused to leave the house in Nutley which they had bought in 1952.

He died in his bed from his third heart attack, two days before they were due to move to New York. He had called me the night before his death and I could hear that something was very wrong. But because I was going to be coming a few days later to help with the move to New York at the weekend, I told him that we could talk more when we met. The very next morning while I was at Harvard doing my research, my wife called to tell me that my father had died. His death was caused, among other things, by my mother's insistence that they move to New York to make her work easier. He died the day before the house sale was to be finalized. It had to be postponed for a week because of his death.

After his death I had to handle all the funeral arrangements. He left no will and had had no plans for the future beyond the impending move to New York. I had to arrange the church, the funeral home, the flowers, etc, and contact the minister, the organist, and sort out the car firm as well as the burial plot at a non-sectarian cemetery (plot numbers 58-59-60, Ferncliff Cemetery, 281 Secor Rd, Hartsdale, N.Y.). I chose the burial plot for my father, to be near Yen Jen-Ying (the man who came to meet my brother and me at the New York harbour) so that my father would have company. My mother said that I should arrange a decent burial for my father but several years later she complained that I had spent too much money on it. I arranged for a service at a local church which my sister Ruth had attended. The top half of the casket was open. I asked the organist of that church to play for the service, and agreed to the music to be played. I asked the minister of that church to allow me to have someone else conduct the service. I asked a family friend who was a missionary in China to serve as the preacher. I engaged for the cars to drive the family and the friends to the cemetery after the service. Then the former missionary said the final words during the burial. Regarding the preparations—my brother arrived two days after our father's death and said "YF (Stanley) is doing such a good job, let him continue doing it."

In Geneva, John Humphrey, Chang's colleague and friend at the UN, made the following entry about Chang's death in his journal for Thursday 25 July 1957: "P. C. Chang is dead. Of all the delegates who came into the Council he was the one with whom I felt most in spiritual intellectual communion. And the man I liked the best. I wish that I had arranged to see him more often in these years since his retirement. He was a scholar, and in a way an artist although he performed his functions well in spite of these superior gifts. What a giant he seems in contrast with the time-servers."[8] According to Habib Malik, the son of Charles Malik (Chang's colleague at the UN). Charles Malik did not mention anything in his diary about Chang's death on the relevant dates, which may indicate that he did not know about it when it happened or that he did not feel the need to mention anything about it in his diary. The dates of the diary that Habib Malik read were 13 July to November that year (1957), then around the period of December 1958 on the tenth anniversary of the UDHR, and then again around December 1968 on the twentieth anniversary of the declaration.

After Peng Chun Chang's death, Stanley was the only child living near the family home in Nutley and the only one who could help with the practical arrangements immediately. His sister Ruth was living with her family in Baltimore, and their elder brother Chen Chung was in California. Stanley described the time immediately after their father's death:

> The other remarkable thing which my mother did, in addition to the family's long flight from Tientsin to Kunming in 1937, happened after my father's death in 1957. Because my father died intestate, American law required that his estate be divided up, one-third to the widow and two-thirds to the children. My mother sent me 5,000 dollars, which means that the estate was worth 30,000 dollars. So she gave away 20,000 dollars to her children, keeping only 10,000 dollars for herself. She was 59 years old and did part-time clerical work until she retired and had to live off a state pension. But when she died in 1986

her entire estate was worth 250,000 dollars. She had been successful on the stock-market. Before she died, she asked me not to tell the other children how much money she had. However, the lawyer who notarized her will told me that my siblings had to be informed of the size of my mother's estate. So I told Chen and Ruth that there was enough money for us to be able to help our sister Ming-Ming for a number of years.

Stanley's mother died in 1986 in California, where all four of the children would eventually also come to live. In her final years, their mother suffered from Parkinson's disease, during which time her eldest daughter, Ming-Ming, was an enormous help to her. Stanley had previously asked his mother if she wished to be buried in the same grave as his father at Ferncliff Cemetery on the east coast, but she had said no. Her wish was that her ashes should be scattered on the Pacific Ocean. (However, as she requested, her name appears on the plaque at Ferncliff Cemetery. The plaque was remade at the expense of her estate, according to Stanley.)

Stanley Chang

Since this book relies to a great extent upon the reminiscences of Peng Chun Chang's youngest son, Stanley (Yuan-Feng) Chang, it is important that some key events in his own biography also be reviewed here.

Like his two older siblings, Chen Chung (1927–2014) and Ruth (1923–), Stanley Chang (1928–) chose to study science at university and had a successful career as a researcher and teacher at a number of American universities. For much of his life, Stanley has also followed his father in maintaining a wide range of cultural interests. Like his father before him, he is deeply involved in literature, ballet, opera, and classical music, and he himself admits that the way in which he devotes his energies to his various areas of interest closely resembles how his father systematically cultivated his own various passions. Stanley learned the piano from a young age, including some of the most demanding pieces. By virtue of the family's stays in China, Turkey, Chile, and the United States, Stanley also grew up multilingual.

Stanley has evidently played a key role in helping to keep the Chang family together. He was able to reconcile his mother with his elder brother

Chen after a serious falling-out over his sister Ming-Ming's living arrangements. He also helped his brother at the time of his first marriage by overcoming their father's skepticism through sheer force of argument. When their sister Ruth was about to marry, Stanley, unlike their father, took the time to engage with her deliberations over the marriage. He also became very close to their mother and in her twilight years helped her to take care of Ming-Ming. Their mother was also very close to Stanley throughout his childhood. When Stanley contracted TB in his leg in the 1930s, she cared for him, teaching him mathematics and other subjects while he was confined to bed for long periods.

Because of the tumultuous events in China that followed on Japan's attacks during the 1930s, Stanley was unable to complete his schooling in China. As a result, he was forced to compensate later in life for this gap in his education. Once the family left China, however, he was unable to develop his competence in areas such as reading and writing Mandarin. His knowledge of Chinese worsened the longer they stayed in the United States. Stanley was primarily educated in British and American schools. He took his first degree at Purdue University in the United States, subsequently taking a doctorate in applied physics at Harvard. By virtue of living in close proximity to his parents for several years during the 1940s and 1950s, he gained good insight into their lives and even, to some extent, into his father's work for the UN. In connection with the latter, Stanley was granted a unique opportunity to attend as a listener during the first working meetings on the UN Declaration in the summer of 1947 at the UN's temporary premises on Long Island.

While in Cambridge, Massachusetts, in 1955, Stanley met his future wife, Hanping Chu, at a party arranged by the Chao family, who were good friends of their parents. Stanley socialized frequently with their daughter Iris (Rulan), who went on to become a distinguished musicologist at Harvard. (After P. C. Chang died, Stanley kept up the close relationship with the Chaos for over twenty-five years.) The idea was that Hanping would come to the party so that the Chao family could introduce her to a different man, but fate had decreed otherwise. That year, Stanley and Hanping were married, and they went on to have two children, a son, Leon, and a daughter, Claire. Stanley recalled that Peng Chun Chang was not unfriendly toward Hanping when he first met her, but he nonetheless felt that there was a certain coolness or distance between them. Chang did not offer either financial support or words of encouragement for the wedding, which Stanley and Hanping instead had to arrange with help from Hanping's father. Like Chang, Mr. Chu had come as a scholarship student to the United States, where he had had a successful career in banking, working for the International Monetary Fund in Washington, D.C., where the family subsequently moved.

Peng Chun Chang was at first opposed to the marriage. He later refused to go to Washington, D.C., where the wedding had initially been meant to be held, because Chang did not want to meet any representatives from the Chinese mission. The wedding was eventually held in a chapel in Harvard Yard in Cambridge in November 1955. In attendance were Hanping's and Stanley's parents, the family's good friend Y. R. Chao and his wife and daughter Iris, as well as her husband Ted Pian, a famous physicist from MIT. During the ceremony, Stanley was anxious lest his father make a scene, but the moment passed without incident. There was an unpleasant moment during the wedding reception, however, when Peng Chun Chang told off Stanley's brother-in-law for pouring too much alcohol into Stanley's glass. This incident, which Stanley found excruciating, subsequently led to Stanley giving up alcohol entirely.

In the 1960s, '70s, and '80s, Stanley evidently enjoyed a happy family life and made strides in his career, including at universities in Lincoln, Nebraska, and in Claremont, California. He divorced his wife, however, after she became mentally ill in the early 1990s. Hanping died in 2011, and Stanley relates that he misses her very much.

For long periods, as has been noted, Stanley's relationship to his father was obviously very difficult and complex. He described his father's attitude toward him as "feudal." Stanley has related how it took many years before he could view his father in a more forgiving light, given his demanding parenting style and behavior toward the family. Stanley explained that he and his father never really had the chance to bond because Stanley was doing graduate work at Harvard during the last years of his father's life. At the same time, it is clear that Stanley Chang has in recent years reflected deeply on his father's professional contributions, especially in connection with his work at the UN. There is no doubt that he has a profound admiration for his father's work on the UDHR and his multifaceted talents. Stanley has told me in our communications that he has striven to remember as much as possible about his father's life in order to give a full and nuanced picture of all his talents and shortcomings.

In 1998, Stanley and John Humphrey's widow were invited to a special event in Paris to commemorate the fiftieth anniversary of the signing of the UN Declaration. The Chang family had decided that only Stanley would attend the event in view of the fact that it was he who had been with their father on Long Island when the UN Declaration had begun to be drafted. Stanley felt deeply honored to be able to attend the anniversary, where he met, among other dignitaries, France's foreign minister. Nonetheless, he was disappointed that so much of the anniversary events were focused on Eleanor Roosevelt and René Cassin. The Paris jubilee also reactivated long-dormant memories of his own presence at the initial drafting stages of the UN Declaration.

PART II

THE IDEAS BEHIND THE UN DECLARATION

CHAPTER 5

Peng Chun Chang and the UN Declaration of Human Rights

The following memoir comes from Peng Chun Chang's son Stanley, who, aged eighteen, found himself part of a world-historical event by virtue of being probably the sole witness to the discussions of Eleanor Roosevelt's writing group during their initial phase in summer 1947.

> I was the only witness that summer in 1947 when my father was vice-chairman of the writing group that would compose the UN Declaration of Human Rights. The group met for several weeks at Sperry Gyroscope Plant in Lake Success on Long Island. The auditorium held around 400–500 people, and I always sat in the second row, near the exit on the right between the rows of seating. As far as I'm aware, I was the only auditor since I never observed anyone else come in and listen during those weeks.
>
> The writing group sat round a table set up on a stage, and there were five people in particular who caught my attention. Apart from my father, there was Eleanor Roosevelt, the acting chairperson, a Frenchman (René Cassin), a Canadian (John Humphrey), and a Lebanese (Charles Malik). As soon as any questions came up relating to formulation or logical organization, the other members of the working group expected my father to be able to give an answer. Although Mrs Roosevelt was the chair, in reality it was my father who managed the greater part of the negotiations. That is to say, she handed over most of the work to my father and, at times, was so passive as to give the impression of not even being present.

> My father had more or less forced me to attend and listen to the writing group's discussion because it was his view that I would thereby be present at the making of world history. As an eighteen-year-old, however, I felt that these people were simply wasting time with all their discussions and arguments. What I remember best from all those meetings were the interactions between Roosevelt, my father, Malik, Humphrey, and Cassin. I don't remember so many details from the discussions themselves. I found the month-long meetings phase increasingly tedious. After a few weeks, I managed to persuade my father to let me leave the auditorium now and then to talk with my father's chauffeur, who later taught me to drive his car. During the journeys home to Garden City, where our family was living at that time, my father would sit silently in the car, never making any reference to the meetings which he had attended.

Between 11 and 27 June 1947, eighteen meetings took place in Long Island in which P. C. Chang and his son Stanley participated. Since none of the delegates themselves are still alive at the time of writing (2018), Stanley Chang is almost certainly the only living witness to the drafting phase of the UDHR. We will return in due course to some of his more striking recollections.

The group to which Stanley Chang referred was thus a writing committee that initially consisted of Charles Malik, a Lebanese philosopher with a doctorate from Harvard; Stanley's father Peng Chun Chang; Mrs Roosevelt; and John Humphrey, a Canadian law professor. The group was subsequently made larger on the basis of the delegates' particular strengths and national origins. Apart from Roosevelt, Chang, Malik (and Humphrey as its secretary), the group's primary asset was the French representative, the legal expert René Cassin, who had worked for Charles de Gaulle as part of his government in exile in London. In total, the main delegates at the June meeting were as follows: Roosevelt, Chang, Cassin, Malik, Humphrey, William Hodgson (from Australia), Santa Cruz (from Chile), Geoffrey Wilson (from Great Britain), and the Soviet delegate, Vladimir Koretskij.

The UN and the UN Declaration

The UN Declaration of Human Rights is intimately bound up with the creation of the United Nations, an international organization which for many people today represents the closest humanity has come to creating a global government. For its part, the UN Declaration is the closest humanity has come to formulating a global ethics that transcends the various cultures of the different nations.

How did this ambitious global project of creating the United Nations and UN Declaration begin? If one applies a narrow time perspective and considers the creation of the UN against the backdrop of the Second World War, the UN can be traced back to a series of international meetings between the leaders of countries fighting the Axis powers. A key preliminary meeting occurred in August 1941, when American president Franklin D. Roosevelt met with the British prime minister Winston Churchill on the American cruiser USS *Augusta*.[1] This meeting would result in the drafting of the Atlantic Charter, which comprised a number of fundamental freedoms—freedom from want and fear—that had earlier figured in Franklin D. Roosevelt's famous address to Congress in January 1941. In it, Roosevelt had spoken of four fundamental human freedoms, including, as well as those already mentioned, the right to freedom of expression and freedom of religion.

Roosevelt's address to Congress had a tremendous impact. The four fundamental freedoms were referenced increasingly during the 1940s, being subsequently expanded in various documents into "human rights and fundamental freedoms." They then became a central component of the UN Charter in 1945. The preamble states that fundamental human rights should be respected while article 62 in the UN Charter states the respect and promotion of fundamental freedoms. President Roosevelt was one of a number of politicians who were working for the creation of the UN in San Francisco. His speech about the four freedoms was also an inspiration for the UN Commission on Human Rights, which would later be chaired by his widow, Eleanor. Chang was among the authors who wanted the preamble to the declaration to contain a reference to these freedoms, a desire that was subsequently realized in the preamble's second sentence.[2]

The League of Nations had not had a vocabulary of this kind at hand in the 1920s and 1930s but had instead mostly alluded to the rights of ethnic and national minorities. The international labor organization, the ILO, also referred to human rights within working life. The 1926 Slavery Convention had also been signed, on 25 September. According to the American historian Samuel Moyn, Franklin D. Roosevelt's speech about the four fundamental freedoms was the beginning of a discourse on human rights and fundamental freedoms, right up to the creation of the UN and the UN Declaration in the

1940s (private communication, October 2015).³ To be sure, there had been historical precursors of the notion of human rights—principally in the form of concepts of human beings' natural rights, particularly during the French Revolution of the late 1700s and the French Declaration of the Rights of Man and of the Citizen in 1789.⁴ But the fact that the very formulation of universal human rights emerged on such a broad front in the mid-1940s was probably due for the most part to Franklin D. Roosevelt's speech to the United States Congress.

In 1944, representatives of the governments of China, Britain, the United States, and the Soviet Union met at Dumbarton Oaks, in Washington, D.C., with a view to creating a new international organization for peace and security. After this meeting, representatives from other countries that had fought Germany, Italy, and Japan were invited to an additional meeting in San Francisco, held in spring 1945, at which the United Nations was formed. At both of these meetings, participants formulated the terms of the UN Charter, which included principles relating to human rights, something China had pushed for particularly strongly.⁵ Participants at the San Francisco meeting also expressed a desire that a human rights commission be created under the leadership of the United Nations Economic and Social Council, ECOSOC.⁶

Following the UN General Assembly's first meeting in London in 1946, the Economic and Social Council appointed Eleanor Roosevelt as chairperson of a small working group tasked with ascertaining how a commission on human rights might be organized. One of the commission's key tasks was to produce an international bill of rights.

In January 1947, when the Commission on Human Rights met for the first time, Roosevelt was elected chairperson, while Chang was appointed as vice-chair and Malik as rapporteur.⁷ Britain's representative, Charles Dukes, nominated Chang on the basis of his wide-ranging expertise on human rights. That this should have been Dukes's rationale is interesting since Chang's publications did not include any text that explicitly addressed human rights, even if he had previously conducted research into ethics and pedagogy, something that in itself was a clearly relevant merit for writing the UN Declaration. Chang had also been involved in the practical politics around human rights issues, not least through his involvement in development issues during his time as a diplomat in Chile. He had also shown a keen interest in questions concerning cultural interactions during his time as a diplomat in Turkey. His active role in the struggle against Japan's colonial ambitions in China during the 1930s was also an obvious merit in this context.

The members of the commission came from Chile, China, France, India, Iran, Lebanon, Panama, the Philippines, the Soviet Union, Britain, the United States, Uruguay, and Yugoslavia. At the meeting it emerged that several of the commission's delegates were ideologically very far apart, so that it would be simpler if a preliminary draft were to be prepared by Roosevelt, Chang, and Malik with the help of the commission's secretary, the Canadian law professor John Humphrey.

It would later become apparent that the various representatives were also divided when it came to how much room for maneuver each had been given by their respective countries. Some of the most intransigent representatives came from the Eastern Bloc. For his part, Chang belonged to those who had been given the most negotiating space. As the country he represented—the Republic of China—became increasingly drawn into a civil war that prevented it from taking much interest in human rights debates at the UN, Chang acquired greater latitude and found himself able to articulate his own personal opinions to a quite considerable degree. This situation was unique among the various delegates and principal authors of the document, who, unlike Chang, were continually required to check with their governments at home about not only issues of principle but even minor changes in terminology.

The Work on the UN Declaration

Previous scholarship on the UDHR typically mentions the first working meeting between Roosevelt, Chang, Malik, and Humphrey in 1947, a meeting that took place in the living room of Roosevelt's apartment on Washington Square in New York City. Roosevelt had suggested that they meet for tea. In his memoirs, John Humphrey related that during tea the original suggestion, that the group should write a draft declaration of rights, was quickly abandoned because of the radical philosophical and ideological differences that emerged between Chang and Malik. Among other things, Chang had proposed that Humphrey should put his work duties to one side and instead spend six months studying Chinese philosophy. Humphrey's interpretation of this statement by Chang was that Western ideas should not be allowed to overshadow the work of drafting a declaration. Although he addressed the remark to Humphrey, Chang was all the while looking at Malik. The latter, who was a Greek Orthodox Christian and positively disposed toward Catholicism and natural law theory, responded with a long exposition on the philosophy of Thomas Aquinas. Before tea was over, the group thus agreed that Humphrey alone would be tasked with formulating a first draft.[8]

In her memoirs, published in 1958, Eleanor Roosevelt described the meeting and the circumstances around it as follows:

> In the period that I presided as chairman of the Human Rights Commission we spent most of our time trying to write the Universal Declaration of Human Rights and the Covenants, and there were times, it seemed to me, when I was getting in over my head. The Officers of the Commission had been charged with the task of preparing the first draft of the Declaration, and I remember that on one occasion, thinking our work might be helped by an informal atmosphere, I asked this small group to meet at my apartment for tea. One of the members was the Chinese representative, Dr. P. C. Chang, who was a great joy to all of us because of his sense of humour, his philosophical observations and his ability to quote some apt Chinese proverb to fit almost any occasion. Dr. John P. Humphrey, a Canadian who was the permanent head of the Division of Human Rights in the U. N. Secretariat, and Dr. Charles Malik of Lebanon, one of the very able diplomats at the United Nations, were also at the meeting.
>
> They arrived in the middle of a Sunday afternoon, so we would have plenty of time to work. It was decided that Dr. Humphrey would prepare the preliminary draft, and as we settled down over the teacups, one of them made a remark with philosophic implications, and a heated discussion ensued. Dr. Chang was a pluralist and held forth in charming fashion on the proposition that there is more than one kind of ultimate reality. The Declaration, he said, should reflect more than simply Western ideas and Dr. Humphrey would have to be eclectic in his approach. His remark, though addressed to Dr Humphrey, was really directed at Dr. Malik, from whom it drew a prompt retort as he expounded at some length the philosophy of Thomas Aquinas. Dr Humphrey joined enthusiastically in the discussion, and I remember that at one point Dr. Chang suggested that the Secretariat might well spend a few months studying the fundamentals of Confucian-

ism! But by that time I could not follow them, so lofty had the conversation become, so I simply filled the teacups again and sat back to be entertained by the talk of these learned gentlemen.[9]

Roosevelt's recollections are interesting in that they reveal how at an early stage profound philosophical differences emerged between the drafting committee's two leading figures, Chang and Malik, which made it impossible for these individuals to assume sole responsibility for producing a preliminary text.

Roosevelt's drafting committee was subsequently augmented by representatives from Australia, Chile, the Soviet Union, Britain, and France. In the scholarship, René Cassin, France's representative, is usually considered as one of the key architects of the UDHR. Roosevelt's drafting committee convened for the first time on 9 June in the premises on Long Island mentioned by Stanley Chang in his account cited above. The basis for the first meeting was a 408-page text compiled by the Canadian professors John Humphrey and Emile Giraud. An inventory of previous human rights documents, this text also included a proposal for a collection of human rights articles. So as to be able to complete the text in peace and quiet, Humphrey locked himself away in the Lido Beach Hotel (popularly known as the Pink Lady) on Long Island.[10]

With Humphrey's and Giraud's text as its starting point, together with suggestions from the governments of Panama, Chile, and Cuba, the committee chose to work up a more structured text. The task of writing this text fell to René Cassin, who, after a long weekend in June, came up with a proposal.[11] During the summer of 1947, this working draft was the object of intensive discussion by the members of the drafting committee. The meetings that Stanley Chang attended took place in the UN's temporary premises on Long Island. During the construction of the UN's permanent headquarters between 1947 and 1952, the UN had its headquarters in the Sperry Corporation's facilities at Lake Success, Great Neck, on Long Island, largely because of its proximity to Manhattan.

At the second session of the Commission on Human Rights, in Geneva in November 1947, a decision was made about how the "international jurisprudence" of human rights would proceed. The work was divided into three categories: (1) work on the Declaration; (2) work on a more binding set of conventions; and (3) implementation measures, namely, how the various states and other key actors would secure human rights in reality. During the commission's third session in July 1948, the preamble and most of the articles emerged, and the commission decided to accord the same emphasis on civil, political rights as on social, economic, and cultural rights. The Latin American and Eastern Bloc countries were particularly keen to underscore the importance of socioeconomic rights, albeit from entirely opposed ideological starting points (Marxism for the Eastern Bloc, and Catholic social ethics and natural law for the Latin Americans). The commission also took under consideration a number of commentaries from various governments, though these were relatively few in number and tentative in nature.[12]

The Economic and Social Council then decided that it would be best if only one declaration were presented to the UN's General Assembly. The main reason was the favorable climate that had prevailed around the work on the declaration in consequence of the horrors of the Second World War still being fresh in the memories of several of the parties involved. Waiting to present the declaration until a binding text for the convention had been hammered out entailed a risk that the favorable climate of discussion would be dissipated by the tensions of the emerging Cold War. The result was that the UN General Assembly adopted the UN Declaration on 10 December 1948 in the Palais de Chaillot, Paris, with forty-eight votes for, none against, and eight abstentions—Belarus, Czechoslovakia, Poland, the Ukraine, the Soviet Union, Yugoslavia, Saudi Arabia, and South Africa. That same week, on 9 December, the UN General Assembly also adopted the Convention on the Prevention and Punishment of the Crime of Genocide, and the following year, in August 1949, it adopted the Fourth Geneva Convention, intended to protect civilian populations in wartime.

With the passage of time, the decision to present the General Assembly with the declaration alone was revealed to have been very shrewd, given the tremendous tensions that lay below the surface when it came to converting the articles into a more binding law or convention text. Chang provided a good description of the climate of ideas and opinion that he regarded as characteristic of the various parties involved in the UDHR and that ultimately succeeded in achieving a surprisingly high degree of unity with regard to the contents of the articles. Chang claimed that humanity finally stood on the threshold to a new, more human era—"a new humanism"—after the myopia, or "shortsightedness," of the past 150 years.[13] According to Chang the purpose of the declaration was to set up a moral standard toward which mankind might aspire.[14]

For Chang, it was important that the UN acted *now* and that the organization agreed upon a declaration of rights because the time was right for such a declaration. The inspiration for all efforts to create a new human rights document was the ideal of human freedom and dignity. According to Chang, the fact that human rights had been incorporated into between thirty-five and forty national constitutions around the world clearly indicated that, despite deep philosophical and ideological differences, a consensus on human rights could be achieved. However, like several other delegates, Chang wanted the UN General Assembly to consider and finalize the UN Declaration prior to finalizing the text of a binding convention. For Chang, there were a number of reasons:

1. A binding convention would give powerful countries an incentive to intervene in other countries.
2. The most pressing requirement for the international community was to create a declaration able to protect humanity after two world wars. Moreover, drafting the text of a binding convention would be a very time-consuming process.
3. Ascribing legal obligations would threaten the universality of the document because the presence of binding contents might deter some states from voting *for* the declaration.

For all these reasons, Chang proposed, the procedure as regards the rights documents should be as follows: first, a declaration, then a convention and a proposal for implementation measures. The commission shared this view and decided accordingly.[15] At the end of 1948, the only realistic course of action was to present a declaration to the General Assembly. By the early 1950s, the climate around human rights issues also changed as a result of the escalation of the Cold War and dramatic developments such as the Korean War. The relatively broad unity around the UDHR gave way to more open conflicts over the development of the text of a binding convention.[16]

It would take another six years for the commission to submit a proposal for texts for the convention (1948–1954), a further thirteen years for them to be adopted (1954–1966), and finally an additional eleven years before at least thirty-five states ratified the texts of both the Covenant on Economic, Social and Cultural Rights and the Covenant on Civil and Political Rights (1966–1977). From the beginning, the idea had been that a joint convention text would be submitted but, because of ideological antagonisms between East and West, two covenants were eventually adopted in 1966.

The states that initially adopted a positive stance toward the rapid drafting of a convention text in tandem with the development of the UDHR were Australia, India, and Britain. Chile, Egypt, France, and Uruguay took a more compromising view, which meant keeping the door open for having a parallel text for the convention. Albeit for different reasons, the United States, the Soviet Union, Yugoslavia, and China were particularly vocal that only one text of the declaration should be presented. In part, they did not want such a text to be drafted in haste, but the Soviet Union and the United States were also especially disinclined to accept an international legal document that might be used in order to intervene in their respective domestic affairs.[17] In other words, given these profound differences of opinion it was an extraordinary achievement on the part of Eleanor Roosevelt, Peng Chun Chang, and their collaborators to push a draft text of the UDHR through all of the various levels of the UN system. (One could also claim that that it was an advantage that the UDHR "only" became a declaration and not a binding convention because conventions often include "security clauses" and limitations.[18])

Before the text of the declaration could be put to a vote in the General Assembly, it needed to pass several crucial committee stages. First it had to be approved by the Commission on Human Rights and then circulated for comments among the various member states. These comments were then returned to the drafting committee. The revised document then had to be sent back to the Commission on Human Rights, which would then allow the Economic and Social Council to decide whether the text was ready to be presented to the General Assembly. When the text reached the assembly, it would be scrutinized by the Third Committee for Social, Humanitarian and Cultural Affairs before being voted on in the General Assembly.[19] Chang himself participated in 142 meetings on the UN Declaration at these various levels.[20] The challenge of pushing the text through was exacerbated by a series of political factors.

Obstructive and Facilitative Factors for the UDHR

One obstructive factor for the creation of the UDHR was of course the deep ideological, cultural, and religious differences between the different states. The member states of the UN consisted of thirty-seven so-called Western Christian states, eleven states in which Islam played a central role, four "Buddhist" states, one "Hindu" state, and China, with its Confucian tradition, as well as the six states of the Soviet bloc. Given the sensitive ethical and political issues that Roosevelt's working group had to take into consideration when drafting the text, this radical pluralism posed an obvious challenge, both positively and negatively. A central task of the working group was therefore to try to reach agreement so far as possible on the rights articles despite the fact that delegates had such profound cultural, religious, and ideological points of departure.

For the Muslim states, one particularly controversial article was Article 18, the right to freedom of religion, an article in whose drafting Malik and Chang were deeply involved. The article included the right to change one's religious affiliation. This formulation met with opposition from Muslim states because renouncing one's faith in Islam was not permitted by Muslim tradition. Even so, Saudi Arabia was the only Muslim state to abstain from the vote in the General Assembly; the other Muslim states voted for the UDHR. Pakistan's foreign minister, Sir Muhammad Zafrulla Khan, who persuaded the other Muslim states to vote for the declaration, played a crucial role in this context.[21]

Charles Malik's son Habib offered some interesting observations on the origin of the UDHR's key Article 18 on freedom of religion:

> My father wrote the actual wording of Article 18 and it was adopted by the drafting committee as it was. His reasons for spelling out the right to change one's religion have to do, to my mind, with his experiences as a native non-Muslim living in a predominantly Muslim milieu in the Arab Middle East. He saw at first hand how non-Muslim communities throughout history had been systematically relegated to second-class status through the *dhimmi* system, and so he wanted to stress religious freedom as an inviolable right. But there is another side to this. Islam regards opting out of the faith as apostasy (*ridda*), which according to Islamic *sharia* is punishable by death. Many of my father's young philosophy students in the late 1930s and the early 1940s at the American University in Beirut were so influenced by him that a few freely took the bold step of converting to Christianity (Catholicism for the most part). They exercised their right to change religion, and he felt this needed to be stated emphatically as an integral part of religious rights, so he did so and it was accepted. Later, he successfully lobbied the Saudis to cast an abstention instead of a no

vote, which is what they were planning to do mainly because of this clause in Article 18.[22]

Chang was also very interested in Article 18, perhaps because of his involvement with Christianity during his student years in the US and his turn toward Chinese philosophy and agnosticism in later years. Further, Chang had shown an interest in intercultural contacts and cultural change in several of his writings before he started to work at the UN. He was particularly engaged with the question of why China had not faced the same kind of problems of religious conflicts and discrimination as the West (something we will return to in Chapter 8). From a traditional Confucian perspective a key concept has been harmony instead of sameness. The concept of harmony also "opens up" for various tolerant policies in comparison to the concept of sameness.[23] Chang was eager to stress the importance of "pluralistic tolerance," which was according to him a condition for harmony and peace in a society (as well as relations based on benevolence and justice).[24] Like Malik, Chang also emphasized the importance of the right to *change* one's beliefs as a necessary precondition for religious freedom. However, Chang thought that the right to hold religious beliefs implied the right to change them. Hence, it was sufficient to say "the right to freedom of thought, religion and belief."[25]

An additional controversial article for the Islamic nations was Article 16, which dealt with the rights given to women in marriage. This article assumed that women and men should have equal rights in marriage, an assumption that stood in conflict with common Islamic views at the time.

Another serious obstacle for the work on the UDHR was that the Cold War had also grown colder, with the United States and the Soviet Union adopting an increasingly confrontational stance and opposed political agendas. The crisis in Palestine made itself felt and was a source of anxiety given the relations between some of the working group's members. Tensions were, in other words, high in the Middle East after the British abandoned their Palestine Mandate and the struggle toward the creation of a state of Israel became stronger.[26] Malik, who was a Christian Arab, sided with the Arab League, while Cassin, who was a French Jew, was openly Zionist. Conflicts had also emerged between China and Korea, and the Berlin Blockade had begun.[27] China was in the throes of a civil war that the Communists were winning. Despite all these problems, the core members of the UN's Commission on Human Rights managed to agree on a text and to push it through all the various levels of the UN system.

The main players in Roosevelt's working group were a highly professional team, and many of them had extensive experience with diplomatic work. They were thus able to overcome personal antagonisms and ideological differences in order to show a united front to the UN General Assembly and hence get the UDHR adopted.

As noted earlier, Roosevelt and several of her collaborators had a special incentive to present and secure the adoption of a declaration in the General Assembly. The mood was "now or never." The delegates included in their number several people with direct personal experience of having been subjected to extraordinary cruelty. The Holocaust and the Second World War remained powerful memories that served to foreground the essential issues at stake in the UDHR. This was a declaration that would emphasize the very antithesis of the horrors which had been inflicted by the Axis Powers. The authors of the document were thus highly motivated to contribute to the formulation of a rights document that would prevent genocide and world war from ever occurring again.

Eleanor Roosevelt had also put forward the view that an important reason why it had not proven possible to maintain world peace during the first half of the twentieth century was that the international community lacked clear norms for human rights. Although human rights had more functions than merely maintaining peace—for example, the protection of people's fundamental needs and the "humanizing of man" (this was Chang's idea)—the creation of peace and the avoidance of war were very important goals of the UDHR.[28] Eleanor Roosevelt articulated this goal as follows: "Many of us believed that absence of clear and unambiguous human rights principles around the world were one of the principal causes of friction between different states, and that recognition of these human rights could be a cornerstone upon which peace might be constructed."[29] However, Roosevelt also claimed in the same vein as Chang that "the Declaration is an educational declaration, and the only way we can guarantee that these rights will be observed is by doing a good job educationally."[30]

Several of the delegates also demonstrated valuable leadership qualities when negotiations were in danger of collapsing. Eleanor Roosevelt's considerable diplomatic abilities are well attested.[31] But Charles Malik also revealed an extraordinary ability to deal with crisis. He led the work of the General Assembly's Third Committee (Social, Humanitarian, and Cultural Affairs). Each of the draft articles was examined very closely; the minutes of the Third Committee ran to over nine hundred pages. Article 1, in which Chang took a particular interest, was the subject of very fierce debate, with discussion of it taking six days. Eventually Malik began using a stopwatch to limit each commentator to three minutes, a suggestion that originated with a Swedish delegate, Ulla Lindström.[32]

The Drafting Team of the UN Declaration

The scholarly literature often emphasizes that the UDHR was a collective creation involving hundreds of individuals. This statement seems credible if one reads the UN documents from the various sessions of the Human Rights Commission, the drafting committee, the Economic and Social Council, and the so-called Third Committee. Even so, there are grounds for saying that a number of individuals appear to have played an especially important role by making special complementary contributions: Eleanor Roosevelt, Peng Chun Chang, René Cassin, Charles Malik, and John Humphrey. Other figures who are also often named in this context are the Filipino diplomat Carlos Romulo, the Indian women's rights activist Hansa Mehta, and the Chilean legal expert Hernán Santa Cruz.

Roosevelt, Chang, Cassin, Malik, and Humphrey appear to have been especially decisive figures in the committee work, on two counts in particular. First, they were more or less present at all of the critical deliberations as well as being involved in the writing process from the very start. Second, they were also very active with respect to the document as a whole, making a number of vital contributions to its key articles and pivotal characteristics. They are followed in importance by Santa Cruz, Romulo, and Mehta. Santa Cruz played an important role in emphasizing socioeconomic rights. Like Chang, Romulo was a leading critic of the Western states' colonial policies, while Mehta had a significant part with regard to women's rights. Other delegates also made important contributions, such as the delegates from several Latin American countries more generally, who also emphasized socioeconomic rights, and the delegates from the Eastern Bloc, who highlighted socioeconomic issues as well as questions about discrimination.

In the secondary literature, Roosevelt, Cassin, Chang, and Malik are often considered to be the principal "critical authors," or drafters, of the document. Yet it should also be stressed that the committee secretary, John Humphrey, also played an important role in collating the historical materials that he submitted to the drafting committee.[33] Were one to adopt a narrow definition of the concept of author (or "critical author"), one might narrow the group yet further. It is true that Roosevelt played a very important role by virtue of her personality and her diplomatic abilities, but she was not involved in writing the actual text to the same degree as other members of the core drafting team. Malik and Chang, who were philosophically the most experienced and astute on the team, made substantial contributions to the key sections—such as the preamble and Article 1—and to the character of the document as a whole. For their part, Cassin and Humphrey, the group's legal experts, provided crucial textual underpinnings, with Cassin in particular playing a key role in the organization of the text.

An analogy can usefully be drawn here with the research group associated with the so-called Higgs boson particle, which, despite its proper name, was theorized collectively. The main authors of the UDHR came from an array of backgrounds and marshaled an array of different kinds of expertise and perspectives, all of which contributed to the document as a whole.

René Cassin (1887–1976) was a skilled rhetorician and lawyer. Schooled in the French legal tradition, his political experience included working for de Gaulle's government in exile in London during the Second World War. He had been a soldier in the First World War and had also worked for the League of Nations. During the World War I, Cassin was seriously wounded and was physically disabled for the rest of his life. Moreover, he had been involved in organizing an international veterans' movement after the First World War. During the Second World War, most of his family had died in Nazi concentration camps, and he himself would have been executed had he returned to France during the Vichy regime. After the end of World War II, he served as France's delegate on the UN Commission on Human Rights from 1947 to 1948 and on its drafting committee. In 1949, he became the vice-chairman, and in 1955 the chairman, of the Commission on Human Rights. He was also appointed as a judge on the European Court of Human Rights in 1959, becoming its president in 1965. In 1968, Cassin received the Nobel Peace Prize for his contributions to human rights.

As discussed in Part I, Chang was a highly multifaceted individual with a wide range of interests (literature, theater, music, pedagogy, philosophy) and diverse professional experiences (director, author, teacher, researcher, school administrator, diplomat). He, like Cassin, suffered from physical complaints (in Chang's case, heart problems) and had also directly experienced major conflicts and war between China and Japan in the 1930s.

Charles Malik (1906–1987) was a philosophy professor and diplomat from Lebanon who had a deep knowledge of various theological and philosophical traditions. Malik remained Greek-Orthodox all his life, but he had a profound admiration for Catholicism, theologically as well as philosophically. He particularly admired Thomas of Aquinas. He had a clear ecumenical bent and maintained an open attitude toward the three major traditions in Christianity.[34] He had pursued his doctoral studies under the philosopher and mathematician Alfred North Whitehead at Harvard and had also studied under Martin Heidegger at Freiburg in Germany in the 1930s. Rising anti-Semitism in Germany caused him to move to the United States, where he continued his studies. On the basis of his appearance, Germans assumed that Malik, an Arab, was Jewish, as a result of which he was subjected to violence and discrimination during his time as a student in Germany. He was a rapporteur for the Commission on Human Rights during the drafting of the UDHR, succeeding Eleanor Roosevelt as its chairman. He went on to become chairman of ECOSOC as well as of the General Assembly's Third Committee, which met eighty-one times between September and December 1948 to debate the articles of the UDHR. That Malik held these two key positions during the final phases of the work on the UDHR was to be of great importance when the time came to vote on the declaration in the General Assembly.

Eleanor Roosevelt (1884–1962) was politically very active in a range of issues including civil rights and women's rights. The range of her political engagement emerges clearly in the "My Day'" newspaper column, which she wrote, six days a week, between 1935 and 1962. In it, she dealt with every imaginable topic, from everyday tasks in the household to dramatic events such as the Japanese attack on Pearl Harbor and the atomic bomb. Roosevelt was the United States' representative to the UN General Assembly (1946–1952) and chairman of its Commission on Human Rights (1947–1948) during the period in which the UN Declaration was drafted. She came from a privileged family in New York. The fact that her deceased husband Franklin D. Roosevelt had been president of the United States was a huge asset for the group working on the UDHR insofar as she enjoyed a close relationship with his successor, President Harry S. Truman. Eleanor Roosevelt had also endured human suffering close at hand, not least in consequence of her husband's polio and physical disability during the last years of his life, as well as of his various infidelities. She had grown up with her grandmother after the early deaths of her own parents. One of her brothers also died young, and her father Elliot was severely afflicted with alcoholism toward the end of his life.

The Canadian John P. Humphrey (1905–1995) was an experienced legal expert with a wide knowledge of the world's various legal traditions. A law professor at McGill University in Montreal, he had taken an interest in international law from an early stage in his scholarly career. Both his parents died while he was a child, and he lost an arm at a young age. Humphrey had also had to endure a great deal of bullying and exclusion while attending a private boarding school. It was perhaps he of all the members of the Commission on Human Rights who became closest to Peng Chun Chang. He expressed his contribution to the UDHR in a modest and humble way in his memoir—"I was no Thomas Jefferson."[35]

It is striking just how many of the individuals involved in drafting the UN Declaration had themselves undergone suffering at various times of their lives, something that may account for their deep commitment to the task in hand.[36] These circumstances may also shed light on why several of the authors in the core team fought to ensure that social and economic rights were included in the declaration and that vulnerable groups should be accorded protection under its provisions.

The Result of the Negotiations: The UN Universal Declaration of Human Rights

The declaration can be viewed as an extension of several centuries of work on human rights with respect to practical politics as well as theory. As regards the former, key precursors included the antislavery movement of the eighteenth century, the efforts of trade unionists from the late nineteenth century to improve dire working conditions, the struggle for equal vote in elections, and the various women's movements. In the more theoretical domain, a profound influence was exerted by philosophical notions of natural rights, not least as these latter had informed previous rights declarations such as the American Declaration of Independence of 1776, the United States Bill of Rights, and the French Declaration of the Rights of Man and of the Citizen in 1789.[37]

This Enlightenment legacy was Chang's point of departure when arguing over the various articles of the UDHR (even though he was skeptical of introducing "the metaphysics" of natural rights into the document). Chang's view was that the commission and the drafting committee could safely draw upon this tradition when it had to define what human rights meant and which rights were particularly central. Those working on the declaration had also drawn inspiration from a number of other sources in the early 1940s, including the American Law Institute's "Statement of Essential Human Rights" (1945). The British writer H. G. Wells wrote the book *The Rights of Man* in 1940, which was also influential for the human rights discussions. There had also been a precursor to the UDHR in the American Declaration of the Rights and Duties of Man, also known as the Bogotá Declaration, which was signed in April 1948 and particularly emphasized that human rights should be formulated in tandem with moral obligations.

From a historical perspective, it can be argued that the function of human—or, put differently, natural rights—has been to take away from the state or monarch something that is then labeled sacred or inviolable, such as certain fundamental human entitlements. In other words, human rights have been treated as something that transcends any individual ruler or prevailing legal system and that can serve as a critical corrective to current legislation and policies. In Chinese thought, reference is frequently made to "the mandate of heaven," (*tian ming*) which has fulfilled a function that approximates to the notions of human or natural rights. The doctrine of "mandate of heaven" has usually been interpreted as the claim that heaven gives the mandate to rule and heaven can take it away if the king does not rule well.[38] For example, throughout history, natural disasters have been treated by many people as a sign that a political leader has lacked legitimacy or that he or she has lost the approval conferred by heaven's mandate.

In addition to these historical-philosophical roots, a number of proximate events and experiences lay behind the birth of the UN Declaration. Perhaps the most important catalysts of the UN Declaration were the Holocaust and the Second World War. Numerous commentators have argued that it was precisely these horrific episodes in the history of humanity that ultimately led the various states to unite over the key elements of the UN Declaration. Whenever there was disagreement on a central issue, reference could always be made to the crimes against humanity that had been committed by Nazi Germany and its allies. The next stage of the argument would be to observe that the purpose of the declaration was to ensure that nothing of this kind would ever occur again.[39]

Both during and after the Second World War, it had become obvious to the international community that existing laws and models for democracy—in the form of majority rule—were insufficient to prevent rights violations and atrocities by an individual regime. Hitler had come to power by means of a general election in the early 1930s, only to suppress democracy and the rule of law in Germany. The authors of the UN Declaration had also noted carefully how fascist regimes had invoked crises and states of emergency as a ploy for abolishing human rights. What was therefore needed was a universal ethics of rights to which every state was required to adhere in both its legislation and its policies.

Certain fundamental rights, such as the rights not to be tortured, not to be subjected to slavery or discrimination or an unfair trial, were now to be regarded as inviolable even by the invocation of a state of emergency. This idea also applied to the internal "belief aspect" of the right to freedom of religion (*forum internum*) in contrast to religious practices (*forum externum*). For the restriction of rights that were not absolute in nature, such as the right to freedom of expression, extremely strong reasons would need to be adduced. History had shown that the rights which authoritarian leaders sought to restrict first was the right to freedom of expression; after that, they would set their sights on restricting and abolishing the others.[40]

The History of the UN Declaration—A Success Story?

The UN Declaration is today one of the most translated documents in the history of the world and is available in more than 440 languages as well as the UN's own official languages—Chinese, English, Russian, French, Spanish, and Arabic. The UDHR can be compared with the most translated document, the New Testament, with over 1,300 translations, and the Jehovah's Witnesses' *Listen to God and Live Forever*, with over 580 translations.

The UN Declaration, which will shortly turn seventy-five years old (in December 2023), can today be described as a success story as measured by its impact on social debate, the establishment of norms, legislation, and on subsequent conventions, declarations, and organizational work.

The postwar period—especially after the adoption of the UN Declaration in 1948—has seen the emergence of a series of expanded rights declarations and binding conventions by the United Nations and other global and regional agencies. In 1966, as noted above, the UN Declaration was supplemented by two conventions: the Covenant on Civil and Political Rights and the Covenant on Economic, Social, and Cultural Rights. Additional key conventions include the International Convention on the Elimination of All

Forms of Racial Discrimination (1965); the Convention on the Elimination of all Forms of Discrimination against Women (1979); the Convention against Torture and Other Cruel, Inhuman or Degrading Treatment or Punishment (1984); the Convention on the Rights of the Child (1989); the Convention on the Rights of Persons with Disabilities (2006); and various regional legal instruments such as the European Convention on Human Rights (1950), the American Convention on Human Rights (1969); and the African Charter on Human and Peoples' Rights (1986). The UDHR has thus come to stand as a powerful inspiration for an array of rights conventions and declarations in the postwar period. Eleanor Roosevelt's contention that the declaration would become a new Magna Carta for humanity has been confirmed in several ways. The French drafter René Cassin said in his Nobel lecture in 1968 that "it [the UDHR] is the first document of an ethical sort that organized humanity has ever adopted, and precisely at a time when man's power over nature became vastly increased because of scientific discoveries, and when it was essential to decide to what constructive ends these powers should be put."[41]

A global civil community of human rights has also emerged, with voluntary organizations such as Amnesty International, Oxfam, Greenpeace, Human Rights Watch, and Doctors without Borders making substantial contributions. International human rights bodies such as the International Criminal Tribunal at The Hague are also signs that a global way of thinking about human rights is increasingly taking an institutional form. The Canadian researcher and politician Michael Ignatieff has rightly noted that human rights today represent a moral lingua franca that is available to individuals and interest groups seeking a foundation for their political demands.[42]

And yet the text of the declaration is far from having been realized in practice, despite such notable achievements as decolonization, the struggle against racial discrimination, and the abolition of apartheid in South Africa in 1994, the passing of some authoritarian and military regimes in Latin America, as well as the fall of the Iron Curtain in 1989—and with it—the collapse of most of the communist dictatorships of Eastern Europe.[43] Sadly, however, many grave human rights problems persist in the world. Countries such as North Korea, Iran, Russia, China, and Turkey impose comprehensive restrictions on freedom of expression and other freedoms, and in many countries, members of various minorities are subjected to serious discrimination and violence.

The Properties of the UN Declaration

How, then, should we understand the UN Declaration's extraordinary success? In the first place, it is a very well written, structured, and internally coherent text that many people regard as almost comprehensive. Second, it has a special tone that conveys to readers the same feeling of timelessness that one finds in the literary masterpieces of world history. Speaking on the occasion of its sixtieth jubilee, the Irish poet and Nobel laureate Seamus Heaney praised the document's literary qualities. The UDHR, he argued, was to human beings' moral consciousness what the gold standard had been to the monetary system.[44]

It is true that the UN Declaration did not become legally binding since it is not a convention. It was "merely" a declaration. But the UN Declaration has come to be a moral guiding star for much of the human rights work that is ongoing in the world today. A great source of inspiration for all of the UN conventions that have been adopted in the postwar period, it is considered the closest thing to international common law as regards human rights. The fact that the UDHR has also been widely considered to be a clarification, an exposition, and an instantiation of those articles of the UN Charter that address rights has conferred on the declaration a unique authority in the world community and within the UN itself. Article 68 of the UN Charter explicitly articulates a desire to create a human rights commission with the task of drafting an international human rights declaration and an international bill of rights.

What made the UDHR such a landmark was that the individual, the single human being, for the first time in history was accorded a status within international law. To be sure, the League of Nations had to some extent shown the way with Article 23 of its covenant. This article stated that members of the League would ensure fair working conditions for men, women, and children. The League of Nations would also act as a monitor to ensure that the rights of various minorities were respected. But never before had so broad a collection of rights—civil, political, socioeconomic, and cultural—been ascribed to an individual simply by virtue of being a human being.

This latter notion—by virtue of being a human—also introduced into this context the word "universal." In other words, rights in the UN Declaration applied to *all* people. No person should be discriminated against as regards their rights on the basis of race, skin color, gender, language, religion, political or other opinions, national or social origin, property, ancestry, or status more generally. Claims to rights were to be directed not solely to states but also to other parties, including individuals, groups, organizations, and schools, all of whom had a responsibility to respect the observance of human rights, not least through education, "naming and shaming," and information campaigns. Chang was also deeply involved in these clusters of issues relating to discrimination and the universality of rights as well as the implementation of human rights, among other things, through education.

Taking human rights as a starting point meant opposing various collectivist perspectives in the realms of morality and politics. Protection of the individual human being's dignity always lies at the heart of any human rights ethics. Chang also strongly emphasized the fundamental rights and dignity of human beings in the same spirit as various European Enlightenment philosophers, and it was arguably he who most forcefully advocated that respect for human dignity should be included in the preamble to the UDHR.[45] From a rights perspective, individual human beings' fundamental rights—for example, to life, freedom, and integrity—cannot be sacrificed for the "common good," whether the latter is defined in terms of national utility or, as with utilitarianism, the maximizing of happiness more generally. What characterizes human rights, apart from their universality, is thus their morally paramount function in relation to other ethical considerations.[46]

As the legal expert Ove Bring has also contended, one might say that international—or universal—human rights commitments as a whole are special in relation to other international agreements and commitments. States that sign or ratify human rights norms are in the first instance or primarily obligated to respect these norms, not with regard to each other, but with regard to their own citizens.[47]

On several counts, then, the UN Declaration is a remarkable text. It was created at the start of the Cold War, a period characterized by powerful ideological antagonisms between the victorious powers in the East and the West. Despite this global polarization, these states managed to agree upon a set of rights articles that were highly ambitious for their time. (As some writers would claim later, some of the human rights of the UDHR express aspirations rather than enforceable rights that have clear monitoring and implementation mechanisms.[48]) As we recall the rights addressed by the UN Declaration are civil, political, socioeconomic, and cultural. In this it differs from the 1950 European Convention on Human Rights, for example, which is concerned solely with civil and political rights—with the exception of the subsequent protocol amendments that address other rights, such as the right to education. The Commission on Human Rights in the UN thus chose to ascribe the same priority to two different kinds of rights—civil and political (so-called *rights of option*) and economic, social, and cultural (so-called *rights of claim*).⁴⁹ A life of human dignity—and hence respect for human dignity—requires not only a guarantee of political freedoms and civil rights but also respect for an array of rights within the social, economic, and cultural spheres. Put differently, one might argue that the UN Declaration is concerned with guaranteeing two distinct phenomena, namely actions—and, with them, the possibility for actions—and essential "products" or resources that are important for living a life of human dignity.

Chang articulated a similar distinction when discussing the UN Declaration's "culture and science" article, that is, Article 27: "Everyone has the right freely to participate in the cultural life of the community, to enjoy the arts and to share in scientific advancement and its benefits." The declaration, he argued, should not only guarantee the consumption or enjoyment of cultural creations but also the individual's own actions and participation in the process of cultural creation.⁵⁰ This principle was to be adopted by the UN's Commission on Human Rights and had an impact on the formulation of the article. Chang was insistent upon the importance of all-rounded personal development, which can be presumed to include the ability to participate in cultural and scientific activities.

Depending upon which phenomena one focuses on within the human rights discourse—human needs, interests, abilities, and opportunities for action—it is possible to speak of separate functions of various rights. A number of rights have the purpose of *protecting* human beings from external threats to their fundamental needs and interests. Other rights have, in contrast, the purpose of *developing* human beings' capacities, while others have the function to *strengthen* people's opportunities for action in such a way as their capacities can find expression in both word and deed. It is also possible to ascribe to the UDHR *as a whole* the function of being a morally pedagogical instrument, something that Chang often emphasized when talking about "the humanization of man" through the declaration.

To this can be added the fact that the UDHR has its point of departure in two kinds of interests that, according to the British philosopher Rowan Cruft, are vital to all people: first, the individual interests of a single human being, which directly justify specific human rights such as the right not to be subjected to torture or slavery. Here reference need only to be made to *one* individual when legitimizing the right in question. Every single individual has these rights, regardless of his or her relation to other people.[51] But there are also those interests that every human being has in relation to other people and that together can be considered as the basis for demanding a human right. For instance, all people have a substantial interest in being able to enjoy culture and science and in sharing in the joint benefits that cultural activities in society can offer. One might therefore say that on the basis of these collective benefits—culture and science—every person has the right to be able to enjoy cultural and scientific education. Several articles in the UDHR refer to the value or benefits of this latter kind; for example, education, culture, science, politics, or membership in an organization that requires the participation of many people. Chang was also very much involved in ensuring that all of these different rights and benefits were guaranteed by the UN Declaration.

The Multicultural History of the UN Declaration

An additional reason for the declaration's success is the multicultural nature of its history. Its text was written with the involvement of people from different countries and cultures. The text has, in other words, democratic representativeness and, with it, a resonance in an array of countries around the world. This pluralism also included different experiences of various forms of oppression and suffering. One of the darkest instances of this latter had been, of course, the European experience of Nazism, something that René Cassin had experienced firsthand. Another was Japan's policies of colonial aggression and militarism, which Chang and others had also experienced personally.

There was a broad consensus among all those involved in the commission, the drafting committee, the Economic and Social Council, and the Third Committee that clarity and comprehensibility should be a defining feature of the document. Representative of this perspective was the statement made by the Swedish delegate Ulla Lindström that "it has often been said in committee that the Declaration of Human Rights was intended for the man in the street."[52] Like Malik and Cassin, Chang was also very anxious that the text should be nonacademic, conceptually lucid, well-structured, short, and concise.[53]

It may be added that at the time of the UDHR's drafting there did not exist a clear definition of human rights as a concept. The authors of the declaration were referring to something that was more or less taken for granted.[54] Human rights are rights that human beings have by virtue of being human. No distinction should be made on the basis of religion, nationality, gender, or language, for example. Chang's view was that it was unnecessary to come up with an agreed-upon definition of human rights in order for the articles to be binding. Presumably he felt that it was easy to give examples of human rights but that there might be disagreement about what it was that made them human rights. Just as it was unnecessary to require unity about the basis for human rights in order to be able to accept the UDHR, so, too, was it unnecessary to require unity about the necessary and sufficient conditions for usage of the concept.

Apart from his references during the writing of the UN Declaration to Enlightenment-era conceptions of rights, the closest Chang came to giving an explicit definition was in a description of the completion of the UDHR he gave in a speech in October 1950. In this address, Chang underscored the fundamental nature of human rights and their cross-cultural legitimacy. Human rights documents do not apply to things like road traffic, customs duties, or narcotics; they are about human rights alone, and no one can claim that such rights should be qualified. Chang argued that it was important to distinguish between abstract rights—human rights—and the ways in which to realize those rights, and not to put them on the same logical level.[55] The authors of the UDHR also sought to formulate the articles in a general fashion so that they could be interpreted and applied in new situations in the future. For example, René Cassin's proposal that the preamble to the UDHR refer more concretely to the atrocities committed by the Fascist regimes during the Second World War was not accepted, and the preamble included instead the more general phrase "barbarous acts which have outraged the conscience of mankind."

One issue of relevance to all these points is the document's intercultural and universal nature. The UDHR can be said to be an intercultural document in *three* senses. First, people from a range of countries and regions worked together in writing the document. Second, the UDHR contains principles that emphasize the importance of culture for people's self-identification and well-being as well as of understanding and tolerance, which transcend the boundaries of the group. The UDHR also has a substantial article on freedom of religion (Article 18), which emphasizes the right to practice religion, individually as well as collectively, in both the private and the public sphere.

Third, the document is intercultural in that it can be regarded as the result of intercultural dialogue. Some of its authors—Chang especially—tried to achieve a consensus on fundamental freedoms and rights even though the delegates came from visibly different ethical and cultural traditions. One important area of unity that emerged during the discussions in the Human Rights Commission was that human rights should be able to be justified from several philosophical outlooks, not just one or two.

Chang was also interested in the idea of "the intercultural" in all three of these senses. He would also make a clear contribution to each of these dimensions, as we will see in due course. He sought to ensure that the document would enjoy as much support as possible from the various peoples of the world. What is more, he wanted the UDHR to articulate principles of tolerance and religious freedom. The article dealing with freedom of religion, he argued, expressed one of the most central freedoms in human history. He additionally sought to justify the articles in such as way that representatives from different cultures would be able to accept so far as possible the documents within the framework of their own traditions.

This goal of ensuring that the UDHR would be an intercultural document—in all three senses—was closely linked to the goal of making it universal. The document should be accessible to everyone—its language should be as simple and clear as possible—and it should be able to be justified and accepted by most of the delegates on the Commission on Human Rights and by humanity at large. Hence, it should not be biased in terms of religion. Finally, it should be universally applicable, regardless of whether people were living within a nation-state or not.

It may therefore be concluded that Chang was supportive and even a strong promoter of the UDHR's core features, such as the document's universal and intercultural nature, its religious neutrality, its inclusion of the concept of human dignity, and its broad understanding of the content of human rights as well as the document's formal qualities and logical structure. He was also closely involved in the debate over the document's implementation. In Chapters 6, 7, and 8 each of these contributions will be examined in greater detail.

CHAPTER 6

Chang's Ideas About Ethics and Human Rights

Chang presented his ideas in all of the UN bodies that have already been mentioned in connection with the writing of the UN Declaration, which is to say the Third Committee, the Economic and Social Council, the Commission on Human Rights, and the so-called drafting group. As vice-chairman of the Commission on Human Rights and active coauthor of the UDHR, Chang had a special role in the Chinese delegation. However, he was not China's sole representative; there were other prominent Chinese delegates who contributed to the work on the UN Declaration, even if their contributions seem modest in comparison with Chang's.

The Chinese Presence in UN Bodies

Among the other Chinese delegates to the UN, special mention must be made to John C. H. Wu (Wu Jinxiong), who represented China in Chang's place at the commission's second meeting in Geneva in 1947.

Wu was a well-known legal expert in China who had studied in the United States, France, and Germany. At the time of the Geneva meeting, he was China's ambassador to the Vatican. René Cassin had wanted to have the meeting in Geneva; he was keen for there to be a UN meeting on "Francophone soil," not least since he expected the European—and Francophone— context to make the climate of discussion more favorable to him. From the very start, this proposal met with fierce resistance, including from Roosevelt and Chang. Instead of taking part in the Geneva meeting, Chang chose to attend a meeting of the Economic and Social Council.

According to Pierre Étienne Will, a French sinologist who has studied the archives in Taiwan for the period of correspondence between the UN delegates and the republican regime, the Geneva meeting was, paradoxically, one of the few occasions when the Chinese delegation communicated clearly with its regime at home.[1] John C. H. Wu, who was Christian, stated that the commission seemed to be well versed in the Confucian principle that "what you do not wish for yourself, do not do to others," instead of the positive formulation, "do to others as you would have them do to you," which is a well-known dictum of Christianity. Previously, during his "Christian youth period," Chang had also declared a preference for the positive formulation of this reciprocity principle ("do to others as you would have them do to you") over the negative version ("what you do not wish for yourself, do not do to others"). (See Chang's article "The Gospel in China.")

What else did the Chinese regime's communications to John C. H. Wu contain? In its letters to him—seemingly the only official correspondence relating to the Geneva meeting—the government in Nanking stressed that he should above all convey the impression that there were no significant problems with minorities in China, particularly regarding Xinjiang. Additionally, he should say that several of the key rights being discussed in the UN context had already been included in the new Chinese constitution of 1946. He should also point out the importance of people's natural rights as something that chimed well with Chinese traditions as well as call attention to the political ideal that "within the four seas, all men are brothers."

There were two further points that the regime wished its representative to emphasize. The first was China's meritocratic examination system for the recruitment of civil servants, which guaranteed fairness in the form of equal opportunity. Last but not least, the regime wanted John C. H. Wu to highlight the fact that China had not succumbed to extremism of either the left or the right. The country was instead striving to find a balance or "middle course." At the Geneva meeting, the Chinese also proposed a kind of minideclaration comprising ten articles, which condensed a larger number of rights articles into just a few by means of abstraction and generalization. Only one of these articles included social and economic rights, in other words, the right to a decent living. While the proposal was not accepted, it did encourage the delegates to try to use formulations that were as concise as possible.[2] For his part, Chang did not have much correspondence with the regime at home, despite serving as vice-chairman of the Commission on

Human Rights. According to Will, the archive contains a report, cabled to Nanking after the first meeting of the drafting group in the summer of 1947, in which Chang relates that China—that is to say, Chang—has been very active in making interventions on every article. This broadly matches both the notes from the UN meeting on Long Island in the summer of 1947 and Stanley's memories of the summer sessions, that is, that his father had been very active. The meetings in summer 1947 seem also to have been highly significant in that several important ideas were introduced then—for example, Chang's concepts of "two-man mindedness," or "sympathy for others."[3] As will be seen, Chang in fact acted with a high degree of independence in all of the UN bodies. He rarely consulted with his government about either the articles or the other contents of the UN Declaration. Because of his extensive knowledge of similar political and ethical questions, and his deep engagement with the UN project, he presumably had a very clear idea of what he wanted to say and where his work at the UN was directed.

It can reasonably be assumed that Chang's independence with regard to his government at home was something that facilitated his work with the UN on the issue of human rights. The nationalist republic was of course anything but democratic (in the sense of liberal democracy), and its policies were already in violation of a number of human rights.[4] A special culture and identity had also been developing in several of those involved in writing the UN Declaration, which may account for why they saw themselves primarily as agents within a new, United Nations context. What is more, the regime at home had its hands full with serious internal conflicts and thus paid no great interest to human rights issues at the UN.

Stanley Chang went on: "With regard to my father's ideas and opinions, he was capable of expressing them without paying any real consideration to the opinions of the Chinese government. Nor did I ever see him reading coded telegrams in New York in the way that he did during his time as a diplomat in Turkey. (The code was written in five-digit sequences.)" Some scholars who have written about Chang and the other key individuals in the drafting process of the UN Declaration have focused in particular on the meeting of the Third Committee in autumn 1948. It was scheduled just before the UN Declaration was presented to the General Assembly on 10 December so that all countries that were members of the UN could have an opportunity to discuss its text.[5] Several of the debates that took place in the Third Committee during the fall were also highly interesting in that they dealt with issues of principle and thus had a summative aspect. Chang had a mediating role during the discussions, and he managed to present constructive compromises.[6]

Notwithstanding, there were clearly many other interventions in different settings and at earlier stages that also usefully shed light on the main concerns of the writers of the declaration. Given what has already been noted, it is not too much to say that many of Chang's statements in UN settings increasingly came to represent his own personal opinions. It is thus perfectly reasonable to try to reconstruct Chang's *own* views on ethics, particularly human rights, on the basis of this UN material. Some of his statements were official in nature, of course, and this was something Chang also highlighted in his argumentation. Some of these were general in nature and broadly matched Chang's own views. It is not too much of a stretch, then, to say that several of these statements can also be considered as Chang's own.

Chang's Significance for the UDHR

Like Charles Malik, who was also one of the principal authors of the UDHR, Chang was interested in the more overarching issues related to the declaration, such as its philosophy, ethical justification, and function. He was also particularly interested in its central sections, such as the preamble and Article 1. He was deeply preoccupied with how the document could be implemented and with what strategies were realistic and reasonable in order to realize those human rights.

Chang articulated a kind of anti-metaphysical pragmatic philosophy that contrasted starkly with Charles Malik's Thomism and natural rights doctrine. It also contrasted with the Eastern Bloc's Marxism and atheism as well as with the so-called official Christianity of countries such as Brazil and the Netherlands. Chang's rights philosophy also ran counter to those countries, such as Britain, that primarily emphasized civil and political rights and did not wish to highlight socioeconomic ones. He was clearly opposed to the kind of "liberal atomism" that viewed the function of human rights as being primarily to protect the property and freedoms of the individual. At the same time, Chang was an advocate of essential freedoms, such as freedom of religion and expression, and he often referred to the civil and political rights that had been claimed during the Enlightenment period in Europe.

It is striking that Chang, who made so significant a contribution to the UDHR, came from a country that in the 1940s was openly authoritarian and

Figure 1. Family picture from 1906 in China. Poling on the left (30 years old), Peng on the right (14 years old). The father, Jiu-an (63 years old), is flanked by Poling's children.

Figure 2. Peng as PhD student at Columbia University, 1919.

Figure 3. Picture from Peng and Ts'a's wedding at the Union Theological Seminary in New York. They married in 1921.

Figure 4. Peng and Ts'a in their house at the Nankai campus before the Japanese bombings in 1937.

Figure 5. Nankai University, the first building built in 1919 before the Japanese bombings.

Figure 6. Family picture in Hong Kong 1940 just before the departure to Turkey. In the middle, Ts'a and Peng, to the left Chen and Ruth, and to the right Yuan-Feng (Stanley) and Ming-Ming.

Figure 7. Peng and Ts'a at Turkey's national day during their stay in Turkey.

Figure 8. Peng's installation as ambassador in Santiago, Chile, 1942.

Figure 9. Peng and Lord Ernest Bevin in London, 1946.

Figure 10. Peng and Anthony Eden in London, 1946.

Figure 11. Poling and Peng in New York before Poling leaves for China on a boat, 1946.

Figure 12. Family picture in New York from 1948. From the left, Yuan-Feng (Stanley), Ruth, Chen, Ming-Ming, Ts'a, and Peng.

Figure 13. Chang deeply concentrating during a debate on the Universal Declaration in the UN.

Figure 14. From the left, Peng's good friend Y. R. Chao, Ts'a, Hu Shi, Hu Shi's wife Jian Dongxiu, and Peng.

was violating human rights in a number of ways. It was not a state that had cherished human rights thinking in the same way as England, France or the United States. Nor did the concept of human or natural rights have an exact equivalent in the Chinese context, even if Chang did try to show that the equivalents of a certain kind of human rights thinking could be found in the philosophy of Confucius, Mencius, and others. However, China was not the only country involved in the writing of the UDHR that was itself violating human rights. Delegates from several western European countries and the United States represented states that had also violated human rights flagrantly, for example, by racial discrimination and colonialism.

Chang also stood out because of his educational background, which has already been described. While other key authors of the UDHR—such as Cassin, Humphrey, and Santa Cruz—had been trained in the law, Chang was a humanist who had studied subjects such as philosophy, pedagogy, literature, and drama. For instance, he had taken two master's degrees from Columbia University, where he had also taken his doctorate in the philosophy of education. It was a humanistic background that he shared with Charles Malik. One can speculate as to the importance for the writing of the UDHR of Chang's special background. A number of Chang's colleagues—such as John Humphrey— believed that it was precisely his special cultural, educational, and professional background—and, not least, his personal characteristics—that enabled him to make so profound a contribution to the Commission on Human Rights. Chang himself stressed the importance of being a scholar and educator for understanding the international scene, and this idea could also be applied to his specific work within the UN. Chang expressed the following points about the importance of education in understanding the contingencies of conflicts in the world from the point of view of a "school man" in 1938:

> You know we school men, and school women . . . have been given various kinds of heavy responsibilities. We have been asked to be the preservers of cultures, the transmitters of cultures, psychologists in the use of various techniques, the humanists in the general sense of that word, taking care of the larger social implications of the educational process. May I say that, from the point of view of the school man, it seems as though a new duty is going to be thrust upon us. That duty is to be statesmen as well. Especially in this age we have to understand the international scene in order that we, as school people, can do our work as well and intelligently and exactly.[7]

Chang stressed also in this context the importance of freedom for intellectual exploration concerning international affairs and what scholars can do to increase it. Chang identified here three factors that are not so beneficial for the free exploration of international problems (apart from the fourth factor—the suppression of freedom of intellectual exploration from actors in countries governed by people who claim certain ideologies). Chang said:

> Now why is it that the margin of freedom for intellectual exploration has become narrower (than 50 years ago)? I think one of the factors surely is *urgency*.... When problems are too urgent then we have to take the thing that is at hand. There is no time for free exploration. Under these circumstances, such as all of us have gone through during times of war, for instance, we would not be left free by others to think for ourselves.... Another factor that is not so good for free exploration of international problems is the factor of what we might call *localization*: localization in our interests, localization in our understanding. A third factor may be *over-specialization*—that is, over-emphasizing one thing.... It seems as though, as school people, when we think of these various problems, we must somehow in our educational process break down the urgency by a cool, comprehensive view of things. When other people shout slogans we, the school people, should not use them. When other people say it is either this kind of "ism" or that kind of "ism" ... it seems as though it is our important duty, as school people, not to shout with them. And, of course, regarding localization, it is also our duty to introduce more comprehensive views of the world.[8]

Chang was also a strong advocate of freedom of speech and the freedom of the press. For him these freedoms were of special interest for Chinese people since he regarded democratic freedoms as deeply rooted in China's history. He was also eager to pay attention to the fact that Chinese people happened to be not only inventors and originators of the printed word but also champions for its unharnessed dissemination.[9] Paper-making started very early in China and some scholars suggest that it started as early as the 2nd century BC, in the regions of south and southeast China.[10] In 1948 at a UN meeting in Geneva Chang stressed that: "The printed word since its very inception has been the greatest enemy of tyrants and autocrats. Little wonder, in their attempt to subjugate the people, they first turned their wrath on the makers of the printed word. Emperor Chin Shih-huang, builder of the Great Wall of China, was surely a forerunner of all dictators and tyrants who have suppressed the freedom of speech. It was he who put to death scholars whose writings he did not like, and it was he who ordered all books to be burned. He tried to put an end to the freedom of thought and information by suppressing the printed word and its authors. And what was the result? He failed miserably and his dynasty was overthrown. Dictators, whenever and wherever found, may well take note of his experience! The history of China in the past two thousand years is replete with statesmen, scholars, and poets who preferred imprisonment, exile and even death to not being free to vent to their own thoughts and beliefs."[11] This form of argumentation—presenting a normative statement on the basis of a historical exploration (often with China in focus) was common for Chang in the UN setting.

Almost all of the so-called core group of authors—some of whom, such as Hernán Santa Cruz, were close to him—spoke very positively of Chang, both as a person and as a delegate in the drafting group. This included not only Roosevelt and Humphrey but also, paradoxically, Charles Malik, who, despite their deep differences of opinion, voiced his warm appreciation for Chang's intellectual capacity and his important contributions to the formulation of the UDHR. John Humphrey recorded his first impressions of Chang in his journal: "The vice-chairman was P. C. Chang who also represented China in the Economic and Social Council. I was at first put off by his somewhat gruff manner and his inhibited criticisms of the Secretariat, but I soon learned to appreciate his great human qualities and we became friends."[12] Humphrey also wrote the following journal entry for 17 May 1950 about Chang while they were attending a meeting of the UN Commission on Information and Press Freedom in Montevideo: "We [Humphrey and his wife Jeanne] went for a long walk with P. C. Chang tonight. He is worried about his intervention at this afternoon's meeting. In spite of his long experience and intellectual powers Chang is in many respects still a boy. This indeed is the source of his particular charm. I have seldom seen anyone more worked up emotionally then he was this afternoon when he accused American journalists of reporting on China without either perspective or knowledge."[13] The only person in the core group who, excepting a few comments on his style of writing, did not have anything very positive to say about Chang, either as a person or his contributions to the work, was René Cassin. For his part, John Humphrey stated that Chang "was a formidable intellectual force and in intellectual capacity he far surpassed all the rest of us on the Committee."

Hernán Santa Cruz also had the following to say about Chang in his memoirs:

> China's seat, the fifth of the five great powers, was held by Professor P. C. Chang, one of the most original personalities ever to pass through the UN. His knowledge of Mandarin was combined with a deep knowledge of Western culture. He had a degree from Clark University and a doctorate from Columbia University and had been a professor at the University of Chicago. He had also been a Minister at China's embassy to Turkey and had been its ambassador to Chile. He was involved in revising the English in the version which had been drafted by delegates from Anglophone countries, and every time someone referred to something as being new Chang would always make them disappointed by showing that all ideas are at least two thousand years old. In every UN body in which he participated, he distinguished himself by his unique style. He was listened to and respected on the Commission for Human Rights, where he became vice-chairman under Eleanor Roosevelt and where he made an important contribution to the development of the Universal Declaration.[14]

Making an important contribution to the writing of a document can mean different things, however. The usual interpretation would be that the individual in question has been influential with respect to most of the articles of the declaration as well as for its style, arrangement, and structure. Another interpretation would be that the author has been influential with respect to the "core articles" in the declaration. Implicitly, he or she has been important in connection with the qualities that are seen as having particular significance for the document. His or her ideas have thus been *congruous* with the document's central qualities. Chang was important in all four aspects. He emphasized that the document should cover a range of rights, including civil, political, socioeconomic, and cultural. In other words, he was not only engaged with particular articles and rights issues but had interests that ranged across the entire field. He also made contributions to a number of central articles.[15]

He was particularly involved with Article 25, which emphasizes a decent standard of living, Article 23 on the right to work, Article 27 on the right to culture (as both consumer and creator), Article 26:2 on the right to full development of the human personality, Article 18 on the right to freedom of religion, Article 2 on the right not to be discriminated against, Article 21 on the right to equal access to public services, as well as the fundamental first article, which articulates the UDHR's view of humanity. He also helped to ensure that the word "dignity" should have a prominent place in the declaration. The word "benevolence" in a Confucian vein was also used by Chang when he justified the inclusion of economic and social rights in the UDHR.[16]

Because of his experiences as a teacher, Chang was particularly interested in the right to education. He was responsible for the inclusion of the word "fundamental" in Article 26:1: "Everyone has the right to education. Education shall be free, at least in the elementary and fundamental stages." According to Chang, many adults had never had the chance to attend school regularly, and by including the word "fundamental," he wanted to emphasize the importance of adult education. This idea was doubtless influenced by China's particular educational problems and by the fact that large numbers of its adult population had received no elementary education. According to Chang (something he expressed in a previous writing 1934), "Education should be prolonged to include adult life. This is particularly necessary in times of social change, such as are now going on in China, when the adults are quite as unprepared in the new situation as the young are and the adult has a much more important part to play than the child."[17]

As already noted, Chang was also involved in the formulation of Article 26:2, which declares: "Education shall be directed to the full development of the human personality."[18] For Chang, development of the personality incorporated an array of dimensions: social, cultural, spiritual, scientific, and material. Following Chinese traditions, he sought to avoid making a hard distinction between spiritual and material. On previous occasions, Chang had also taken culture to include economics, politics, social organization, and culture in a more artistic sense.[19] Education in its broadest sense, Chang believed, was also a matter of enhancing the quality of life. On this view, the goal of developing human personality on a broad front thus serves to make a series of other human rights relevant. Chang also believed that it was more reasonable to speak of "the free development of one's personality" than to speak of "freely developing one's personality." It is a good question why he preferred the first formulation. One possible explanation is that it does not exclude the role of environment and "inner" qualities in the development of personality. The second formulation more strongly emphasizes individual freedom in the development of personality, that is, that an individual actually is and should be his or her own "life architect."[20]

Chang also played an influential role in the formulation of Articles 27:1 and 27:2, which address people's right to enjoy the fruits of artistic, literary, and scientific activities as well as their opportunities for participating in such activities. According to Chang, the phrase "to share in scientific advancement and its benefits" came from the sixteenth-century philosopher and author Francis Bacon—a statement that has amazed a number of commentators.[21] However, Chang was presumably referring to Bacon's classic work *The New Atlantis*, in which he argued for the importance of science for *all* of society.

The Cuban delegate Perez Cisneros took Chang to be arguing that protection of the creations of an individual artist, author, or scientist represented the realization of *everyone's* interests—as both consumers and producers. There was, in other words, a substantial common interest in literary, artistic, and scientific works being *directly* available to all people in their "authentic" and original form, which is to say that one should strive to protect the "integrity" of the original works. That was why this article belonged in the UDHR. The Cuban delegate made this statement shortly after Chang's own intervention, and the fact that Chang himself did not subsequently correct Cisneros's comment can be taken as grounds for assuming that he had correctly interpreted Chang's position. The proposal by China that then became Article 27 of the UDHR reads: "Everyone has the right freely to participate in the cultural life of the community, to enjoy the arts and to share in scientific advancement and its benefits" (27:1). It goes on: "Everyone has the right to the protection of the moral and material interests resulting from any scientific, literary or artistic production of which he is the author" (27:2). Article 27 was special in that it emphasized the rights of all to *share in scientific advancement*. This can be interpreted as stating that citizens should be granted the opportunity to be, not only cultural consumers and producers in a more artistic sense of the word, but also participants in scientific endeavor.[22]

Another important point with which Chang was involved concerned the relationship between rights and duties. He emphasized that the declaration should not be interpreted in an individualistic fashion but rather that it should convey the importance of one's duties toward other human beings and to society at large.[23] He was therefore very pleased with the final formulation of Article 1 since, in his view, it struck a happy balance between the rights of the individual at the start of the clause and the reference to brotherhood—or community—at the end.[24] According to Chang, the articles of the UDHR would have been regarded as more selfish in spirit if they had not been preceded by reference to "a spirit of brotherhood" in the first article: "All human beings are born free and equal in dignity and rights. They are endowed with reason and conscience and should act towards one another in a spirit of *brotherhood*" (italics added).

Chang believed that it was logical that the declaration, after itemizing all the various rights, should also conclude with a reference to duties (in Article 29:1). He also sought to introduce a reference to the duties of the individual into Article 28: "Everyone is entitled to a social and international order in which the rights and freedoms set forth in this Declaration can be fully realized."[25] This proposal was, however, rejected. Chang wanted the declaration to be imbued with duties in a number of ways, an ambition that has been surprisingly downplayed by some commentators. The political scientist Johannes Morsink, for example, has argued that Chang's idea that duties should be present at the end and not at the beginning of the UN Declaration can be read as an attempt to reduce the priority accorded to duties in the document.[26] However, as the above comments suggest, this is a questionable reading.

For Chang, as for several delegates on the Commission on Human Rights, it was important that rights should be exercised in accordance with other moral considerations. Apart from the fact that rights always correspond to duties, there were other qualifications or limitations. He stressed that the limitations on the exercise of the rights and freedoms should not appear at the beginning of the declaration before those rights and freedoms themselves had been set forth.[27] Chang also introduced the notion of *general welfare* in Article 29:2 as a legitimate restriction on the exercise of rights and freedoms in the declaration. The list of restrictions took the form of society's legitimate demands for just or fair requirements of morality, general welfare, and public order. These restrictions were defined within the framework for a democratic society and were determined upon the basis of a legislative order whose aim was also to guarantee recognition of and respect for the freedoms and rights of others.

What has often been pointed out in the secondary literature is that several of these restrictions suffer from a lack of precision, which makes them susceptible to different interpretations.[28] What ought to be included in the concept of general welfare? One danger is that the concept is given a consequentialist interpretation in ethics which disregards the weighty moral significance that from the very start had been meant to be associated with human rights. Chang's role with regard to the restrictions placed on these rights was thus ambiguous. On the one hand, he introduced the concept of general welfare as a restriction on rights, which did not serve to strengthen the rhetoric around rights in relation to other ethical considerations such as teleological ones (for example maximization of welfare or utility). On the other hand, he wanted to dispense with the general and manipulable concept of morals as a restriction since it was, he felt, already covered by the rights and freedoms of others.[29]

In general, Chang was very interested in the logical structure of the UDHR and exerted himself to explain how the various articles related to each other. He expressed interest in the document's logical disposition in a number of ways. For instance, he stated that there should not be any interruption in the articles' organic progression from the right to life and other freedoms to the protection of those rights, which found expression, among other places, in its references to civil rights. Further, he was eager that one should not mix different ideas or principles in the same article. Chang also made an influential presentation of the structure of the UDHR, which was subsequently used in a great many contexts: "Articles 1, 2, 3 express the three principal ideas of eighteenth-century philosophy. Article 1 expresses the idea of brotherhood, Article 2 the idea of equality, and Article 3 the idea of freedom. Article 3 articulates a fundamental principle which is then defined and clarified in the following nine Articles.... [I]n this series of articles, the idea of freedom is developed gradually; first, it is applied to the individual, then to the family, and finally to the nation." These remarks were interesting because they also explained why Chang was hesitant to change certain articles (and the order between them), since the formulations and their structure had stood the test of time according to Chang and revealed an organic unity of the Universal Declaration.[30] During his final years at the UN, Chang also reflected more generally on the UDHR's relationship to the UN Charter and the project of writing a binding text for the convention.[31] He argued that where the UDHR represented an application of the UN Charter, a convention would represent an application of the UN Declaration. Chang had good grounds for this distinction, not least in view of the fact that a convention would provide greater precision for ratifying states as regards what exactly they were committing themselves to.

Chang was also very involved in the formulation of the preamble to the declaration, and he lobbied hard for it to include a philosophical statement of position that would explain the subsequent articles. In the present instance, it was especially important that the declaration highlighted the profound difference between human beings and animals. By "philosophical statement of position," Chang meant that the preamble should include overarching ethical concepts or moral principles that would justify the articles that followed. It was thus not a matter of philosophy or theology in the sense of natural law or theism. But according to Chang the preamble should include a philosophical anthropology in the sense that it should highlight what is special or unique about human beings in comparison to animals. In this, as noted already, Chang was anxious that the concept of human dignity should be included in the preamble; this was subsequently realized by foregrounding the dignity of the individual person. In other words, the preamble should emphasize respect for each person's dignity as a human being. Hence, a standard should be established "with a view to elevating the concept of man's dignity and emphasizing the respect of man; that principle should be embodied in a preamble to the International Bill of Rights."[32] Chang also stressed that the principle of equality should be examined, bearing in mind the concept of human dignity.[33]

One might say that the notion of respect for human dignity was important to emphasize in light of all the talk about human beings having fundamental equality, something Chang had underscored (4 February 1947, Commission for Human Rights). This equality should take into consideration all the independent choices that a person makes, while also recognizing the necessity of protecting human beings in difficult and unforeseen circumstances—especially concerning basic welfare and legal protection (17 November 1948, Third Committee). Chang believed that it was important to include the phrase "unforeseen circumstances" in order to encourage people's self-reliance and sense of responsibility.[34]

Unlike the Soviet delegation, which wanted to include the formulation "right to social security" in Article 25, Chang also wanted a more general formulation, "right to security," so that it might also cover a range of circumstances such as disability, illness, and old age. Chang's view was that *social* security had already been addressed in the declaration.

At this point, it may be remarked that Chang to some extent anticipated the subsequent discussions of equality and human dignity by the American philosopher Ronald Dworkin and others. Dworkin sought to devise precisely such a notion of equality (*equality of resources*) that might take into consideration people's free choices at the same time as it acknowledged the involuntary and difficult circumstances that can present themselves in the lifetime of a human being.[35]

Initially, Chang had also wanted the text of the declaration to be shorter, just ten articles, with a commentary on each and a description of their implementation. This suggestion did not find wider support. It can be noted that this minimalist rights proposal chimed badly with Chang's more overarching thinking about the document. In discussions of the various articles—including the article on religious freedom and that on a decent standard of living—he exerted himself to be as concrete and exhaustive as possible so as to reach out to the great majority of the world's population. (For example, Chang wanted to talk about food, housing and clothing in the case of decent living.) A coherent text, rather than one divided into three parts, also promised to give the UDHR a stronger "identity."

During the work on the UDHR, Chang strove always to make the declaration clear and simple to understand so that it could be a document for all of humanity. In other words, it should be as striking as possible and accordingly as concise as possible. Thus it would not be a declaration comprehensible only to legal experts, diplomats, and scholars.[36] A study of Chang's contributions indicates that he was continually focused on particular wordings and ways in which to find more "economical" formulations. In his concluding address before the General Assembly in Paris just prior to the vote on the UDHR, Chang also stated that he had made special efforts when revising particular words in the text, something he traced back to Confucius. As he explained:

> I have been asked whether I would persist in presenting drafting amendments up to the gates of Heaven—if that is the place where I am destined to go. Is this meticulousness merely academic? Please permit me to quote a passage from a Chinese thinker. This is from the *Analects of Confucius*: "It is absolutely necessary to rectify terms. When terms are not rectified, statements will not be clear. When statements are not clear, no measures can be accomplished. When measures are not accomplished, propriety and music (the basic institutions for the maintenance of harmony and order) cannot prosper. When propriety and music do not prosper, the people will not know how to move their hands and feet." Now we can see how important it is that terms should be rectified. Of course, order and harmony among men can only be based on the Rectification of Terms. Can we not see that all the contentions in the world are somehow derived from either intentional or unintentional confusion in the use of language?[37]

According to Chang, every antagonism in some way had its origins in an intentionally or unintentionally confusing linguistic formulation. For Confucius, the reformation of states can only begin once things have been given their proper name, that is to say, when moral qualities acquire their proper "colors." One should not glorify arrogance with the word "dignity" any more than one should encourage deceit by calling it circumspection.[38]

During his time as Chief of the Chinese Delegation to the UN Conference on Freedom of Information in Geneva in 1948, Chang was also eager to emphasis the quality of information and not only the extent of freedom of information. Chang stated: "All measures aimed at the improvement of the quality of information deserve our hearty support. There must be accuracy and diligence in the collection of facts and in regard to interpretation—which is all important—there must be a Will to be Fair!"[39]

Chang was important for the document in the sense that large sections of it were *congruous* with his overarching philosophy. The UDHR was broad in its content, religiously neutral, universal, and intercultural in a number of regards, containing as it did civil, political, economic, and social rights as well as obligations. Moreover, he underscored the importance of a series of ways to realize human rights, such as education and legislation. All this was to find its way into the UN Declaration. In many instances, Chang also managed to counteract deadlock and conflict in the working group by means of his humor and ready quotations, which often came from Chinese tradition. His rhetorical abilities and experiences from the theatrical world were also assets during the UN negotiations, which called for a special "scenic presence" and facility for argument.

The UN Declaration from Chang's Perspective

Because a number of authors were involved to a more or less decisive degree in the drafting of the UDHR, the document can be considered a kind of point of intersection between different perspectives. Can a study of Chang's ideas provide a new perspective on the UDHR? The question is an important one in light of Chang's special qualities. Together with Charles Malik, he was the most philosophically disposed of the key authors of the UDHR, and he had, in a quite different way from the other writers, reflected on the philosophical issues that had been actualized by the writing process.

Again with the exception of Malik, Chang was also the only member of the drafting group who, by virtue of his doctoral studies and teaching background, had experience in the area of pedagogy and practical instruction in schools and universities. It was no coincidence that he viewed the UDHR as a project of moral pedagogy.

Another, quite different reason was his perspective on the world and the human rights violations of the Second World War. For several of the authors of the UN Declaration, such as René Cassin and Charles Malik, the crimes of Nazi Germany in particular had provided a grim backdrop to the writing of the UDHR. When discussing the UDHR, Nazi Germany and the Holocaust are often taken to be its self-evident starting point.[40] For Eleanor Roosevelt and the United States, Japan was also a sensitive topic because of the US's use of atom bombs against Hiroshima and Nagasaki. It is not hard to imagine that these latter, dramatic events also predisposed the US in some measure to downplay Japan's role in relation to the other Axis powers—principally Germany—in UN discussions of the UDHR.

For Chang, however, Japan was an extremely important framework of reference in discussions of rights, even if he often chose not to mention Japan by name in UN meetings. For the most part, he spoke of the atrocities that the Axis powers had committed, which was natural, of course, given that they had acted in concert. Stanley Chang claimed that his father seldom mentioned Japan in the 1940s, not least because of his frail health. After his heart attack in Chile, Chang completely changed his lifestyle and tried to the best of his abilities to avoid becoming embroiled in discussions that were particularly charged for him, such as Japan's role during the Second World War and its previous attacks on China. According to Stanley, he was largely successful in this aim. As a consequence of his deep engagement in China's struggle against the Japanese Empire, Japan and its participation in the Second World War were inescapable points of departure for Chang's thinking on the contents and functions of the UN Declaration. Colonialism in the broader sense of the term was also a key point of departure for Chang's involvement in the UN Declaration.[41]

It was remarked earlier that a Eurocentric perspective has often neglected Japan's global role in the atrocities committed during the Second World War. Japan was "only" one of the Axis powers, whereas Nazi Germany was its central agent by virtue of being located in the heart of Europe. If we view the Second World War from the east, however, Japan's actions become far more central. It can be added that Japan's role in the Second World War and its colonial policies still remain a highly charged issue in the Far East, an issue that, by contrast, has been clearly downplayed in Europe and the United States.

Man's Inhumanity to Man

Certain challenges, which were emphasized in various ways by the authors of the declaration, were directly connected with the work on the UDHR. There were three types of challenges that these authors had to deal with during the drafting process: brutality by one human being toward another; the implementation of the UN Declaration, and the task of finding agreement in diversity, that is to say, formulating ethical common denominators despite the ideological, philosophical, and religious pluralism among the delegates and the drafters.

One major challenge in which Chang was particularly involved was the following: how to explain the attempt to draft a rights document whose primary purpose is to protect humanity from acts of cruelty committed by humanity itself. For many, human beings occupy a special position in the world by virtue of their reason, their free will, and their consciousness. This perspective assumes that humans have a specially protected status in comparison with other living creatures. The purpose of the UDHR was, in other words, to formulate rights that could protect people from different, systematic threats. A few in the Commission on Human Rights, such as the Brazilian delegate Austregesilo de Athayde, categorically asserted that man was created in God's image and thus deserved particular respect and consideration.[42] At the same time, the great problem after the Second World War was precisely the fact that human beings had been the cause of all of the barbarities with which we associate this period. The phrase "man's inhumanity to man" was used frequently by Chang during the initial discussions of the UDHR in the summer of 1947. When he spoke about cruelty or morally reprehensible actions, he was referring primarily to bestial instincts, selfishness, and intolerance. His son Stanley offered the following recollection of the summer sessions at Lake Success when his father was working with Eleanor Roosevelt, René Cassin, Charles Malik, and John Humphrey to set the parameters of the ongoing drafting project: "During these meetings my father often quoted Robert Burns on "man's inhumanity to man," and so it became fixed in my consciousness." According to Chang, human nature was divided: a good, human part, and a brutal, animal part. He was not inclined, in other words, to consider human beings as an unequivocally "holy" or completely good creature. In Chang's view, the eighteenth-century philosophers in Europe had realized that human beings to a large extent were animals, but that there was also a part of their makeup that separated humans from animals. This was the truly human part and it was good. The good part of human beings should thus be given special prominence, developed, and protected. The purpose of the UN Declaration was, accordingly, to protect and strengthen the good part of humanity—which is to say, its capacity for sympathy for others or, put differently, the humanization of man—and hence, to promote humanity's moral stature. This would occur when human beings became more aware of their fundamental obligations toward each other, moral duties that corresponded to human rights. The overarching perspective of the UN Declaration was thus to respect human dignity, which in Chang's terminology included the human capacity for sympathy and identification with one's fellow human beings.

This notion of the humanization of man by means of the UDHR had obvious points in common with the ideas of the Chinese philosopher Mencius about human beings' inner capacity to become more human by means of moral growth. In other words, Chang stressed that Enlightenment philosophers and Mencius had certain points in common regarding the nature of humanity (Mencius VI.A.14).[43] Chang's belief in the divided nature of humanity was hardly an original idea. What was new, however, and in the context, fruitful, was that Chang assigned to the UDHR a special ethical function—the humanization of man—and that this was understood as a refinement of the human capacity to sympathize with others.

Chang wished to contrast this dualistic view of humanity with philosophies that either emphasized that human beings are "neutral" from birth or considered human beings as wholly brutal or evil. The third alternative, which Chang thereby excluded in a more implicit fashion, was the view of human beings as thoroughly good. It is safe to assume that the first and third alternatives are unrealistic given the historical experience of human evil. The second alternative is also unrealistic in view of the fact that humanity has unquestionably been a source of much good throughout history. If human beings were unrelentingly brutal or evil, it would seem pointless to create a document whose purpose was to protect humanity from itself.

Which historical precursors can be identified with the clause relating to man's inhumanity to man to which Chang alluded? In 1673, the German historian Samuel von Pufendorf argued that human beings throughout history had caused more suffering to other human beings than all other factors combined. With the advent of the new era, many philosophers had begun to differentiate between the cruelties of nature and those caused by humanity directly.[44] According to Pufendorf, the latter category exceeded the former by an order of magnitude. As the Scottish poet Robert Burns wrote in his famous poem "Man Was Made to Mourn: A Dirge" (1784): "Man's inhumanity to man / Makes countless thousands mourn!"

In the popular imagination, the phrase "man's inhumanity to man" is often associated with Burns's poem. In it, Burns took as his point of departure all the economic and social injustices that had defined human history since time immemorial. The poem has subsequently acquired a wider application, also becoming associated with war and genocide. A very early precursor of Burns's phrase can be found in the commentaries on evil and oppression in Isaiah 3:5: "And the people shall be oppressed, every one by another, and every one by his neighbor." The Roman author Plautus (255–184 BC) also declared that "Man is no man but a wolf to a stranger" or alternatively "A man is a wolf not a man, to another man which he hasn't met yet."[45] A similar sentence has become a well-known saying throughout history namely, "A man is a wolf to another man" (*Homo homini lupus*).

During the postwar period, a number of writers and politicians have, in different ways, invoked the more general statement of man's inhumanity to man. In the 1960s, Martin Luther King also spoke of man's brutality to man, particularly in connection with the murder of four African-American girls when the Ku Klux Klan bombed a church in Birmingham, Alabama, in 1963, and also in connection to the Apartheid regime in South Africa.[46]

It is interesting to note here that Chang, who was so unwilling in other contexts to refer to philosophical and theological views of humanity, on this occasion chose to take as his starting point precisely such a view. The primary addressee of the UN Declaration was the good part of every human being. The purpose of the declaration was, in other words, to rein in the bestial part of humanity so as to allow the good part to gain the upper hand, that is to say, to strengthen people's sympathy with their fellow human beings.

The preamble to the UDHR also states that "*whereas* disregard and contempt for human rights have resulted in barbarous acts which have outraged the conscience of mankind. The General Assembly proclaims this Universal Declaration of Human Rights as a common standard of achievement for all peoples and nations." These statements refer to the principal reason for the writing of the declaration. It was to guarantee all of the rights that could protect human beings from similarly barbarous acts in the future. Chang stressed that the notion of human rights arose at the time when despots and tyrants ruled over men.[47]

Chang also argued that disregard and contempt for human rights—not ignorance of them—had been the real problem during the Second World War. The word "ignorance" had been used by certain delegates, but Chang and the Russian delegate Pavlov opposed its usage.[48] It would certainly be possible to use a broad conception of knowledge as the antithesis of ignorance in this context and to argue that knowledge of human rights entails (1) an awareness of what human rights are, both as a category and individually; (2) an insight into why they are morally reasonable; (3) the internalization of this knowledge in a way that permeates one's personality and, consequently; and (4) that one acts in accordance with them. One might say, then, that Chang was primarily speaking about (1) and (2) when he argued that it was not ignorance which had been the true cause of the problem of human rights.

If one were to take Chang's distinction between bestial and human sides more literally, however, it could be asked how well the phrase "disregard and contempt" accords with the notion that it was above all the bestial side of human beings that had been the source of all of the catastrophes endured by humanity during the Second World War. Rather, it would seem that some cruelties and atrocities truly are "human" in the sense of presupposing some forethought and "empathy" with the victim's needs and values precisely in order to cause maximal harm to that victim. Chang also ascribed to human beings their own responsibility for many of their acts; in so doing, he took it as obvious that a human being has the power to do both good and evil. Another interpretation, which may bring Chang's various statements into harmony with each other, is that the notion of humanity's bestial side is here being used in a more figurative sense, as a designation for the brutal aspects of humanity.

For those involved in drafting the UDHR, fascism, evil and the Holocaust were of course the self-evident points of departure for their codification of human rights. However, other authors of the UDHR, such as Charles Malik and René Cassin, spoke to a far lesser extent than Chang did about human nature and humanity's good and bad sides in the context of the brutal events of the Second World War. Admittedly, Cassin also spoke of the "spark" that is unique to human beings and that prompts them to act, as well as of their capacity to form their own convictions, and he repeatedly emphasized the necessity of arguing that all humans have the same fundamental nature.[49] In the case of explanations for the brutality of the Axis powers, however, Cassin did not make reference to a specific view of humanity in the way that Chang did. Malik talked mainly about man's proper nature (which was good), and he did not want to highlight or emphasize the animal nature.[50]

These differences in principle between Chang, Malik, and Cassin are surprising in view of the fact that Malik especially had a clear tendency in other contexts to talk about metaphysics and natural attributes and rights. However, on this matter—the threat to humanity—Malik and Cassin spoke more in terms of different nationalities and the state's capacity for violence. Using the terminology of the English philosopher Thomas Hobbes, Cassin described Nazi Germany as a Leviathan state, that is to say, an authority and brutal state formation that had to be resisted. He also mentioned perverted forms of romantic nationalism as constituting a threat to the integrity and freedoms of the individual. The purpose of the UN Declaration was to formulate rights that could protect the individual against state formations and nationalist ideas of this kind. One purpose of the struggle for human rights is, in other words, to free men and women from the depredations of Leviathan states.[51]

In the same vein, Charles Malik talked about collectivist ideologies and state doctrines that devalued the status of the individual, declaring that man was not created for the state, but that the state exists for the sake of man.[52] Malik was eager to stress "the supremacy of man over all society and all social claims."[53] He went on to argue that "the greatest danger in our time comes from a collectivism which demands the erasure of the individual person as such, in both their individuality and their fundamental inviolability."[54] In addition, Malik talked about the dangers of totalitarianism and fascist regimes.[55] And yet Malik and Cassin also spoke of the importance of changing other people's mindsets so that they would not fall victim to social pressure and totalitarian tendencies. Cassin wrote later in his memoir that "in the eyes of the Declaration's authors effective respect for human rights depends primarily and above all on the mentalities of individuals and social groups."[56] Malik would later on claim in 1968 in Geneva that "Men, cultures and nations must first mature inwardly before there can be effective international machinery to adjudicate complaints about the violation of human rights."[57]

However, it was only natural that the authors of the declaration should have offered different formulations of how such political improvements should be realized, given the differences in both their diagnoses of humanity's predicament and their explanations for why humanity had experienced such catastrophes during the Second World War. Since Cassin's and Malik's focus had primarily been state institutions and collectives, and the risks entailed by their monopoly on violence with regard to the individual's human rights, it was important to restrain them by political-structural and legal means as well as through ideological change. National independence would also be circumscribed by means of an international rights order in which the UDHR occupied a central position.

Because Chang's primary focus was on individuals and their predisposition to do good as well as evil, these methods were to become pedagogical and psychological in the broadest sense. According to Chang, one of the primary purposes of the UDHR was precisely the humanization of man. It should be mentioned in this context that Chang did not want to make a too sharp distinction between the state and the individual.[58] This statement could be interpreted in the following way. Individual citizens have duties toward their community or state. A well-functioning republic could also be seen as a precondition for the well being of the citizens.

A reasonable strategy would be to advocate a combination of Malik's, Cassin's, and Chang's ideas in order to counteract a climate that risked producing still greater brutality in society. According to Stanley, his father also said many times to him that nations behave like children. In this case, Chang probably assumed that states often are self-centered and short-sighted in international politics and that they frequently react in ways that could be seen by one another as exaggerated. This statement from Chang made it clear that for him it was an urgent task to create an international organization, such as the United Nations, in order to constrain "the immature actions" of the member states on the basis of an international morality such as the Universal Declaration.

It should also be noted that Chang's conception of the UDHR's primary function articulated a perspective that was clearly individualistic and pedagogical. The primary aim of the human rights project was to "raise the standard of man" or the humanization of man.[59] Other authors had placed greater emphasis upon the UN Declaration's primary function as being to curtail the actions of states against their own citizens. In other words, the UDHR would offer a critical corrective by which the actions of state institutions could be assessed. A common perception was also that war and conflicts between states had their origins in the absence of a clear framework composed of human rights.

However, these differing understandings of the UN Declaration's function(s) were not in opposition to each other. The reasonable alternative is, rather, that they can be combined. The priority of a particular function can, however, explain why this or that particular aspect of the UN Declaration is emphasized at any given point. From Chang's perspective on humanizing humanity, the particular focus should be socialization, tolerance, compassion, and sympathy. They involved the right to religious freedom and social rights, including the right to education. If curtailing the state's monopoly on violence was the main concern, then the principle of state jurisdiction moved center stage. It would involve the right to impartial treatment in a court of law and the right not to be subjected to arbitrary arrest.

Inherent Natural Human Qualities

Given his conception of the UDHR's principal function—to be a tool for moral education and to humanize humanity—it was also important for Chang to emphasize the qualities he had in mind when referring to human beings' capacity and incapacity in connection with the moral and pedagogical goals of the UDHR. In this regard, it made perfect sense for Chang to speak of human beings having *inherent and natural* capacities for doing good, that is to say, a capacity for showing sympathy toward other people.

Chang was inspired by the Chinese philosopher Mencius's assumption that human beings possess a natural capacity to identify themselves with the desires and needs of one's fellow human beings.[60] According to Chang (in his previous writings), Mencius taught that the nature of man was good and that the difference between man and animals, though very small, should be stressed and could be cultivated. Chang said that one of the implications of this teaching of the essential goodness of the nature of man is the fundamental respect for what is "human" in all men.[61] Elsewhere (and later), however, Chang clearly seems to have been skeptical about using formulations such as inalienable or inherent qualities.

Commentators have taken very different views on Chang's ideas about human beings having inherent or natural qualities. In a recently published essay, the German sinologist Frédérick Krumbein argued that Chang was not entirely opposed to the idea of invoking human beings' "inner or internal qualities." Chang was a member of the committee that drafted the preamble to the declaration and was responsible for similar phrasing being used in the first sentence of the preamble.⁶² However, there are also differing views on this matter, even if Chang ultimately did not oppose the majority when the preamble was finalized. Charles Malik's son Habib—who has in his possession his father's collected journals, which are as yet unpublished—communicated the following to me:

> A point of friction between Chang and my father concerned the Preamble to the Declaration. It was Malik's version which was ultimately adopted, not René Cassin's longer and less reader-friendly version. And Malik's version was accepted in its entirety even though Chang had serious objections. However, Chang's criticisms were ignored by Eleanor Roosevelt and the others. It may be speculated as to whether this left a bitter taste in Chang's mouth with respect to my father. If I remember rightly [this is confirmed by Malik's diary], Chang's criticisms related to the Preamble's containing terms with a metaphysical meaning, such as inherent, internal, inalienable. Many of these terms had been used in previous Declarations such as France's Declaration of the Rights of Man and the American Declaration of Independence. My father used these expressions in the Preamble and then carried over some of his particular suggestions into subsequent Articles in the Declaration. For instance, he proposed the theist concept of *created*. *Endowed* then became the compromise term since it allowed the phrase to be expanded using whichever metaphysics best fit the philosophical point of departure in question ("endowed by God, nature, chance" etc.). Chang and Malik also disagreed sharply on Thomas of Aquinas's philosophy versus the Chinese alternatives which Chang chose to introduce.

For its part, the Chinese delegation (and Chang, presumably) advocated a preamble entirely free of terms such as "inalienable" and "inherent." The preamble proposed by the Chinese delegation read: "Whereas the peoples of United Nations have reaffirmed their faith in fundamental human rights, in the dignity and worth of the human person, and in the equal rights of men and women, the General Assembly resolves to state in a solemn declaration of the essential rights and fundamental freedoms of the human being and adopts the following declaration."

It is a good question as to why Chang was willing to use words like "inner," "inherent," and "natural" in connection with the good—or evil—parts of human beings and why he was opposed to Malik's rhetoric of inalienable, inherent rights in the first sentence of the preamble to the UDHR ("Whereas recognition of the inherent dignity and of the equal and inalienable rights of all members of the human family..."). Perhaps it derived ultimately from Chang's understanding of the very function of the declaration: the moral, pedagogical project of "humanizing humanity" or increasing man's moral stature.[63] Words such as "natural" and "inherent" had a special relevance in this context because they brought into focus the conditions for this moral and pedagogical project. Nor is it entirely possible to disassociate oneself from metaphysical or philosophical anthropological assumptions about humanity if one's starting point is that humans have an inviolable value—or a dignity, a free will, and a moral conscience. Let us call this a "thin" metaphysics. It is possible to reach agreement about humanity's good side having these qualities or capacities without involving other metaphysical assumptions, such as that God created human beings—a more substantial, or "thick," metaphysics about which there is far less consensus.[64]

In the case of the declaration, Chang can be interpreted as having advocated a so-called thin metaphysics against a thick one because the latter would have created disunity about the document. One obviously problematic issue, however, was where to draw this line of demarcation between thin and thick metaphysical ideas. For Chang, as noted earlier, this line should be drawn on the basis of what it did and did not require in terms of the moral and pedagogical project associated with the UDHR. Nor was he entirely positive about including the words "born with" in Article 1 of the declaration. He wanted to remove any associations with Rousseau and the notion that human beings are originally creatures of good and that certain attributes are thus inner, or internal (a formulation Chang wished to avoid). Chang also claimed that if the word "born" was deleted, the question of whether human rights began at birth or at conception would not arise.[65] On the other hand, if the words "born with" were indeed to be introduced into the article, he wanted to also include "and remains." It may be asked how Chang's criticisms of terms such as "inalienable" can be reconciled with this latter addition. If one accepts that "born with" is to be followed by "remains," human rights are something that cannot be lost during one's lifetime and are thus inalienable. Terms such as "inalienable," "inviolable," "internal," "inherent," "inner," and "natural" could also be viewed as a conceptual family that had a metaphysical significance. If something is inalienable, it must be natural, internal, and necessarily tied to the individual. These observations may explain why Chang was generally negatively disposed toward all these formulations with regard to the UN Declaration.

Implementation of the UN Declaration

In preceding chapters I have addressed the issue of whether the declaration was actually intended to protect people from their fellow human beings. According to Chang, then, the primary addressee of the delegation was "a human being's good part": how this part could resist and triumph over the evil part. Additionally, a central challenge of the UN Declaration was how to realize the document's goals within the foreseeable future in view of the fact that there was neither a world state nor a strong UN able to implement the declaration and that individual states were openly driven by self-interest. For Chang as for several other delegates, it was unrealistic—and perhaps also undesirable—to put one's faith in a world government: realization of human rights would have to happen within the framework of nation-states and through the global community's creation of a fresh international collaboration in the new UN organization. Given that the drafters conceived the Universal Declaration as a common standard of achievement for all peoples and nations, it was not only international law and institutions that were pivotal for the fulfillment of human rights but also national laws.[66]

Equally unrealistic was the idea of a confederation of states with some kind of joint police force. At an early point during his studies in the US, Chang had voiced his skepticism toward the idea that patriotism for one's own country was merely a brief transition phase in human history. As he had argued in *The Chinese Student Monthly* in 1912:

> There are philosophers ... who assure us that, in the future, patriotism will be regarded not as a virtue, but merely as a mental stage toward a state of feeling, when our patriotism will include the whole human race and all the world. This may be so; but the age of which these philosophers speak is still several thousands of years distant. In fact, philosophers of this type are so very advanced that they are of no practical service to the present generation. As things are now are and

have been for two or three thousand years past and are likely to be for two or three thousand years to come, the words "home" and "country" mean a great deal. Nor do they show any tendency to lose their significance. The "prodigal son" and the "man without a country" are despised with more severity to-day than ever before. If there was ever a time when your loyalty to your home and your country is valued most and esteemed most highly, it is no other time than today. All facts and experiences clearly show that those philosophers who venture to assert that patriotism will be regarded less and less as a virtue, are doing nothing short of "building castles in the air."[67]

In another early essay from 1920 Chang also emphasized the importance of cooperation between liberal movements in various countries, especially liberal student movements around the world, in order to achieve a sustainable peace.[68] In an essay written in 1942, Chang also stated that all people should strive to be both distinctly national and at the same time creatively modern.[69] For Chang, then, neither citizenship of the world nor a world-state were realistic prospects. Instead, the focus must be on a nationalism that could counteract narrowly local interests in China and safeguard their common cultural frameworks. What stands out clearly from Stanley Chang's accounts is that his father in different ways articulated a "Great China," or "centrist," attitude later in life, that is to say, a conception of China as the Middle Kingdom. Such thinking and perspective also sat awkwardly with notions of a more global citizenship.

It is interesting to note, however, that as early as 1912, in his early student years, Peng Chun Chang was meditating on the meaning, possibilities, and desirability of a kind of world community and global citizenship. Similar thoughts were to recur later during his work with the UN and the UN Declaration (see Chapter 5). He hoped that a new kind of loyalty could be fostered in humanity if the UN succeeded in bringing peoples together in order to solve key common problems. What was important, according to Chang, was that people did not become preoccupied with national pride, prejudices, and drawing boundaries in ways that obscured areas of shared, global agreement.[70] At a UN meeting on 10 June 1948, Chang argued that people had responsibilities to human society in general and not just to their own countries.

During his time at the UN, Chang also made important contributions to the issues around implementing the UDHR. Again and again, and particularly after his work on the UDHR, he emphasized that the UN Declaration and Covenants should not be regarded negatively, that is to say, that its agents and bodies should not focus solely on complaints about violations of human rights and on the implementation of punitive procedures. A reasonable amount of attention should also be directed toward its positive dimensions, that is to say, its promotion and protection of, and instruction, as well as toward preventative work. Education and international cooperation should be central, in other words, with regard to the realization of human rights.[71] According to Chang, experience from other social spheres had shown that complaints and strict discipline were not the sole, or the best, means of achieving positive goals. Chang stressed that the sounded way to progress was to use the Universal Declaration as an instrument for the promotion of ideals.[72]

To this effect Chang quoted several apt Chinese proverbs: "Political stability takes more than good intentions and achieving results takes more than just laws." Chang held that the main purpose of the UDHR was to "build up" better people, not primarily to punish those who had violated human rights. The most effective way to rectify the world's "failings" was to achieve a common standard of precisely the kind that the architects of the UN Declaration were striving to realize. On this point, Chang can be said to be invoking what is now a commonplace view of norms and the realization of values. Moral upbringing aims to get people not only *not* to do certain things but also to actively help create positive conditions. For this reason, it is not sufficient merely to emphasize strategies such as protection, correction, and penalties; encouragement and promotional measures are also called for such as education and cooperative international measures. If legislation and penalties are made the centerpiece of the effort to realize human rights, then the state will also become the primary guarantor of those rights. By contrast, the modern view is that responsibility for promoting and guaranteeing human rights lies with a far wider group of agents, one including not only states but also groups, organizations, companies, and individuals (something that is clearly stated in the UDHR).

According to a common Confucian view, recourse to laws and the administration of justice should also be considered a last resort, to be used only when all other informal avenues have failed to resolve a conflict of interest. An illustrative statement is the following: The Master said, in hearing litigation, I am no different from any other man. But if you insist on a difference, it is perhaps that I try to get the parties not to resort to litigation in the first place (*Analects* 12.13).

Chang drew on another Confucian saying when he spoke about the conditions for peace.[73] Chang related politics to ethics and ethics to education as if they were Chinese boxes: "To promote peace in the world, there must be order in the various countries. To achieve order in the countries, it is important that families (social relations) be regulated. To regulate families, people need to be cultivated. To cultivate people, their hearts must be healed. To heal their hearts, their thoughts must be honest. To have honest thoughts, people need to extend their knowledge. To extend their knowledge, people need to draw closer to things as they truly are."

Finding Agreement in Diversity

A third key challenge that drafting the UDHR posed was the following: How can the commission and the drafting group reach agreement on the contents of the UDHR given the religious, philosophical and ideological diversity in the world? This challenge is also related to the preceding one of implementation of the UDHR. For the question of its realization to be meaningful, there has to be sufficiently broad agreement about the actual content of the declaration.

Chang expressed optimism about "the problem of pluralism" and about reaching ethical agreement in diversity. In his concluding address on 10 December 1948, when the General Assembly was to vote on the UDHR, Chang declared: "Our gratifying and historic agreements have occurred when the real subject of Human Rights is held unconfusedly before our minds and hearts. Our clinging and wrangling disagreements have come from tangential excursions prompted by what are often narrowly conceived as 'political' preoccupations." It is not entirely clear what Chang meant here by "political preoccupations," but in light of his statements in other contexts it may be taken to be a reference to national self-interest and political calculation. Chang's understanding of the function of the UDHR also suggests that certain ideological and religious debates were irrelevant, divisive, or ill-advised with respect to human rights. In the discussion of the first challenge, I proposed that the desirability of counteracting human brutality or inhumanity toward fellow human beings was an obvious common denominator, regardless of one's ideological, philosophical, or religious conviction. What was meant by people's brutality toward their fellow human beings was also abundantly apparent in light of the brutality with which the Axis powers had waged war, in particular the racism and genocidal policies of Nazi Germany. Moreover, Chang noted that it is a sad truth that people generally work together better in time of war than in peace.[74] Following on his earlier meditations in the 1930s about how cultures can meet constructively, Chang also actively sought to reach an intercultural understanding about the articles of the declaration.

In another setting—the UN Conference on Freedom of Information—Chang formulated some guidelines for the work on international agreements and conventions:

> The great and important tasks before us must be looked at in their proper perspective. Our generation is now attempting to jump the great hurdle from national communities into a world community. Let not the over-dramatized conflicts blind us from seeing the possibility for quiet and constructive efforts out of the turmoil. Now in conclusion, may I humbly suggest four words and four only, to be constantly before our minds in our strenuous deliberations. The first word is Purpose which must be "for the relief of man's estate." We should constantly keep in mind that Purpose is for the welfare of men. The second word is Program. In regard to the program, I would like to suggest it should always be practicable, concrete and creative. ... The third word is Patience. We should give more than a sprinkle of human forbearance in our debate. And fourthly and lastly, Perspective. Again may I remind you of that saying, "to revivify the old in order to understand the new." Only thus can we obtain a proper perspective.[75]

Chang's view of the preconditions for reaching agreement about ethics and human rights despite metaphysical, religious, and ideological differences is strongly reminiscent of the kind of thinking that characterized a parallel investigation into human rights for UNESCO whose leading light was the French moral philosopher Jacques Maritain. During this investigation, Maritain had stated that "we are in agreement about rights with the proviso that no-one asks us why." According to Maritain, we can reach agreement not on the basis of common speculative (metaphysical) ideas, but when it is a matter of practical ideas that can serve as guidelines for action.[76] His statements strongly recall Chang's prioritizing of "an art of living" in place of metaphysical speculations. Maritain also had another revealing description of the UN declaration and its articles. He viewed the thirty articles as strings upon which one might play different pieces of music. It was, in other words, more of an ethical framework that might be reconciled with an array of different philosophies.

Criticism of the Universality of Human Rights

The three challenges mentioned above could be considered as a basis for questioning the human rights project represented by the UDHR. However, as we have seen, Chang believed that there were ways to counter these challenges. Despite its misdeeds throughout history, humanity very much deserved to be protected. It was also possible to find ethical common denominators amid the ideological and religious plurality, and there were ways to implement the UN Declaration despite the absence of a "world government."

Chang was therefore involved in responding to some of the more central problematizations of the UN Declaration and its point of departure in human rights thinking. In particular, he called into question the culturally relativistic critique of human rights.[77] This critique came from two separate quarters. In the first place, it had been formulated at an early stage by the American Anthropological Association, which argued that the rights principles in the UN Declaration merely reflected the West's community of values and thus had no applicability to non-Western countries and their cultures.[78]

After the creation of the UDHR, there was another culturally relativistic critique of the idea that the declaration would be applied universally, this time from a quite unexpected quarter, namely the colonial powers of France, Belgium, and the Netherlands. These states argued that non-self-governing territories or colonies were not sufficiently mature for the UN Declaration, or, put differently, that its principles were not suited to the conditions of social life in these territories.[79] Critics of the UDHR's universalism here relied upon a so-called civilization argument that held that only the West had attained the quite different level of civilization that was required for human rights to have applicability.

Chang was clearly skeptical about these culturally relativistic lines of argument. He contended that the whole idea of human rights was that they should be applicable universally, regardless of whether the peoples in question lived in nation-states or colonized territories. He also believed that human rights could be acceptable from different cultural starting points. The preamble to the declaration was to state that human rights should be recognized and applied among the peoples of the member states and the people in territories under those states' jurisdiction. In other words, Chang felt that reference to Western civilization was clearly inappropriate in this context. For him, the value of Western civilization had been problematized in spectacular fashion by the most recent world war in Europe and the racist policies of Nazi Germany. Belgian and French arguments about the colonies' inability to accept human rights, he argued, were nothing more than European prejudices cloaked in the rhetoric of civilization.[80] His attitude was that this so-called classic Eurocentric view of civilization, whose imperialistic logic and ethnocentrism he underscored, represented the principal obstacle to universal application of human rights.[81]

Chang additionally argued that there were also no grounds for believing that people in colonies did not want to have human rights. If human rights were intimately connected with being human, as the French delegation and others had claimed, it could reasonably be asked why a particular level of civilization should present a barrier to the universal applicability of rights. It was true, Chang noted, that differing scientific, technological, and other advances created unequal conditions for the realization of human rights, as, for example, with countries' different educational facilities and legal systems. It did not follow, however, that less developed regions should be exploited by outsiders or that they should not have human rights as a moral guiding principle. Acceptance of universal human rights was premised on the rejection of culturally relativistic thinking, a mode of thought that clearly could have had quite different origins.

An additional premise for the defense of human rights, according to Chang, was tolerance toward the different life philosophies and religious convictions to be found around the world. Uncompromising dogmatism had historically been the cause of great suffering by fueling conflicts and giving them an ideological basis. If harmony in the human family were to be attained and humanity to be saved, it was of the utmost importance that all people "in a spirit of genuine tolerance" learned to accept each other's different convictions.[82]

As Chang saw it, there was a widespread tendency around the world to presuppose a standardized way of thinking and a single mode of life. With such an attitude, a temporary balance could be reached only by distancing oneself from the truth and resorting to coercion. No matter how coercive such measures might be, it was impossible to achieve a more enduring balance in this way. Human thinking, Chang contended, had consistently manifested an impatient desire to enforce conformity. This tendency had been especially pronounced following the First World War. For Chang, one of the main purposes of the UN Declaration was thus to promote a *pluralistic tolerance* in humanity that recognized the value of people having different views on life, ways of living, and cultural frameworks, a pluralism that could also enrich their cultural life.[83] It is not entirely clear what Chang meant here by "a standardized way of thinking." Given Chang's situation at the UN, a number of interpretations are possible, none of which necessarily excludes the others. One possible allusion is to the social ideals held up by authoritarian communist groups. Another is to the efforts by the colonial powers (or authoritarian states) to force their religions and ideologies upon other parts of the world.

Chang's ideas about the universality of human rights nonetheless constitute a restriction on pluralism insofar as they must apply everywhere and for all people. In some sense, then, these ideas about human rights represent a uniform way of thinking that must have global validity.

Chang also believed that colonialism and exploitation were a "burden" for the colonizing powers as well as for the colonized themselves. Even the former suffered as a result of the corrupting effects of power.[84] Appropriating material possessions and seizing political power by unjust means entailed, in other words, a moral loss. The implication of such a perspective from the point of view of historic, corrective justice was that both victim and aggressor needed to be healed and thereby enter into new, more constructive relations with each other. In these statements, Chang gave a "new" interpretation of the (in)famous poem title "The White Man's Burden" by Rudyard Kipling. The burden for the Western countries was in other words also a *moral* burden for them, according to Chang. He further said that an argument that was often linked to the notion of the white man's burden was "that the culture of the peoples of Europe was somehow superior to that developed elsewhere and that the European was responsible for spreading his enlightened civilization over the less 'civilized' regions of the world."[85] However, one problem with this argument, according to Chang, was that the imperialistic nations did not pay attention to the fact that preindustrialized nations or people could also be highly cultured.

CHAPTER 7

Chang, Malik, and Cassin

The work on the UN Declaration was characterized by a series of disagreements between the delegates—ideological, philosophical, national, and religious, as well as cultural differences in a more general sense. Areas of disagreement included how civil and political rights related to social and economic rights, the document's religious neutrality, the justification for the document, the status of collective rights, the place of responsibilities, the relationship between individuals and the state or the community, the implementation of the rights, and a series of specific issues related to the formulation of the articles and their sequence.[1] As regards implementation, there were substantial disagreements between two blocs in particular. Some states, the Soviet Union included, argued that implementation of the UDHR should be left to the individual state. Many states instead wanted the international community and the UN to create an oversight mechanism and a system that might coordinate a response to the violation of human rights.[2]

In addition to these larger divisions, there were a number of personal antagonisms and conflicts within the so-called core group of authors.

Chang and Malik

As has been mentioned already, Chang enjoyed relatively good relationships with his coauthors for long periods of time, with the exception of occasional eruptions, particularly during the escalation of the civil war in China. Chang had constructive relationships with Roosevelt and Humphrey for much of the writing process, even if Humphrey on a few occasions showed irritation with Chang's mood swings.[3] Roosevelt, Humphrey, and Chang also shared each other's values to a considerable degree on many issues, for instance, on the significance of socioeconomic rights and the importance of education for fulfilling the objectives of the declaration. With Malik, however, Chang seems to have had substantial differences of opinion as well as personal incompatibilities that at times made working together difficult. As John Humphrey recorded in his diary: "I had lunch with Malik. He, Cassin & Mrs Mehta are now leading the fight. P.C. Chang's role I regret to have to say is quite negative. Incidentally, P.C. Chang and Malik hate each other."[4] Humphrey, who generally gave highly positive opinions of Chang, made an unusual observation here. Humphrey had also speculated during other phases in the writing process about why Chang was not being constructive, particularly when debating with Malik. His explanation was that Chang's mood swings were due primarily to his ill-health and his anxiety about political developments in his own country.

It should be emphasized that two people could have entirely different political convictions and personalities but nonetheless be in agreement about the principal contents and disposition of the UN Declaration. By the end of the drafting process in autumn 1948, Chang and Malik were showing a more united front in order to get the document through the General Assembly. Malik ultimately toned down his religious references so that the document could be approved by as many parties as possible. For instance, he had wanted to include a reference to "the Creator," but this reference was removed, largely upon the insistence of Roosevelt and Chang.[5]

Charles Malik also lobbied hard for a clause protecting minorities, an issue that lay especially close to his heart as a citizen of multireligious and multiethnic Lebanon. However, his ideas about the rights of minorities failed to convince the other members of the drafting group. In his diary entry for 15 June 1948, he recorded his disappointment: "I fought for the inclusion of an Article on minorities. Proposed the mildest form: "Cultural groups will not be denied a right to self-determination." Lost. The Americans and the South Americans completely opposed to the idea."[6] Chang, however, who did not support Malik's formulation, stressed that the Commission on Human Rights should not give the impression that it had completely ignored the issue of minority rights for ethnic and religious groups. For example, Article 26, which dealt with the right to education, contained a clause supporting religious minorities.

It is not entirely clear what Chang's intentions were here, but it seems likely that the right for parents to decide their children's education in Article 26:3 should be seen as a way of preserving cultural traditions and thereby maintaining the cultural identity of various religious and cultural groups. Additionally, Article 26:2 states that education should promote understanding, tolerance, and friendship between all nations, races, and religious groups, which is of clear relevance for minorities. It should also be added that the UN Declaration contains a series of articles that are of relevance to various minority groups even though they are formulated in individual terms. One such is Article 2, which deals with antidiscrimination; others include Article 18, on the right to religious freedom, and Article 27, on the right to a cultural life.

The controversy over having an article in the UN Declaration about minorities had primarily taken place between countries with a long historical presence of minorities, such as Lebanon, and so-called immigrant societies, such as the US. An ambitious proposal for an article about minorities would have emphasized the importance of ethnic national minorities having their own schools and cultural and religious institutions as well as being able to use their own languages in the media and in contacts with state and local authorities.[7] Eleanor Roosevelt, who was in the vanguard of the opposition to minority rights, argued that such an article risked undermining the unity of pluralistic societies and preventing the process of integrating new immigrants.

Chang and Malik were nonetheless in agreement about many articles in the declaration, such as Article 18 on the right to religious freedom. In their view, it was also important to stress the right to change one's religion or religious conviction, if religious freedom was to be realized. However, Chang was less inclined to spell out this explicitly in Article 18. He claimed that the right to freedoms such as freedom of thought, belief, and religion implied the right to change them. Hence, it was enough to state people's right to these freedoms.[8] Malik thought instead that it was urgent to express the right to change one's belief and religion explicitly for specific political and ethical reasons.[9] Malik's proposal was later on accepted. Chang and Malik agreed also about the dangers of materialism and consumption society in the world, and they both emphasized the importance of education, culture, and immaterial values. As events turned out, however, and as previously noted, there emerged a number of oppositions to the preamble and the disposition of the articles.

Charles Malik's son Habib had the following to say about the relationship between his father and Chang, which may offer grounds for modulating Humphrey's statement that Chang and Malik hated each other:

> Despite their differing convictions about human nature, natural rights, and the fundamental nature of reality, and whatever their po-

litical roles, both men were diplomats at heart. They genuinely wanted to achieve practical results and to produce a UN Declaration. Both wanted to find ethical common denominators for the UN document, and this made it possible for them not to let their philosophical differences take over. They also had difficulties putting up with each other in the daily work. Despite all this, they continued to work together, both within and outside the committees, and they ate lunch together many times, as my father recorded in his diary.[10]

Conversely, the American legal scholar Mary Ann Glendon has argued that the quarrels between Chang and Malik did not really stem from differences in their respective philosophical convictions: "I do believe that the differences of opinion between Chang and Malik ultimately had less to do with their different attitudes towards Thomism than with their different personalities."[11]

What were the sharpest points of disagreement between Chang and Malik? Although Chang was dissatisfied with the final version of the preamble that Malik had produced, he had to bow to the majority. Habib Malik speculated that this may have left a bitter taste in the mouth for Chang because the preamble to the UDHR was such an extremely central part of the text of the Declaration. Chang was continually on his guard against formulations that could be interpreted in a Christian or theistic light as well as formulations that could be interpreted in terms of natural law. His position on this matter was far removed from Malik's own. Malik's diary notes include the following entry with regard to his conflicts with Chang over the writing of the preamble:

> Missed my morning flight and was forced to take a later plane to New York from Washington D.C. On the plane, I worked on the Preamble, which I finished. What a dreadful person Chang is—filled with hate, poisonousness, and bitterness. My text for the Preamble was largely adopted. Cassin made a few contributions. Chang wants to remove the word inalienable merely because I put it in. The Article I have proposed on the right to a good social and international order does not seem to have been much more successful.[12]

Malik went on to describe the conflict with Chang in his entry for the following day: "Arguing with Chang today. He agreed to remove the parentheses around 'inalienable.' Lunch with Chang and Hyde. Chang is not practical.

He is unable to look beyond himself, either."[13] Malik's statement that Chang opposed the word "inalienable" merely because Malik had proposed it can be read in several ways. Since Chang and Malik had clashed earlier over the presence in the UN Declaration of ideas taken from natural law and Christian theism, it is conceivable that Chang was continually suspicious of Malik's suggestions for formulations. Chang was well aware that Malik took Christianity as his point of departure and that he had previously sought to give the UDHR a theistic basis. The word "inalienable" could also be given a theistic connotation by virtue of its place in the preamble ("recognition of the inherent dignity and of the equal and inalienable rights of all members of the human family") Because Chang wanted the document to be as universal as possible, he was continually on his guard against any attempt to smuggle metaphysical or theological phrasing into the UDHR, which may have been one reason why Chang wanted the term "inalienable" to be removed from the declaration. At this particular point in time, the mood between Chang and Malik was tense. Presumably, then, Chang was negatively disposed toward Malik in a number of their work settings. Chang ultimately conceded, however, and agreed to allow the inclusion of the word "inalienable", something that the other main authors also agreed to. It was thus Malik's proposal for the preamble that was adopted as the final version, in preference to Chang's suggested changes and to Cassin's proposed text, whose specific references to "recent atrocities" were seen as far too concrete for a document intended to be "eternal."

It should be added, however, that Malik admired Chang and that he was not afraid of voicing this admiration in official settings. A case in point is the following statement he made while chairman of the Third Committee just prior to the UDHR's submission to the General Assembly on 10 December 1948. In his address on 9 December, Malik praised the representatives on the Commission on Human Rights for their various contributions to the declaration, paying particular tribute to Peng Chun Chang. Malik declared: "I regret not being able to mention by name or to honour all of those who have participated in the writing [of the UDHR] to the present moment, and yet I must nonetheless mention my old rival P. C. Chang, who has succeeded in broadening our horizons with his repeated observations drawn from oriental philosophical traditions and oriental philosophy, and who has revised many of our Articles using his unique writing style."[14] According to Habib Malik, his father and Chang complemented each other in their respective emphases. Thanks to Malik's particular concern with personal political rights and freedoms and Chang's with socioeconomic rights, the UDHR is a rich and wide-ranging document. In his concluding address to the General Assembly, Malik also took pains to highlight all of the substantive contributions made by the members of the drafting group, including the contributions from the Russians, something that attests to the fact that he, too, appreciated the inclusion of socioeconomic rights.

Chang and Cassin

Chang's and Malik's relationship has dominated the secondary scholarship on the creation of the UDHR in several respects, particularly the philosophical aspects of the document. As already noted, their conflicts of personality were also widely attested.

By contrast, there is a striking near silence in the secondary literature as regards Chang's relationship to another key author of the UN Declaration, René Cassin. In all of the monographs and articles on the genesis of the UDHR that I have read, I have encountered only bland references to the fact that Chang and Cassin were both actively involved in writing the document and that they went about their work in different ways. Cassin, who, unlike Chang, was in a position to write his memoirs late in life and to describe his work on the UDHR in numerous lectures, mentioned Chang only on a few occasions and always briefly and in a rather neutral tone.[15]

In my correspondence with Chang's son Stanley, it was thus a great surprise to learn how tense the relationship between Chang and Cassin had been. What makes it especially surprising is that Chang and Cassin shared a number of perspectives on what the UDHR should contain that proved that they could reach substantial agreement in spite of their personal and national differences. Let us now turn to some of these common denominators.

For example, when Chang wanted the preamble to the declaration to include references to respect for human beings and their dignity, Cassin lent his support. Cassin was also keen to underscore the differentiating "spark" that separated humans from animals and that gave the former a special moral status but also obligations. Cassin's desire for the declaration to carry the designation "universal" rather than "international" also chimed with Chang's view that its text should be universally applicable to all people, regardless of whether or not they lived in nation-states. Originally made by Haiti, this proposal was subsequently supported by Cassin. At the same time,

Cassin showed himself to be in the first instance loyal toward his own government, arguing—in line with France's official position—that a so-called colonial clause should be inserted into a new UN convention on human rights.[16] This colonial clause would mean that human rights should be applied differently in states and in colonies.

Both Cassin and Chang referred to the importance of how the French Enlightenment had conceptualized freedom. They were nonetheless concerned that the UDHR should not merely imitate previous rights documents. Chang and Cassin were also united in their view that the authors of the UDHR faced a major pedagogical challenge in that the document needed to be a text that all people could understand and accept. In other words, the UDHR needed to be free of concepts and formulations whose meaning was known only to legal specialists, philosophers, or diplomats. Cassin was also positively inclined toward Chang's addition of a social-emotional quality to human beings ("conscience" and "act towards others in a spirit of brotherhood") as an adjunct to human beings' rational side in Article 1.

Both also had a non-individualistic view of human beings, emphasizing the importance of social relations for human identity and self-realization. Cassin and Chang were concerned, too, to underscore the socioeconomic rights in the declaration, a view they also shared with Roosevelt, Santa Cruz, and Humphrey, among others. Additionally, Chang and Cassin were part of the secular group of authors who opposed the inclusion of religious elements in the UN Declaration. They would later argue for the right of individuals to appeal to international bodies, something that the superpowers opposed. With regard to Article 27, Cassin and Chang endorsed both participation in and enjoyment of culture. Cassin also initially agreed with Chang's proposal (concerning "the problem of the structure of the UDHR") that the best way to begin the writing process would be to consider not the substance (i.e., the tentative articles) but the overall "plan" of the bill, beginning with thoughts for a preamble.[17] Given these points of agreement, it can reasonably be asked why they should have come into conflict. Is there any basis for Stanley's belief that his father was negatively disposed toward Cassin?

The Conflict Between Chang and Cassin

A number of points of difference and rivalry between Chang and Cassin were particularly striking. Both Cassin and Chang often assumed the role of interpreter of the UDHR's overarching purpose and structure, something that says much about how each man viewed his own role in the creation of the document. Both considered themselves architects and educators of the UN Declaration. Cassin had initially used the analogy of a temple when describing the properties of the UDHR—a temple with steps, a roof, and pillars that represented the different components of the UN Declaration (or it was described in terms of a portico and columns).[18] Chang, as noted earlier, had also described the logical progression of the articles in the document.

While Cassin repeatedly emphasized the authority of the state and its importance for the realization of human rights, Chang underscored the fact that rights always came before state authority.[19] On this point it seems clear that Cassin was strongly influenced by France's centralist state traditions. What is more, he was not enamored of Chang's proposal to introduce an article in the declaration affirming the right of all citizens to take part in an examination that would open a path to employment by the state. According to Cassin, this proposal was far too specific to be able to be included in the text of the declaration; instead, it ought to be moved to a commentary text. Chang felt strongly that the clause should be approved, and it is safe to assume that he was quite disappointed that so few of the other delegates supported him on this issue. John P. Humphrey was an exception. Chang also wanted the UN Declaration to consist of as few articles as possible. For his part, Cassin argued that the number of ideas should determine the number of articles, not the other way around: "We should not assume that the declaration should only include such and such number of articles."[20]

Cassin and Chang also had divergent views on Europe and cosmopolitan thinking. Chang's view was that during the eighteenth century a cosmopolitan tradition had enabled many European thinkers to draw on China's political, economic, and cultural life but that this tradition had been lost in the century which followed. Chang's negative characterization of the nineteenth century was doubtless based upon China's painful experiences during that period, including the Opium Wars and the destruction of the Summer Palace of Yuanmingyu-an, outside Peking, in 1860 during the Second Opium War. Chang's hope was that this new, twentieth-century experiment with human rights might revive the eighteenth-century cosmopolitan tradition.

Cassin argued that Chang was right about the cosmopolitan tradition of the eighteenth century. However, he claimed that this tradition had been revived in the twentieth century by several European countries. Nor did Cassin embark on any comparative studies of ethics in order to make the UDHR more universal and morally reasonable in the same way as Chang. His sole point of departure was European rights philosophy, principally that of Enlightenment France. Just before the vote on the UN Declaration, Chang also stated that he wished to acknowledge his particular gratitude to Cassin for the exemplary and authoritative way in which he had informed the assembly about French ideas of fundamental freedoms and human rights during the eighteenth century.[21] In the context, it is unclear whether he was being ironic. Given Stanley Chang's view that the Frenchman Cassin regarded everything French as superior, an ironic reading of Chang's statement cannot be wholly ruled out. For his part, Cassin was on record as saying that Chang's special style of writing had left its mark on the UN Declaration.

Cassin and Chang found themselves on opposite sides when it came to the implementation of the UDHR in one particular respect. Cassin claimed that the immediate introduction of human rights law in the colonies could create general disorder. In other words, one should not ascribe the same kinds of rights to countries that found themselves at different stages of development.[22] However, according to Cassin, certain fundamental rights, such as the right to life, were completely universal and should apply in all territories, whether colonies or not. Unlike Chang, Cassin believed that the right to life should refer only to physical existence. Chang for his part believed that it was also important to emphasize the goodness of life itself in the concept of the right to life and in the development of human life.[23] Cassin was presumably skeptical about Chang's formulation since it opened the possibility for controversies about what the goodness of life might signify. The key thing was that the UDHR stressed that the physical existence of a human being had a special claim to protection, about which there was agreement to an entirely different degree than there was on the meaning of the goodness of life.

Cassin had not voiced any real skepticism about France's having colonial possessions because he believed that the latter would benefit from French values, nor does he seem to have seen any contradiction between involvement in human rights and France's possession of colonies: colonies were a vehicle for spreading French values in the world, that is to say, French conceptions of human rights and freedoms.

Chang, unlike Cassin, was a keen advocate of anti-colonialism, and he emphasized that all human rights should be realized everywhere and immediately.[24] Japan, in addition to the European colonial powers, was the particular object of Chang's critique of colonialism. As noted already, he was also suspicious of the cultural relativism defended by France and the other colonial powers. Chang was skeptical of their presumption that indigenous people did not desire human rights.[25] That Cassin made himself a spokesperson for the European perspective in the drafting group may also have constituted a major point of disagreement with Chang. What lay behind Chang's efforts with the UDHR was a desire to settle accounts with the injustices of European and Japanese colonialism. Moreover, Cassin was to be a loyal ally of de Gaulle in the 1950s and would defend his increasingly more authoritarian rule. For Cassin, the breaking point came only when de Gaulle officially criticized Israel.[26]

One can also speculate about the competition between Chang and Cassin for influence in the Commission on Human Rights. After the session on Long Island in the summer of 1947, it was decided that the drafting group should go to Geneva and continue its work there during the autumn. Cassin was very positive about this proposal since it meant that the group would be on European soil. The idea was that there should be three working groups in Geneva. One would continue working on the declaration, another would take responsibility for a draft text of a convention, and a third would submit proposals for implementation measures. Eleanor Roosevelt initially suggested that she herself should be involved in the work on the Universal Declaration, together with representatives from China, the Soviet Union, the Philippines, Panama, and Belarus. Following this decision, Cassin protested, arguing that, instead of working on the text of a convention, he should work on the declaration itself because he had already been involved in its drafting for such a long time. Following Cassin's request, it was also decided that France and China should change places. China would now join the convention group while France would join the declaration group.

Given that the declaration group was likely regarded as a more central group than that working on the convention—the development of a declaration being viewed as a more realistic project than the authoring of a convention—it may be assumed that Chang was disappointed at being forced to change places with Cassin. The declaration group was also the group that Eleanor Roosevelt had chosen to join. Although only speculation, this nonetheless fits with the pattern of reaction described by Stanley Chang, that is, that Chang and Cassin had an openly competitive relationship within the Commission on Human Rights. As events turned out, Chang was not part of the Chinese delegation in Geneva. Instead he chose to be part of another UN meeting, that of the Economic and Social Council, despite the importance of the Geneva meeting. Another delegate from China served as a temporary replacement. This was also one of the few occasions when Chang was not included in discussion of the UN Declaration and the International Bill of Rights. Another was the May meeting of the drafting committee in 1948, when Chang's stand-in took his place.

When Cassin arrived in New York for the first time in 1947 to take part in the UN's Commission on Human Rights, he was keen to give France and Europe a leading role in the drafting of the UDHR. He was an outspoken French nationalist with a deep admiration for French traditions, something that continued to inform his life even after the end of the Second World War, and he had also declared in various settings that he regarded France as an intellectual leader in the world. In other words, Cassin belonged to a generation of Frenchmen who placed enormous faith in what they held to be France's unique contributions to Western civilization and the world as a whole. (In his Nobel lecture in 1968, Cassin stressed at the end of his speech that "my country imbues me with a love that overflows its borders. And the more French I am, the more I feel a part of mankind."[27])

When Cassin came to the US and the new setting of the UN, just prior to the start of the drafting work on the UN Declaration, he was met by a perspective that was quite different from the official French one, not least from Chang and the Filipino delegate, Carlos Romulo, who fought for the Asian countries to have an important say over the contents of the UDHR.[28] Presumably, Chang's and Cassin's strongly nationalistic—and regional—perspectives were a stumbling block in their relationship, a possibility that has also been considered by Chang's son Stanley.

It is interesting to note that John Humphrey, Eleanor Roosevelt, and Charles Malik do not mention any conflicts between Chang and Cassin in their biographies and diary entries. What does recur consistently in their remarks on Chang's work, however, is the deep disagreement between Malik and Chang, particularly with regard to Article 1 of the UN Declaration and the preamble. I have asked Habib Malik about his father's diary entries for the summer 1947 sessions at the Sperry Gyroscope Plant. According to Habib Malik, those entries make no reference to any conflicts in the drafting group between Chang and Cassin or to any more substantial conflicts in general. Nevertheless, Stanley Chang had the following to say about the negotiations on Long Island in 1947:

My father introduced me to Mrs Roosevelt and good old Malik (my father called Charles Malik "good old Malik" to differentiate him from Jakob Malik, the Soviet delegate). I and Mrs. Roosevelt and Charles Malik had only pleasant meetings and greetings for each other. As for Malik, I found him a friendly person whom my father could relate to, including with the help of humour. Things were very different with the Frenchman, however. I remember very tense debates between my father and René Cassin. There was always very fierce disagreement between them. The Frenchman, who thought that French ideas were best, always wanted to joke about and diminish the importance of my father's allusions to Confucius, and he accused my father of always wanting to make this the most important thing in the drafting of the UN Declaration. My father know how to use humour in order to win debates. But with the Frenchman, he simply hated him and for the most part was unable to hide it with humour. Hiding his mood was not my father's strong suit, either. But he could do it when it was a question of someone on his own level. However, I can tell you that he had utter contempt for the Frenchman. He could not fend him off with jokes, as he did with other people. With the Frenchman matters were always in deadly earnest, and arguments with him demanded all my father's debating skills. My father was shaped by what you might call a "Middle Kingdom attitude", which meant that he believed that China as a country was the centre of the world. That is to say, everything else lay either west or east or south or north of China. This attitude may also explain why my father had such fraught conflicts and bruising exchanges with the Frenchman Cassin during the debates over the content of the UN Declaration. For Cassin, everything French was simply the best.

Admittedly, Stanley Chang's memories are of events far removed in time, but they recurred regularly and with great clarity in my correspondence with him during 2015. The fraught relationship between Cassin and Stanley's father is something to which Stanley continually returned when describing the meetings in the Sperry Gyroscope Plant. One could also speculate that the supposedly bad relations between Cassin and Chang might just be explained by the fact that both men were outspoken nationalists who identified deeply with the cultural traditions of their respective countries. It would certainly be reasonable to assume that Chang's "Middle Kingdom attitude" put him on a collision course with the nationalistic attitudes of several other delegates. Nonetheless, it seems as though his relation to Cassin, in particular, became especially charged as a result of both men's deeply nationalistic convictions.

According to Stanley Chang, his father had a very strong desire to stand out in different settings. As Stanley put it: "My father's presence always commanded respect." According to Jay Winter and Antoine Prost, authors of a biography of René Cassin, Cassin was also prone to vanity and he often sought the acclaim of those around him.[29] Some of his colleagues also regarded him as a person who was always trying to ensure that his own opinion prevailed. John Humphrey, for example, stated in his memoir that Cassin was "always so preoccupied with pressing his own point of view."[30] What is more, particularly during the final years of his life, he was anxious to present himself as the most important person involved in the drafting of the UDHR. Reading his own writings, it is easy to jump to the conclusion that it was Cassin himself who was responsible for the first draft of the UDHR while in fact it was a collective creation.[31] These characteristics may also explain why Chang and Cassin had such difficulties with each other professionally as well as on a more personal level.

Chang and Cassin had different educational backgrounds and life experiences. Chang was a humanist through and through whose main interests included literature, theater, history, and philosophy, while Cassin was a lawyer. Chang did not speak French and Cassin did not speak English as fluently as Chang, whose English outshone even that of most native speakers. Stanley Chang has told me that both his father and mother spoke English with no trace of an accent. Chang also strove to be as concise as possible in his arguments about the articles of the declaration, while Cassin was more prolix. Chang was fond of using metaphors, something Cassin did not do to anything like the same degree. While Chang had shuttled between different activities and places around the world all his life, Cassin had always worked along particular constant trajectories, such as the development of an international legal system centered on France. There was also a clear line in Cassin's career connecting his early involvement in the League of Nations to his later work for the United Nations and the Council of Europe.

In light of Stanley Chang's recollections, it is interesting to speculate about what in particular Cassin and Chang might have crossed swords over. Stanley knew his father and his typical reactions well. Stanley was continually present in his father's working milieu during the two years when the UDHR was being drafted. Stanley has also explained that after his father's first heart attack in Chile in 1943, his father made great efforts to keep his temperament in check. Chang thereby restrained himself in order to avoid outbursts of temper. According to Stanley, his father was largely successful in this effort for much of the 1940s. Chang presumably did not reveal his irritation with Cassin to the other members of the group, despite the fact that their relationship had soured. Further evidence that Chang was trying to restrain himself is provided by a family conversation at dinner in the early 1950s. During the meal, Stanley's older brother Chen Chun said that Peng asserted things with an authority that was actually meaningless. Stanley expected that this statement would cause his father to explode with rage, but to his surprise his father said nothing. (When asked what the family used to talk about at mealtimes more generally, Stanley replied that they mostly did not talk very much at all, "silence being a virtue.")

For reasons of health, Chang was thus practicing a kind of anger management while working on the UDHR and in other settings. Chang's wife, who knew about her husband's problems with maintaining face and adapting himself to the strict professional role of the diplomat, also convinced him to take a break from his UN work and, now and then, to rest up in somewhere other than New York, including a visit to Wisconsin in 1951.[32] In other words, Chang tried to maintain a professional demeanor during even the most trying situations, something that is also confirmed by Malik's diary entries on Chang's relationship with Malik. Stanley also offers some observations on his father's difficulties with the role of diplomat. According to Stanley, his father was a direct person who gladly said what he thought, someone who was not fond of the evasive manner required of those working in a diplomatic capacity.

At the same time, agreement on fundamental issues does not necessarily make for friction-free relationships. Despite the fact that Chang and Cassin were ultimately in relatively broad agreement about the content and disposition of the UDHR—especially with regard to the UN General Assembly—there were nonetheless deep divisions between them, divisions that stemmed primarily from their national, professional, and personal differences.

CHAPTER 8

Chang's Intercultural Ethics and the UN Declaration

At an early age Chang became deeply interested in the issue of cultural encounters, particularly between his own country, China, and the outside world. In his lifetime he also gathered experiences from many countries and cultures. Early on, he also became interested in questions of ethics and philosophy, something that found a new outlet in his involvement with the UN Declaration. Among the main authors of the UDHR, it was he who most vigorously defended the notion that the document should be grounded in more than one ethical tradition, precisely in order to make the UN Declaration a universal document that could be implemented globally. Chang's ideas about intercultural ethics also anticipated the American philosopher John Rawls's notion of overlapping consensus.[1] Chang proposed, as Rawls would later, a way in which to describe the conditions needed to achieve a *just or fair consensus* in a setting characterized by philosophical, religious, and ideological pluralism—"to find unity in diversity."

Creative Changes and Intercultural Dialogues

In writings published before he began work on the UDHR, Peng Chun Chang argued that one needed to be careful not to overemphasize the cultural differences between Eastern and Western countries. Far from there being some homogeneous and monolithic West implacably opposed to the East, there were in fact many Easts and Wests. There could be common denominators between a Western grouping and an Eastern, just as other groups could be riven by conflicts. Chang thought that wide terms such as "East" and "West" usually are good hiding places for all sorts of prejudices.² Instead of talking about an encounter between West and East, Chang wanted to talk more concretely about learned habits, group behaviors, the "spirit" of a culture, and different forms of national expression. By thinking in these terms, we can also conceive of constructive intercultural meetings between all of those groups whom we happen to represent. For instance, according to Chang, the humanistic attitude in Chinese tradition appeared to be more "modern" than the prevailing outlook on life in medieval Europe.

Chang expressed a similar stance toward "ideological conflicts." In an article published in 1938—"Civilization and Social Philosophies"—Chang made the following comments upon the political/ideological divides in Europe:

> While in Europe I noticed certain countries claiming to be ruled by certain kinds of ideologies. Certain people may be shouting from the ideological platforms against certain other countries. As a matter of fact, their own country may, at that very moment, still be carrying on very good economical relations with that country. I think you understand what I mean. So this matter of ideologies is not so very reliable to go by. It seems as though the further we get away from the enunciators of ideologies, the more weight we give to the ideologies. The closer you get to them, then, the plainer you will see certain flexibilities in what they say. Now, that is a general observation. Usually, among the great masters themselves of certain schools of thought, there is not so much really bitter quarreling. It is really among their disciples'disciples'disciples—then the quarrel becomes worse. Thus when we actually get close to those countries, we find that the so-called ideologies themselves do allow a good deal of flexible manipulation, according to the time and needs of a special situation. So it seems that as though it behooves us to be careful not to define the ideologies in too close and too definite a fashion.³

It should be emphasized in this context that Chang was very skeptical of talking in terms of different "isms" and using these "isms" in order to describe the politics in a certain country in a general way. Chang stated further that "we must not be persuaded by too sweeping a statement, especially in our educational process, to classify countries definitely according to certain definite "isms." It is not so simple. I have found very good friends in countries which are supposed, for the time being, to be not so friendly to my country. This is surprising. It shows that many things we hear and read in the newspapers are sometimes what we call facades. Too many of the so-called ideologies are facades. We, as educated people, should try to go behind the ideologies, behind the three F's—force, face, and farthings."[4]

Chang used these three F words to describe the challenges that he thought "ideological politics" raised at the time when he wrote his article. Unfortunately the political situation in Europe deteriorated after 1938, and Chang's hopes of finding constructive cooperation and compromises between certain countries became more and more unrealistic.

In his early writings, Chang drew on China's history and present circumstances in order to formulate some interesting ideas about cultural interactions.[5] These ideas can also be applied when making sense of his work on the UN Declaration. What characterizes cultural contacts in the modern era, according to Chang, is that they are, in contrast to cultural encounters of the past, far more rapid and involuntary.

According to Chang, it is possible to distinguish three phases of a culture in transition. As his main example, he invoked the cultural changes undergone by China in the last two hundred years.[6] He alternated between descriptive and normative accounts of the different phases. In his descriptive mode, he declared that the phases are of regular occurrence; in normative mode, that the third phrase is preferable to the two preceding phases.

Chang thus identified three phases in China's societal transformation. First, a period of *self-sufficiency*, during which cultural influences from without were ignored and regarded as largely irrelevant for China's social development. These periods were characteristic of a time when China had practically no economic interaction or cultural exchange with the outside world. Chang criticized this approach for being overly conservative and cautious. The defenses made of this approach had on several occasions been disproportionately zealous in view of the acute social need for change in the areas of economics, education, and technology.[7] The last decades of the imperial dynasty in China provides an illustrative example of this kind of historical phase. As noted in Chapter 1, right up until the final years of the dynasty, China had persisted with antiquated educational strategies of rote learning and a heavy emphasis upon law and politics instead of science and technology. China's failure prior to 1900 to keep up with Europe as regards social modernization was to be explained in large part by this attitude of self-sufficiency. Other contributing factors behind China's protracted process of modernization was (as mentioned before) the country's size in relation to Japan and the fact that China also lacked the kind of top-down command structure that had been a defining feature of Japan's decision-making capacity.

Roughly one generation ago—that is, at the end of the nineteenth century, according to Chang's calculations—the first phase had given way to one of *hurried borrowing* in which isolation had been replaced with the frenetic import of ideas from overseas. For Chang, both of these tendencies were problematic. Self-sufficiency created a static and self-centered society while forced borrowing paid no respect to the identity-creating aspects of the old traditions. According to Chang, the greatest problem in this context was the impatient and combative desire for rapid change—particularly among territories that had already been modernized to some degree. The era of forced borrowing had primarily taken place between the late 1800s and the 1920s, when Chinese students began to travel overseas to study. When they returned to China, they brought with them Western ideas that they applied in a rapid fashion without making any serious comparative study of the organic structure of the various societies. According to Chang, such ideas ought never to be accepted without comparative studies if one wanted to avoid "acute indigestion." This was also a point that Chang would later raise in the UN context. He said that too much advice from foreign experts on how to improve the situation in China may "lead to a certain amount of indigestion."[8] Chang claimed in an article published in 1931 that:

> At the beginning of the twentieth century certain of the young scholars felt great dissatisfaction. Things were moving slowly, consequently there was a movement of doing away with all traditional ways. The thought become prevalent that everything from abroad must have a higher value. But this theory and manner of working did not succeed because things could not be transplanted. Things could not be taken over in a day. Western things could not be altogether copied, so for the past ten years a new attitude has come to the front, a new method of evaluation, judging thing perhaps seemingly in a piecemeal, slow manner but fundamentally working on the idea of fitting things on a firm foundation. We may characterize it as a relative point of view.[9]

In other words, Chang endorsed the view that it was possible to be thoroughly modern but at the same time creatively Chinese.[10]

The third and more constructive phase was what Chang wanted to call *creative adjustment*.[11] A creative adjustment comprises a number of elements: (1) an attentiveness to emergent dissatisfaction with existing cultural frameworks and customs, and with it a growing desire to understand one's own cultural starting points; (2) a broad comparative overview of different alternatives for achieving stimulus and inspiration; and (3) a liberating inventiveness. The broad overview of different alternatives was not meant to produce hurried borrowing or some kind of imitation of the West, as China had been guilty of during the first twenty years of the twentieth century. Another example of hectic imitation had been Japan's importing of Western technology, which it had used for destructive ends, such as the creation of a massive arms industry.

The *liberating inventiveness* was liberating in the sense of detaching itself from sluggishness, strict traditionalism, and an especially problematic view of culture. This conservative view of culture presupposes that cultural phenomena cannot be disrupted or changed, and it downplays the internal heterogeneity of culture. Instead, as Chang argued metaphorically, cultural phenomena are treated as objects that have fallen from the sky or as glasses that can be moved around a table. The view of culture that Chang instead articulated treated cultural phenomena as things that could be analyzed and disrupted—albeit not for destructive purposes but, rather, to achieve a greater understanding of those phenomena's multifaceted nature and origin. According to Chang, the circumstances in which alternative cultural phenomena had emerged thus ought to be analyzed in order to identify the limits to the scope of those cultural trends. Chang was eager to stress that the Chinese had never been averse to the introduction of foreign intellectual influences. Chang said, "When the value of these is clearly demonstrated, the Chinese have shown themselves to be willing learners and ready adapters of the imported ideas for the enrichment of their own culture."[12] This phenomenon was especially clear in the case of Buddhism from India and modern experimental science from the European nations that had had a quite decisive role in the intellectual transformation of China. During his time as a student in the US, Chang also argued that Chinese society did not regard Christianity as a strange or foreign belief system. He was more inclined to talk about how Christian ideas might enrich China in different ways, so long as Christian missionaries were respectful of domestic traditions.

It is interesting to note in this context that Chang at an early stage, that is to say, in the 1920s and 1930s, articulated a line of thought that has become increasingly valued in debates over interculturalism and multiculturalism, particularly in the West in the last few years.[13] Recently, that debate has been characterized by a problematizing of essentialist conceptions of culture and cultural attitudes that pay no heed to either the cultural pluralism inherent in various traditions or the similarities between traditions.

Chang claimed that we needed to grasp the importance of change during our lifetime. We should therefore start by striving to gain a clear understanding of our era's most acute needs. Beneficial cultural change thus requires people to confront their most urgent needs in those particular situations in which they find themselves. Chang did not specify more closely what he meant by acute or urgent needs. Presumably he had in mind that circumstances have to show what those needs are—for instance, a change in attitude or social organization, or technological and scientific development. Chang's teacher John Dewey was similarly evasive when referring to people's needs and goals. Dewey claimed that one's own understanding of which means are reasonable also affects one's conception of which goals are desirable.

In order to understand what takes place during the social transformation of a society, Chang argued, it is important to keep in mind something that we often take for granted when using the words "transformation" or "reorganization." For the most part, it is a matter of a change *from* something, *through* something, and *to* something. A transformation can thus be problematized in three different ways. The key questions are: Is it really reasonable to leave this stage? If so, is it reasonable to do so in this particular way and for this particular "destination"?

Intercultural Dialogues and the UN Declaration

How did Chang's earlier ideas about cultural influence find expression in his work on the UDHR? The following are possible examples:

1. Rising dissatisfaction with the lack of a global ethic and international institutions capable of sustaining that ethic. Previously, there existed only limited examples in the form of national and regional institutions and agreements. The League of Nations was considered a failure in several regards by virtue of its failure to prevent war and conflicts. This organization had also not succeeded in promoting human rights to any notable degree—even if it did create protection for the rights of certain

minorities. Humanity had endured the cruelties of war, colonialism, ethnic cleansing, and genocide as well as more general violations of human dignity in the form of racism and discrimination. For these reasons, there was an acute need for a new international peace organization as well as for agreements in the form of human rights protections.
2. A wide-ranging, comparative overview that could inspire the drafting of a new rights document. It was important that any new declaration should not be an imitation or repetition of existing rights documents. Those had been developed under specific historical circumstances that differed from the situation in which the authors of the UN Declaration found themselves. The preliminary task of making a wide-ranging, comparative inventory was initially given to John Humphrey, who prepared an overview of previous rights documents throughout history.
3. A liberating inventiveness with regard to the UN Declaration's contents and function. For Chang especially, this meant emphasizing the document's moral and pedagogical function, to humanize humanity or—put differently—raise the moral stature of man. Such moral elevation might be attained through greater awareness of humanity's own moral obligations. By learning about human rights, human beings might also come to see which obligations were particularly vital. A significant function of the UDHR was also to prevent brutality to one's fellow human beings, and this was taken to be an important point of agreement among the delegates and key authors in the drafting group.

What, then, were the consequences of Chang's ideas about a liberating inventiveness for the writing of the UN Declaration? Chang claimed that certain questions, such as metaphysical problems about the nature of reality, were not suited to being discussed in this context. These questions were generally insoluble (and intractable) and also did not lend themselves to rounds of voting. Metaphysical and theological notions could also reflect culturally biased perspectives. Bias of this kind might restrict fundamental freedoms such as freedom of conscience and freedom of religion as well as reduce the universality and representativeness of the UDHR. In other words, Chang always saw the immediate task at hand as being to ensure the document's universality. In principle, all human beings should be able to feel that the declaration belonged to them.

For Chang, it was also unclear what metaphysical notions about the fundamental nature of humanity and reality could contribute to the UDHR's primary function: namely, to humanize humanity or raise the moral stature of man. In effect, such notions seemed irrelevant to the project. When Chang talked about the kinds of questions that should be excluded from discussions of the UDHR's content, he often had in mind theological, philosophical, and metaphysical questions. These problematics applied above all to humanity's fundamental nature, origin, and place in the universe. The available answers to these questions—such as theism and materialism—were often articulated by various delegates on the UN Commission on Human Rights.

How reasonable, then, were Chang's ideas? If, unlike Chang, we were to maintain that theology and metaphysics should have a place in the writing of the UDHR, one would need to acknowledge that even though full consensus is impossible to reach on such issues—by means of empirical science and logic—it may nonetheless be possible to reach a certain degree of agreement on the basis of special criteria for rationality, such as simplicity and compatibility with other kinds of knowledge. If this more limited kind of agreement is possible, therefore, it is not because of cultural bias or narrowness. Several advocates of human rights also believe that some conceptions about the fundamental nature of human beings may be of considerable relevance for the UDHR project, since such notions can lend extra weight to its demands for justice. Another objection to rejecting metaphysics or theology out of hand in relation to ethical reflections is also that such ethical reflections often presuppose certain assumptions about the nature of human beings, for instance, that they possess autonomy, conscience, and rationality.

Aside from these arguments—*insolubility, bias,* and *irrelevance*—Chang also used *irony* in his critique of those individuals who wanted the UDHR to contain religious and metaphysical elements. When the Dutch representative wanted to introduce a formulation about humanity's divine origin into the preamble, Chang replied that so important a point could not possibly be merely *one part* of a section or article; stating so essential a truth required instead a separate article in the declaration. He also said that in the case of important questions like these, it was necessary to put the matter to a vote, one that reflected the total number of inhabitants in each country. But as certain delegations had pointed out, it was impossible to decide so important a problem by a vote that would only reflect political factors. Chang expressed his hope that in view of all these complications, the delegate from the Netherlands would be willing to withdraw his proposal.[14] In his ironic commentaries, Chang sought to direct listeners to the unreasonable consequences that his opponent's approach would entail if it was carried through to its logical conclusion. An additional, more or less implicit argument was that fierce disagreements and conflicts could easily arise if metaphysical questions were made the subject of voting rounds in the Commission on Human Rights.

At the same time, Chang did not want the document to alienate people with strong religious and metaphysical convictions. The challenge thus became to find compromises or agreements that were acceptable to most of the delegates. A good illustration of this approach can be seen in the phrasing of Article 1. "All human beings are born free and equal in dignity and rights. They are endowed with reason and conscience and should act towards one another in a spirit of brotherhood." Chang's interventions were decisive for the Third Committee's decision to remove the phrase "endowed by nature," which had been the wording of the previous Geneva text. He argued that removal of these words would circumvent theological and philosophical questions that could not or should not be included in a declaration that aimed to be universal. Chang hoped that his colleagues would show the same restraint as he and the Chinese delegation had with regard to asserting culturally specific practices and ideas. China was also a very large country that represented a considerable fraction of the world's population. Despite this, it had chosen not to assert its own cultural paradigm or customs in relation to the drafting of the UN Declaration. Chang here cited an array of cultural practices that were highly valued in China, such as "decorum," his point seemingly being that if China could show such restraint with respect to its own cultural practices, then other states ought to do the same with respect to issues of metaphysics. The unstated implication here was also that voting or majority decision should not determine the way in which similar issues were settled. Decisions should instead follow the principle of respecting different perspectives and finding an acceptable area of agreement, despite one's cultural and national starting point. (Chang's colleague Malik wanted to change the words "by nature" to "by their nature" in order to avoid the interpretation that "nature" referred to something distinct from human existence. However, this idea was also voted down since the Third Committee in the end wanted to avoid any reference to "nature.")

It is interesting to note that when Chang talked about Chinese restraint, he was essentially referring to manners and social codes, since Confucian philosophical traditions do not presuppose metaphysical standpoints in the same way as, for example, Christianity. Such restraint was thus comparable to a Christian not lobbying for the UDHR to have a distinctly Christian metaphysical underpinning.

Conversely, phrases such as "by God," "by nature," and "by chance" are connected with "endowed with," which made the sentence open to quite different metaphysical interpretations. For Christians, this connection could also be entirely necessary since, for them, reference to God accounted for humanity's great and inviolable value. Moreover, the phrase "endowed with" was a compromise insofar as some delegates had wanted to have the more openly Christian theistic formulation "created with." For Article 16:3 of the UDHR, on the family, Charles Malik also wanted to include a theistic framework using the notion of "created." "Endowed with"—or "imbued with"—was a formulation that almost all of the delegates could accept by virtue of the fact that it left open whether the endowing had been done by God, nature, or something else. Nonetheless, it is fair to say that the word "endowed" can easily give the impression of one agent equipping another with certain capacities, which is to say, an impression that accords conveniently with a theistic worldview.[15] During the drafting of Article 1, Chang claimed that for Western civilization, the era of religious intolerance had now come to an end. The first sentence in Article 1 should thus refer to neither God nor nature. Those who believed in God could still find the idea of God in the powerful statement that all human beings are born free and equal and have been endowed with reason and conscience, even if the clause "by God" had been removed. Others would be able to interpret and accept the sentence in other ways.[16] According to Chang, there was thus no contradiction between the eighteenth-century idea of humanity's benign nature and the idea of a soul given to man by God, since the notion of God carried a special emphasis upon the *human* part of human nature as being in contradistinction to the brutish, animal part. An original and ingenious solution, it was accepted by the drafting committee and subsequently by the Commission on Human Rights.

Religion in Europe and China

What, then, were Chang's views about the relationship between religion and politics? Chang was in the habit of making comparisons between Western and Chinese philosophical traditions and historical experiences with regard to the relationship between religion and politics. He stressed that China had never had religious problems in the same way as the West, problems that incidentally had been exemplified by Europe's religious wars, its colonial policies, and the fraught relationship between religion and science. He underscored how easily religions could be misused for political ends, and because of this he wanted to particularly highlight and criticize the way in which the Christian church had endorsed the colonial project by having missionaries constitute the first "wave" in the European states' campaigns of colonization. This statement from Chang was a reply to Saudi Arabia's criticism of Article 18 (freedom of religion). Hence, Chang endorsed freedom of religion and the right to change one's belief or religion (he called it one of the most essential freedoms) but admitted at the same time that missionaries from the West had not always limited themselves to their religious mission.[17]

According to Chang, a number of eighteenth-century philosophers in Europe had been deeply impressed by the fact that China had not suffered from the kind of religious discrimination and intolerance that had afflicted several European countries.[18] Why, then, do China and Europe have such different histories in this particular respect? A number of sinologists, such as Professor Willard J. Peterson,[19] have claimed that Chinese governments have historically not had the same kinds of problems with religious intolerance as Europe because the role of religion in China has been quite different for several thousand years. Admittedly, religiously inflected conflicts have blown up now and then in China, but the problem has never attained the same intensity and scale as in Europe. So long as religious leaders in China did not organize their members for political ends, the country's governments were able to tolerate many varieties of religious conviction and practices. Because religious denomination was also not used politically to create a "we and they" division, the Chinese population—from the man on the street to the emperor—could, in principle, be Buddhist, Muslim, Taoist, or Christian. From a Western standpoint, according to Peterson, this "indifferent" attitude toward religion could be interpreted as a kind of religious tolerance.

According to this perspective, it is therefore important to emphasize that religion has historically not had the same public and political significance in China as it has in Europe. However, it may be noted that over the centuries there have been several bloody political mobilizations in China with religious aspects, something that Chang—like Peterson—omits to mention in his remarks. Examples of such movements include the Yellow Turban Rebellion, the Red Turban Rebellion, and the Taiping Rebellion. The first of these had ties to Taoism and occurred during the Han Dynasty between 184 and

205 AD. The rebellion, which acquired its name from the yellow headgear worn by its members, originated in a farming crisis and was defeated after several years of fighting. The Red Turban rebels, who fought against the Mongol Yuan dynasty between 1351 and 1368 AD, were associated with the White Lotus Movement and Manichaeism. Their uprising also had its origins in social problems, this time caused by tax increases to pay for the military. Unlike the Yellow Turban Rebellion, this one succeeded in toppling the dynasty.

The third uprising, the Taiping Rebellion, which took place between 1850 and 1864 and claimed millions of lives, has gone down in posterity as one of history's bloodiest uprisings. This rebellion, too, had been triggered by worsening economic conditions and burdensome taxes. Hong Xuiquan, its leader, defined himself as a Christian and had also been influenced by shamanism.[20] The uprising was suppressed with the help of the colonial powers because Shanghai—their most important economic possession—had been threatened. Yet this uprising was to haunt the Qing dynasty, something that eventually led to its persecution of a number of Christian groups during the final years of the dynasty, prior to the establishment of the republic in 1912. It should be mentioned in this context that Chang actually referred to the Taiping Rebellion when reflecting on the history of China in the nineteenth century in his book *China at the Crossroads*.[21]

There are those who might argue that Communism in China has had an almost religious function in official life since the Second World War, a perspective that would also explain the regime's uncompromising attitude toward religious groups such as Falun Gong in recent years. In Chang's own time—the republican period—religions provided the basis for various forms of social community, and one of the first measures taken by Mao and the Communists after assuming power was the banning of religion and churches on the grounds that they were in competition with the Communist Party. The view of China as a region fortunately unaffected by conflicts deriving from religion is thus untrue. Even so, there is some truth to the claim that religion has never had the same official importance in China as in European countries during the same historical periods.

Chang also noted that 1859 marked the beginning of the conflict between religion and science in the West, thanks to the publication of Darwin's theory of evolution in *The Origin of Species*. The debate it provoked, Chang argued, had created unnecessary conflicts that continued to make themselves felt, not least within the UN committee. In order to highlight how unnecessary this conflict was, Chang invoked the way in which China had addressed "the problem of religion." In China, the issue of how to live had always taken center stage and been prioritized over metaphysical questions relating to the causes and fundamental conditions of life. This principle was exemplified by China's philosophical tradition, in which Confucius and Mencius had been the guiding lights. Chinese philosophy, according to Chang, was premised upon belief in a unitary cause which was articulated in the human realm by what Chang termed pluralistic tolerance, a concept that we have encountered in previous chapters. This kind of tolerance was necessary in order to avoid acute conflicts and to promote kindness, justice, and amicable relationships.[22]

Was Chang's comparison between Chinese philosophical traditions and non-Chinese or Western traditions persuasive in this respect? So as to gain a more nuanced image of non-Chinese worldviews other than that which Chang held up, it is important to stress that most religions involve more than just instructions to the faithful on how to situate themselves with regard to what is divine in their world. A number of religious belief systems also include ethical precepts and concrete directions about how to behave. For example, in the Christian tradition there are ethical rules in the form of the Ten Commandments, the New Testament, and the catechism. While several religions and churches rely upon metaphysical notions about the nature of reality and its fundamental causes, these do not necessarily reduce the priority of ethical norms in everyday life. However, Chang's claim can be admitted in the sense that disagreement over issues that are divisive and virtually insoluble will easily arise so long as metaphysical concepts remain central to theological, ethical and philosophical debates.

Chang also held that the best way to witness the magnificence of the divine is to try to live rightly, something that included adopting an attitude of pluralistic tolerance toward one's fellow human beings. He regarded this as a distinctly humanistic outlook. It means respecting the spirit or the divine *as if* it existed and thereby becoming conscious of people's obligations toward each other. The most important thing was therefore to emphasize how much this respect meant for humanity, not to focus upon the nature of the divine— the latter, according to Chang, being something about which we ought to humbly admit we know nothing. This was precisely what it meant to be human. This agnostic declaration of Chang's was taken from Confucius.

Confucius had also been generally considered a secularly oriented philosopher who was more interested in the art of living than in theological questions about the existence of God.²³ For Confucius the social world of humans was more essential than "other-worldly concerns."²⁴ In the 1930s and 1940s, Chang became increasingly curious about Confucius's writings, an interest that presumably influenced his more general engagement with questions of ethics, religion, and outlook on life. When he openly discussed Confucius's attitudes toward spiritual matters and religious ceremonies, Chang thus cited *Analects* 6:22 ("Respect the Spirit as if the Spirit were there"), which Stanley Chang recalls his father repeating frequently to the children.

Chang and Christianity

What, then, was Chang's relationship to Christianity for most of his life? We noted earlier that he was active in Christian student circles while a student at Clark University. The fact that his religious activism waned after his years studying in the US may be the reason why so few commentators have considered his religious activism during those early student days. The Christianity-inflected essays that he wrote as a student were also published in student newspapers with very small circulations. In those essays, Chang primarily emphasized Christianity's ethical imperatives in the form of faith in an absolute, inviolable human value and in the potential for Christianity to be reconciled with and to complement Chinese traditions.

In his address "The Gospel in China," given at the major Christian-Chinese student convention in Missouri in 1914, Chang voiced his hope that most of China's social problems would disappear if every citizen managed to follow three central Christian precepts.²⁵ These precepts were to follow in Jesus Christ's ideal of self-sacrifice and brotherhood; to seek always to act on the understanding that each person has a unique and infinite value; and to approach God as a loving father and to have the faith to follow His will. Chang emphasized that it was through Christianity in the first instance that our understanding of human worth had been revolutionized, because Jesus Christ had argued that the most marginalized members of society should be accorded the same value as the most privileged. Moreover, Chang argued, the notion of human value acquired a special significance and force in the Christian doctrine of immortality. In another article, titled "A New World: A New Attitude," which appeared a year later, Chang contended that democracy in the true sense of the word meant recognition of the divine value of individual human beings as they were.²⁶

Several of these ethical motifs would recur in Chang's later reflections upon human rights in the UN Declaration, albeit without their religious connotations. The desire to do good to others and the society in which one lived (the notion of brotherhood), reciprocity as a principle of human relationships, and the idea of the supreme and unique value of the individual human being—these were all notions that Chang explicitly invoked in the debates about the UN Declaration.

That Chang at early stage in his life could be described as Christian does not fit the image of him that has been circulated among his various commentators, namely that he was the member of the Commission on Human Rights and the drafting group who made the most number of contributions derived from Eastern and Confucian perspectives on the human rights problematic.

When asked how religiously active Chang was in the 1930s, '40s, and '50s, Stanley Chang offered the following answer:

> My father was never involved in religious activities during all the time I lived with him. Something he said to me now and then was "Ru Tsai," which means "as if present."
>
> I was supposed always to act on this principle, of "God as ever-present." My mother was raised as a Methodist so when I went to college I also described myself as Methodist. My parents did not discuss any religious matters with us children during our upbringing, which now perhaps seem strange. An exception was a statement that my father made in connection with the Old and New Testaments during my stay at home in Nutley sometime between 1952 and 1954. It was a simple, straightforward statement: "The Jewish God was severe and vengeful, while the Christian God is forgiving and kind." Since that time I have always felt sorry for the Jewish people.

This last statement by P. C. Chang reveals that even at the end of his life he retained a positive affinity for the Christian concept of God, even if he was not active in any Christian church in the 1950s.

Given Chang's religious activities in the 1910s while a student in the US, it may reasonably be asked what happened to those convictions. His engagement with Christianity seems to have been limited to his years as a student, when he wrote articles with a Christian framework and took part in bible study groups and Christian student conferences. And yet Chang's involvement in

Christianity is strikingly absent in the 1920s, 1930s, and 1940s. One possible explanation is the influence of his brother Poling during Chang's youth. Poling himself was an active Christian who, as noted already, was more a father to Chang than a brother. As also noted before, the scholarship program to the US was also based on the hope that its students would make a commitment to Christianity. The longer Chang studied in the US, the more his religious zeal appears to have cooled. Among other factors, he was coming into contact with a university world in which agnostic and secular thinking were commonplace, not least in the form of the pragmatic philosophy of John Dewey, Chang's teacher at Columbia University.

Chang's writings of the 1920s, '30s, and '40s also offer little evidence to suggest any involvement in religion and interest in Christianity. However, he does enjoin respect and tolerance for other religious faiths, an attitude that is illustrated by the short eulogy he gave in 1947 at the funeral of a friend, Timothy T. F. Lew, where he expressed his admiration for his friend's religious commitment:

> According to Confucius, a man can be immortalized by his accomplishments in three respects: 1) in virtue, 2) in works, 3) in words.
>
> In the matter of virtue Dr Timothy Lew had been a good friend to all who knew him. In the matter of works, he achieved a good deal in the field of religious education and helped to strengthen the foundations of the growing Christian church movement in China. In the matter of words, he has edited many outstanding publications, and is well known as an author, translator and interpreter of both Eastern and Western cultures.[27]

This statement can plausibly be read as implying that Chang was willing to highlight Lew's contributions to the Christian church in China and that he viewed them as deserving to be foregrounded in the context of Lew's lifelong professional activity.

It is illuminative here to draw a parallel between Chang and his teacher at Columbia University, John Dewey. Dewey has been described as one of the least religious "pragmatist" philosophers in the United States. He was also critical of both militant atheists and militant religious groups.[28] With regard to militancy, Dewey took a critical view of the elevation of individual human reason. Instead, he thought that human beings should be characterized by humility toward their limited capacity for understanding and toward their place in the universe. There is a similarity here with Chang's rejection of the dogmatic refusal to compromise. The fact that Dewey's philosophy was to be called into question by Communists may also have influenced Chang's own decision to distance himself from Communism later in life.

John Dewey grew up in a home that was deeply affected by evangelical revivalism, a situation that also has suggestive parallels to Chang's upbringing by his Christian brother, Poling. Dewey became increasingly critical of religion as his studies and researches progressed. In effect, he wanted to do away with the supernatural and metaphysical components of religions while retaining the ethical and humanistic aspects of church life. This, too, strongly recalls Chang's own intellectual growth. Later in life, Chang also wanted to retain the ethical perspective of religion, something that found expression in, among other things, Chang's axiom, "Live as though God exists," which he often repeated to his son Stanley.

Dewey's criticism of the elevation of the situation of the individual human being—whether as an elevation of either human reason or as an elevation of an individualistic outlook—also offers suggestive parallels with Chang's own thinking. Chang can be read as arguing that Chinese philosophical traditions take a *holistic* view of human beings and nature, with the former being considered an integrated part of the latter. He readily echoed the view that human beings' happiness and prosperity are the result of successful adaptation to their immediate environment.[29] Chang claimed that the Greeks had "fixed the chains of anthropocentrism upon us" but that they also gave us an antidote in science.[30] His references to the art of living and his downplaying of metaphysical considerations also tallied with his teacher John Dewey's pragmatic philosophy, which emphasized the intimate relationship between thought and action.[31]

Chang as Confucian?

In recent years, scholars writing on Peng Chun Chang have sought to promote the idea that his main contribution to the UN Declaration was a Confucian perspective.[32] The following is a representative statement of this position: "Peng Chun Chang was generally regarded as one of the sharpest philosophical minds among the delegates. He was a noted Confucian humanist, philosopher, diplomat, playwright, and director, who had held diplomatic posts in Turkey and Chile. He had developed an enthusiasm for promoting Chinese culture and was also given to making connections between Islam and Confucianism."[33] Given Chang's many references to Confucian ideas—particularly in connection with his UN work—it is perhaps natural to call him a Confucian humanist and thinker. However, in recent years, this prevailing view of the presence of Confucian thinking in Chang's statements and writings has been called into question.[34] Commentators taking this view have contended that Chang did not often mention Confucius or other Chinese philosophers in connection with the drafting of the declaration. On the contrary, Chang's statements attest to very different influences, including ideas that to some degree ran contrary to his supposedly Confucian roots. Some have argued that it is doubtful whether Chang influenced the UDHR in a Confucian direction since the document is so manifestly premised on Western rights traditions. For instance, Chang often emphasized the importance of liberal freedoms and a strand of rights thinking that originated in the European Enlightenment. Additionally, he underscored that individuals can flourish in the encounter between several traditions and not only within the framework of their own culture, a view that he shared with Eleanor Roosevelt.[35]

The American legal expert Mary Ann Glendon has tended to emphasize the more multifaceted nature of Chang's thinking, although she concedes that Confucianism was an important point of reference for him.[36] Glendon has also made the following statement about Malik's ideas and his relationship with Chang:

> Malik's ideas were very varied and so, too, were Chang's. They were working together on a project that was very complex in which there was room for compromises and improvisations. This was not a project where one could apply a fixed theory, the problems had to be allowed to speak for themselves and so a more gradualist approach was thus called for. The idea that Malik's philosophy was based on Thomism came from people like Eleanor Roosevelt, who used the term as shorthand for Malik's perspective.[37] . . . Although Malik was familiar with Thomas of Aquinas's philosophy, Malik had a doctorate in philosophy from Harvard, his approach to the drafting committee had been inspired by many different philosophical strands. To call him a Thomist was somewhat reductive, a bit like saying that a

Jewish diplomat was Talmudic. I also do not think that the differences of opinion between Chang and Malik had very much to do with Thomism, it was more about their different personalities.[38]

Glendon's remarks are illuminating and highlight an important dimension of the drafting of the UDHR. The various key authors of the document were undoubtedly highly aware that the writing of the declaration was not a matter of creating an ethical theory or applying an ethical theory to a certain body of material. Rather, it was about successively trying to arrive at reasonable proposals—including compromises—in light of the delegates' different cultural, ideological, and philosophical starting points and the specific problems at hand.

Despite all this, one should probably not downplay Malik's Thomist and natural rights thinking or Chang's "Confucianism." This is important to emphasize in connection with the drafting process and its influence upon certain formulations in the UDHR. Recall the quotations from Eleanor Roosevelt's notes on when she invited Malik, Chang, and Humphrey for tea in her apartment in Washington Square. What emerged clearly there was that Malik believed that the drafters of the UN Declaration should acknowledge the intellectual framework of Christianity, particularly the philosophy of Thomas of Aquinas. For his part, Chang recommended complete immersion in classical Chinese philosophy.

Chang's ambition that the UDHR should have the moral-pedagogical function of humanizing humanity (or raising the moral stature of man)—in which raising awareness of the individual's obligations played a key role—also aligned well with a Confucian perspective on morality. According to Chang, Confucius's chief emphasis was upon human responsibility and reciprocity. He also stressed the importance of understanding other men and showing sympathy with them. Further, Confucius meant that learning was the chief joy of life, there "learning" was not only referring to "learning from books" but also to a comprehensive learning that included social behavior and the understanding of men. This broad form of learning continues throughout life.[39] The idea of the priority of the people over government in Article 21 in the UDHR was also something that Chang endorsed and that was in tune with Confucian traditions.

However, Chang's ideas about this moral function of the UDHR could clearly be combined with other perspectives than merely Confucianism. We noted earlier that there were also a number of points in common between

Chang's philosophical approach and John Dewey's pragmatism. They had similar views on democracy and the role of education in society, and they also endorsed an anti-metaphysical stance in ethics.

Chang was keen, too, that the concepts of acting in the spirit of brotherhood and of the individual's obligations to society should be included in the document, something that fit well with a Confucian outlook. Moreover, Chang's emphasis upon socioeconomic rights was compatible with the Confucian idea that a prince should safeguard the welfare of his people. But Chang also wanted the UDHR to be influenced by other ethical traditions in addition to Confucian thought such as the Enlightenment ideas about fundamental rights and freedoms.

Confucianism and Human Rights

It may be worth pausing for a moment on this question of Confucianism's relationship to human rights thinking. It is customary to differentiate between Confucianism as a philosophy and Confucianism as a state ideology or praxis. We will here be focusing primarily on the former. As regards the latter (Confucianism as a state ideology), Confucianism during the Mao Zedong era was seen as too bound up with the old kingdom of China, an association for which it was heavily criticized. This was especially obvious during the Cultural Revolution of 1966 to 1976.[40] In the 1990s, however, Confucianism in China was increasingly viewed as a way of promoting social cohesion, order, and harmony, and, moreover, as a basis for civic morality and loyalty to the state (or the Communist Party).

The relationship between Confucianism as a philosophy and human rights is, however, ambiguous. While some aspects of Confucianism clearly stand in an uneasy relationship with the idea of human rights, others support it. For example, Confucius's writings, *The Analects*, do not emphasize the importance of autonomy or the equal and general right to political participation and influence on the part of the general population. However, they do foreground human beings' material needs and the importance of the sovereign meeting such fundamental needs on the part of the people. Social virtues are important as well as loyalty to one's family, and emphasis is also placed on the prosperity, order, and harmony of society.[41] In spite of these convergences between Confucian ethics and human rights a number of sinologists, such as Willard Peterson, argue that there is an underlying opposition between Confucian ethics and human rights ethics. Peterson expressed this opposition as follows:

> I think part of the problem is in what I understand to be fundamental to Western notions of human rights. These are protections, granted by those in power (at least nominally) to those with less power, as promised protections from abuse of power. This kind of concept is in Magna Carta, the US Bill of Rights, etc. For Confucius, such a promise of protection from abuse does not come up. A good ruler, especially an ideal ruler, by definition does not abuse his power by mistreating those under his control. Similarly, a good father does not abuse his power over his family; there are no "rights" that a family member has against the father, and no "rights" that protect a subject from abuse by a superior. For Confucius, the idea that a law enshrining a granted right (right to free speech, right to trial by one's peers, etc.) would protect one from an abuse of power would be naïve.
>
> Perhaps the big problem in bringing "traditional" China into the discussion on human rights is the role of the law (by which "rights" are enforceable through sanctions). In the Chinese traditions, laws are imposed as standards by those with power over those with less or no power. Expectations of moral behavior might serve as a check on the behavior of someone with power; some might appeal to precedent and tradition. Perhaps the Roman tradition (down to the present day) gives more of a role to "laws," including laws that make a claim about checking abuses by those with more power.[42]

Peterson's remarks are very interesting, and he represents a particular school of thought on the relationship between Confucian ethics and human rights, that is, "incompatibilism." Another doctrine, "compatibilism," claims instead that Confucian ethics and human rights stand in a more harmonious relationship to one another.[43] How did Chang's philosophy relate to these two schools of thought? Chang obviously thought that Confucian thought could *enrich* human rights ethics through concepts such as benevolence or sympathy for others (see the section *Two-Man-Mindedness* below). Well known human rights such as welfare rights could also be *supported* by Confucian ethics, according to Chang. One might also say that Chang stressed the role of education more than that of law and punishment when he talked about the fulfillment of rights generally, which seems to be reasonable given his Chinese and Confucian background. Chang had also claimed that: "China is one of the first amongst nations to cherish the ideals of human rights and freedom. These ideals have been woven into her long and continuous civilization from the earliest rulers down to Dr. Sun Yat-sen, the Founder of the Chinese Republic. The Chinese people today accept these ideals as anything but foreign."[44] Chang based these thoughts mainly on Mencius who advocated the right to revolution against unjust rulers and feudalistic systems.

On the other hand, Peterson's remarks fit a conception of human rights that imagines that human rights are primarily meaningful in the context of law, an idea that can be questioned on the basis of different functions of human rights and their possible methods of fulfillment. Chang also claimed that the purpose of the declaration was to create better human beings, not merely to punish those who violate human rights.

The usual Confucian skepticism toward a rhetoric of rights stems from the view that it can undermine traditional social structures, structures that rest upon shared understanding and trust. Repeated reference to rights within families—and other primary units of social organization—can thus create distance between their members and also have a divisive effect upon the family's sense of community. The Confucian approach has also emphasized that people should be aware of the law's limited capacity to direct human behavior as well as of its complete inability to regulate human character.[45] In response to a proposal from Uruguay Chang argued that a formulation such as "prescribed by law" should not be applied in the case of concepts such as moral education and recognition of the rights of others. By contrast, he explained, this kind of phrasing could be relevant for concepts such as public order.[46]

Confucian ethics has frequently spoken of living in accordance with conventions (*li*) and on the principles of the five relations (*wu lu*), that is to say, son–father; husband–wife; older–younger brother; ruler–ruled; and friend–friend. According to Confucius, it was important to respect all these roles or positions in order to achieve social order in society. In other words, an egalitarian human-rights perspective posed a serious challenge to most of the social hierarchies that have been historically encouraged by common forms of Confucianism. The only one of the above relations in the Confucian world of ideas that has an egalitarian basis or flavor is that of friend–friend.[47] Perhaps this relation might also provide the foundation for a more egalitarian mode of thinking in Confucian ethics, if it were to be given greater prominence among the other relations emphasized by Confucianism. Relatives can also be friends, for example. However, in the work on the UDHR, the problematic of rights was primarily centered on the concepts of human being and citizen and—with the exception of ruler–ruled, which is associated with the concept of citizen—not those relations addressed by Confucius. Chang here aligned himself with the egalitarian viewpoint in rights ethics, as did several of the other delegates. Every person and citizen was thus endowed with *equal* rights (and obligations).

Confucianism does, however, include principles that are compatible with the demand for human rights. The negative formulation of the Golden Rule found in Confucian philosophical traditions, "Never impose on others what you would not choose for yourself," is a good example.[48] In an early essay, Chang had argued that people's selfishness must be counteracted not only by such a maxim but also by Jesus's more positive formulation, "Do unto others what you want them to do to you."[49] This is yet another illustration of how different ethical traditions—here, Confucian and Christian—can work in tandem and contribute to more genuinely ethical insights, something that chimes well with Chang's ideas about an intercultural ethics. Other formulations within Confucian ethics that are compatible with human rights include the notion that all people within the four seas are brothers and that the ultimate scope of morality is everything under the heavens. The precept that a noble person is not a tool constitutes another moral valuation that sits well with human rights thinking and the principle of human dignity, which was elaborated by the German Enlightenment philosopher Immanuel Kant, that is, that human beings should primarily be treated as ends in themselves and not merely means.[50]

Pierre-Étienne Will's Analysis of Chang's Philosophy

One of the most thought-provoking recent analyses of Chang's contributions to the UN Declaration, one that reveals the multifaceted nature of his thinking, has been presented by the French sinologist Pierre-Étienne Will.[51] Will claims that Chang was far too clever and cosmopolitan merely to act as Confucianism's ambassador to the UN. Such a reading, he argues, misses what is subtle and original in Chang's argumentative strategies. According to Will, Chang made use of *three* strategies when arguing for a particular formulation in the text of the declaration.

First, Chang wanted to prevent the UDHR from becoming a document that citizens from non-Western states would fail to see themselves in. He thus wanted to use formulations that could be viewed as general, inclusive, and neutral. Accordingly, as we noted earlier, he was firmly opposed to phrases that could be interpreted in theistically—terms such as "created by"—and he was against references to the doctrine of natural law being included in the declaration.

Second, Chang adopted a more positive strategy intended to foreground the contributions made by different ethical traditions, all in order to strengthen the UDHR's universal validity and legitimacy. Presumably, Chang also believed that it would be easier to implement the UDHR if elements of the declaration found an "echo" or a counterpart in different traditions. For example, notions of social and economic rights had a natural home in Chinese philosophical traditions. Chang approvingly cited Confucius's statement that when "the great or the right way [*Ta Tao*] dominates or prevails, the world becomes a better place for everyone." All people—young or old, healthy or sick, those with parents and those without—should be cared for.[52] And third, Chang used classical Chinese proverbs as a means of finding compromises or emphasizing a particular perspective.

Two-Man-Mindedness

Chang also argued that the second clause of Article 1—that human beings should act in a spirit of brotherhood—was compatible with the traditional Chinese notion that all people should show kindness and respect to each other.[53] Only by means of such an attitude could people raise themselves to become truly human. One of the most important contributions made to the UDHR by the Chinese philosophical traditions that Chang advocated was the inclusion of the word *ren* (two-man-mindedness), an expression usually translated as kindness, sympathy toward others, or humaneness. The word *ren* was introduced into Article 1 with the help of the word "conscience" in order to emphasize not merely human beings' cognitive capacity but also their socio-emotional skills and capacity to see things from other people's perspective.[54]

Chang treated this social ability (of *ren*) as the natural goodness in people, our innate capacity for empathy toward each other. The word *ren* is a combination of two words, "human" and "two," a combination that has a profound connotation in the works of Confucius and Mencius.⁵⁵ According to Chang, Confucius also stressed the notion of *reciprocity* as the most salient ethical concept. To highlight human beings' capacity for considerateness toward and empathy with their fellow humans as being a key human attribute also makes possible an open and inclusive approach to what it is to be human, in contrast to concepts that focus instead on cognitive capacities.

What more precisely were Confucius's ideas on this question? According to Confucius, to be able to "stand up," a person must be familiar with his or her social milieu. (Confucius expressed this in terms of being able to stand up only after reaching the age of thirty.) To be able to stand up, argued Confucius, it was necessary to adapt oneself to other people by means of mutual respect and understanding.⁵⁶ The notion of reciprocity was thus key for Confucius, and it also found its way into his negative formulation of the Golden Rule: "Do not do to others things which you do not wish others to do to you."

The writings of Mencius (the book *Gaozi*) also emphasize humanity's moral nature by means of the pairing consciousness-heart, denoting that which separates people from animals. According to Mencius, all humans share an innate goodness, a disposition to do good, which can be developed through education and self-discipline.⁵⁷ Mencius illustrates *ren* with the following revealing story. A person endowed with *ren* would immediately try to save a child in danger of falling down a well. That rescue would not be based upon any thought of social recognition or validation or because the person in question was acquainted with the child's parents. Rather, it would be the expression of a fundamental sympathy with someone in danger.⁵⁸

In the secondary literature, there is an array of different suggestions as to how to translate *ren*, "two-man-mindedness," or *lianqxin*—since English lacks any simple or obvious equivalent. (*Liangxin* often stands for "benevolent heart" or "good-hearted.") The standard translation these days is "benevolence," but "being humane" is also an accepted alternative. The latter accords well with Chang's idealistic view of humanity. The good, human part expresses sympathy for others. In the drafting group, René Cassin felt the word could also be associated with Rousseau's notion of compassion, but this latter term was not ultimately chosen to convey the sense of *ren*.⁵⁹

The notion of two-man-mindedness implicitly stands in contrast to that of one-man-mindedness, a designation for egoism, individualism, and selfishness. Chang wished to use the concepts of *ren* and two-man-mindedness in order to emphasize a capacity to identify with other people's needs and interests and to show compassion and a more profound kind of engagement, by which other people's worries and pleasures become one's own. Chang's choice of the term "two-man-mindedness" in this concrete context was especially felicitous. The concept denotes a dialogue and a relation of sympathy between *two* people, as is reflected in the fact that when all is said and done, we interact with those around us on an individual basis: *you* is thus always a concrete person. According to Chang, this good side of human beings needs to be cultivated so as to counteract the animal aspects of human beings that lead to brutality.

From this perspective, it was also natural or reasonable that Article 1 should contain a reference to brotherhood—or community—something that can be said to rest upon this capacity for sympathy with one's fellow human beings. However, the term that ultimately came to be used to express Chang's thinking was "conscience." For a number of commentators, this word was a highly unsatisfactory translation since conscience is primarily associated with an inner moral tribunal, not the capacity for sympathy for one's fellow human beings.[60] Chang accounted for his own acceptance of the term, despite its not being the optimal translation, as follows: "I think that the word *conscience* which has been proposed by the British representative is a very good word. I was searching for a suitable term and perhaps this words is as good as any other, at least for now. I was about to propose a kind of sympathy which includes compassion, whatever that is, a natural phenomenon. If I cannot find a better term, and until I do so, I therefore accept the word *conscience*."[61] In other words, it is striking that Chang accepted this translation of *ren* in terms of conscience. He did not return to the question and provided no alternative translation. That said, it should be noted that Chang had some grounds for accepting the term "conscience." "Conscience" conveys the sense of having been brought up in a manner that is respectful of other people's welfare. Its opposite term is a person entirely lacking in empathy who has no feelings of obligation toward fellow human beings.

How was Chang able to distinguish here between contributions to the UDHR that were culturally partisan and contributions that came from different cultures but that nonetheless shared some universal values? One possible answer would be that the latter did not comprise proposals that risked affecting the inclusive character of the entire document. Rather, they provided depth to people's understanding of questions that had struck a chord with a number of delegates in the writing group. With regard to the concept *ren*, or two-man-mindedness, for example, Eleanor Roosevelt had already argued that Article 1 of the declaration needed to refer to the social, emotional qualities of human beings in addition to their rational sides. Chang's proposal thus fitted in well with this discussion.

Conceptualizing Rights in the Enlightenment

Not only did Chang refer to Chinese philosophical traditions, he took pains to highlight the key ethical contributions made by other traditions stemming from the European Enlightenment. He also pointed out the convergence or complementariness in how these Chinese traditions related to other traditions. According to Chang, the idea that there is a good, human side to human beings—which more or less corresponds to sympathy for one's fellow human beings—can also be found in the writings of eighteenth-century European philosophers. On several occasions, he made reference to Enlightenment philosophers, particularly French philosophers such as Voltaire, François Quesnay, and other physiocrats. He also cited the names of a number of representative Englishmen, including Edward Gibbon, Oliver Goldsmith, and Joseph Addison. According to Chang, Voltaire in particular had been inspired by Confucian philosophy and political concepts from China such as anti-feudalism, the right to overthrow an unjust ruler, and the importance of religious tolerance. The meritocratic character of the Chinese state (with public examination for the offices) was also something that impressed Enlightenment philosophers. Intellectual merit instead of birth or origin should determine one's career.[62] Hence, Chinese ideas had been intermingled with European thought and sentiment on human rights at the time when that subject had been first speculated upon in modern Europe.[63]

Visits to China by European Jesuits in the seventeenth and eighteenth centuries initiated a period of cultural exchange as a result of which European philosophers became acquainted with the work of Chinese philosophers. A number of philosophers and writers, such as Gottfried Wilhelm Leibniz, Johann Wolfgang von Goethe, and Pierre Bayle, remarked positively on Chinese society. Bayle argued that Chinese civilization offered clear proof that ethics could exist without the apparatus of a religion.[64] Chang also praised the French Enlightenment philosophers, arguing that the present discussions of human rights and freedoms had their basis in ideas that they had articulated. In this respect there was no need to reinvent the wheel.

In his concluding address on 10 December 1948, Chang made the following statement about the emergence of the idea of human rights in eighteenth-century Europe and China's influence thereon: "About one hundred and seventy years ago, when human rights were first promulgated in the Western world, the emphasis naturally was on the "Rights" to be demanded, but we also must not forget that these Rights were "Human" in contrast to the "Divine Right of Kings" prevalent up to the Eighteenth Century in Europe. Chinese thought imported into Europe in that period became known to all the thinkers of the age. The Chinese contribution to the emphasis on the "Human" in the struggle for Human Rights is well known and does not need to be stressed here again."[65] Chang also discussed how the word "human" in the concept of human rights had another connotation in addition to simply standing in contrast to the rights of sovereigns, that is to say, rights that were regarded as divinely conferred upon rulers. The contrast here stemmed from how a person had rights by virtue of being a human being. Chang also felt that the emphasis should be put on the *human* aspect of the notion of human rights. People must be continually aware of the fellow human beings with whom they shared their society. This observation followed naturally upon Chang's understanding of *ren* and sympathy toward others and his emphasis upon the humanizing of humanity. This was clearly an inspiration from Confucian ethics. At times, he was also more interested in using a phrase such as "art of living" instead of "rights." The rights rhetoric to which he referred was more or less taken for granted when he discussed notions of duty, benevolence, and moral upbringing.

Chang's references to the importance of the Enlightenment for human rights were clearly reasonable, and many scholars have argued that it was precisely during this period that people in the West began in earnest to struggle against aristocratic privilege and monarchical absolutism.[66] Powerfully inspired by the scientific revolution, intellectuals in the west began a questioning of ecclesiastical and royal authority that was to continue for two hundred years. These intellectuals argued for the right to life; to freedom of thought, conscience, religion, and expression; to political freedom; and to private property. All across Europe, feudalism was further weakened and slavery began to be questioned by increasing numbers of people.

* * *

Chang's historical narrative should nonetheless be qualified. The idea of natural rights in fact had an earlier provenance than Chang suggested and harked back to the so-called medieval canonists and their commentaries on

Roman law and the place of the individual as the primary subject of the legal system.[67] The European Enlightenment also brought with it a breakthrough for notions of religious tolerance by focusing increasingly upon the relationship of the individual to God. In the wake of the Peace of Westphalia in 1648, there was also a growing ambition to find a common, nondenominational language for use by Catholics and Protestants in the various states, a development that also served to promote religious freedom.

When Chang talked about the Enlightenment's importance for the evolution of the concept of human rights, he was focusing primarily on French Enlightenment philosophers, rather than Immanuel Kant, John Locke, or Thomas Paine. This is rather curious, particularly given both Kant's central importance for any understanding of the idea of an inviolable human value or dignity and Locke's influence on religious tolerance and political freedoms. Chang referred to the notions of rights that permeated the American Declaration of Independence yet without making explicit mention of any American thinkers—a surprising omission given that his encounter with the Western intellectual tradition had primarily taken place under the auspices of a study visit to the United States.

What made the French philosophers so interesting to Chang was probably the fact that they had been deeply influenced by Chinese philosophical traditions and the experiences of the French Jesuits during their various visits to China. For Chang, it was especially important to assert the Enlightenment ideas of freedom in connection with the inclusion of civil and political rights by the UDHR. In the case of social provisions and of welfare rights more generally, he wished instead to foreground the significance of China throughout history.

It is a fair question how compatible Chang's references to Enlightenment understandings of natural rights were with his skepticism toward the concept of natural rights in the UN Declaration. Such concepts recur frequently in the writings of several Enlightenment philosophers. How can we reconcile these positions? It is likely that what Chang meant was that normative ideas about freedom, equality, brotherhood, and suchlike should be included in the UN Declaration, but that metaphysical ideas about objective natural rights should not.

Chang was thus arguing that different countries' respective experiences could enrich the UN Declaration. Enlightenment France had contributed the concepts of equality, freedom, and fraternity. China had taught the world quite different things. Its traditions were clearly aligned with the concept of human rights, as, for example, in Mencius's arguments about the people's superiority to their ruler and the right to rebel against a sovereign who was unsuited for office. If a regime or ruler did not treat its subjects well, the mandate of heaven could be transferred to someone else. On this traditional view, natural catastrophes could be a sign that a ruler was unjust. In such cases, the people were entitled to rise up. The regime which had preceded the Zhou dynasty, namely the Shang dynasty (1600–1046 BC) had thus lost the mandate of heaven, according to representatives of the Zhou dynasty. The expression "mandate of heaven" originates in the Zhou dynasty period (1046–256 BC). The preamble to the UDHR also states that human beings have the right to "recourse, as a last resort, to rebellion against tyranny and oppression" in the absence of a state able to protect their human rights.

At this point it may be asked to what extent Chang was idealizing Chinese history. To be sure, there had been thinkers, such as Mencius, who articulated the idea of circumscribing the power of the sovereign, and the notion of the mandate of heaven enjoyed broad popular currency. The Chinese emperor was nonetheless "alone" in his autocratic exercise of power, unlike those European sovereigns who during certain periods were crowned by the Pope.

If we adopt the concept of *bricolage* proposed by the American ethicist Jeffrey Stout, we might say that Chang advocated a similar view of the UDHR. Stout used this concept to describe Martin Luther King's great capacity for borrowing from more than one ethical tradition for the purposes of organizing a broad coalition with the goal of democratically reforming a United States segregated by race. In King's case, these included ethical insights from the Bible and a tradition of natural rights thinking, which formed the basis for his and the civil rights movement's demands for equal treatment, regardless of skin color.[68] In Chang's case, it was a matter of borrowing from different ethical traditions to enable as wide-reaching a consensus as possible about the rights articles in the UN Declaration and to ensure the UDHR's universal legitimacy. For Chang, it was principally a matter of French Enlightenment ideas and Confucian intellectual traditions.

Chang's Use of Chinese Proverbs

The third argumentative strategy of Chang's that Will identified is the former's use of Confucian and Chinese proverbs as a way to underscore a point or achieve a compromise. As John Humphrey put it, Chang was a master of the art of compromise, someone who often used the pretext of drawing on a quotation from Confucius in order to present to the commission an idea that would allow them to avoid deadlock in the negotiations.[69] Here are a few representative examples that Chang offered to create a spirit of compromise among the delegates: "'Sweep the snow in front of one's own door. Overlook the frost on others' rooftiles. That made for good neighbours."[70] Chang also wanted to specially emphasize the need for weighing any additions carefully before making them part of the committee's text. An apt Chinese proverb in this context was, "Questions that have been allowed to mature slowly are free of sharp corners."[71] Regarding confrontation in a conflict and the choice between hard and soft approaches, he offered the following statement: "It is about fighting with clenched fist on one hand and with soft glue on the other."[72] The idea behind this saying was that the soft approach always trumps one that is harder and more inflexible and fragile. Chang stressed that several adages from the Chinese tradition were quite modern and clearly relevant for the current political situation. Chang cited as examples: "Heaven sees as we people see; Heaven hears as we people hear," and "The people come first, the State or Institutions next, and the Rulers last." Further, "It is more dangerous to stop the mouths of the people than to stop the torrents of the river. The torrents will rush on and carry away the dykes, but in regard to the people, the numbers hurt will be multitudinous." According to Chang through such adages we could see good warnings against attempts to harness the freedom of speech.[73]

Last, Chang often used metaphorical phraseology as a way to press a point. As was mentioned before, Chang used metaphors such as children's diseases when he talked about the political development of specific states, such as China at certain stages in its history. Further, as we noticed before, he described states as "children" when he made comments about their behavior in international politics.

Extending Will's Analysis

Will's analysis of Chang's argumentative technique is illuminating and would seem to be adequate in light of many of Chang's statements in the UN about the UDHR.[74] Even so, a few additions and corrections are in order.

The first, complementary point can be exemplified in two different ways. First, it can be said that intercultural unity becomes achievable and reasonable when an ethical opinion can be justified by means of—or is compatible with—different views of humanity. Article 1 offers an example: "All human beings are born free and equal in dignity and rights. They are endowed with reason and conscience and should act towards one another in a spirit of brotherhood." Chang was greatly interested in this article because it was a key one, that is to say an article that asserted the UN Declaration's view of humanity in an overarching fashion. Chang argued that the idea of human beings as autonomous, rational, and morally aware beings in this article was compatible with the concept of God, and thus compatible with different theistic traditions, since the concept of God placed a specific emphasis upon the so-called human aspects of human beings. It was not necessary for the article to refer to human beings as having been created in God's image, as had been claimed by the Brazilian delegate Austregésilo de Athayde and others.[75] Chang also assumed that this notion of human qualities was compatible with how secular humanist traditions viewed humanity.

Chang's argumentative strategy here is strongly reminiscent of John Rawls's idea of *overlapping consensus*. On the basis of this idea, Rawls contended, one can argue for religious tolerance, for instance, using a range of different philosophical starting points: partly from the Protestant concept of faith, which emphasizes that inner religious conviction must be genuine and not compelled, and partly from liberal notions of human freedoms, in which freedom of religion is regarded as a fundamental freedom.[76] Like Rawls, Chang allowed disunity over the justification for ethical principles—such as human rights—in order to achieve as broad a consensus as possible on the UDHR.[77]

Second, it can be said that Chang allowed the UDHR to be open and inclusive with regard to different metaphysical concepts. The document could potentially speak to everyone so long as it allowed for each person's own metaphysical and philosophical assumptions. Returning to Article 1, it might be argued that "endowed with" reason and conscience—the latter, in Chang's terminology, "sympathy for others," or, in Chinese, *lianqxin*—could be complemented with different views of reality. In this way, the door was left open for "by God," "by nature," "by chance," and so forth, without the necessity of specifying a particular metaphysical basis for human beings' rational and social empathetic capacities. For Chang, it thus became important that the

UN Declaration contained no concepts of a metaphysical nature that made the document acceptable solely to certain philosophical or cultural traditions. Such concepts also actualized questions that were insoluble for human reason. Here Chang's thinking recalls Rawls's argument that a theory of justice cannot be based on "comprehensive conceptions of the good" or inscrutable metaphysical standpoints.

We might also include on Chang's list of intercultural strategies his ideas about the primary function of the UDHR. As already noted, Chang saw this function as being to humanize humanity or "raise the moral stature of man." In view of humanity's experiences in recent years, Chang argued, it was necessary that the preamble emphasize that which differentiated human beings from animals and that it safeguard the dignity of human beings in this respect. In his moral-pedagogical project, it was unnecessary to refer to any "explanatory metaphysical concepts" since these were irrelevant to the purpose of the document. The great challenge of the UDHR, to deal with human beings' brutality toward other human beings, was connected to this moral-pedagogical function. For Chang, this challenge was one of the most serious that humanity had faced during its history. Presumably it was for this reason that he argued that the attempt to meet this challenge represented an ethical common denominator for all those for whom the UDHR was intended.

The UN Declaration—The Result of Compromise?

The literature on the UDHR describes it as the product of an international compromise. Yet the word "compromise" sometimes has a negative connotation since it carries associations of cowardice and submissiveness. On this view, someone who compromises is vulnerable to accusations of being spineless and failing to fight for their beliefs. The Spanish philosopher George Santayana (1863–1952), whom Peng mentioned in his conversations with Stanley, articulates a common attitude toward compromises: "Compromises are repugnant to passionate people because they can be seen as defeats, and they are repugnant to intellectuals because they look like confusion."[78] Santayana's view of the negative value of compromises is open to question, however. The key issue is what the compromises are about. In certain situations, a compromise may well be the most reasonable solution. In our everyday lives, too, we are always having to adapt our interests to each other in order to reach negotiated settlements. On other occasions, however, compromise can be the expression of submissiveness when it involves the repeated abandonment of our deepest convictions. Realizing the UDHR was a highly complicated project, from early on several of the delegates had to learn the art of give and take, even when it came to deeply cherished beliefs.

It was also the first time that a global rights document of this kind had been drafted with the individual at its center—and this, moreover, at a highly charged moment and with delegates from quite different cultural and political traditions. As noted earlier, it is clear that people with a tendency toward compromise can sometimes give voice to a fear and an unwillingness to stand up for their ideals. In many cases, however, a willingness to compromise can give rise to "ideal solutions." If both parties champion unrealistic and narrow-minded proposals, compromises can turn out to be the golden mean.

Chang, as noted, has been described in the literature on the UDHR as the master of compromise, in the positive sense of the word. Helped by his personal style, including his fondness for humor, his ready ability to find equivalents for concepts taken from different traditions, and his overarching strategy for the UDHR—that the document should be an instrument of moral education—Chang succeeded in dismantling ostensibly insurmountable obstacles to negotiation. A representative assessment of Chang is offered by his colleague John Humphrey: "He was a master of the art of compromise and, under cover of a quotation from Confucius, would often provide the formula which made it possible for the commission to escape from some impasse."[79]

What does compromise mean under such circumstances? One relevant and neutral sense of the word is that both parties must give up something in order to gain something new and valuable.[80] This sense of a compromise is limited insofar as a compromise can also cover situations in which neither party gains anything new but both are forced to give up something in order to gain anything at all. In the present context, however, the first sense of the word is adequate.

All parties to the creation of the UDHR had something very substantial to gain, namely a document that would promote peace and order in the world and prevent human beings behaving brutally toward one another. To this end, it was thus vital that the UDHR be a universal, inclusive, and religiously neutral document. In other words, the secularism that has often been associated with the document had more to do with pragmatism and a spirit of compromise than with any critical, Western view of religion with roots in Enlightenment thinking. Chang, who was agnostically inclined, also believed that religion and metaphysics applied to questions that exceeded the capacities of human reason.

The UN Declaration was also meant to be simple to understand and easily applicable to the moral-pedagogical project of *humanizing* humanity. Given these ambitions, it was necessary for several of the delegates to accept that some cherished religious or metaphysical ideas would not find their way into the UDHR. Accordingly, impartiality and a willingness to remove more culturally specific elements were required. Moreover, Chang focused on concepts such as equality, respect for human dignity, and the right not to be discriminated against, as well as on *pluralistic tolerance* and freedom of religion, all of which pointed toward universality and broadly impartial involvement in the document's creation.

An important question is, of course, whether all parties viewed the compromises as reasonable and just to the same degree. Some parties perhaps had to sacrifice more than others and might thus feel that the compromises had not been equal in kind. In other words, it was perhaps not possible to realize fully the goal of regarding all parties' metaphysical and religious convictions as compatible with the contents of the document.

In the case of Article 1 and the clause "endowed with reason and conscience," the removal of the words "by God" and "by nature" can be regarded as an impartial proposal insofar as both theists and materialists were forced to tone down their metaphysical assumptions equally. Chang interpreted "by nature" in a materialist sense and counterposed this phrase to a religious doctrine of creation. This can be problematized, of course, if one holds that "by nature" can also be understood in nonmaterialist terms, surely a reasonable assumption. "Endowed with" can also be considered a more or less successful compromise solution in comparison with "created with," since both theists and materialists can accept the first formulation, while the latter is acceptable only to theists. According to Chang, by including the clause "in a spirit of brotherhood," Article 1 also finds a balance between an emphasis on individual interests and an emphasis on more collective interests and duties to one's fellow human beings.

Introduction of the concept of a free, rational, independent being in Article 1 also had to resonate with a number of the delegates in a manner that would be felt to be reasonable and impartial. The concepts seem also to be compatible with a theistic conception of God, as Chang claims. For many Christians, however, it is the idea that human beings have been created in God's image that makes human value sacred, absolute, and inviolable. Removal of this reference thus risks reducing the powerfully normative perspective of Article 1 in the eyes of Christians. This is a general criticism that can be leveled at those authors who sought to remove all religious references from the UDHR.[81] At the same time, these must be weighed against the desire of nonreligious parties to ensure that the UDHR bore no traces of religious influence. Chang's preference for the concept "a rational being with conscience" was thus a reasonable compromise insofar as these concepts could be accepted by both religious and nonreligious delegates.

As regards the attitude of different religions toward Article 1, Chang limited his perspective to religions or conceptions of the divine that resembled those of theism. From the perspective of those other religions that articulate a more hierarchical view of humanity—or presuppose the existence of more than one god, or no god at all, as understood by the theistic faiths—it is unclear whether the religion in question has any closer relationship to the concepts of freedom, rationality, and independence as the salient properties of a human being.

For a philosophy that seeks to formulate rules for the art of living but not to formulate a metaphysical system, the UDHR's lack of obvious metaphysical assumptions is attractive. A Confucian philosophy thus lies very close to the UDHR since its primary focus is the art of living rather than metaphysical questions. Chang was also a driving force in the drafting process and clearly had very fixed views on the direction that the work on the UDHR should take. Taking religious neutrality as its starting point and with a focus on ethics instead of metaphysics, the document acquired properties that accorded well with Chang's own philosophical outlook.

It was therefore decisive for the broad acceptance of Article 1 that the various parties felt that they did not need to put brackets around too much of their own private or culturally specific convictions. While they might perhaps view the proposed formulation as according only imperfectly with their fundamental beliefs, they nonetheless saw that the document had certain valuable attributes that could compensate for the absence of their "full" metaphysical convictions. Achieving this balance was no easy task, however, especially when the representatives of certain religions maintained that religion and its truths ought to take priority over scientific rationales and over concepts such as religious neutrality.

Chang did not focus solely on compromises and other constructive solutions to issues relating to the formulation and understanding of the major articles of the UDHR, such as Article 1. He was also focused on highly concrete wordings—which, needless to say, also had far-reaching implications, depending on the article in question. An illustrative example is offered by Article 2, the so-called antidiscrimination article, which forbade discrimination on the basis of factors such as sex, nationality, and property.[82] The Soviet delegates wanted to add social status according to property. For their part, the delegates from the United Kingdom wanted to delete the word "property" since the word "status," as they saw it, already covered property. Chang therefore proposed "property or other status." The Soviet Union also wanted to include class, something that the United States opposed. Chang replied that class, too, was covered by "or other status." This suggestion was subsequently accepted. All of this shows the commitment that Chang brought to the task of making the UN Declaration a document that most of the delegates could accept.

Chang also tried to reconcile positions that at first glance seemed to be far apart. Concerning Article 27, which dealt with the right to culture, Chang stressed that the protection of art or culture in its original form fulfilled the interest of both the individual artist and for mankind as a whole. In other words, it is in the interest of everyone to protect "the integrity" of the creation.

CHAPTER 9

Chang's Triumphs, Defeats, and "Blind Spots"

What, then, were Chang's most obvious triumphs and defeats with the UDHR? When referring to the triumphs and defeats that resulted from his various proposals or formulations for articles, we may have one of two things in mind. First, those articles of formulations that Chang himself authored or was principally responsible for. Second, more generally, those articles that he supported—regardless of whether he had authored them—and how they were received during the final drafting phase of the UN Declaration.

If we ask the question of whether Chang truly succeeded with regard to the content of the UDHR, a fairly clear image appears. In most cases— particularly those which we might call significant for the UDHR—Chang got his way. He sought continually to ensure that the document was universal and religiously neutral, and in this respect he can be said to have largely succeeded. As several colleagues, including Charles Malik, came to realize, Chang maintained a hawklike vigilance against formulations that could potentially be interpreted in religious or philosophical terms, and he struck down every attempt to smuggle them into individual articles. His pragmatic and agnostic outlook meant that his primary focus was on a rights ethic that could be accepted by people of almost any faith.

Chang was anxious that the authors of the UDHR should not spend too much time on abstract philosophical expositions with regard to the concept of human rights or metaphysical ideas related to the concept. He repeatedly made reference to the rights legacy that had already been formulated by the Enlightenment philosophers of the eighteenth century and to the ideas about rights that had found expression in declarations about human rights such as the French Declaration of the Rights of Man and of the Citizen. It was there, he believed, that modern conceptions of human rights had originated.

In this context, it is interesting to note that, according to Chang, some of these ideas had partly originated in China. The questioning of absolute sovereign power and feudalism in China had inspired Voltaire, among others, to reevaluate political relations in his own country.[1] One indirect consequence of Chang's insistence on excluding metaphysical concepts was also that the UDHR increasingly came to resemble a document whose fundamental concepts chimed well with the ideas of Confucianism. The latter included the view that "the art of living" is more important than speculations about metaphysics and questions about reality in its entirety. Accordingly, it seems clear that Chang did not compromise his fundamental convictions. If we assume that his primary goal with the UDHR was to humanize humanity and for the document to contain an art of living rather than a metaphysics, he was largely successful in imposing his will.

And yet, in referring to human beings as free, sensible, and morally conscious beings that differ in kind from animals, Chang showed that he could not manage without at least a "thin" metaphysics or philosophical anthropology. In this context, as we have already seen, he introduced the core concept of *ren* (two-man-mindedness) or sympathy for others, although this was inadequately translated in Article 1 as "conscience."

For the preamble, Chang thus emphasized the necessity of including the words "respect for other human beings' dignity" and of highlighting the profound difference between humans and animals. For instance, he talked about the respect that should be shown to human beings at "the human level."[2] One of Chang's most important contributions was that he took very seriously the problem of inhumanity towards one's fellow humans. The primary point of departure for the drafting of the UDHR was that human beings have a good, human side that should overshadow their brutish animal side. What is more, the purpose of every kind of social and political education was, in the first instance, the voluntary acknowledgement of other people's rights, not the imposition of various laws and restrictions. In addition, Chang wanted the preamble to include references to Franklin D. Roosevelt's freedoms, a request with which the Commission on Human Rights complied—unsurprisingly, given that its chairman was Eleanor Roosevelt (and also because of its reasonableness).[3]

Chang was jointly responsible for several key articles in the declaration, such as the right to education, the anti-discrimination article, the right to freedom of religion, the right to an adequate standard of living, and the right to a rich and flourishing cultural life. He was also a driving force behind the foregrounding of duties or obligations in the declaration, securing the emphasis upon brotherhood in Article 1, and the reference to individuals' responsibilities toward both each other and society in large in Article 29. Moreover, he was actively engaged in the disposition of the declaration, as is attested by the location of duties in the penultimate article: "Everyone has duties to the community in which alone the free and full development of his personality is possible." According to Chang, it was logical that the declaration should mention duties only after it had enumerated all the rights. The introductory Articles 1 and 2 were fundamental to the whole declaration. For this reason, it was not desirable that the concept of duty be introduced at the start of the UN Declaration, since human rights were to occupy center stage in the declaration's opening section.

Chang was also on the winning side of the debate over the realization of an international bill of rights. The idea, which subsequently became a reality, was that the General Assembly should first pass the text of the declaration and only then—when the time was felt to be right—the texts of the various Conventions.

In summary, it could be argued that Chang played a key role in the final formulation of the contents of the UDHR. Chang was involved in practically all of its central articles and their defining attributes. His contributions are also regarded as extremely valuable by many commentators today. The qualities of universality and religious neutrality have made the UN Declaration extraordinarily effective in the world, particularly in societal debates. Chang's broad conception of what constitute human rights—that they should include civil, political, socioeconomic, and cultural rights—is also a highly valued approach in many parts of the world today, even if some neoliberal critics now argue that human rights ought to have a narrower scope.

We noted earlier a congruence between the document and Chang's main ideas and intentions. Universality, religious neutrality, a broad conception of rights, a balance between individual rights and duties and an instructive style—Chang helped to ensure that all these characteristics became part of the document. What is more, he did so with only minimal compromising of his own Chinese cultural heritage.

Chang's Defeats in the UDHR Drafting

However, Chang did not get his way with regard to the introduction to the declaration and the formulation of a number of articles. Some of these defeats were more unfortunate than others. Among the proposals of Chang's that were not ultimately accepted was the right to petition, a particularly significant defeat since this right was especially valued and could trace its roots back to England's Magna Carta of 1215. Although Chang had proposed this right during the drafting committee's first session, it did not find its way into the final version of the UDHR. In the second session, the proposal had also been supported by Cuba and France. One reason why the majority of states objected to the inclusion of such a right in the declaration was that they identified a lack of clarity about what the scope of such a right might be, that is to say what kinds of petitions could be made. If such a right could also be asserted with regard to the UN or some international court, critics argued, national courts could conceivably become subject to an international rule of law that had not yet been properly developed.

Another of Chang's ideas that fell on deaf ears was the right to employment in the civil service by means of examination. He argued that such a right, given the fact that more societal functions were becoming more public in nature, could serve as a means of achieving a more complete democracy. Just as representative parliamentary rule could be seen as the realization of the democratic form of government, so might this method be viewed as a way to achieve democracy in society more generally. His thought was that the selection of candidates for these posts on the basis of merit might widen the social basis of such key public positions, in contrast to selection on the basis of social origin and contacts. According to Chang, this kind of selective system had existed in China ever since the days of the Han dynasty. Article 18 of the new Chinese Constitution of 1946 also contained such a right, namely the right to be examined for consideration for employment by the state.[4]

The objection to Chang's proposal was that the right being proposed was more of a concrete measure than a universally applicable right. Moreover, the Soviet delegates felt that this proposal would encourage socially skewed recruiting practices since only a limited proportion of the population had the education required in order to be able to succeed in this kind of examination. A key question that should also be asked is whether Chang's idea of a right to meritocratic selection criteria for civil servants was really more about states realizing the rule of law and administrative justice than the promotion of democracy. Chang's proposal emphasizes the importance of choosing people for civil service appointments on the basis of relevant evaluative criteria, which, for him, meant particular merits or expertise. The proposal thus sought to achieve justice—and nondiscrimination—by preventing nepotism. Chang deserves credit for recognizing that these objectives are of a general nature and that they could thus justify their inclusion in a rights declaration. In such cases, rights could perhaps have been formulated in a more general fashion, for example, "the right to be evaluated on the basis of criteria relevant to civil service appointments."

While several of Chang's ideas about the preamble to the declaration did find a hearing—such as his views on respect for human dignity—his proposal to remove metaphysical terms such as "inalienable" or "innate" did not find a sympathetic audience. This is perhaps not a source of regret for many people today. To be sure, Chang was right that these expressions "reek" of metaphysics. He was, as already noted, extremely insistent about removing from the UDHR every kind of metaphysical reference that could be given a theistic or natural rights slant. At the same time, there was a desire on the part of many delegates to give real weight to human rights in the declaration. These were neither conditional nor subject to compromise or horse trading. Using formulations such as rights being "innate" or "inalienable" was thus a way to give voice to this strongly moralistic attitude.

Although Chang was also opposed to the inclusion of the word "born" in Article 1, it was ultimately retained. The article reads: "All human beings are born free and equal in dignity and rights. They are endowed with reason and conscience and should act towards one another in a spirit of brotherhood." Chang believed that it would be best if the drafters of the declaration began with a clean slate, rather than working from the premise that human beings were originally good. This attitude contrasted sharply with the ideas of the Enlightenment philosopher Jean-Jacques Rousseau that human beings were born good.[5] At the same time, Chang himself argued that human beings had both a good and a brutal side, something that seems to contradict his statement that the drafters of the UDHR should "start with a clean slate" when describing human nature. Chang can perhaps be interpreted as arguing that the drafters of the UDHR should not commit themselves to a fixed view on human nature by virtue of having chosen terms such as "born with." In other words, the issue of whether human beings are predisposed to goodness or evil is something that requires further discussion and analysis.

Eleanor Roosevelt's and Chang's proposal to remove the word "alone" in Article 29:1 also failed to secure majority approval: "Everyone has duties to the community in which *alone* the free and full development of his personality is possible" (emphasis added).[6] Doubtless they wished to remove the word "alone" in order to keep the door open for a plurality of communities, not merely that society or cultural tradition in which a human being is born and raised. Reading between the lines, one discerns here a liberal perspective on human beings as capable of development or as receiving their identity through a range of differing life choices.

Chang was also unsuccessful in his efforts to push for a shorter declaration comprising only ten articles, something the Chinese delegation had argued for.[7] He had also stated that he wished the text of the UDHR to have no more than twenty articles. Nonetheless, a number of formulations in the Chinese text served as inspirations for the final UN Declaration, for example, Article 20: "Everyone has the right to freedom of peaceful assembly and association." The short Chinese text was characterized by concise formulations with very few illustrations and concrete examples. Chang was also against the right to paid vacation (Article 24) being included in the declaration, because he saw it as far too concrete a proposal to be included in a declaration of this kind. On this issue Chang was also forced to concede.

Yet examination of Chang's interventions during the work on the UN Declaration reveals that on several occasions he pushed for a greater degree of concretization. The critical question is thus to what degree China's shorter declaration squares with Chang's more overarching ideas about the content of the UDHR. For example, the phrase "freedom of religion" does not appear in the declaration proposed by the Chinese delegation, which instead refers only to freedom of conscience or belief. However, Chang lobbied for the concept of religion to be included in the UN Declaration on the grounds that one could not be too explicit with regard to bringing the document's contents and message to as many people as possible. In this particular context, in other words, there was virtue in seeking concretization rather than generalization. In the case of socioeconomic rights, Chang was also clearly inclined to speak in concrete terms such as the need for food, clothes, and lodging, since these problems are extremely acute for a large part of the world's population. The fact that the degree of concretization of the articles was determined on a case-by-case basis may account for Chang's remarks in this respect.

Chang's Blind Spots and Moral Limitations

The impression given is thus that Chang was progressive in official contexts with regard to human rights, and a number of commentators have tended to describe him as a social liberal in the broad sense of the term. A memo from the US State Department in 1947 notes that "Chang is one of China's leading liberals . . . probably not a member of the Kuomintang and in any case not active in the party."[8] In light of Chang's poor relationship with the Chinese delegation and his attitude toward Chiang Kai-shek, the statement seems warranted. Chang had been influenced by liberal attitudes in a number of ways with regard to the relationship between citizens and the state. Stanley Chang has also confirmed that his father was not a member of the Kuomintang. Peng Chun Chang also resigned from his post as a representative for China in the UN when the Kuomintang government moved to Formosa after the civil war. It will be recalled that the main reason for his resignation was that he thought "the new regime" undemocratic.

It is an interesting question whether Chang ever voiced opinions that did not square with his various statements in connection with the drafting of the UDHR. In other words, did he ever make any eye-opening assertions that would be hard to reconcile with his passionate involvement in the cause of human rights? For instance, did Chang defend any Chinese customs that others would have considered inhumane? How did Chang behave on the issue of human rights in daily life? Stanley recalled: "My father was far from perfect. He was prejudiced about many things. I often wonder how he managed to reconcile everything that was inside him with his public appearance. He once said to my brother, 'Why should you have a happy life when I haven't?' My brother's comment about our father was made when we were both undergraduates. When my father spoke about having had a bad life, I am sure he meant the beatings he got from Uncle Poling." We should remember that Chang grew up in a time of historic upheaval in China and that he was influenced by a number of traditions and different circumstances during his upbringing. He evinced no particular interest in the rights of women or minorities, at least not within the framework of the UN Declaration. The former—women's rights was something that Roosevelt and the Indian delegate Hansa Mehta, for example, were deeply involved in. Charles Malik's involvement, too, extended to rights for minorities. It is obvious that Chang was influenced by a traditionally patriarchal family ideal, one that remains characteristic of social life in China despite campaigns in the early twentieth century such as the May Fourth Movement.[9] He also had a "Centralist" attitude, which held that (majority) Chinese culture was superior to many other cultures.[10]

There is also one example of Chang defending a Chinese custom that many people have regarded as inhumane, namely *Mui Tsai* (Cantonese for "little sister"). In his journal entry for 18 July 1949 in Geneva, John Humphrey described a breakfast meeting with Chang at which they discussed *Mui Tsai*. The British delegation had described this practice as forced slave labor, something that deeply irritated Chang, who instead felt that it could be described as a form of adoption. However, Chang's statement to Humphrey about *Mui Tsai* does not reveal precisely how he viewed this practice. Whatever the case, it was not, as far as he was concerned, a question of slavery.[11]

The debate over *Mui Tsai* is interesting insofar as it illustrates how even the most fundamental rights in the UDHR, such as the right not to be subjected to slavery—which has also become *ius cogens*, or international common law—could give rise to very different interpretations and problems of delimitation among the delegates.

The issue of slavery in China has also been a controversial subject for a long time and it is not entirely clear whether slavery in various forms was practiced in China during certain periods. According to a very strict definition of slavery—people treated as cattle to be bought and sold—China for very long periods of time did not tolerate slavery. According to the sinologist Willard J. Peterson, however, slavery as a concept encompasses other practices, a number of which were exemplified in China for several centuries.[12] If slavery is taken to include forced servitude requiring labor, regardless of whether this was the result of a court verdict or a commercial transaction—parents selling their children into indentured labor—then China did indeed tolerate it for extended periods. If slavery is taken to mean that individuals can be born into a subordinate status of this kind in consequence of their mother's status, then China also exemplified this practice until at least 1950. In the eighteenth century, Chinese governments devised laws intended to liberate children born to those living in such slave-like circumstances, which indicates that there clearly were people who were not free. If these people were given the same surname as members of the family that they served, this did not really change their status or conditions of life.

According to Peterson, however, it was this latter state to which Chang was most likely referring when he said that they were adopted. These individuals were members of a family but had no possibility of leaving that family, marrying someone of their choosing, or having the legal status of free people. In effect, they were indentured servants, not employees who could leave their family whenever they wished. One may well ask to what extent Chang allowed his cultural frame of reference and his nationalism to affect his judgment on this urgent question. There can be no doubt that on certain issues, despite his universalistic and cosmopolitan ambitions for the UDHR, he was deeply influenced by his Chinese background. From a human rights perspective, however, it was highly problematic that Chang defended *Mui Tsai* as a form of adoption.

In private, Chang clearly voiced his loyalty to Chinese traditions in a way that today would unquestionably be regarded as traditional and old-fashioned. Stanley relates that when his brother Chen Chung decided to marry Marjorie, an American, in 1951—something Peng Chun Chang deeply disliked because it would break the Chinese bloodline—his father quoted Confucius in support of his position: "You children must maintain Chinese traditions and Chinese culture. According to Confucius, there can only be peace and prosperity if order prevails. Everyone has their particular role. The Emperor can only rule if he treats the people justly and benevolently. For their part, the people must follow the rules that come from antiquity."

In other words, Chang was completely opposed to interracial marriages and wanted his children to marry people from China. Stanley thought it was strange that his father could hold this view in light of the fact that he had helped to write the UN Declaration, one of whose articles stipulates the right to marry a person of one's own choosing (Article 16). According to Stanley, this was the only answer that his father gave: "How could your brother maintain Chinese traditions? And what about our family history? We are Nan-Kai!" When his brother married Marjorie in California, neither their father nor mother came to the wedding. It may be that Chang's nationalist Chinese attitude caused him to worry about how the Second World War had served to split up so many families in China and undermine their traditional rituals.[13] As has been noted, Stanley also came in for criticism from his father in relation to his own marriage, despite the fact that he had chosen to marry a Chinese woman. Chang was firmly opposed to the marriage. (However, Stanley's brother Chen Chung and his wife Marjorie later visited the family in Nutley during the fall of 1952. As Stanley put it: "Time heals all wounds. Finally my father was able to reconcile himself with the facts of life as they were. Neither he nor my mother fully accepted my brother's wife, but they were civil towards her and treated her without malice.")

In his earlier writings, Chang had also expressed his appreciation of a more traditional family ideal. It was an ideal that subordinated the individual wishes of its members to the family's best, above all with the care of the elderly taking center stage. As a result of increased mobility, the growth of individualism, and a cult of youth in an economy now being subjected to market forces, the traditional family structure had been shattered, Chang believed, resulting in ever fewer family units. In a piece written in 1934, Chang also voiced his appreciation for arranged marriages based on the careful deliberations of wise parents. He cited approvingly that "in the old family system marriage was above all arranged by parents. Wise parents identified which circumstances were most beneficial for the children's happiness and their grandchildren's wellbeing. To be sure, there were many examples of unhappy marriages but those individuals had been brought up to suppress their own feelings in order to adapt socially."[14]

This text was included in an early version of Chang's book *China at the Crossroads*. Yet this quotation was omitted from the later edition of the book.[15] Chang, who evidently married entirely in accordance with his own wishes, was thus fully determined to exert an influence on his children's choice of spouse. As we recall from Chapter 1, Chang also wrote a play "The New Order Cometh" in 1915, which expressed an appreciation for a more modern form of marriage based upon romantic love.

Another illustration of Chang's family ideal was his prioritizing of his eldest son Chen Chung over his younger son and his daughters. According to Stanley, there was no question but that their father treated the eldest son completely differently. Stanley related that when his elder brother was applying to college in the United States, his parents encouraged him and accompanied him on campus visits to Harvard and elsewhere. They were also very happy and encouraging when Chen Chung got into Harvard. When it was Stanley's turn to apply to college, he did not receive the same encouragement from his parents, who initially also failed to give him any practical assistance. For instance, Stanley applied to various Ivy League schools but without success. Afterward, however, his father helped him to get into Purdue University, where one of his father's friends was employed.

When Stanley applied to graduate school at Harvard in the 1950s and was accepted, his father was not in the least pleased. The response he got was, "Are you an elitist?" According to Stanley, his father was more concerned that he should stay at home and help him with the house in Nutley. However, Stanley also recalled the following events: "In 1949, my father and I went to my brother's graduation at Harvard. My father read my brother's diary and I did nothing to stop him. Later, when I told this fact to my brother, he was furious and told me he would have stopped our father if it was my diary he had been reading.... In the summer of 1950, when my brother was courting his girlfriend Marjorie, I spent many days arguing with my father about the question of marriage to an American girl. It was my way of repaying my brother for what I had failed to do when my father read his diary."

As already mentioned, Peng Chun Chang was not significantly involved in the care and upbringing of the eldest child, his disabled daughter Ming-Ming. Her principal support would be her mother and her siblings, particularly Stanley. Stanley went so far as to say that his father continually kept Ming-Ming at arm's length. He also related that his father was careful to emphasize the Confucian ideals that describe the responsibility of each person to do their best on the basis of their particular position in life. During their time in Turkey, both sons were encouraged by their father to learn the Confucian rules for living. According to Stanley, Chang also manifested an elitist attitude toward people around him, speaking more naturally and relaxedly with those he regarded as being of his social station. His upbringing in a society clearly marked by different class and social hierarchies is amply evident here.

It is interesting to note that in his various statements as educator, philosopher, author, director, and diplomat—particularly within the UN system—Chang mostly articulated what we even now would call progressive and liberal views, views that reflected common perceptions of human rights. The great exception, however, were the so-called family issues in which Chang in very explicit fashion defended old Chinese traditions, a defense that directly clashed with his otherwise liberal statements. He was clearly deeply affected by the traditional Chinese family structure and its openly patriarchal aspects. Nonetheless, he was a champion of rights for orphans, whose existence was a painful reality in China following the Second World War and the war with Japan.

The traditional patriarchal family ideal has occupied a central place in Chinese culture throughout history and down to the present day. According to this ideal, a father should always remain the head of the family and the eldest son his "prince regent." It is therefore not strange that Peng Chun Chang should have been affected by this ideal given that he—unlike his own children, who had grown up in the West—had been formed by domestic Chinese family traditions. To be sure, there had been a number of reforms in the twentieth century, such as the outlawing of binding women's feet in the 1920s. Particularly in the big cities during the period of the republic, women had also found new avenues for education and employment as well as more general freedoms. Although the Nationalist Party—the Kuomintang—had in fact done very little to change traditional gender roles, the party accepted, in theory at least, that women had the same civil rights as men. In Mao Zedong's time, attempts were also made to change the Chinese family ideal, though the challenge proved to be almost insurmountable. It is true that educational opportunities for women improved in the 1950s, particularly in medicine and teacher training, but a number of features of the traditional Chinese family ideal nonetheless lived on in many parts of the country.[16]

More generally, it is fair to say that the family, gender roles, and sexuality are particularly explosive issues in the world today, particularly when these issues are discussed in relation to religious views. In other words, the most divisive issues in many pluralistic societies today are ethical questions relating to family life in civil society, not questions relating to liberal democracy, rule of law, and the legality of state governance.[17] Chang's attitude was thus hardly unusual for his time, nor indeed would it be in today's world.

Chang's Relation to China and Its Cultural Traditions

Most of the delegates involved in drafting the UDHR experienced an obvious tension between their identification with their native cultural traditions and the project of creating a document with intercultural and universal ideals. This was particularly true of Chang, as we have remarked. The challenge mentioned earlier, "to find unity in diversity," is related to this challenge. How could all these delegates, each with a starting point in their own national traditions, come up with ethical common denominators?

In all his arguments over the UDHR and also in his earlier writings and lectures, Chang was highly appreciative of his native country and Chinese traditions, which resulted in an uncritical attitude toward some of its customary practices. He was in many respects an obvious Chinese nationalist who directed criticism outward, toward the European colonial powers and Japan. Chang's upbringing, education, and professional engagement in the Nankai Schools, which was a focal point of Chinese nationalism during the period of the republic, may also explain his nationalist fervor. According to Stanley, his father was deeply influenced by what can be called a Middle Kingdom attitude (or a "Centralist attitude")—that is to say, that other countries lay to the west, east, north, and south of China—and he revealed this in different ways in his encounters with people from other countries.

In other words, even though Chang strove to make the UDHR a universal and religiously neutral document, his deep identification with and appreciation for all things Chinese became apparent on many occasions during debates at the UN. In his arguments for the content of certain articles, he also referred to what he believed were universally applicable Chinese insights from which other countries had much to learn. As already noted, he made frequent use of quotations from Chinese philosophers such as Confucius and Mencius.

One may ask how much Chang himself really needed to compromise with regard to his fundamental convictions and deep identification with China's cultural heritage. To oversimplify somewhat, we might say that Chang articulated *four* strategies in the context of harmonizing his deep identification with and affection for his country and its traditions, and the universal project of the UDHR and its "new" rights articles.

First, Chang asserted that Chinese philosophy—and, more specifically, Confucius—was primarily directed toward the art of living, not metaphysical speculations. Keeping the UDHR free of explicitly metaphysical components was thus entirely in keeping with a "Chinese or Confucian starting point." The UN Declaration primarily contained ethical concepts of rights and duties. By contrast, the rhetoric of rights itself had no obvious historical counterpart in Chinese tradition. However, Chang associated these rights very closely with the moral maturity of humanity and its awareness of its duties, a device by which the UDHR acquired a clearer correspondence with elements of Chinese philosophy. In sum, Chang made a virtue of necessity: the absence of metaphysics opened the door to ethics and "the art of living, Confucius-style" becoming the defining features of the UN Declaration.

Second, Chang campaigned for a "thin metaphysics" as presupposed by the document's reference to human beings as free, rational, and compassionate creatures. For Chang, the UDHR's primary function was also to humanize humanity. It was inevitable that so morally pedagogical a project would proceed from certain philosophical-anthropological assumptions regarding human nature, such as the human capacity for sympathy with others. This project was also something that fit well with Chinese ethical traditions.

Third, as noted already, Chang pointed out that a number of insights which clearly had a Chinese origin–such as *ren*, or the importance of sympathy with one's fellow human beings—also had considerable universal applicability and that the document would benefit from their inclusion.

Fourth—and following on from this—Chang argued that insights which ostensibly originated in Western culture, such as Enlightenment notions of rights, in fact contained elements that had originated in China. Like antifeudalism, the widespread understanding of the right to revolt against an unjust absolute sovereign had its roots in Chinese philosophy and attitudes. Time and again, Chang took pains to underscore that French Enlightenment philosophers such as Voltaire had read the writings of Confucius and that the latter had affected their thinking.

To summarize, Chang's points of departure as regards the content, disposition, and functions of the UDHR closely followed in the traditions of Chinese philosophy, which did not have the same kind of explicitly metaphysical premises as Christianity and other natural rights philosophies. Chang had thus not been forced to compromise on a number of his fundamental convictions when the UDHR was approved by the UN General Assembly.

Stanley, too, has often reflected on Chang's zealous advocacy, in more or less reasonable ways, of his Chinese cultural inheritance:

> As for my father's private moments, there were many occasions when he was capable of saying things to my mother (never to me!) that made me wonder how he could hide these feelings from the rest of the world. But he was very cautious in what he said in official settings. He was prejudiced against everyone who did not have Chinese roots. For him, China was the centre of the world. According to my father, the philosophies created by the ancient Chinese philosophers, which had been passed on down through the generations, constituted the only true and right model for ruling a great country.[18]

Conclusion

Peng Chun Chang can in many respects be described as a cultural mediator between his own country, China—or, more precisely, his region—and the West, principally Europe and the United States. Both cultural movements—from the West to China, and from China to the West—shaped Chang's life to varying degrees but with particular force during certain periods. In the 1910s, he had a so-called period of immersion in which he dedicated himself through study at American universities to deepening and broadening his knowledge of Western intellectual traditions, in addition to gaining field-specific knowledge. As a student in the United States, he was also actively involved in Christian student groups, an interest that seems subsequently to have evaporated. At the same time, he became involved in the political and cultural condition of his native country, in part through theatrical productions with an overtly socio-political theme.

Cultural Mediation Between East and West in Both Directions

For much of the 1920s in particular, Chang sought to spread ideas from the West to China—in particular through pedagogical ideas, science, literature, and theater. In the 1930s, by contrast, he focused intensively upon presenting China to the outside world, including how it had historically viewed the West, and upon Western relations with China. He was keen to spread knowledge of Chinese history and China's cultural life, and he pointed out that for much of its long history, China had been a pioneer in different fields and more advanced both materially and culturally than large parts of the Western world. In the 1930s, Chang evinced a desire to communicate the reality of the situation then facing China, a situation largely defined by the ongoing war with Japan. During this decade he shuttled between China, Europe, and the United States, trying in various ways to mobilize support for China among the Western powers.

Chang had fixed views on what constituted "good" or "bad" intercultural communication, as he did on "good" or "bad" cultural exchanges. Good cultural communication showed respect for domestic traditions, neither slavishly imitating ideas from without nor rejecting them out of hand. Chang's cultural mediation expressed itself in a number of different ways. For certain periods, he was active as a lecturer at various organizations and universities, particularly during his time in the United States. At other times, particularly in the 1920s, he sought to implement ideas from the West (mainly from the United States) in projects in China with which he was involved, particularly in schools and universities. He also wrote articles and books intended to convey ideas and experiences from the West to China and, in similar fashion, from China to the West. He translated books of Chinese poetry into English.[1] While a diplomat in Turkey, he evinced a keen interest in the relation between Chinese culture and Islam and Arabic cultural patterns.[2]

From having worked primarily in a bilateral mode along these two separate axes, Chang became involved in increasingly multilateral fashion during the mid-1940s after he joined the UN's drafting team for the UDHR. On several counts Chang's life can be thought of as a journey whose apex—writing the UDHR—was the largely unforeseen outcome of his preceding activities. One might say that "things fell into place" in the mid-1940s as Chang's previous attainments turned out to be key qualifications for the great task of helping to write the UN Declaration. His cosmopolitan life, wide-ranging educational background, teaching skills, stylistic facility, his background in theatre and performance and interest in cross-cultural encounter were obviously relevant for the discussion and drafting of this document.

In this book I have sought to show that Chang's role in the drafting of the UDHR was critical in a number of regards. He made a decisive contribution to the content of several key Articles, such as Article 1. He was closely engaged with the formulation and defense of a series of Articles, particularly those dealing with welfare issues, education, and cultural life. He was also involved in debate strategies relating to the document's contents as well as to questions about the UDHR's function. Logical structure and stylistic issues were close to his heart. Put simply, it would be hard to find another author of the document who had the same impact and the same ecumenical and intercultural approach as Chang's. The person who come closest in this respect is the Lebanese philosopher Charles Malik, who at the end of the writing process endorsed the various contributions of the different writers. It in no way diminishes the importance of either Eleanor Roosevelt and John Humphreys or the contributions of the other authors of the UDHR such as René Cassin to say that Chang stands out as the key figure for all of the attributes now considered significant for this document: its universality, its religious neutrality, and its focus on the fundamental needs and the dignity of individual human beings. The idea that the UDHR should be a basis for "the art of living" was also an idea that Chang strongly endorsed. The issues in which Chang took a special interest have also turned out to have a critical importance in the world today.

Chang was highly active when it came to rebutting the perennial critiques of human rights thinking, such as the culturally relativist critique which held that the UDHR merely expressed the values of a particular cultural formation—that of the West—and that the document accordingly lacked universal objectivity. He was also opposed to ideologies and philosophical tendencies which denied pluralism and the value of different cultural traditions. Finally, Chang attacked those critics who argued that talk of human rights was a proxy for selfish individualism. Instead, he connected it to moral duties and empathy for one's fellow human beings.[3]

After completing the drafting of this rights document, Chang's personal life took a turn for the worse as a result of professional difficulties compounded by health problems at home. He lost his political and professional appointments and even his native land, eventually dying, bitter and almost friendless, in a small satellite town to New York.

Chang—Professional Hero

It may be asked how closely Chang's work reflected his life. When considering the congruence between an author's biography and his work, one can start by imagining a *total* congruence between the two. Their actions reflect, continually and evenly, ideals that they also articulated in both their writings and various political contexts. Touching on this issue in his book *Courage*, the former British prime minister Gordon Brown has spoken of *sustained altruists*, those people who for much of their life allow altruism to define their daily actions, privately as well as publicly.[4] It goes without saying that historically this group has always been small in number. The notion of a consistent altruist was not applicable to Chang or to most of the other authors of the UN Declaration. There existed profound discrepancies between Chang's ideas and actions in certain regards—particularly, as we have seen, in the relation between his public and private lives. Chang espoused an almost archaic, hierarchical view of family, particularly if we take his son Stanley at his word. According to Stanley, his father raised both sons in a way that likely differed little from how Chang himself had been brought up by his elder brother Poling.

In his daily life, Chang also evinced an obviously elitist view of social relations and, as noted already, more easily related to people he regarded as of the same social station as himself. His upbringing in a patriarchal social climate may also account for why he never took women's rights particularly seriously while working for the UN. This was also true of several of the other men in the drafting group. However, in his theatrical activities, Chang had shown an interest in women's rights by producing Henrik Ibsen's play *A Doll's House* in China several times. And he had worked at Nankai University, which from early on admitted both male and female students.

Chang was heavily influenced by a view of China as the Middle Kingdom, and he placed particular emphasis upon the country's thousand-year traditions. According to Stanley, when Chang met people from other countries he did not conceal his pride in coming from the Middle Kingdom. His father, Stanley explained, was clearly shaped by his schooling in China, particularly the nationalistic education that he had received at the Nankai School. At the same time, he had respect for religious and cultural pluralism and for tolerance in general. He believed that China—at least from a long historical perspective—could be a model country in its treatment of the "religious problem." Chang saw this problem as a matter of creating harmonious relations while avoiding serious conflict between different religious groups within a society.

In view of these qualifications and reservations about ideals versus practice in Chang's life, it is perhaps more accurate to use the term "professional hero," a term (also taken from Gordon Brown and Frank Farley) that designates someone who has made a heroic contribution by virtue of their extraordinary professional commitment—in Chang's case, as an educator, cultural mediator, and UN diplomat.[5] To this can be added his deeply private involvement in philosophical and literary matters that often also overlapped with the issues which engaged him in his professional capacity as teacher, theatrical producer, scholar, and diplomat.

In Chang's case, then, there was a *partial* congruence between life and work. In other words, he failed in several instances to live up to his ethical ideals, above all with regard to his family. As Stanley explained: "The UN Declaration of Human Rights may be a perfect document but my father was far from perfect. He was a bigot and harboured prejudices about more than you would think." There was, however, a strong congruence on the professional level. Chang was a brilliant and multifaceted person who, for essentially all his life, involved himself in important projects of universal human significance that reflected his other writings and areas of interest. Whether it concerned politics, theater, literature, education, or philosophy, Chang threw himself into it with the same frenetic originality and attention to detail. In all his activities, he evinced a humanistic outlook and a powerful faith in human freedoms and the possibility of overcoming difficult challenges.

For much of his working life, Chang took a critical stance toward politically authoritarian approaches, with regard to which he was profoundly influenced by the liberal ideas in which he had become immersed during his study years in the United States. It was thus both natural and predictable that Chang became increasingly ill at ease with the regime that he represented at the UN and that he later accused of "fake" democracy. Yet the fact that the regime was on its last legs during the period when Chang was involved in drafting the UN Declaration granted him a degree of independence that practically no other delegate enjoyed with respect to their national government. Many of the interventions that he made about the content of the UN Declaration can thus be presumed to be his own. After all, according to Stanley, he was never a member of the nationalist Kuomintang party and, indeed, was critical of Chiang Kai-shek as leader.

Broadly speaking, Chang was a social-liberal thinker who emphasized both civil-political and socioeconomic rights. While a student, he was also deeply influenced by the pragmatic philosophy and democratic theories of John Dewey among others. These ideas accorded well with Chang's interpretation of Confucian philosophy as focusing more on the art of living than on metaphysical speculations about human nature and the fundamental causes or conditions of reality. As we have seen, from an early stage Chang's thinking ran along lines similar to those of modern political philosophers in the social-liberal tradition as articulated in the writings of the American philosophers John Rawls and Ronald Dworkin. Rawls's notion of an overlapping consensus had an earlier counterpart in Chang's writings while

Dworkin's endorsement of human dignity resembled Chang's ideas concerning dignity and equality. Chang's conception of justice is strongly reminiscent of the American philosopher Michael Walzer's notion of *complex justice*. Moreover, he sought to find ethical common denominators among the delegates by emphasizing the importance of combatting brutality and injustice, an idea that subsequently found an advocate in the Latvian-American philosopher Judith N. Shklar.[6]

Chang accordingly distanced himself from a fully market-economic society that encouraged individualism and materialism. He was skeptical of human rights thinking that could be interpreted as the expression of selfish individualism. His starting point was quite different from those rights theorists whose models are premised upon individuals and the demands for freedom and property rights that these latter make on society.[7] For Chang, the focus of rights discussions should instead be the humanizing of human beings and raising awareness of the individual's duties and natural sympathy toward his or her fellow human beings.

Chang also sought to emphasize the role of education and positive measures, not merely laws and regulations, in promoting human rights.[8] Chang claimed that emphasis should be placed not on restraining people through restrictions, but on educating them. The purpose of all social and political education was the voluntary recognition of the rights of others. That is the ideal which the Declaration should express, according to Chang."[9]

His overall thinking here resembles the Indian philosopher and economist Amartya Sen's ideas about the realization of human rights.[10] Chang's ideas about cultural and civilizational differences also recall Sen's ideas in their emphasis upon how certain ethical notions could be discerned in quite different civilizations and cultural groupings.[11] It simply made no sense, according to Chang and Sen, to compare East and West with regard to ethical ideals because there existed so many "Easts" and "Wests," each of which had its own starting point. In his own life he also strived to understand different cultures and learn from their differences and similarities. These personal experiences obviously influenced his writings on intercultural communication and ethics. As an educator he paid special attention to the importance of education for constructive political reforms. A typical statement from Chang is the following: "It may be interesting to note that whenever the Chinese are faced with any problem the first thing they think of is to try to approach it through educational means."[12]

Why Did It Take So Long for Chang to Begin to Be Recognized?

One issue that presents itself in this context is why it has taken so long for Chang to be recognized as a Chinese pioneer of human rights, and why attention has instead tended to be directed toward the other authors of the UN Declaration. A number of factors can be adduced. As already noted, China and human rights issues have become increasingly topical. That a Chinese philosopher and diplomat was one of the most important drafters of the UN Declaration has thus been growing in political significance, not least for those interested in problematizing the adoption of the UN Declaration as a document with marginal relevance for countries outside of the West.

This last factor may account for why a good number of writers on the UN Declaration have paid little or no attention to Chang. In effect, he has been marginalized in the secondary literature because his home country, the Republic of China, was long regarded as an authoritarian state with weak human-rights traditions. The latter has shown itself to be a truth in need of qualification, however. While it is true that the Republic of China was no paradigm from a democratic perspective, there has been a lively debate over human rights in twentieth-century China that goes back to the founding of the republic in 1912.[13]

For obvious reasons, Chang's contributions to the UN Declaration and his work for the UN have attracted relatively little interest in the People's Republic of China since 1949 because his name has been so closely connected with the Republic of China. This perspective needs to be reevaluated, however, since during the 1940s Chang was in fact representing *one* country at the UN: China. Later generations of Chinese ought therefore to take pride in the fact that China's representative to the UN played so prominent a role in the writing of the UDHR.[14] Chang also decided to quit his work as diplomat at the beginning of the 1950s because he thought he was merely representing a "fake democracy" on an offshore island. Moreover, at places such as Tsinghua University, Chang was eclipsed somewhat by more famous Chinese scholars who had also studied in the US through the Boxer Indemnity Scholarship Fund. The introduction of human rights concepts in the legal and political discourse in the People's Republic of China was also a rather late phenomenon. The concept of human rights was mainly introduced in official political debates through the White Paper on Human Rights from 1991, which also recognized the Universal Declaration of Human Rights.[15]

By contrast, Chang's role as a theatrical director and playwright has received more attention in China in recent years. One reason why Chang and his family have also elicited interest in the People's Republic of China is that the famous Nankai University in Tientsin has been so closely associated with the Chang name, because Chang's older brother Poling was responsible for cofounding the university. Peng Chun Chang himself also played a key role in helping to establish the university, working for several years there as a teacher, administrator, and professor.

Another reason for why the authors of studies of the UDHR have partly overlooked Chang is that China historically has not been associated with rights traditions to the same extent as the West. The following statement by the Chinese philosopher Chung Shu Lo is fairly typical of how a number of Chinese ethical traditions have been characterized in the secondary literature: "The fundamental ethical concept in Chinese social and political tradition is the realization of the individual's duties towards neighbours, rather than the assertion of rights. Rights violations will best be remedied by the realization of mutual obligations."[16]

At first glance, it thus seems slightly paradoxical that someone primarily associated with theater and literature, who represented an authoritarian state lacking any obvious human rights traditions, should have become one of the most important authors of the UN Declaration. Yet Chang had specialized in pedagogy as student, researcher, and teacher, and this expertise was highly relevant to the drafting of the UDHR. People with quite different traditions than that of Western liberalism can also bring fresh perspectives to the understanding of human rights. This precept is confirmed by the career of Peng Chun Chang.

Chang died in 1957, earlier than several of his cowriters of the UN Declaration, including René Cassin, Charles Malik, John Humphrey, and Hernan Santa Cruz, all of whom lived to see the 1960s and 1970s, and some even the 1980s. A number of Chang's colleagues thus lived to see the UDHR evolve into the text of more binding conventions, a process that resulted in the UN conventions of 1966. They had the opportunity to travel the world and describe their work for the UN. Most of the aforementioned also wrote memoirs in which they related what they had contributed to the declaration and the UN's work subsequently. Eleanor Roosevelt, who died in the early 1960s, had a special position by virtue of her role as chairman for the Commission on Human Rights, which also explains why her name has always been so closely associated with the UDHR. Charles Malik and John Humphrey also kept diaries, which Chang seems not to have done regularly, aside from a few years in the 1920s. Cassin wrote also a memoir and was clearly outspoken about his role on the Human Rights Commission. For these reasons, some scholars may have emphasized the special importance of Cassin, Malik, Humphrey, and Roosevelt as key drafters of the UDHR.[17]

The widespread perception that the Universal Declaration has its main origin in Western liberal thought may also have contributed to the negligence of Chang's contributions to the document. In addition, according to the human rights scholar Samuel Moyn, the concept of human rights was introduced and "skyrocketed" rather late in the broad public debates (i.e., during the '70s), which may also explain that the general as well as the academic interest in human rights and the Universal Declaration has been a rather slow process.[18]

A final conceivable reason for the tardy interest in Chang in relation to the UN Declaration is that, compared to René Cassin and Charles Malik, he made fewer interventions in the years 1947–1948. I have made a rough estimate of the number of speeches referenced in William Schabas's anthology of contributions during the drafting of the UN Declaration. René Cassin made over five hundred speeches and Charles Malik over three hundred. Chang's speeches numbered more than two hundred, which is in fact a significant tally compared to the other authors, such as Hansa Mehta and Carlos Romulo. Chang's role as vice-chairman in the drafting group may have made him more reticent in certain situations, such that his comments were at times limited to conclusions, stylistic questions, and the document's logical structure. These were important questions, admittedly, particularly given that the pedagogical principle underlying the UN Declaration was that it should be a document easily understandable by the general public.

The Relevance of New Material for Understanding Chang and the UDHR

By way of conclusion, it should be asked how the new material in this book has changed our understanding of Peng Chun Chang and his involvement in the UDHR. What new picture emerges from my interviews with Stanley Chang, Chang's own writings, statements from his colleagues and from the studies of the secondary literature? One of my ambitions has been to examine in as comprehensive fashion as possible everything that Chang wrote in

English—particularly regarding the ideas that relate to his work on the UN Declaration.

Those critical of the UDHR's claim to universality have referred to the fact that the non-Western delegates—Chang and Malik, for example—had studied at Western universities.[19] This training meant that they were deeply influenced by Western liberal traditions. In effect, the declaration has been accused of expressing these values and, accordingly, been treated as irrelevant to other cultures and regions.

In stark contrast, Stanley's account portrays Chang as someone who was deeply affected by his Chinese upbringing, not least by his education in the nationalist Nankai Schools. The charge that he was primarily influenced by so-called Western values, which in turn found expression in his work with the UDHR, is therefore unwarranted. In his arguments about different articles, Chang made statements containing an array of references to different intellectual traditions. Given this background, it is also incorrect to characterize Chang's contributions to the UN Declaration as offering only Confucian and Eastern perspectives. Chang had a motley educational background, adopting from wildly different sources values and ideas that he saw as universally applicable. Chang also had an aversion to contrasting large civilizational entities with each other or comparing their values precisely because such generalizations elided tremendous internal diversity.[20]

There has been a tendency in the scholarly literature to foreground Chang's conflicts with Charles Malik during the writing process.[21] If Stanley Chang can be taken at his word, the most serious conflict was in fact between Chang and René Cassin. Their openly nationalistic approaches and striking differences of personality undoubtedly contributed to their difficulties in achieving a relaxed working relationship on the Commission on Human Rights. It is clear from Stanley's accounts that Chang also had a Middle Kingdom attitude, something that may account for why Chang clashed in particular with René Cassin, a nationalistic Frenchman. This attitude may also explain why Chang in different ways sought to be part of the drafting of a rights document that overlapped substantially with a number of Chinese philosophical traditions.

Stanley Chang's memories from the first drafting period on Long Island in the summer of 1947 attest to the fact that his father played a crucial role in the writing process and that Eleanor Roosevelt at times took a more passive role. A survey of the secondary literature also indicates that Chang was not only an important presence at meetings—as a person to whom others often referred matters—but also that his contributions to the UDHR were unquestionably substantial, particularly with regard to the fundamental features of the UDHR. These findings directly contradict those accounts that have foregrounded the role of Eleanor Roosevelt and other individuals, such as John Humphrey, Charles Malik, and René Cassin, in the creation of the UDHR.[22]

Stanley Chang's recollection of his father's life and relationship with his family and the world at large offers a portrait of an extremely complicated individual struggling with many inner conflicts that often spilled onto the family's life. This image of Chang stands in stark contrast to those more hagiographic accounts that limit their focus to Chang's positive qualities, including the depth and range of his education and the multifaceted nature of his life.[23] The fact that Chang during the process of drafting the UN Declaration so frequently alluded to humanity's dual nature—a good part and a bad—undoubtedly reflected a deeper existential problematic of his own.

Stanley Chang also mentioned that, in the debates on Long Island about the UN Declaration, his father often invoked Robert Burns's poetic dictum about man's inhumanity to man. Chang's use of this particular poem sheds further light upon how he viewed the project of the UN Declaration—as having been written primarily in order to bolster humanity's good side against its own bestial side.

The new information supplied by Stanley gives an insight into Chang's attitude toward Communism and the leader of the republic, Chiang Kai-shek. Chang was obviously not a Communist. Indeed, when discussing political developments in China, he described Communism as a disease of childhood. In an article published in 1931, Chang also stated that the group who endorsed revolution on the basis of the communist doctrine was chiefly composed of certain of youths who were dissatisfied with present conditions.[24] Yet, if Stanley is to be believed, he was no more sympathetic to Chiang Kai-shek and Kuomintang. Chang also acted very independently of his government. According to Stanley, his father in principle had little communication with his government during his time at the UN, something which confirms that many of his statements to the various UN committees regarding the content of the UDHR were his own opinions. Another highly illuminating item of information provided by Stanley Chang is that his father left the Chinese mission at the UN because of the lack of real democracy in Taiwan.

Another aspect of Chang's life that very few commentators have addressed is his religious involvement. What emerges from a survey of his early essays and from conversations with Stanley Chang is that Chang's attitude toward religion—and specifically Christianity—changed radically during the course of his life. From having been religiously active in Christian student groups during his university studies as an undergraduate in the United States, Chang's perspective became almost agnostic for the greater part of his adult life.

Chang's growing agnosticism undoubtedly also played a significant part in his rejection of religious and metaphysical elements in the UDHR. It was thus not only the desire for universalism that lay behind his demand for religious neutrality, that is, that the document should be accessible for all people, regardless of their religious background, but also the view that religious questions lie beyond the scope of human reason, that nothing can be said with certainty about God or any religious reality—that is to say, an agnostic point of view. Beginning in the early 1920s, when Chang returned to China, he also showed a growing interest in classical Chinese philosophy. Until the 1950s, Chang seems to have focused his attention on philosophers with a high degree of societal engagement, such as Confucius and Mencius. During his last years, his interest seems to have shifted more toward "introverted" philosophers within Taoism. According to Stanley, his father regarded Chinese thinkers such as Confucius and Mencius less as religious figures than as individuals whose core ideas were academic and ethical. In conclusion, the many interviews with Stanley that form the basis for this study can be said to have provided a great many factual details about the lives of Chang and his family that have not previously been available to scholars.

Chang and the World Today

It is a fascinating question as to how Peng Chun Chang would have reacted to the dramatic political events that are shaping the world in 2023, seventy-five years after the completion of the UN Declaration. Although the question is hypothetical, it allows us to evaluate the connection between his ideas to the world today. How would Chang have viewed the present global political challenges as well as the ongoing developments in China? For instance, the global polarization that has arisen against a background of religious fundamentalism and extremism runs directly contrary to Chang's advocacy of pluralistic tolerance and the right to freedom of religion. His strong emphasis upon secularism and religious neutrality in relation to the

UN Declaration also sends a clear signal to those politicians in recent years who have sought to blur the boundary between private involvement in religion and official state policy.

Developments in China in the last few decades would undoubtedly have worried Chang in several ways. To be sure, given his national pride and strong identification with China's territories and their thousand-year traditions, he would have welcomed some aspects of this development, notably China's fast growing importance in world politics.

He would also have viewed favorably the resurgent interest in Confucius in China during the last few years—with the proviso that the Confucian intellectual legacy was made more liberal. Chang would likely also have been pleased to see the measures taken to combat corruption. But the notion of a wide-ranging national sovereignty able to suspend human rights, like the prioritizing of economic rights above civil and political rights, fits badly with Chang's larger vision of human rights, the universality of the UN Declaration, and the UN's intended role in world politics. Chang was also a passionate advocate of civil and political rights and was clearly unwilling to subordinate these to socioeconomic rights. He was an energetic advocate of a democratic state with freedom of speech, free and open elections and the rule of law. He would definitely have been skeptical about a one-party system and the leadership cult. He also believed that human rights had a universality that superseded the legal system of any single state. One development in China about which Chang would likely have been extremely critical is the spread of market-economic thinking and of materialistic values more broadly. These form a stark contrast to Chang's emphasis upon the non-material values and the prizing of social community and education above material consumption.

Chang's prediction that Communism would be a passing phase also proved to be wrong. Far from being diseases of childhood that would be quickly overcome, Communism and the domination of the Communist Party continue to assume new forms of expression in Chinese society today.

APPENDIX

A NOTE ON SOURCES

In view of the paucity of written material on Chang's life and work, the main sections of this book can be described as a critical reconstruction on the basis of "fragments." For much of his life, Chang himself evidently had little interest in keeping a journal or making notes. During his final years of working at the UN, from 1948 to 1952, the Republic of China was involved in a civil war, and after Communist forces seized power, its government was forced to relocate to the island of Formosa. During these years Chang also took more of his own initiatives and provided his government with only a very sparse account of his activities. It would therefore seem that there is very little official material from this period that describes Chang's activities, something that has been confirmed by the archival researches of the French sinologist Pierre Étienne Will.[1]

Most of those who knew Chang personally are no longer alive. However, through correspondence with Chang's only surviving son—the physics professor Stanley (Yuan-Feng) Chang (b. 1928)—I have been able to gain access to information unavailable to previous writers on Chang. This information particularly concerns his relationship to the Republic of China and its leader, his relationships with the other authors of the UN Declaration, and, more generally, his persona and everyday habits and attitudes, as well as the key events in his life. My exclusive access to the information provided by Chang's son has been very important for the narrative of this book.

Stanley Chang's memories of his father's reflections upon various complicated political and ethical questions—including those connected to the UN Declaration—are by their nature fragmentary and inconclusive. Much time has passed since the 1940s and 1950s, and according to Stanley Chang, he and his father only ever discussed such matters infrequently. What is more, Stanley's knowledge of Chinese got worse the longer he stayed in the United States. Even so, a number of things relating to his father appear with particular clarity from the conversations Stanley recalled, including Chang's relationships with several of the UN delegates, such as René Cassin. Although Stanley Chang's personal relationship with his father was extremely complicated, it is clear from his accounts that he had a profound admiration for his father's professional abilities and deep learning, and he identified with the challenges faced by his father in his work for the UN.

Ideally, I would also have been able to talk with some of Peng Chun Chang's close friends, some relatives of the same generation or older, or his colleagues, so as to ask them about Chang's areas of interest, opinions, and attitudes on various questions, as well as about the first thirty years of his life. The fact that none of them are still alive has made this an impossibility. It would also have been desirable to have had access to notes made by Chang in conjunction with his work for the UN. This, too, seems to have been an impossibility. Nonetheless, written remarks by several of Chang's sometime friends and colleagues, such as Charles Malik and John Humphrey, shed new light on his actions and thinking in certain areas.

Stanley Chang's own memories of his father come primarily from the second half of the 1930s and from the 1940s and 1950s. The information that I have received from Stanley regarding his father's life from the 1890s up to 1940 are for the most part things that he has been told by Chang himself and other relatives. I have also gleaned additional information about Chang's life from a document that was privately produced and circulated by Chang's daughter Ruth Cheng and her husband Sze-Chuh Cheng.[2] This text, together with information provided by Stanley, have been my main source for identifying the chronology and key events in Peng Chun Chang's life.

My contact with Stanley Chang has enabled me to gain a highly personal insight into Peng Chun Chang's life. Being in correspondence with Chang's son has provided entirely new dimensions to this project, as I hope is apparent from the resulting book.

Because previous biographical accounts of Peng Chun Chang have been so limited in scope, my conversations with Stanley Chang have been able to fill in many gaps. Needless to say, it is problematic from an evidentiary point of view to rely upon a single source, particularly one with a so personally inflected and complicated image of his father—and in relation to events that also took place many years previously. The passage of time problematizes Stanley's memories of some details in particular, which means that some information provided should probably be taken with a grain of salt. Nonetheless, a good deal of the information with which Stanley has provided me has been consistent and exhaustive, and in light of the difficulty of obtaining supplementary information from other sources, correspondence with Stanley Chang has been an extremely valuable addition to the writing process. What has emerged from that correspondence is a rounded picture of Peng Chun Chang that is both consistent and credible.

My correspondence with Stanley has principally consisted of questions posed by me about the key events in Chang's life. I have also asked about Chang's thoughts about and attitudes toward significant issues and individuals whom he encountered in his life. Stanley's answers have in turn led to the actualizing of new questions, and so forth. Being able to present images of Peng Chun Chang and his life from the perspective of his son is unquestionably valuable in its own right and something that no other source could have replaced. For the most part, therefore, I have chosen to present Stanley's stories about his father as direct quotations, some of which I have then glossed and commented. My goal has been to put these statements into context by referring to the historical circumstances, particularly in China, in which the Chang family found itself at the moments in question. Collectively, these memoirs create an "aura" or framework around Peng Chun Chang's life and times.

Another ambition has been to strike a reasonable balance between Stanley's everyday observations and his more overarching reflections about his father's thinking and statements on key political and ethical issues. Some of Stanley's descriptions of how Chang spoke and acted in various everyday situations may additionally provide new perspectives on Chang's fundamental personality traits and life choices. Because Stanley was one of the four children who were physically closest to their father for an extended period in the late 1940s and early 1950s, he gained a unique insight into Chang's life during and immediately after his years at the UN. Although Stanley concedes that for periods of time he became distant from his father—and that they discussed serious political issues only rarely—he nonetheless gained important glimpses into his father's political thinking. Stanley has related that what he best remembers are the conversations between his father and mother when the latter was helping Chang transcribe materials related to his work.

My primary source for Chang's statements at the UN has been William A. Schabas's relatively recent anthology on the debates about the UN Declaration.[3]

Chang's books and articles published in English have also been a point of departure for the conceptual studies in this book. Chang appears not to have published many articles in Chinese, and those he did, seem to have been concerned mostly with the theater and literature.[4]

NOTES

Introduction

1. Since Chang himself wrote his name as Peng Chun Chang or P. C. Chang, and this is how he is generally known in the Western world, I have retained this spelling. I also refer in the same way to his relatives in the US. His brother, on the other hand, spelled his name Chang Poling. The use of different transcriptions in the book—Hanyu Pinyin and Wade-Giles—is because the authors I refer to in the text have used different systems.

2. Chang's name has shown up now and then in connection to some of the anniversaries of the United Nations and the UDHR. For example, in 1997 Hillary Rodham Clinton mentioned in a speech in the UN that Chang, who helped draft the Universal Declaration, stressed that human rights had counterparts in Confucian traditions. She presumably praised Chang in this context for making the UDHR more universal. (Hillary Clintons's remarks to the United Nations, New York, 10 December, 1997, The President's Interagency Concuil of Women.)

3. Glendon, *World Made New*, 211.
4. Chang, "Shakespeare in China," 399.
5. Chang, "Wither China," 3.
6. See, for example, Ignatieff, "Human Rights, Global Ethics and the Ordinary Virtues," 3–4 and Ignatieff, *The Ordinary Virtues*.
7. Urquhart, "Mrs. Roosevelt's Revolution."
8. Hobbins, Review of *A World Made New*, 380–381.
9. Chang, *China at the Crossroads*, 47.
10. Malik, *Challenge of Human Rights*, 249.
11. Hobbins, *On the Edge of Greatness*, vol. 2, 191.
12. Glendon, *World Made New*; Winter and Prost, *René Cassin and Human Rights*.

Chapter 1

1. Lary, *China's Republic*, 64.
2. Mitter, *Modern China*, 25–27.
3. After the 1911 Revolution and the regime change the Chinese population growed from 436 million in 1910 to nearly 542 million in 1949. See Wang, "China's First Revolution," 129.
4. Ibid., 23.
5. Hayes, *Introduction to Japanese Politics*, 18.
6. Chang, "Education and Scientific Research," 424.

7. Shih, "Chang Poling," 10. During the late Qing period there were also suggestions to change the constitution and introduce a constitutional monarchy. See Wang Chaohua, "China's First Revolution", 126.
8. Chang, *How Nankai Began*.
9. Lee, *Zhou Enlai*, 57.
10. Elman, *Civil Examination and Meritocracy in Late Imperial China*, 318.
11. According to Confucian ethics, the family is also the core of the communal life in a society. See Sim, "Confucian Approach to Human Rights," 341. Given this perspective it can be seen as somewhat peculiar that Chang did not talk about his own family background with his son Stanley to any large extent. However, the traditional Confucian view was that the family was "patrilineal" which means that the family line was detected through the male from a founding male ancestor. This phenomenon may to some extent explain Chang's special focus upon his father. See Gardner, *Confucianism*, 101.
12. Stanley Chang's comments throughout are from Cheng and Cheng, *Peng Chun Chang*.
13. Ibid.
14. Chang, *How Nankai Began*.
15. Ibid.
16. Boorman, "Chang Poling"; Shih, "Chang Poling," 5.
17. Shih, "Chang Poling," 10.
18. Kampen, "Olympic Games and Human Rights."
19. Chang, *How Nankai Began*.
20. Lee, *Zhou Enlai*, 191.
21. Peng Chun Chang's brother Poling has generally been much more well known than Peng among people in China for a long time, not at least because of his role in creating Nankai University and for being a pioneer in the context of Chinese Olympics.
22. Some of the other universities that were allowed to keep their original names were Beijing, Tsinghua, Wuhan, Zhejiang, Xiamen, North Eastern, Sichuan, and Yunnan. After 1949, all Christian universities in China, such as the famous St. John's and Yenching University, were abolished. Some of their houses and staff later became integrated into the officially accepted universities. The buildings of the Yenching University, for example, became part of Beijing University.
23. Cheng and Cheng, *Peng Chun Chang*.
24. Lee, *Zhou Enlai*, 66.
25. Humphrey, *Human Rights & the United Nations*, 139.
26. The China Institute was created in 1926 by a distinguished group of scholars all of them connected to Columbia University, namely, John Dewey, Hu Shi, Paul Monroe, and Kuo Ping-Wen. The purpose of the institute ever since its beginning has been to advance understanding of Chinese culture and politics.
27. Chang, *How Nankai Began*.
28. Zhou, *Influences of Boxer Indemnity Reparations*.
29. Grieder, *Hu Shi and the Chinese Renaissance*.
30. Lary, *China's Republic*, 67.
31. Bevis and Lucas, "Chinese Students in U.S.Colleges," 32–33.
32. Lary, *China's Republic*, 64.
33. Chang, "National Ideals."
34. Chang, *China at the Crossroads*.

35. Chang, "National Ideals," 20.
36. Chang, "China's Real Situation," 86.
37. Chang, "Brief Survey of the Principle of Extraterritoriality," 403.
38. Ibid., 400–401.
39. Ibid., 402. The system of extraterritorial rights (or personal law) had been introduced in China after the 1842 Treaty of Nanjing, and it ended in 1943 when the British and the Americans accepted to relinquish these rights for their citizens in China. Kuomintang (KMT) also achieved tariff autonomy in 1929. The principle of extraterritoriality meant that foreigners living in China were not subject to Chinese jurisdiction if they had committed an offense against the law or were involved in legal disputes. However, Stalin did not renounce the Russian privileges in China and they continued until 1955 when Khrushchev cancelled them. See Chang, *China at the Crossroads*, 110; and Wang, "China's First Revolution," 135.
40. *Cornell Daily Sun*, vol. 34, no. 6, 27 September 1913.
41. Chang, "Gospel in China"; Chang, "Christian Leadership"; Chang, "Chinese Students."
42. Chang, "China's Desire to Retain the Best in Her Own Civilization."
43. Ibid., "Chang believed that China also needed leaders of Christian character."
44. Chang, "Old Ideas and New in China," 729.
45. Hobbins, *On the Edge of Greatness*, vol. 2, 127.
46. Craft, *V. K: Wellington Koo and the Emergence of Modern China*.
47. Chang, "Chinese Themes on the Stage"; Chang, "Shakespeare in China."
48. Chang, "Chinese Themes on the Stage," 218.
49. Ibid., 222.
50. Cheng and Cheng, *Peng Chun Chang*.
51. Ibid.
52. Pomfret, *Beautiful Country and the Middle Kingdom*, 139; Ye, *Seeking Modernity in China's Name*.
53. Goldstone, *Revolutions*, 79–80.
54. Dikötter, *Age of Openness*, 67.
55. Goldstone, *Revolutions*, 80.
56. Mackerras, *China in Transformation, 1900–1949*, chap. 14.
57. Lodén, *Rediscovering Confucianism*, 166.
58. Chang, *China at the Crossroads*, 157.
59. Mackerras, *China in Transformation, 1900–1949*, 40.
60. Chang, "Rising Consciousness of Civic Responsibility Among the Students of China."
61. Ibid., 382.
62. Xingzhi, *Transformation of Chinese Traditional Education*, 102.
63. Chang, "Redirecting Educational Effort in China," 286.
64. Ibid., 291.
65. Ibid., 290.
66. Ibid., 289
67. In his later work on the Universal Declaration of Human Rights, Chang paid special attention to Article 26 (the Educational Article). In this article (26:2), it is stressed that "education shall be directed to the full development of the human personality . . . (and) it shall promote understanding, tolerance." This article reveals an ideal of education that emphasizes the moral dimensions of education, an ideal that coheres well with Confucian ideas.
68. *Milwaukee Journal*, 2 March 1921.

69. Davin, *Mao*, 12.
70. Cheng and Cheng, *Peng Chun Chang*.
71. Ibid.; Greider, *Hu Shi and the Chinese Renaissance*.
72. The North China Famine of 1920–1921 was the most severe famine since the 1870s and affected 20 to 30 million people serously in provinces such as Zhili, Henan, and Shandong. The famine was mainly caused by harvest failure and food crises. Chang also made comments on the causes of this famine: "The last famine in China and all other famines for the last five hundred years, are the result of the destruction of forests, and carry a warning to America." See *Southern Lumberman*, vol. 104 (1921), 38.
73. Liu, "Professor Lydia H. Liu on Human Rights Pioneer and Columbia Alum P. C. Chang."
74. *The Detroit Educational Bullentin*, vol. 5, 1921.
75. Dudley, "Notes from the P.S.A. Annual Dinner." The poem is from Yen Yu, *Tsang-Lang Discourse on Poetry*.
76. Chang, *Education for Modernization in China*.
77. Ibid., 20–22.
78. See, for example, "Two Lectures," in Cheng and Cheng, *Peng Chun Chang*.
79. Chang, "Speaker Explains Manchurian Case," 5.
80. Willing, "Review of *Education for Modernization in China*."
81. *Today with Mrs. Roosevelt*, episode 14: 14 May 1950. Eleanor Roosevelt and her guests (among them P. C. Chang) discuss the United Nations and its relation to human rights.
82. Wager, "Review: *Education for Modernization in China*."
83. Chan and Egan, *Pragmatist and His Free Spirit*, 280.
84. Twiss, "Confucian Contributions to the Universal Declaration of Human Rights," 104–106.
85. Ching-Sze Wang, *John Dewey in China*; and Dewey, *Impressions of Soviet Russia*.
86. Chang, *China at the Crossroads*, 176.
87. Zheng, *Zhang Boling zhuan*.
88. Lary, *China's Republic*, 65–67.
89. Chang, *China: Whence and Wither?*, 114–115.
90. Twiss, "Confucian Contributions to the Universal Declaration of Human Rights," 104–106.
91. Li, *Peng-Chun Chang, American Pragmatism, and the Universal Declaration of Human Rights*, 27.
92. Svensson, *Debating Human Rights in China*, 133.
93. Ibid., 132.
94. Hartman, *Det pedagogiska kulturarvet*, 313–314.
95. Chang, *China: Whence and Wither?*, 115.

Chapter 2

1. Luo, *Inheritance Within Rupture*, 168.
2. *Columbia Alumni News*, vol. 13, 1921.
3. Chatterjee, "Tagore," 36.
4. Fei and Yangeng, *Poling and P. C. Chang*, 206.
5. Chang, *New Drama and the Old Theater*, 455.

6. Jin, *Chinese Theatre*; Cheng and Cheng, *Peng Chun Chang*.
7. Mackerras, *China in Transformation, 1900–1949*, chap. 6.
8. Mitter, *Modern China*, 44–45.
9. Ibid.
10. Wright, *History of China*, 135.
11. Mackerras, *China in Transformation*, chap. 7; Lary, *China's Republic*, 104.
12. Gardell, "Chiang Kai-shek har fått en sen revansch" (Chiang Kai-Shek got a late come back).
13. Chang, "'Second Phase' of China's Struggle," 216–217.
14. Chang, "Civilization and Social Philosophies," 11.
15. Lary, *China's Republic*, 105.
16. Neary, *Human Rights in Japan, South Korea and Taiwan*, 103.
17. Lary, *China's Republic*, 94.
18. A. C. Scott, *Mei Lan-Fang: The Life and Times of a Peking Actor*, 108–109.
19. Cui and Li, "Peng Chun Chang."
20. Cheng and Cheng, *Peng Chun Chang*.
21. Ibid.
22. Jin, *Chinese Theatre*, 104.
23. Tian, "Gordon Graig, Mei Lanfang and the Chinese Theatre."
24. Chang, "Speaker Explains Manchurian Case," 5.
25. Lary, *China's Republic*, 130–131.
26. *Milwaukee Journal*, 18 November 1931.
27. The Lytton Commission (1931–1932), led by Earl Victor Bulwer Lytton, was appointed by the League of Nations to determine the cause of the Japanese invasion of Manchuria in September 1931 after the Mukden incident. After a six-week visit by the commission to Manchuria, a report was written (the Lytton Report), which was presented in September 1932. The report stated that while both parties—China and Japan—had responsibility for the escalation of the conflict, Japan should be seen as the main aggressor. On the basis of the report, the League of Nations decided that the puppet state of Japan (Manchukuo) should not be recognized and that Manchuria should be placed under Chinese rule. However, the report also claimed that Japanese economic interests should be protected. One consequence of the Lytton Report was that Japan withdraw from the League of Nations. See Walters, *History of the League of Nations*, 491–492.
28. Chang, *China at the Crossroads*, 166–167.
29. Cheng and Cheng, *Peng Chun Chang*.
30. Chang, *China at the Crossroads*.
31. Chan and Egan, *Pragmatist and His Free Spirit*, 246–247.
32. Schenck, "Appreciation of Dr. Peng Chun Chang."
33. Ibid.
34. *KA Leo o Hawaii*, 16 January 1936.
35. Chang, "New Year in Princeton," 386.
36. Cheng and Cheng, *Peng Chun Chang*.
37. Chang, *China at the Crossroads*.
38. Ibid., 29–30.
39. Ibid., part 1.
40. Ibid., 120.

41. Chang, "Civilization and Social Philosophies," 10–11.
42. *Exeter & Plymouth Gazette*, 1 May 1936.
43. Mungello, *Great Encounter of China and the West, 1500–1800*, 91.
44. Ibid.
45. I am grateful to Professor Torbjörn Lodén for these remarks.
46. Green, "Review: *China at the Crossroads*"; Latourette, "Review: *China at the Crossroads*."
47. "Chinese Understanding of Music," in Cheng and Cheng, *Peng Chun Chang*.
48. Chang, "Comparison of University Education in United Kingdom and in China." (Translated from Chinese to English by Yi-Ting Chen and Magnus von Platen.)
49. See Chapter 7.
50. Mitter, *Modern China*, 49.
51. Ibid., 50ff.
52. Epstein, *My China Eye*, 80–81.
53. Shih, "Chang Poling," 14.
54. Ibid., 12.
55. The city of Tientsin was under the influence of Japanese control and had extraterritorial rights for the Japanese citizens during 1937. The Japanese army was near the Nankai campus so Japan was evidently aware of what was going on at Nankai University. Nankai's anti-Japanese feelings were, for example, evident in its curriculum and its text books. See Lee, *Zhou Enlai*, 69.
56. Mitter, *Modern China*, 47–48.
57. Chang, "Civilization and Social Philosophies," 5–6.
58. Buchanan, *East Wind*, 66f.
59. Ibid.
60. Ibid., 65.
61. Chang, "The First Year and After," 7.
62. Joas, *Sacredness of the Person*, 186–187.
63. Chang, "The First Year and After," 9.
64. Chang, "Universities and National Reconstruction in China."
65. Chang, "'Second Phase' of China's Struggle."
66. Chang, "The First Year and After," 8.
67. Chang, "Second Phase of China's Struggle," 226.
68. Ibid., 219.
69. Ibid., 216.
70. Chang, "The First Year and After," 9.
71. *China Monthly Review*, vol. 92–93 (1940), 386.
72. Cheng and Cheng, *Peng Chun Chang*.
73. "Two Lectures," in Cheng and Cheng, *Peng Chun Chang*.
74. Holcombe, *The Chinese Revolution*, part 2.
75. Humphrey, *Human Rights & the United Nations*, 136.
76. Cheng and Cheng, *Peng Chun Chang*.
77. Statement by a British diplomat in *British Documents on Foreign Affairs 1940–45*, South America, July 1944–1945.
78. Many scholars assume that there is a tight connection between "believing" (in a religious creed) and "belonging" (to some church or congregation). This thesis was famously chal-

lenged by the British sociologist of religion Grace Davie in her book *Religion in Britain Since 1945—Believing Without Belonging*. Davie claimed that people in Britain had showed (in the postwar period) a tendency to "believe" (that there is "something out there") without engaging in any specific religious activities or groups (i.e., "belonging"). See chap. 6 in her book. This distinction could also be applied to national contexts other than the British one. However, according to Stanley Chang, his parents did not discuss any religious issues with the children, and they did not reveal that they were religious in any obvious way. See Chapter 7.

79. Lary, *China's Republic*, 72, 125f.

Chapter 3

1. Letter from Chang to Soong, T. V. Soong papers, Hoover Institution, Stanford University.
2. "War Against Microbes," in Cheng and Cheng, *Peng Chun Chang*.
3. Walzer, *Spheres of Justice*, chap. 1.
4. Chang, "My View of the United Nations." (translated from Chinese to English by Yi-Ting Chen and Magnus von Platen).
5. Ibid. Chang later on stressed that social, humanitarian, and cultural questions required careful consideration and mutal understanding on the part of the members of the UN (and the Third Committee). If the Third Committee wished to accomplish lasting work, it should therefore make decisions only by a very large majority, if not unanimously (218th meeting on freedom of information).
6. Chang, "China's Stand on Freedom of Information," 25.
7. Stuart, *There Is Another China*.
8. Cheng and Cheng, *Peng Chun Chang*.
9. Silver Bay is a YMCA summer site upstate New York. Stanley's parents used to visit Silver Bay when Stanley and his brother Cheng were working there while they were studying at the Loomis School in Windsor.
10. Sun Yat-sen had introduced a system of balances—legislative, judiciary, and executive, as well as the Examinations Division which was to administer the choice of candidates for the state bureaucracy and the Censorate or Control division that checked the efficiency and the honesty of the government. However, since the introduction of the system in 1928 the military administration and the Executive Division became paramount.
11. Stuart, *There Is Another China*.
12. Lee, *Zhou Enlai*, 192.
13. In the summer of 1946 Chang met Charles Beard in his house in New Milford, Connecticut. During his meeting with Beard, Chang asked him "Has America contributed anything to the advancement of civilization?" Beard answered "Yes I think we have contributed two things. First, we have contributed greatly to the development of technology . . . And secondly, we established a regime of liberty . . . over a vast area." George S. Counts, a distinguised educator from Columbia, joined Chang on the trip and introduced him to Beard who also had a Columbia connection. See Dennis, *George S. Counts and Charles A. Beard. Colloborators for Change*, 157–158. Through his critical question to Beard Chang presumably revealed his scepticism towards American culture and society.
14. Renberg, *Helen Kellers värld*.
15. Lary, *China's Republic*, 166ff; Mitter, *Modern China*, 54–55; Davin, *Mao*, 45–46.

16. Lary, *China's Republic*, 87.
17. Ibid., 129; Goldstone, *Revolutions*, 82.
18. Mitter, *Modern China*, 45.
19. Sun Tzu, *Art of War*.
20. Hobbins, *On the Edge of Greatness*, vol. 1.
21. Ibid., vol. 1, 88.
22. Mitter, *Modern China*, 55.
23. C. C. Chang, "Universal Declaration of Human Rights and P. C. Chang"; Hsia, *My Five Incursions*, 78.
24. Lary, *China's Republic*, 189.
25. Ibid., 186ff.
26. Mitter, *Modern China*, 98.
27. Hobbins, *On the Edge of Greatness*, vol. 1, 5-6.
28. Ibid., vol. 1, 164.
29. Ibid., vol. 2, 175.
30. After the declaration was completed, Chang also became heavily involved in the terms of the binding convention that resulted from it, and he tried in a variety of ways to argue against the colonial powers' refusal to implement the UDHR in their colonies. During his work with the human rights covenants, Chang emphasized many times that the covenants should not go against or downgrade the declaration but should instead fulfil its standards. Chang also voiced the concern that the UDHR should function as a blueprint or inspiration for the work on the convention, and given its status as a binding treaty, one should analyze carefully which articles from the UDHR should be kept in the covenant and which should not be given the specific context. See Third Committee, Two Hundred and Ninety-First Meeting, Fifth Session, 20 October 1950.
31. See, for example, Liu, "Professor Lydia H. Liu on Human Rights Pioneer and Columbia Alum P. C. Chang."
32. Hobbins, *On the Edge of Greatness*, vol. 1, 164-165.
33. Ibid., vol. 2, 22.
34. Malik, *Challenge of Human Rights*, 249.
35. Chang, *China at the Crossroads*, 170.

Chapter 4

1. Chang, "Rising Consciousness of Civic Responsibility Among the Students of China," 382-383; Chang, "Speaker Explains Manchurian Case," 5.
2. Commission on Human Rights, Summary Record of the Sixty-Eighth Meeting, Third Session, E/CN.4/SR.68/, 10 June 1948.
3. Foreword to Cheng and Cheng, *Peng Chun Chang*.
4. Chang, *How Nankai Began*.
5. Papanek, "William Heard Kilpatrick's International Influence," 55-56.
6. Ibid., 55.
7. John Humphrey also mentioned in his diary from June 1955 that Chang was very interested in the philosophy of Lao-Tsu and that he recommended that Humphrey read *The Way and Its Power*. Hobbins, *On the Edge of Greatness*, vol. 3, 155.
8. Ibid., vol. 3, 232-233.

Chapter 5

1. Lundberg, "Debatter i samband med antagandet av den allmänna förklaringen," 62.
2. Will, "La Contribution chinoise à la declaration universelle des droits de l'homme."
3. See also Moyn, *Human Rights and the Uses of History*, 72–73.
4. Roth, *Vad är mänskliga rättigheter?*, chap. 6.
5. Barreto, *Human Rights from a Third World Perspective*, 360.
6. Zhao, "China and the Uneasy Case for Universal Human Rights."
7. Glendon, *World Made New*, 32–33.
8. Ibid, 47.
9. Roosevelt, *On My Own*, 95.
10. Johnson, *Magna Charta for Mankind*.
11. Ibid.
12. Glendon, *World Made New*, 140–141.
13. Economic and Social Council, Summary Record of the Sixty-Ninth Meeting (E/422), 14 March 1947.
14. Commission on Human Rights, Official Records: Drafting Ctte, 2nd Session, 20th Meeting, 3 May, 1948.
15. Glendon, *World Made New*, 84–85; Schabas, *Universal Declaration of Human Rights*; Third Committee, Fifth session, Two Hundred and Ninety-Ninth Meeting, Draft first international covenant on human rights and measures of implementation, A/C.3/SR.299, 31 October 1950.
16. Glendon, *World Made New*, 193–194.
17. Ibid., 139 and 216.
18. Malik, "Charles Malik and the Universal Declaration of Human Rights."
19. Will, "La Contribution chinoise à la declaration universelle des droits de l'homme."
20. Krumbein, "P. C. Chang."
21. Bielefeldt, Ghanea, and Wiener, *Freedom of Religion or Belief*, 57.
22. Habib Malik, personal communication to author, spring 2017.
23. Confucius said: cultivated persons seek harmony but not sameness (*Analects 13.23*).
24. *Third Committee, Summary Record of the Hundred and Twenty-Seventh Meeting*, Draft International Declaration of Human Rights (E/800), A/C.R/SR.127, 9 November 1948.
25. Commission on Human Rights, Summary Record of the Sixtieth Meeting, E/CN.4/SR.60, 4 June 1948.
26. Hobbins, "Review: *A World Made New*," 381.
27. Glendon, *World Made New*, 105 and 209.
28. P. C. Chang, "Statement by Dr. P. C. Chang Before the Plenary Meeting of the General Assembly of the Declaration of Human Rights."
29. Roosevelt, "Promise of Human Rights."
30. Roosevelt, "Making Human Rights Come Alive," 23.
31. Morsink, *Universal Declaration of Human Rights*, 31.
32. Glendon, *World Made New*, 152.
33. Ibid., 66. See also Morsink, *Universal Declaration of Human Rights*, 157.
34. Habib Malik, personal communication to author, September 2016; Glendon, *World Made New*, 125–126.
35. Humphrey, *Human Rights & the United Nations*, 31.

36. McFarland, "Architects of the Universal Declaration."
37. Griffin, *On Human Rights*, 11ff; Tasioulas, "Justice, Equality and Rights."
38. Bol, *Neo-Confucianism in History*, 122.
39. Morsink, *Universal Declaration of Human Rights*, 37.
40. Alfredsson and Eide, *Universal Declaration of Human Rights*, 126.
41. Cassin, "Charter of Human Rights."
42. Ignatieff, *Human Rights as Politics and Idolatry*, 53.
43. Malik, "Charles Malik and the Universal Declaration of Human Rights."
44. Heaney, "Human Rights, Poetic Redress."
45. Schabas, *Universal Declaration of Human Rights*; Commisssion on Human Rights, Summary Record of the Seventh Meeting, E/CN.4/SR.7, 31 January 1947.
46. Orend, *Human Rights*, 20.
47. Bring, "Notion of Human Rights and the Issue of Cultural Relativism," 546.
48. Sunstein, "Rights of Passage."
49. Cassin, "How the Charter on Human Rights Was Born," 5.
50. Third Committee, Summary Record of the Hundred and Fifty-First Meeting, A/C.3/SR.151, 22 November 1948.
51. Cruft, "Human Rights as Individualistically Justified," 58.
52. Morsink, The Universal Declaration of Human Rights, p. 34.
53. Third Committee, Summary Record of the Hundred and Third Meeting, A/C.3/SR.103, 15 October 1948.
54. Eide and Alfredsson, *Universal Declaration of Human Rights*.
55. Third Committee, Two Hundred and Ninety-Fifth Meeting, Draft First International Covenant on Human Rights and Measures of Implementation, A/C.3/SR, 27 October 1950.

Chapter 6

1. Will, "La Contribution chinoise à la declaration universelle des droits de l'homme," 297–366. See also *China and the United Nations*. Report of a Study Group set up by the China Institute of International Affairs (New York: Manhattan Publishing Company for Carnegie Endowment for International Peace, 1959).
2. Krumbein, "P. C. Chang."
3. Drafting Committee of the Commission on Human Rights, Summary Record of the Eighth Meeting, E/CN.4/AC.1/SR.b, 17 June 1947.
4. Mackerras, *China in Transformation, 1900–1949*, 113.
5. Glendon, *World Made New*, 147.
6. Ibid.
7. Chang, "Civilization and Social Philosophies," 6.
8. Ibid., 7.
9. Chang, "China's Stand on Freedom of Information," 27.
10. Robinson, *Writing and Script*, 132.
11. Chang, "China's Stand on Freedom of Information," 28.
12. Humphrey, *Human Rights & the United Nations*, 23.
13. Hobbins, *On the Edge of Greatness*, vol. 2, 54.
14. Santa Cruz, *Cooperar o Perecer 1941–1960*, 120–121. Translated from Spanish to English by Annika Nilsson.

15. See Chang's contributions to the discussions in Schabas, *Universal Declaration of Human Rights* and Krumbein, "P. C. Chang."

16. Drafting Committee of the Commission on Human Rights, Summary Record of the English Meeting, E/CN.4/AC.1/SR.8/, 17 June 1947. See also Svensson, *Debating Human Rights in China*, 203.

17. Chang, *China: Whence and Whither?*, 110.

18. Commission on Human Rights, Summary Record of the Sixty-Ninth Meeting, E/CN.4/SR.69, 11 June 1948.

19. Chang, *China at the Crossroads*, 97–98; Chang, *Education for Modernization in China*, 16.

20. Third Committee, Summary Record of the Hundred and Fifty-Third Meeting, A/C.3/SR.153, 23 November 1948.

21. Donders and Volodin, eds., *Human Rights in Education, Science and Culture*, 276. 1948.

22. Third Committee, Summary Record of the Hundred and Fifty-Second Meeting, A/C.3/SR.152, 22 November 1948.

23. Third Committee, Ninety-Sixth Meeting, Draft International Declaration of Human Rights (E/800), A/C.3/SR.96 7 October 1948.

24. Ibid.

25. Commission on Human Rights, Summary Record of the Sixty-Seventh Meeting, E/CN.4/SR.67, 10 June 1948.

26. Morsink, *Universal Declaration of Human Rights*, 245.

27. Commission on Human Rights, Summary Record of the Seventy-Seventh Meeting, 17 June 1948.

28. Brown, *Universal Declaration of Human Rights in the 21st Century*, 57–58.

29. Drafting Committee of the Commission on Human Rights, Summary Record of the English Meeting, E/CN.4/AC.1/SR.8, 17 June 1947.

30. Morsink, *Universal Declaration of Human Rights*, 234.

31. Third Committee, Summary Record of the Two Hundred and Ninety-First Meeting, A/C.3/SR.291, 20 October 1950.

32. Commission on Human Rights, Summary Record of the Seventh Meeting, E/CN.4/SR 7, 31 January 1947.

33. Commission on Human Rights, Summary Record of the Thirteenth Meeting, E/CN.4/SR 13, 4 February 1947.

34. Third Committee, Summary Record of the Hundred and Forty-Third Meeting, A/C.3/SR.143, 17 November 1948.

35. Dworkin, "What Is Equality?" See also Griffin, *On Human Rights*; and Tasioulas, "Justice, Equality and Rights," for explications of the concept of human dignity, which is currently a pivotal concept in the modern philosophical debates on human rights.

36. Third Committee, Summary Record of the Hundred and Third Meeting, A/C.3/Sr.103, 15 = ct. 1948.

37. Chang, "Statement by Dr. P. C. Chang Before the Plenary Meeting of the General Assembly of the Declaration of Human Rights," December 10, 1948.

38. Ibid.

39. Chang, "China's Stand on Freedom of Information," 30.

40. Morsink, *Universal Declaration of Human Rights*.

41. Liu, "Shadows of Universalism," 407, 416.

42. Morsink, *Universal Declaration of Human Rights*, 285–286; and "Statement by Dr. P. C. Chang Before the Plenary Meeting at the General Assembly of the Declaration of Human Rights," December 10, 1948.
43. Twiss, "Confucian Contributions to the Universal Declaration of Human Rights," 112.
44. Bernstein, *Abuse of Evil*, 3f.
45. Plautus, *Asinaria*, 53.
46. King Jr., Acceptance Speech on the occassion of the award of the Nobel Peace Price in Oslo, 10 December 1964.
47. Malik, *Challenge of Human Rights*, 26.
48. Morsink, *Universal Declaration of Human Rights*, 300.
49. Reinbold, *Seeing the Myth in Human Rights*, 75
50. Malik, *Challenge of Human Rights*, 93.
51. Winter and Prost, *René Cassin and Human Rights*, 317.
52. Malik, *Challenge of Human Rights*, 28, 93f, 156f.
53. Ibid., 157f.
54. Ibid., 28.
55. Ibid., 154–155.
56. Cassin, *La Pensée et L'Action*, 155.
57. Glendon, *A World Made New*, 239.
58. United Nations, *Commission on Human Rights Drafting Committee International Bill of Rights, First Summary Record of the Third Meeting* (United Nations Economic and Social Council, 1947), 195.
59. Malik, *Challenge of Human Rights*, 24.
60. Lodén, "Reason, Feeling and Ethics in the Thought of Mencius and Xunzi."
61. Chang, *China at the Crossroads*, 49.
62. Krumbein, "P. C. Chang."
63. Third Committee, Summary Record of the Ninety-Fifth Meeting, Draft International Declaration of Human Rights, A7C.3/SR.95, 6 October 1948.
64. I am indebted to Professor Göran Collste for bringing this distinction to my attention.
65. Third Committee, Summary Record of the Ninety-Ninth Meeing, A/C.3/SR.99, 11 October 1948.
66. Glendon, "Rule of Law," 10.
67. Chang, "National Ideals," 18–19.
68. Chang, "The Rising Consciousness of Civic Responsibility among Students of China," 384.
69. "Two lectures," in Cheng and Cheng, *Peng Chun Chang*.
70. "A New Loyalty," in Cheng and Cheng, *Peng Chun Chang*.
71. Malik, *Challenge of Human Rights*, 151.
72. Third Committee, Three Hundred and First Meeting, 1 November 1950.
73. "Two Lectures," in Cheng and Cheng, *Peng Chun Chang*.
74. "War on Microbes," in Cheng and Cheng, *Peng Chun Chang*.
75. Chang, "China's Stand on Freedom of Information," 31.
76. Maritain, introduction to *Human Rights*, 9–10n16.
77. Liu, "Shadows of Universalism," 408f.
78. Griffin, *On Human Rights*, chap. 1.

79. Liu, "Shadows of Universalism," 396f.
80. Third Committee, Summary Record of the Two Hundred and Ninety-Fifth Meeting, Draft First International Covenant on Human Rights and Measures of Implementation, A/C.3/SR, 27 October 1950.
81. Liu, "Shadows of Universalism," 396f.
82. Chang, "Statement by Dr. P. C. Chang Before the Plenary Meeting of the General Assembly of the Declaration of Human Rights," 10 December 1948.
83. Twiss, "P. C. Chang, Freedom of Conscience and Religion and the Universal Declaration of Human Rights."
84. Third Committee, Summary Record of the Two Hundred and Ninety-Fifth Meeting, Draft First International Covenant on Human Rights and Measures of Implementation, A/C.3/SR, 27 October1950.
85. Chang, *China at the Crossroads*, 106.

Chapter 7

1. Orend, *Human Rights*.
2. Ibid.; Klug, *Magna Carta for All Humanity*.
3. See the diaries of Humphrey, in Hobbins, *On the Edge of Greatness*.
4. Hobbins, *On the Edge of Greatness*, vol. 2, 174.
5. Glendon, *World Made New*, 161.
6. Habib Malik, personal communication to author, from Charles Malik's diary.
7. Morsink, *Universal Declaration of Human Rights*, chap. 3.
8. Commission on Human Rights, Summary Record of the Sixtieth Meeting, E/CN.4/SR.60, 4 June 1948.
9. See Chapter 5.
10. Habib Malik, personal communication to author, October 2015.
11. Mary Ann Glendon, personal communication to author, 2014.
12. Habib Malik, personal communication to author, from Charles Malik's diary, Monday, 14 June 1948.
13. Glendon, *World Made New*, 119.
14. Ibid., 165.
15. Cassin, *La Pensée et L'Action*, 105, 113.
16. Sluga, "Rene Cassin," 120.
17. Glendon, *World Made New*, 60.
18. Ibid., 174.
19. Third Committee, Summary Record of the Hundred and Thirty-Third Meeting, A/C.3/SR.133, 12 November 1948. Chang also succeeded in introducing the words "shall be" instead of "is" in Article 21:3, which was meant to be a proclamation of a right.
20. Suggestions Submitted by the Representative of France for Articles 7–44 of the International Declaration of Rights (Document E/CN.4/AC.1/W.2/Rev.1).
21. Third Committee, Summary Record of the Ninety-Eighth Meeting, Draft International Declaration of Human Rights (E/800), A/C3/SR.98, 9 October 1948.
22. Burke, *Decolonization and the Evolution of International Human Rights*, 114.
23. Drafting Committee of the Commission on Human Rights, Summary Record of the Third Meeting, E/CN.4/AC.1/SR.3, 11 June 1947.

24. Liu, "Shadows of Universalism," 397.
25. Burke, *Decolonization and the Evolution of International Human Rights*, 118, and Summary Records of the Third Committee of the General Assembly, 295th meeting, 27 October 1950. A/C.3/SR.295, para. 24.
26. Winter and Prost, *René Cassin and Human Rights*, 328.
27. Cassin, "Charter of Human Rights."
28. Sluga, "Rene Cassin," 114.
29. Winter and Prost, *René Cassin and Human Rights*, 241, 352.
30. Sluga, "Rene Cassin," 108; Humphrey, *Human Rights & the United Nations*, 24.
31. Hobbins, "Review of *A World Made New*," 380; Cassin, "How the Charter on Human Rights Was Born," 4.
32. Chang and Cheng, *Peng Chun Chang*.

Chapter 8

1. Bell, *China Model*, 263.
2. Chang, "Intercultural Contacts and Creative Adjustment," 516; Chang, *China at the Crossroads*, 124–125.
3. Chang, "Civilization and Social Philosophies," 8.
4. Ibid., 9.
5. Chang, "Intercultural Contacts and Creative Adjustments"; Chang, *China at the Crossroads*.
6. Ibid.
7. Chang, "Universities and National Reconstruction in China," 249.
8. Third Committee, UK resolution on advising social welfare functions, Fifty-Seventh Meeting, A/C.3/152, 3 October 1947.
9. Chang, "The Cultural Transformation of China," 163.
10. Ibid., 163. Chang identified five trends of Chinese thought concerning political change: (1) Sun Yat Sen's doctrine; (2) the Revolutionary approach represented by the Communists; (3) the Liberal approach of gradual reform that adressed problems such as poverty, corruption, disease, ignorance, and disorder; (4) the Conservative approach that denies that China can travel the same track as the West and that it instead should show reverence to its own past and; (5) Modernization on Chinese terms. Chang presumably favoured the fifth position in combination with the third. See Chang, "Whither China," 1–2.
11. Chang, "Intercultural Contacts and Creative Adjustment," 517–518.
12. Chang, *China at the Crossroads*, 155.
13. See, for example, Parekh, *Rethinking Multiculturalism*.
14. Third Committee, Summary Record of the Hundred and Sixty-Sixth Meeting, Draft International Declaration of Human Rights (E/800), A/C.3/SR.166, 30 November 1948.
15. Roth, *Vad är mänskliga rättigheter?*, 86.
16. Third Committee, Summary Record of the Ninety-Sixth Meeting, Draft International declaration of Human Rights (E/800), A7C.3/SR.96,7 October 1948.
17. Third Committee, Summary Record of the Hundred and Twenty-Seventh Meeting, Draft International Declaration of Human Rights (E/800), A/C.R/SR.127, 9 November 1948.

18. Summary Record of the Third Meeting (of the Drafting Committee of the Commission on Human Rights), E/CN.4/AC.1/SR, 11 June 1947.
19. Willard J. Peterson, personal communication to author, spring 2015.
20. Buruma, *Taming the Gods*, 56–57.
21. Chang, *China at the Crossroads*, 102.
22. Third Committee, Summary Record of the Hundred and Twenty-Seventh Meeting, Draft International Declaration of Human Rights (E/800), A/C.R/SR.127, 9 November 1948.
23. Chang, *China at the Crossroads*, 45
24. Peterson, "Squares and Circles," 51.
25. Chang, "Gospel in China."
26. Cheng and Cheng, *Peng Chun Chang*.
27. *China Institute Bulletin*, no. 47 (December 1947).
28. Bernstein, *Abuse of Evil*, 106–107.
29. Chang, *China at the Crossroads*, 175.
30. Ibid., 173.
31. Twiss, "Confucian Contributions to the Universal Declaration of Human Rights."
32. Ibid.
33. Kao, *Grounding Human Rights in a Pluralist World*, 178.
34. Krumbein, "P. C. Chang."
35. Morsink, *Universal Declaration of Human Rights*, 246.
36. Glendon, *World Made New*, 132–133, 225–226.
37. A similar claim could be made about how Chang is often described as Confucian in the secondary literature.
38. Glendon, personal communication to author, 2015.
39. Chang, *China at the Crossroads*, 45–46.
40. Angle and Tiwald, *Neo-Confucianism*, 210.
41. Confucius, *Essential Analects*.
42. Conversation with Willard Peterson, Spring 2017.
43. Angle, *Contemporary Confucian Political Philosophy*, 167.
44. Chang, "China's Stand on Freedom of Information," 26.
45. Chang, *China at the Crossroads*, 47.
46. Third Committee, 23 November 1948.
47. I would like to thank Johan Lagerkvist for this insight.
48. Tiwald, "Confucianism and Human Rights."
49. Chang, "Gospel in China." The pupil of Confucius—Mencius—claimed on the other hand that "Try your best to treat others as you would wish to be treated yourself, and you will find that this is the shortest way to benevolence," in *Meng Tzu* (7 A4).
50. I am grateful to Torbjörn Lodén for this observation.
51. Will, "La Contribution chinoise à la declaration universelle des droits de l'homme."
52. "Two Lectures," in Cheng and Cheng, *Peng Chun Chang*.
53. Third Committee, Summary Record of the Ninety-Sixth Meeting, Draft International Declaration of Human Rights (E/800), A/C.3/SR.96, 7 October 1948.
54. Drafting Committee of the Commission on Human Rights, Eighth Meeting, First Session, E/CN.4/AC.1/SR.8, 17 June 1947.
55. Chang, *China at the Crossroads*, 46–48.

56. "Two Lectures," in Cheng and Cheng, *Peng Chun Chang*.
57. Lodén, "Reason, Feeling and Ethics in the Thought of Mencius and Xunzi."
58. Ibid.
59. Glendon, *World Made New*, 67.
60. Ibid., 68.
61. Malik, *Challenge of Human Rights*, 70.
62. Buruma, *Taming the Gods*, 30–31.
63. Third Committee, Summary Record of Ninety-First Meeting, Draft International Declaration of Human Rights (E/800), A/C.3/SR.91, 2 October 1948.
64. Israel, "Admiration of China and Classical Chinese Thought in the Radical Enlightenment (1685–1740)," 7.
65. "Statement by Dr P. C. Chang Before the Plenary Meeting of the General Assembly on The Declaration of Human Rights," December 10, 1948.
66. Jacobsen, "Europas kinesiska upplysning"; Mungello, *Great Encounter of China and the West, 1500–1800*, 89.
67. Griffin, *On Human Rights*, 30–32; Tierney, *Idea of Natural Rights*.
68. Stout, *Ethics After Babel*, chap. 3.
69. Glendon, *World Made New*, 44.
70. Third Committee, Summary Record of the Hundred and Fifth Meeting, AC.3/SR.105, 18 October 1948.
71. Third Committee, Summary Record of the Hundred and Fifth Meeting, Draft International Declaration of Human Rights (E/800), A/C.3/SR.105, 18 October 1948.
72. Chang, "'Second Phase' of China's Struggle," 217, 222.
73. Chang, "China's Stand on Freedom of Information," 25–26.
74. Schabas, *Universal Declaration of Human Rights*.
75. Morsink, *Universal Declaration of Human Rights*, 245.
76. Rawls, *Political Liberalism*, 36–37.
77. Ibid., 17.
78. Huxtable, *Law, Ethics and Compromise at the Limits of Life*, 127.
79. Glendon, *World Made New*, 44; Humphrey, *Human Rights & the United Nations*, 17, 23–24, 37.
80. Gutmann and Thompson, *Spirit of Compromise*, 16.
81. Wolstertorff, *Justice*, 245.
82. Sun, "Pengchun Chang's Contributions to the Drafting of the UDHR," 114.

Chapter 9

1. Drafting Committee of the Universal Declaration of Human Rights, Summary Record of the Third Meeting, E/CN.4/AC.1/SR.3, 11 June 1947; Chang, *China at the Crossroads*, 97f; Chang, "Speaker Explains the Manchurian Case," 5.
2. Summary Record of the Seventh Meeting (of the Commission on Human Rights), E/CN.4/4.E/CN.4/W.4, 31 January 1947.
3. Drafting Committee of the Universal Declaration of Human Rights, Summary Record of the Hundred and Sixty-Sixth Meeting of the Third Committee, A/C.3/SR 166, 30 November 1948.

4. Drafting Committee of the Universal Declaration of Human Rights (E/422), Summary Record of the Sixty-Ninth Meeting of the Economic and Social Council, E/CN.4/SR.13, 14 March 1947).

5. Drafting Committee of the Universal Declaration of Human Rights (E/800), Summary Record of the Ninety-Sixth Meeting of the Third Committee, A/C.3/SR.96, 7 October 1948.

6. Morsink, *Universal Declaration of Human Rights*, 246

7. Commission on Human Rights, Drafting Committee, Draft International Declaration on Human Rights (submitted by the Chinese delegation), E/CN.4/AC.1/18, 3 May 1948.

8. Glendon, *World Made New*, 133.

9. Chang, *China: Whence and Wither?*, 114f.

10. Chang claimed in connection to the ideal of a "frontier society," exemplified by the American continental expansion that there is also in China "actual opportunities for expansion, even of the material kind, such as the wide territories in Manchuria, Mongolia, Turkestan, and Tibet, the vast natural resources waiting everywhere to be developed." See Chang, *Education for Modernization in China*, 25. This statement reveals that Chang regarded these territories as belonging to China.

11. Hobbins, *On the Edge of Greatness*, vol. 2, 28. See also Sluga, "Rene Cassin," 118.

12. Willard Petersen, personal communication to author, 2015.

13. Chang, *China: Whence & Wither?*, 115.

14. Ibid., 114.

15. Chang, *China at the Crossroads*.

16. Mackerras, *China in Transformation, 1900–1949*, chap. 11.

17. Roth, *Mångfaldens gränser*, chap. 3.

18. In his article "Civilization and Social Philosophies" from 1938, Chang criticized the attitude of being too proud of one's cultural heritage and having an old civilization. This attitude was, according to Chang, an obstacle against the modernization of China. See Chang, "Civilization and Social Philosophies," 10.

Conclusion

1. Cheng and Cheng, *Peng Chun Chang*.

2. Ibid.

3. Third Committee, Summary Record of the Ninety-Fifth Meeting, Draft International Declaration of Human Rights (E/800), A7C.3/SR.95, 6 October 1948.

4. Brown, *Courage*, 239.

5. Ibid.

6. Shklar, *Faces of Injustice*, 16f.

7. Twiss, "Confucian Contributions to the Universal Declaration of Human Rights," 110.

8. Malik, *Challenge of Human Rights*, 249–250. See also Third Committee, Draft First International Covenant on Human Rights and Measures of Implementaion, Three Hundred and First Meeting, Fifth Session, A/C.3/SR.301, 1 November 1950.

9. Reinbold, Seeing the Myth in Human Rights, Seventy-Fifth Meeting, Third Session, E/CN.4/SR.50, 7.

10. Sen, *Idea of Justice*, 387

11. Sen, *Human Rights and Asian Values*, 190–191.

12. Chang, "China's Stand on Freedom of Information," 29.
13. Svensson, *Debating Human Rights in China*, chaps. 5 and 8.
14. Schabas, "Appreciation of Dr. Peng Chun Chang." However, the Chinese Foreign Secretary Wang Yi expressed the following statements in 2015: "Seventy years ago China was directly involved in designing and building the international order and system with the United Nations as the center piece." This was probably the first time that a senior official from China erased the distinction between the Peoples Republic of China and the Republic of China with reference to the early 1940s. I am grateful to Professor Alastair Iain Johnston at Harvard for bringing these remarks to my attention. Wang Ji, "China's Role in the Global and Regional Order: Participant, Facilitator and Contributor," Speech at the Luncheon of the Fourth World Peace Forum, 2015/06/27.
15. Kinzelbach, "China's White Paper on Human Rights," 3.
16. Lo, "Human Rights in the Chinese Tradition," 187.
17. Roth, "Peng Chun Chang, Intercultural Ethics and the Universal Declaration of Human Rights," 104.
18. Moyn, *Last Utopia*, 4.
19. Mutua, *Human Rights*, 154–155, 178.
20. It is also unwarranted to question the validity of an idea on the basis of its origin. Even though some elements in human rights thinking may have a Western origin it does not prevent it from having universal validity.
21. See, for example, Glendon, *World Made New*, 119.
22. See Morsink, *Universal Declaration of Human Rights*; Glendon, *World Made New*; Winter and Prost, *René Cassin and Human Rights*.
23. See Kao, *Grounding Human Rights in a Pluralist World*, 178; Joas, *Sacredness of the Person*, 31.
24. Chang, "Whither China," 1.

Appendix

1. Will, "La Contribution chinoise à la declaration universelle des droits de l'homme."
2. Cheng and Cheng, *Peng Chun Chang*.
3. Schabas, *Universal Declaration of Human Rights*.
4. Among Chang's few Chinese publications, one could mention some articles that he published in the journal *Rensheng yu wenxue* (1935, vol. 3)—the titles translated in English "A Proposal for Reportage Literature on New Trends in National Reconstruction" and "The Situation in Soviet Russian Drama"; "My View of the United Nations," *Central Daily News* 3, no. 3 (1948); and "A Comparison of University Education in the United Kingdom and in China," *United Commentary Biweekly* 4 (1937).

BIBLIOGRAPHY

Alfredsson, Gudmundur, and Asbjörn Eide, eds. (1999). *The Universal Declaration of Human Rights* (The Hague: Martinus Nijhgoff Publishers).
Angle, Stephen C. (2012). *Contemporary Confucian Political Philosophy* (Cambridge: Polity).
Angle, Stephen C., and Justin Tiwald (2017). *Neo-Confucianism—A Philosophical Introduction* (Cambridge: Polity).
Barreto, Jose-Manuel (2013). *Human Rights from a Third World Perspective: Critique, History and International Law* (Cambridge: Cambridge Scholars Publishing).
Bell, Daniel A. (2015). *The China Model—Political Meritocracy and the Limits of Democracy* (Princeton, NJ: Princeton University Press).
Bernstein, Richard J. (2005). *The Abuse of Evil—The Corruption of Politics and Religion Since 9/11* (Cambridge: Polity Press).
Bevis Brawner, Teresa, and Christopher J. Lucas (2006). "Chinese Students in U.S. Colleges—The First Hundred Years," *International Educator*, November–December, pp. 26–33.
Bielefeldt, Heiner, Nazila Ghanea, and Michael Wiener (2016). *Freedom of Religion—An International Law Commentary* (Oxford: Oxford University Press).
Bol, Peter K. (2008). *Neo-Confucianism in History* (Cambridge, MA: Harvard University Press).
Boorman, Howard L. (1967). "Chang Poling," in Richard C. Howard, Joseph K. H. Cheng, and Howard L. Boorman, eds. *Biographical Dictionary of Republican China* (New York: Columbia University Press), pp. 100–105.
Bring, Ove (2017). "The Notion of Human Rights and the Issue of Cultural Relativism," in James Crawford, Abdul G.Koroma, Said Mahmoudi, and Allain Pellet, eds. *The International Legal Order: Current Needs and Possible Responses—Essays In Honour of Djamchid Momtaz* (Leiden: Brill/Nijhoff), pp. 544–558.
Brown, Gordon (2007). *Courage: Eight Portraits* (London: Bloomsbury).
Brown, Gordon (2016). *The Universal Declaration of Human Rights in the 21st Century* (New York: Open Publishers).
Buchanan, Tom (2012). *East Wind: China and the British Left, 1925–1976* (Oxford: Oxford University Press).
Burke, Roland (2010). *Decolonization and the Evolution of International Human Rights* (Philadelphia: University of Pennsylvania Press).
Buruma, Ian (2010). *Taming the Gods–Religion and Democracy on Three Continents* (Princeton, NJ: Princeton University Press).
Cassin, Réne (1968). "The Charter of Human Rights," Nobel Lecture, 11 December.
Cassin, Réne (1968). "How the Charter of Human Rights Was Born," *UNESCO Courier*, 21 January, pp. 4–6

Cassin, Réne (1972). *La Pensée et L'Action* (Paris: Editions F. Lalou).
Chan, Joseph (1999). "A Confucian Perspective on Human Rights for Contemporary China," in Joanne R. Bauer and Daniel A. Bell, eds. *The East Asian Challenge to Human Rights* (Cambridge: Cambridge University Press.), pp. 212–240.
Chan, Susan, and Zhiping Zhiu Egan (2009). *A Pragmatist and His Free Spirit* (New York: Chinese University Press).
Chang, P. C. (1912). "China's Real Situation," *Chinese Students' Monthly*, 10 December, pp. 83–86.
Chang, P. C. (1912). "National Ideals," *Chinese Students' Monthly*, 10 December, pp. 17–21.
Chang, P. C. (1913). "A Brief Survey of Extraterritoriality, or Consular Jurisdiction in Non-Christian Lands," *Chinese Students' Monthly* 8, no. 6, pp. 400–406.
Chang, P. C. (1914). "China's Desire to Retain the Best in Her Own Tradition," in Fennell Parrish Turner, ed. *Students and the World-Wide Expansion of Christianity* (London: Forgotten Books, reprint, 2013), pp. 244–246.
Chang, P. C. (1914). "Chinese Students in North America," *North American Student* 2, no. 5, pp. 229–231.
Chang, P. C. (1914). "Chinese Themes on the Stage—A Comment on 'Mr. Wu,'" *Chinese Students' Monthly* 10, no. 4, pp. 218–222.
Chang, P. C. (1914). "Christian Leadership and China's Religious Awakening," *Student World* 7-9, pp. 61–63.
Chang, P. C. (1914). "The Gospel in China," in Fennell Parrish Turner, ed. *Students and the World Wide Expansion of Christianity* (London: Forgotten Books, reprint, 2013), pp. 517–520.
Chang, P. C. (1914). "The Prayer of a Chinese," in Ralph E. Diffendorfer, ed. *Thy Kingdom Come: A Book of Social Prayers for Public and Private Worship* (London: Forgotten Books), p. 38.
Chang, P. C. (1915). "A New World: A New Attitude," *Liu Mei Tsing Nien* 1, no. 3, pp. 115–116.
Chang, P. C. (1915). "Shakespeare in China—A Tercentenary Tribute," *Chinese Student Monthly* 11, pp. 396–399.
Chang, P. C. (1920). "The Awakening of China," *Bulletin of the Foreign Policy Association* 1-2, May, pp. 2–3, 6.
Chang, P. C. (1920). "The Rising Consciousness of Civic Responsibility among the Students of China," in *The World's Moral Problems: Adresses at the Third World's Christian Citizenship Conference held in Pittsburgh, PA, 9–16 November 1919* (Pittsburgh: National Reform Association), pp. 382–384.
Chang, P. C. (1921). "New Year in Princeton—A Poem," *Princeton Alumni Weekly* 21, no. 17 (9 February 1921), p. 386.
Chang, P. C. (1923). *Education for Modernization in China* (New York: Columbia University).
Chang, P. C. (1930). "The Present Condition of Chinese Social and Political Life," *Bulletin of the Institute of International Relations* 6, pp. 187–189.
Chang, P. C. (1930). "Some Aspects of Chinese Theatrical Art," in Ruth H. C. Cheng and Sze-Chuh Cheng, eds. *Peng Chun Chang: Biography and Collected Works* (Private publication, 1975), pp. 120–123.
Chang, P. C. (1931). "The Cultural Transformation of China", *Mid-Pacific Magazine* 41, no. 2 (February), pp. 161–164.
Chang, P. C. (1931). "Speaker Explains Manchurian Case" (Transition in China), *Scarsdale Inquirer*, 13 November, p. 5.

Bibliography 277

Chang, P. C. (1931). "Whither China: An Analysis of Trends of Current Chinese Thoughts—An Outline," *China Institute Bulletin*, January, pp. 1-3.
Chang, P. C. (1933). "Education and Scientific Research," *Open Court* 1933 no. 7, pp. 423-432.
Chang, P. C. (1933). "The New Drama and the Old Theater," *Open Court* 1933 no. 7, pp. 453-458.
Chang, P. C. (1933). "Redirecting Educational Effort in China," *Pacific Affairs* 6, no. 6 (June-July), pp. 281-291.
Chang, P. C. (1934). *China: Whence and Whither? An Outline of a High School Unit of Study*, (Institute of Pacific Relations: Honolulu, T. H.).
Chang, P. C. (1936). *China at the Crossroads* (London: Evan Brothers).
Chang, P. C. (1936). "Intercultural Contacts and Creative Adjustment," *Progressive Education* no. 13 (November), pp. 515-520.
Chang, P. C. (1937). "A Comparison of University Education in the United Kingdom and in China," *United Commentary Biweekly* 4, pp. 1-5.
Chang, P. C. (1938). "Civilization and Social Philosophies," in *America and a World at Conflict*, Progressive Education Booklet, no. 9, pp. 5-13.
Chang, P. C. (1938). "The First Year and After" (Summary of a Speech given at the Summer Session, Columbia University, July 13), *Far Eastern Magazine* 2, pp. 7--9.
Chang, P. C. (1939). "The European War and the Far Eastern Situation," *Frontiers of Democracy* 6, pp. 88-90.
Chang, P. C. (1939). "Old Ideas and New China," *Listener* 21, pp. 727-730.
Chang, P. C. (1939). "The 'Second Phase' of China's Struggle," *International Affairs* 18, no. 2, pp. 211-216.
Chang, P. C. (1939). "Universities and National Reconstruction in China," in Edward Bradby, ed. *The University Outside Europe* (New York: Oxford University Press), pp. 243-254.
Chang, P. C. (1942). "Two Lectures," in Ruth H. C. Cheng and Sze-Chuh Cheng, eds. *Peng Chun Chang: Biography and Collected Work* (Private publication, 1975), pp. 143-149
Chang, P. C. (1946). "Three Speeches: A New Loyalty, War Against Microbes and World Significance of Economically 'Low Pressure' Areas," in Ruth H. C. Cheng and Sze- Chuh Cheng, eds. *Peng Chun Chang: Biography and Collected Work* (Private publication, 1975), pp. 150-153.
Chang, P. C. (1948). "China's Stand on Freedom of Information," *China Magazine* 18 (April), pp. 25-31.
Chang, P. C. (1948). "My View of the United Nations," *Central Daily News* 3, no. 3.
Chang, P. C. (1948). "Statement by Dr. P. C. Chang Before the Plenary Meeting of the General Assembly of the Declaration of the Human Rights," 2 October 1948. F. D. Roosevelts Library.
Chang, P. C. (1956). *How Nankai Began* (Unpublished manuscript).
Chang, P. C. (n.d.). "Chinese Understanding of Music," in Ruth, H. C. Cheng and Sze-Chuh Cheng, eds. *Peng Chun Chang: Biography and Collected Work* (Private publication), pp. 172-175
Chang, Y. F. (1996). *Trisha & Stanley* (Pittsburgh, PA: Dorrance).
Chatterjee, Sourabh (2014). "Tagore: A Case Study of His Visit to China in 1924," *IOSR Journal of Humanities and Social Science* 19, no. 3 (March), pp. 28-35.
Chen, Yuan-feng (2013). "The No 1 Play Director Zhang Pengchun and His Early Activities as a Play Director," *Oriental Forum* 2013, no. 2.

Cheng, Ruth H. C., and Cheng, eds. (1995). *Peng Chun Chang: Biography and Collected Works* (Private publication).
Ching-Sze Wang, Jessica (2007). *John Dewey in China* (Albany: SUNY Press).
Confucius (2006). *The Essential Analects: Selected Passages with Traditional Commentary* (Cambridge, MA: Hacket).
Craft. Stephen G. (2004). *V. K. Wellington Koo and the Emergence of Modern China* (Lexington: University Press of Kentucky).
Cruft, Rowan (2015). "Human Rights as Individualistically Justified: A Defence," in Thom Brooks, ed. *Current Controversies in Political Philosophy* (London: Routledge), pp. 45–62.
Cui, Guoliang, and Rong Li (2016). "Peng Chun Chang: A Man who Integrated the Oriental Confucian Thought" with the Universal Declaration of Human Rights," *China Human Rights* (available from http://www.chinahuman rights.org/CSHRS/books/text/t20130419 _1024939).
Cui, Guoliang, and Hong Dong Xiuhua (2003). *On Education and Dramatic Art by Zhang Pengchun* (Tijanin: Nankai University).
Davie, Grace (1994). *Religion in Britain Since 1945—Believing Without Belonging* (Oxford: Wiley Blackwell).
Davin, Delia (2013). *Mao* (Oxford: Oxford University Press).
Dennis, Lawrence J. (1989). *George S. Counts and Charles A. Beard. Colloborators for Change* (Albany: State University of New York Press).
Dewey, John (1929). *Impressions of Soviet Russia and the Revolutionary World—Mexico, China and Turkey* (New York: Teacher's College, Columbia University).
Dikötter, Frank (2008). *The Age of Openess—China Before Mao* (Hong Kong: Hong Kong University Press).
Donders, Yvonne, and Vladimir Volodin, eds. (2007). *Human Rights in Education, Science and Culture: Legal Developments and Challenges* (Farnham, UK: Ashgate).
Donnely, Jack (2003). *Universal Human Rights in Theory and Practice*, 2nd ed. (Ithaca, NY: Cornell University Press.)
Dudley, Dorothy (1922). "Notes from the P.S.A. Annual Dinner," *Poetry* 20, no. 1 (April), pp. 53–56.
Dworkin, Ronald (1981). "What Is Equality? Part 2—Equality of Resources," *Philosophy and Public Affairs* 10, no. 4 (Autumn), pp. 283–345.
Dworkin, Ronald (2011). *Justice for Hedgehogs* (Cambridge, MA: Belknap Press).
Elman, Benjamin A. (2013). *Civil Examinations and Meritocracy in Late Imperial China*. (Cambridge, MA: Harvard University Press).
Epstein, Israel (2015). *My China Eye—Memoirs of a Jew and a Journalist* (Beijing: New Star Press).
Erlanger, Steven (2015). "Are Western Values Losing Their Sway?," *International New York Times*, September 12, p. 4.
Etinson, Adam (2013). "Human Rights, Claimability and the Uses of Abstraction," *Utilitas* 25, no. 4 (December), pp. 463–486.
Fei, Long, and Kong Yangeng (2016). *Poling and P. C. Chang* (Tianjin: Nankai University Publishing House).
Finnis, John (1980). *Natural Law and Natural Rights* (Oxford: Oxford University Press).
Gardell, Carl Johan (2009). "Chiang Kai-shek har fått en sen revansch," *Svenska Dagbladet*, 2 December.
Gardner, Daniel K. (2014). *Confucianism* (Oxford: Oxford University Press).

Glendon, Mary Ann (2001). *A World Made New—Eleanor Roosevelt and the Universal Declaration of Human Rights* (New York: Random House).
Glendon, Mary Ann (2004). "The Rule of Law in the Universal Declaration of Human Rights," *Northwestern Journal of International Human Rights* 2, no. 1, pp. 2-19.
Glendon, Mary Ann. (2011). *The Forum and the Tower—How Scholars and Politicians Have Imagined the World from Plato and to Eleanor Roosevelt.* (Oxford: Oxford University Press).
Goldstone, Jack A. (2014). *Revolutions* (Oxford: Oxford University Press).
Green, O. M. (1937). "Review: *China at the Crossroads*," *International Affairs* 16, no. 2 (March-April), pp. 329-330.
Grieder, Jerome B. (1970). *Hu Shi and the Chinese Renaissance* (Cambridge, MA: Harvard University Press).
Griffin, James (2008). *On Human Rights* (Oxford: Oxford University Press).
Gutmann, Amy, and Dennis Thompson (2012). *The Spirit of Compromise: Why Governing Demands It and Campaigning Undermines It.* (Princeton, NJ: Princeton University Press).
Hartman, Sven (2012). *Det pedagogiska kulturarvet*, 2nd ed. (Stockholm: Natur och Kultur).
Hayes, Louis D. (2005) *Introduction to Japanese Politics*, 4th ed. (Armonk, NY: M. E. Sharpe).
Heaney, Seamus (2008). "Human Rights, Poetic Redress," *Irish Times*, 15 March.
Hobbins, A. J. (2000). *On The Edge of Greatness: The Diaries of John P Humphrey*, 4 vols. (Montreal: McGill University).
Hobbins, A. J. (2002). Review: *A World Made New: Eleanor Roosevelt and the Universal Declaration of Human Rights*, by Mary Ann Glendon, *Journal of the History of International Law* 4, 379-383.
Hocking, W. E. (1948). "Old and New in Moral Philosophy," in John Stuart, ed. *There is Another China* (New York: King's Crown Press), pp. 151-176.
Holcombe, Arthur N. (1930). *The Chinese Revolution* (Cambridge, MA: Harvard University Press).
Hsia, Ching Lin (1977). *My Five Incursions Into Diplomacy* (New York, Great Neck).
Humphrey, John P. (1984). *Human Rights & the United Nations: A Great Adventure* (New York: Transnational Publishers.
Hunt, Lynn (2007). *Inventing Human Rights: A History* (New York: Norton).
Huxtable, Richard (2013). *Law, Ethics and Compromise at the Limits of Life—To Treat or Not to Treat* (Abingdon: Routledge).
Ignatieff, Michael (2001). "The Attack on Human Rights," *Foreign Affairs* 80, no. 6 (November-December), pp. 102-116.
Ignatieff, Michael (2003). *Human Rights as Politics and Idolatry* (Princeton, NJ: Princeton University Press).
Ignatieff, Michael (2017). "Human Rights, Global Ethics and the Ordinary Virtues," *Ethics and International Affairs* 3, no. 1 (Spring), pp. 3-16.
Ignatieff, Michael (2017). *The Ordinary Virtues—Moral Order in a Divided World* (Cambridge, MA: Harvard University Press).
Ishay, Micheline R. (2004). "What Are Human Rights? Six Historical Controversies," *Journal of Human Rights* 3, no. 3 (September), pp. 359-371.
Israel, Jonathan I. "Admiration of China and Classical Chinese Thought in the Radical Enlightenment (1685-1740)," *Taiwan Journal of East Asian Studies* 4, no. 1 (June 2007), pp. 1-25.
Jacobsen, Stefan Gaarsmand (2008). "Europas kinesiske oplysning," *Semikolon* 8, no. 16, pp. 59-70.
Jin, Fu (2010). *Chinese Theatre* (Cambridge: Cambridge University Press).

Joas, Hans (2013). *The Sacredness of the Person—A New Genealogy of Human Rights* (Washington, DC: Georgetown University Press).
Johnson, M. Glen (1998). *A Magna Carta for Mankind: Writing the Universal Declaration of Human Rights* (Paris: UNESCO Publishing).
Kampen, Thomas (2009). "Olympic Games and Human Rights: Zhang Boling and Zhang Pengchun," *EACS Newsletter*, no. 42 (June).
Kao, Y. Grace (2011). *Grounding Human Rights in a Pluralist World* (Washington, DC: Georgetown University Press).
Kinzelbach, Katrin (2016). "China's White Paper on Human Rights—Commentary," *Global Public Policy Institute*, 5 April (available from http://www.GPPL.NET/), pp. 1-7.
Klug, Francesca (2015). *A Magna Carta for All Humanity—Homing in on Human Rights* (London: Routledge).
Krumbein, Frédéric (2015). "P. C. Chang—The Chinese Father of Human Rights," *Journal of Human Rights* 1, pp. 332-352.
Kymlicka, Will (1995). *Multicultural Citizenship* (Oxford: Oxford University Press).
Lary, Diana (2007). *China's Republic* (Cambridge: Cambridge University Press).
Latourette, K. S. (1937). "Review: *China at the Crossroads*," *Pacific Affairs* 10, no. 3 (September), pp. 351-352.
Lee, Chae-jin (1996). *Zhou Enlai: The Early Years* (Standford, CA: Stanford University Press).
Li, Henry (2016). *Peng-Chun Chang, American Pragmatism, and the Universal Declaration of Human Rights*. BA thesis, Harvard College, Cambridge, MA.
Little, David (2015). *Essays on Religion and Human Rights* (Cambridge: Cambridge University Press).
Liu, Lydia H. (2014). "Professor Lydia H. Liu on Human Rights Pioneer and Columbia Alum P. C. Chang" (Columbia University Home Page).
Liu, Lydia H. (2014). "Shadows of Universalism: The Untold Story of Human Rights Around 1948," *Critical Inquiry* 40 (Summer), pp. 385-417.
Lo, Chung-Shu (1950). "Human Rights in the Chinese Tradition," in Jacques Maritain, ed. *Human Rights: Comments and Interpretations* (London: Allan Wingate), pp. 186-190.
Lodén, Torbjörn (2006). *Rediscovering Confucianism—A Major Philosophy of Life in East Asia* (Folkestone: Global Oriental LTD).
Lodén, Torbjörn (2009). "Reason, Feeling and Ethics in the Thought of Mencius and Xunzi," *Journal of Chinese Philosophy* 36, no. 4 (December 2009), pp. 602-617.
Lundberg, Anna (2009). "Debatter i samband med antagandet av den allmänna förklaringen," in Mikael Spång, ed. *Mänskliga rättighete—ett ofullbordat uppdrag* (Malmö: Liber), pp. 61-77.
Luo, Zhitian (2015). *Inheritance Within Rupture: Culture and Scholarship in Early Twentieth Century China* (Leiden: Brill).
Mackerras, Colin (2008). *China in Tranformation, 1900-1949.* (Harlow: Pearson Longman).
Malik, Charles (2000). *The Challenge of Human Rights* (Oxford: Centre for Lebanese Studies).
Malik, Habib (2016). "Charles Malik and the Universal Declaration of Human Rights." Paper delivered at Human Rights and Philosophy: On the Philosophical Origins and Implications of the UDHR, Södertörn University, Stockholm, 16 September.
McFarland, Sam (2016). "Architects of the Universal Declaration: Eleanor Roosevelt, Charles Malik, Peng Chun Chang, John Humphrey and René Cassin," *Chaoyang Law Review* 12, pp. 296-312.

Mitter, Rana (2008). *Modern China* (Oxford: Oxford University Press).Morsink, Johannes (1984). "The Philosophy of the Universal Declaration," *Human Rights Quarterly* 6, no. 3 (August), pp. 309-334.

Morsink, Johannes (1999). *The Universal Declaration of Human Rights: Origins, Drafting and Intent.* (Philadelphia: University of Pennsylvania Press.)

Morsink, Johannes (2009). *Inherent Human Rights—Philosophical Roots of the UN Declaration* (Philadelphia: University of Pennsylvania Press).

Moyn, Samuel (2010). *The Last Utopia: Human Rights in History* (Cambridge, MA: Harvard University Press).

Moyn, Samuel (2014). *Human Rights and the Uses of History* (Cambridge, MA: Harvard University Press).

Mungello, D. E. (1999). *The Great Encounter of China and the West, 1500-1800.* (Lanham, New York: Rowman & Littlefield).

Mutua, Makau (2002). *Human Rights: A Political and Cultural Critique* (Philadelphia: University of Pennsylvania Press).

Neary, Ian (2002). *Human Rights in Japan, South Korea and Taiwan* (London: Routledge).

Nozick, Robert (1974). *Anarchy, State and Utopia* (Oxford: Blackwell).

Nickel, James W. (2014). "What Future for Human Rights?," *Ethics & International Affairs* 28, no. 2, pp. 213-223.

Orend, Brian (2002). *Human Rights—Concept and Context* (Peterborough, ON: Broadview Press).

Papanek, Ernst (1957). "William Heard Kilpatrick's International Influence: Teacher of World Teachers," *Progressive Education* 33/34 (March), pp. 54-60.

Parekh, Bhikhu (2005). *Rethinking Multiculturalism—Cultural Diversity and Political Theory.* (Basingstoke, UK: Palgrave).

Peterson, Willard J. (1988). "Squares & Circles: Mapping the History of Chinese Thought," *Journal of the History of Ideas* 49 (1): pp. 47-60.

Plautus (2006). *Asinaria—The One about the Asses.* Translated by John Henderson. (Madison: University of Wisconsin Press).

Pomfret, John (2016). *The Beautiful Country and the Middle Kingdom: America and China* (New York: Henry Holt).

Rawls, John (1993). *Political Liberalism* (New York: Columbia University Press).

Reinbold, Jenna (2016). *Seeing the Myth in Human Rights* (Philadelphia: University of Pennsylvania Press).

Renberg, Bo (2011). *Helen Kellers värld* (Stockholm: Hjalmarson & Högberg).

Robinson, Andrew (2009). *Writing and Script—A Very Short Introduction* (Oxford: Oxford University Press).

Roosevelt, Eleanor (1948). "The Promise of Human Rights," *Foreign Affairs* 26, no. 3, pp. 470-477.

Roosevelt, Eleanor (1949). "Making Human Rights Come Alive," *Phi Delta Kappan* 31, no. 1 (September), pp. 23-33.

Roosevelt, Eleanor (1958). *On My Own* (New York: Harper Brothers).

Roosevelt, Eleanor (1961). *The Autobiography of Eleanor Roosevelt* (New York: Harper).

Roth, Hans Ingvar (2007). *Vad är mänskliga rättigheter?* (Stockholm: Natur och kultur).

Roth, Hans Ingvar (2010). *Mångfaldens gränser* (Stockholm: Dialogos förlag).

Roth, Hans Ingvar (2012). *Är religion en mänsklig rättighet?* (Stockholm: Norstedts förlag).

Roth, Hans Ingvar (2016). "Peng Chun Chang, Intercultural Ethics and the Universal Declaration of Human Rights," in Göran Collste, ed. *Ethics and Communication—Global Perspectives* (London: Rowman & Littlefield), pp. 95-124.
Russell, Bertrand (1922). *The Problem of China* (London: George Allen & Unwin).
Said, Edward W. (1978) *Orientalism* (New York: Pantheon Books).
Santa Cruz, Hernan (1984). *Cooperar o Perecer: Los anos de creación 1941-1960* (Buenos Aires: Grupo Editor Latino Americano).
Schabas, William A. (2012). "Samuel Moyn, Peng Chun Chang & the Universal Declaration of Human Rights," *PhD Studies in Human Rights* (blog), 13 May. http://humanrightsdoctorate.blogspot.com/2012/05/samuel-moyn-peng-chun-chang-and.html.
Schabas, William A. (2013). *The Universal Declaration of Human Rights* (Cambridge: Cambridge University Press).
Schenck, Norman C. (1933). "An Appreciation of Dr Peng Chun Chang," *Mid-Pacific Magazine* 46-47, p. 55.
Scott, A. C. (1971). *Mei Lan- Fang: The Life and Times of a Peking Actor* (Oxford: Oxford University Press).
Sen, Amartya (1997). *Human Rights and Asian Values* (New York. Carnegie Council).
Sen, Amartya (2009). *The Idea of Justice* (Cambridge, MA: Belknap Press).
Shih, Huh (1948) "Chang Poling: A Tribute," in John Stuart, ed. *There Is Another China* (New York: Kings Crown Press), pp. 4-14.
Shklar, Judith N. (1992). *The Faces of Injustice* (New Haven, CT: Yale University Press).
Siedentop, Larry (2014). "Remember the Religious Roots of Liberal Thought," *Financial Times*, 23 January.
Sim, May (2004). "A Confucian Approach to Human Rights," *History of Philosophy Quarterly* 21, no. 4 (October), pp. 337-356.
Sluga, Glenda (2011). "René Cassin: Les Droits de L'homme and the Universality of Human Rights, 1945-1966," in Stefan-Ludvig Hoffman, ed. *Human Rights in the Twentieth Century* (Cambridge: Cambridge University Press), pp. 107-124.
Sluga, Glenda (2013). *Internationalism in the Age of Nationalism* (Philadelphia: University of Pennsylvania Press).
Stout, Jeffrey (2001). *Ethics After Babel—The Languages of Morals and Their Discontents* (Princeton, NJ: Princeton University Press).
Stuart, John (1948). *There Is Another China* (New York: King's Crown Press).
Sun, Pinghua (2016). "Pengchun Chang's Contributions to the Drafting of the UDHR," *Journal of Civil & Legal Sciences* 5, no. 5, pp. 1-9. .
Sunstein, Cass R. (2002). "Rights of Passage," *New Republic*, 25 February.
Svensson, Marina (2002). *Debating Human Rights in China* (New York: Rowman and Littlefield).
Tasioulas, John (2013). "Justice, Equality and Rights," in Roger Crisp, ed. *The Oxford Handbook of the History of Ethics* (Oxford: Oxford University Press), pp. 768-792
Tian, Min (2007). "Gordon Craig, Mei Lanfang and the Chinese Theatre," *Theatre Research International* 32, no. 2, pp. 161-177.
Tierney, Brian (1997). *The Idea of Natural Rights—Natural Law and Church Law* (Grand Rapids, MI: Eerdemans).
Tierney, Brian (2004). "The Idea of Natural Rights—Origins and Persistence," *Northwestern Journal of International Human Rights* 2, no. 1, pp. 2-13.

Tiwald, Justin (2011). "Confucianism and Human Rights," in Thomas Cushman, ed. *Routledge Handbook of Human Rights* (London: Routledge), pp. 244–254.

Twiss, Sumner B. (2011). "Confucian Contributions to the Universal Declaration of Human Rights: A Historical and Philosophical Perspective," in Arvind Sharma, ed. *The World's Religions After September 11* (Minneapolis: Fortress Press.), pp. 102–114.

Twiss, Sumner B. (2011). "P. C. Chang, Freedom of Conscience and Religion, and the Universal Declaration of Human Rights," in Arvid Sharma, ed. *The World's Religions After September 11* (Minneapolis: Fortress Press), pp. 175–183.

Urquhart, Brian (2001). "Mrs. Roosevelt's Revolution," *New York Review of Books*, 26 April, pp. 32–34.

Wager, R. E. (1924) "Review: *Education for Modernization in China*," *Elementary School Journal* 25, no. 1 (September), pp. 68–70.

Walters, F. P. A. (1960). *A History of the League of Nations* (Oxford: Oxford University Press).

Walzer, Michael (1983). *Spheres of Justice* (New York: Basic Books).

Wang, Chaohua (2017). "China's First Revolution", *New Left Review*, July/August, pp. 125–140.

Wang, Ji (2015). "China's Role in the Global and Regional Order: Participant, Facilitator and Contributor," Speech at the Luncheon of the Fourth World Peace Forum (27 June).

Wen, Haiming, and William Kel'i Akina (2012). "Human Rights Ideology as Endemic in Chinese Philosophy: Classical Confucian and Mohist Perspectives," *Asian Philosophy* 22, no. 4 (November), pp. 387–413.

Wasserstrom, Jeffrey N. (1991). *Student Protests in Twentieth-Century China: The View from Shanghai* (Stanford: Stanford University Press).

Wellman, Carl (2011). *The Moral Dimensions of Human Rights* (New York: Oxford University Press).

Will, Pierre-Étienne (2007). "La Contribution chinoise à la declaration universelle des droits de l'homme," in Mireille Delmas-Marty and Pierre-Etienne Will, eds. *La Chine et la démcratie: Tradition, droit institutions* (Paris: Fayard), chapter 10.

Willing, M. H. (1924). "Review of *Education for Modernization in China*," *Journal of Educational Psychology* 15, no. 5 (May), pp. 325–326.

Winter, Jay, and Antoine Prost (2013). *René Cassin and Human Rights—From the Great War to the Universal Declaration* (Cambridge: Cambridge University Press).

Wolstertorff, Nicholas (2010). *Justice: Rights and Wrongs* (Princeton, NJ: Princeton University Press).

Woods, Kerri (2015). *Human Rights* (New York: Palgrave Macmillan).

Wright, David Curtis (2001). *The History of China* (Westport, CT: Greenwood).

Xingzhi, Tao (2016). *The Transformation of Chinese Traditional Education—Selected Papers* (Leiden: Brill).

Ye, Weili (2002). *Seeking Modernity in China's Name: Chinese Students in the United States, 1900–1927* (Stanford, CA: Stanford University Press).

Yu, Yen (1929). *Tsang-Lang Discourse on Poetry*. Translated by Peng Chun Chang. (Pittsburgh: Laboratory Press).

Yu, Peter K. (2007). "Reconceptualizing Intellectual Property Interests in a Human Rights Framework," *U. C. Davis Law Review* 40, pp. 1039–1149.

Zhao, Jun (2015). "China and the Uneasy Case for Universal Human Rights," *Human Rights Quarterly* 37, no. 1 (February), pp. 29–52.

Zheng, Zhiguang (1989). *Zhang Boling zhuan* [Biography of Zhang Boling] (Tianjin: Tianjin renmin chubanshe).

Zhou, Xiaojuan (2014). *The Influences of the American Boxer Indemnity Reparations Remissions on Chinese Higher Education* (Lincoln: Digital Commons, University of Nebraska).

INDEX

Addison, Joseph, 214
African Charter on Human and Peoples' Rights (1986), 134
agnosticism, 126, 200, 203
altruists, 241–42
American Anthropological Association, 171
American Convention on Human Rights (1969), 134
American Declaration of the Rights and Duties of Man [Bogotá Declaration] (1948), 132
American Law Institute, 132
American University (Beirut), 125
Amnesty International, 134
Analects of Confucius, The, 105, 154, 201, 207
anthropology, philosophical, 153, 165, 226, 237
anti-Semitism, 130
antislavery movement, 131
apartheid, 134, 159
Arab League, 126
Aristotle, 27
Article 1, of UDHR, 3, 152, 180, 224, 227, 240; balance of individual and community, 150–51; debate over, 127–28, 184; drafting of, 197; as key section, 129, 144, 219, 240; phrasing of, 165, 196, 222–23, 226, 229; "two-man mindedness" and, 211, 213–14. *See also* religion, freedom of
art of living, 171, 200, 241; metaphysics versus, 204, 223, 226, 237; rights rhetoric and, 215
Athayde, Austregésilo de, 157, 219
atheism, 203
Atlantic Charter, 117
atomic bombs, 130, 156

Attlee, Clement, 71
Australia, 95, 116, 121, 124
Avare, L' [*The Miser*] (Molière), 59, 73
Awakening, The (Chang), 27
Axis powers, 2, 75, 117, 127; brutality of, 161, 170; Japan's role in, 156

Bacon, Francis, 150
Bayle, Pierre, 214
Beard, Charles A., 90, 263n13
Beijing University, 258n22
Belarus, 122, 183
Belgium, 171
Berlin Blockade, 126
Bevin, Lord Ernest, 90
Bill of Rights, US, 131, 208
Bombs on China (film), 70
Boxer Rebellion, 9, 19; Indemnity Reparation Fund, 19, 37, 46, 70, 100; Indemnity Scholarship Program, 20, 23, 41, 47, 89
Brazil, 79, 144
Brecht, Bertolt, 54
Briand, Aristide, 56
bricolage, 217
"Brief Survey of Extraterritoriality, A" (Chang, 1913), 22–23
Bring, Ove, 136
Britain, 23, 45, 144; as colonial power, 22, 56; Commission on Human Rights and, 119; drafting of UDHR and, 121, 124; Opium Wars and, 10
brotherhood (community), 180, 196, 202, 213, 219; balance with rights of the individual, 150–51; Chinese philosophy and, 211
Brown, Gordon, 241, 242
Buddhism, 124–25, 192, 198
Burns, Robert, 157, 159, 249

Canada, 95
Cao Rulin, 32, 33
Cao Yu, 47, 49
capitalism, 97
Cassin, René, 4, 6, 112, 156, 179–80, 241; Chang's conflict with, 180–87, 248; on human nature, 160–61; importance in drafting team of UDHR, 128; as legal expert, 129, 145; memoir of, 161, 179, 247; Nobel speech (1968), 134; as outspoken French nationalist, 184, 248; proposal for preamble to UDHR, 139; Rousseau's notion of compassion and, 212; in UN Declaration writing group, 115, 116, 121; Zionism of, 126
Centre for the Study of Human Rights Studies (Nankai University), 17
Chang, Chen Chung (first son of PCC), 49, 69, 108, 109, 187; at Harvard, 234, 235; marriage, 233–34
Chang, Marjorie, 233, 235
Chang, Ming-Ming (first daughter of PCC), 45, 55, 68, 104, 110; brain damaged by meningitis, 46; PCC's distance from, 235; in wartime China, 74, 107
Chang, P. C.: art of compromise and, 218, 220–24; Baghdad lectures, 75–77; blind spots and moral limitations of, 231–36; Cassin's conflict with, 180–87, 248; Cassin's working relationship with, 179–80; Chiang Kai-shek and, 51–52, 98, 101, 243; in Chicago, 55–56; on Chinese restraint, 196–97; Christianity and, 201–4, 250; as Confucian, 204–7; cosmopolitanism of, 4; as cultural mediator, 239–41, 242; cultural traditions of China and, 236–38; Dewey's influence on, 40–44, 203–4; on education, 149; in England, 60–64; family life of, 233–36, 242, 249; famine relief and, 38, 260n72; final years and death, 104–9, 110, 246; in Hawaii, 57–59; heart attacks, 74, 78, 96, 106, 107, 129, 156, 186; hobbies of, 25–26, 106; on humanity's dual nature, 5; as human rights pioneer, 4; on ideological conflicts, 189; on inherent natural human qualities, 163–66; intercultural ethics of, 188; Japanese invasion of China and, 66–69; Malik's disagreements with, 119–20, 147, 164–65, 174–79, 248; Mei Lanfang and, 52–55; "Middle Kingdom" or "Centralist" attitude of, 167, 185, 232, 237, 242, 248; on modernization of China, 190–93, 270n10; name variants, 1, 257n1 (Intro.); on nations behaving like children, 162, 218; as professional hero, 241–44; as professor at Nankai University, 45; "propaganda trips" of, 69–73; recognition of achievements of, 245–47; relationship with brother, 13–14, 46, 102, 231; return to China (1916–1919), 30–36; sources on life and work of, 253–55; theatrical interests of, 26–29
Chang, P. C., diplomatic career, 4, 45; family life and, 103–4, 109; outcome of Chinese civil war and, 93–96; retirement from UN (1952), 95, 97, 104, 106. *See also* Chile; Turkey
Chang, P. C., drafting of UN Declaration and, 2, 3, 63, 112, 155–57, 257n2 (Intro.); Chang as "critical author," 128, 129; Chang's personal experiences and, 101; Chang's significance for the UDHR, 144–55; Chinese classical philosophy and, 101, 202; civil war in China and, 82; defeats for Chang, 228–30; Dewey's influence and, 40, 43; education and, 40; formulation of preamble, 152–53; lack of recognition for, 106; at meetings for work on UDHR, 119–24; special role in Chinese delegation, 141; strategies used by Chang, 210–11
Chang, P. C., family life of, 12–13, 75, 87–89; diplomatic travels and, 103–4; raising a family with wife, 45–47; relationship with brother, 13–14, 46, 102
Chang, P. C., in United States, 1, 29, 46, 216, 239, 243; doctoral studies and marriage, 36–38; first period of study (Clark University), 19–26; public lectures, 38
Chang, P. C., writings of: *The Awakening*, 27, 28; "A Brief Survey of Extraterritoriality" (1913), 22–23; *China at the Crossroads* (1936), 57, 60–62, 63, 76, 98, 199, 234; "China's Desire to Retain the Best in Her Own Tradition" (1914), 24; *China: Whence and Whither?* (1934), 57; "Chinese Theatre: Development and Technique" (lecture, 1955), 105; "Chinese Themes on the Stage—A Comment on

'Mr. Wu'" (1914), 26–27; "Civilization and Social Philosophies" (1938), 61, 189, 273n18; "Education for Modernization in China" (dissertation, 1922), 38–40, 60, 76; "The Gospel in China" (1914), 201; *The Intruder*, 27; *The Man in Grey*, 27, 28; *Mei Lanfang in America: Reviews and Criticism* (foreword), 54; *Mu Lan* (play, 1921), 38; "My View of the United Nations" (1948), 85–86; "National Ideals," 21; *The New Order Cometh* (1915), 28–29, 234; "A New World: A New Attitude" (1915), 201; "New Year in Princeton" (poem, 1935), 59; "The Problems of the Pacific" (lecture, 1920), 38; "Redirecting Educational Effort in China" (1933), 34; "The Rising Consciousness of Civic Responsibility Among the Students of China" (1919), 33; "The Second Phase of China's Struggles" (1939), 71–73; "Shakespeare in China" (1915), 1; "The Teachings of Confucius" (lecture, 1921), 46; "Universities and National Reconstruction in China" (1939), 71; writings in Chinese, 255, 274n4; *Xin Cun Zheng* [*The New Village Head*] (play), 31, 47

Chang, Ruth [Hsin-Yueh] (second daughter of PCC), 18, 46–47, 54, 68, 104, 108, 254; education and career of, 109; on father's heart attacks in Chile, 78; on father's relationship with family, 103; in wartime China, 74, 107

Chang, Stanley [Yuan-Feng] (second son of PCC), 5, 12, 20, 143, 249, 253–55, 258n11; biography of, 109–12; career of, 49; on Cassin's conflict with PCC, 179, 182, 185–86; on challenges to PCC's position at UN, 93–94; on Chang family's escape from Japanese invasion, 66–69; on community of scholars, 70; on creation of WHO, 84–85; on Dewey's influence, 41; on diplomatic travels, 77–78, 80–81, 104; on drafting of UN Declaration, 115–16; on father's heart attacks in Chile, 96; on father's library, 48; on father's religious attitudes, 202; on father's views of Chiang Kai-shek, 51; on "Great China" attitude of PCC, 167; higher education of, 234–35; on imperfections of PCC, 231, 243; on last years of father's life, 106–8; on life in

Turkey, 74–75; on Nankai Schools, 17, 18–19; on negotiations at Sperry, 184–85; on opera performance at China Institute, 54–55; on Pearl Harbor attack, 74; recollections of mother, 37–38; relationship with father, 87–89, 111, 253; on time immediately after father's death, 108–9; on travels of PCC, 58; on universities in China, 17–18; on Windsor boarding school, 87

Chang Poling [Shouchun] (older brother of PCC), 12, 45, 90, 204, 242, 257n1 (Intro.); Chiang Kai-shek and, 52; China Institute and, 41; Christian faith of, 23–24, 203; in Communist China, 86–87; death of, 18; Dewey's influence and, 42; Japanese invasion and, 66; Kuomintang regime and, 18; memorialization of, 105; Nankai Schools and, 57, 86, 246; Olympic Games and, 15–16, 258n21; PCC's relationship with, 13–14, 46, 102, 231; at Teachers College, Columbia U., 31

Chang Xihu (son of Chang Poling), 66
Chao, Y. R. (Zhao Yuanren), 20, 42, 48, 106, 111
Chaplin, Charlie, 54
Chen Duxiu, 32
Cheng Sze-Chuh, 254
Chen Heqin, 20–21
Chen Ning Yang, 20
Chiang Kai-shek, 9, 16, 30, 98, 101; Chang's critical attitude toward, 243, 249; Chinese civil war and, 90; Japanese invasion and, 69; Northern Expedition and, 49–50; second Chinese Revolution and, 50–52; Xi'an Incident and, 64–65
Chile, 119, 121, 124
Chile, Chang's diplomatic post in, 4, 5, 45, 77–81, 96, 102, 109; Chang's first heart attack and, 74, 78, 96, 156, 186; development issues and, 118
China: absence of religious conflicts in, 126; absorption of conquerors by, 98–99; Christian universities in, 258n22; contributions to human rights, 216–17; corruption in, 28, 50, 59, 91, 100; cultural traditions of, 236–38; drafting of UDHR and, 124, 183, 196–97, 245; foreign influences adopted by, 192; Han dynasty, 198–99, 228; history of Western relations

China: absence of religious conflicts in (continued) with, 60, 62; human rights failings of, 4, 134, 145; Japanese occupation of, 54; Japan's historical relationship with, 61; May Fourth Movement, 31–36, 232; as Middle Kingdom, 167, 185; Ming dynasty, 100; minority rights in, 142; modernization in, 10; Muslims in, 75–76; Nankai Schools, 14–19, 27; national identity of, 24; Olympic Games (2008) in, 15–16; railroad system, 22, 52; religion and politics in, 197–201; Shang dynasty, 217; slavery in, 232; social community forms in, 42; universities in, 17–18, 64, 71–72, 258n22; warlords/warlord period, 29, 30; Yuan dynasty, 199; Zhou dynasty, 217. *See also* modernization, in China; Qing (Manchu) dynasty

China, People's Republic of, 63, 93, 134, 246; Cultural Revolution (1966–1976), 207; human rights concepts in, 245. *See also* Communist Party, Chinese (CCP)

China, Republic of, 9, 23, 119, 253; in 1910s, 29–30; Chiang Kai-shek and, 49–52; Constitution (1946), 228; declaration of (1912), 11, 199, 245; flight to Taiwan, 82, 253; loss of civil war with Communists, 92–93; notion of nation-state and, 63; revolution of 1911 and, 30, 37; United Nations (UN) and, 82, 141–44. *See also* Kuomintang (KMT)

China at the Crossroads (Chang, 1936), 57, 60–62, 63, 76, 98, 199, 234

China Institute (New York), 18, 26, 105, 258n26; opera performance at, 54–55; ties to Boxer Indemnity Scholarship Program, 41

"China's Desire to Retain the Best in Her Own Tradition" (Chang, 1914), 24

China: Whence and Whither? (Chang, 1934), 57

Chinese language: Cantonese, 36, 232; Mandarin, 36, 37, 110; Shanghainese (Wu), 36–37

Chinese opera, 53–55

Chinese Revolution, The (Holcombe), 76

Chinese Student Monthly, 21

Chinese Students' Christian Association, 23

"Chinese Theatre: Development and Technique" (Chang lecture, 1955), 105

"Chinese Themes on the Stage—A Comment on 'Mr. Wu'" (Chang, 1914), 26–27

Ching Ling, 80

Chin Shih-huang, Emperor, 147

Christianity, 23–24, 39, 126, 142, 198; Catholicism, 120, 122, 130, 216; Chang Poling's Christian faith, 23–24; Chang's attitude toward, 201–4, 250; Chinese attitude toward, 192; ethical rules within, 200; Greek Orthodox, 120, 130; Malik's Thomism, 120, 126, 130, 144, 178; metaphysics and, 196–97, 238; Methodism, 79, 80, 202; Protestantism, 216, 219; student groups, 239

Chungking, city of, 68, 73, 83

Chung Shu Lo, 246

Churchill, Winston, 117

Cisneros, Perez, 150

civilization, European prejudices and rhetoric of, 171–72, 173

"Civilization and Social Philosophies" (Chang, 1938), 61, 189, 273n18

civil and political rights, 102, 136–37, 152, 174; economic rights prioritized over, 251; European Enlightenment and, 144, 216; as rights of option, 137

civil rights movement, US, 217

civil service, in China, 11, 13, 70, 87, 95

civil war, Chinese, 4, 10, 82, 92–93, 253; Chang's attitude toward, 97–99; China's representation at UN and, 93–96; collapse of KMT–CCP coalition, 91–92

Clark University, 23, 25, 26, 36, 51, 79, 148; Chinese scholarship students at, 20–21; Christian student circles at, 201; debate team, 77; degrees in psychology and pedagogy, 19–20; honorary doctorate for Chang, 71

Cold War, 105, 122, 123, 126, 136

Colombia, 79

colonialism, 21, 156, 173, 182, 194

Columbia University, 20, 28, 34, 36, 37, 55; Chang's doctoral studies at, 36, 38; Chang speech given at (1938), 71; Chang's teaching position at, 82; China Institute and, 26; Dewey as Chang's teacher at, 203; honorary doctorate for Chang, 86, 148;

Philosophical Club, 41; Teachers College, 20, 31, 105
Commission on Human Rights, UN, 1, 25, 86, 128, 183; approval process for UDHR and, 124, 126; Chang as vice-chairman of, 83, 118, 129, 141, 142–43, 148; "culture and science" article and, 137, 138; four fundamental freedoms and, 117; on "international jurisprudence" of human rights, 121; members' qualifications for, 96; preamble and articles, 122; rights of minorities and, 175; voting rounds in, 196
Communism, 1, 4–5, 18, 50–51, 52; authoritarian social ideals and, 173; Chang's critical attitude toward, 204; Chang's criticism of, 43, 97–99, 249, 251; Chinese revolution (1949), 50; coalitions with Kuomintang (KMT), 49–50; collapse in Eastern Europe, 134; quasi-religious function of, in China, 199
Communist Party, Chinese (CCP), 207, 251; coalitions with Kuomintang (KMT), 65, 73, 90–91; creation of (1921), 32; Long March, 64; suppression of religion under, 199; Xi'an Incident and, 64–65. See also China, People's Republic of
"compatibilism," (concerning Confucianism and human rights), 208
complex justice, 244
compromise, 218, 220–24
Confucian philosophy, 21, 44, 120–21, 125; art of living and, 223, 226; benevolence concept, 149; Chang as Confucian, 204–7; changing Communist views of, 207; on conditions for peace, 169; on conflict resolution, 168–69; education and, 35; European Enlightenment philosophers influenced by, 214; five relations principle, 209; focus on the human being, 40; Golden Rule, 27, 210, 212, 271n49; harmony versus sameness, 126, 265n23; human rights and, 207–10; metaphysics and, 196; proverbs, 217–18; secular ethics of, 62
Confucius, 12, 84, 89, 101, 105, 185, 237; China's resurgent interest in, 3, 251; civil service in China and, 11; human rights thinking and, 145; "problem of religion" and, 200; on rectification of terms, 154–55; as secularly oriented philosopher, 200–201; societal engagement of, 250; "two-man mindedness" (ren) and, 212; Voltaire and, 238
conscience, 44, 180, 223; in Article 1 of UDHR, 151, 196, 197, 211, 219, 222, 226, 229; European Enlightenment and, 215; freedom of religion and, 230; as inner moral tribunal, 213; outraged conscience of mankind, 139, 159; rejection of metaphysics/theology and, 194, 195; "thin" metaphysics and, 165; "two-man mindedness" (ren) translated as, 226
Convention on the Elimination of All Forms of Discrimination against Women (1979), 134
Convention of Peking (1905), 10
Convention on the Prevention and Punishment of the Crime of Genocide, 122
Convention on the Rights of the Child (1989), 134
Convention on the Rights of Persons with Disabilities (2006), 134
Convention against Torture and Other Cruel, Inhuman or Degrading Treatment or Punishment (1984), 134
Council of Europe, 186
Counts, Geroge S., 263n13
Courage (Brown), 241
Covenant on Civil and Political Rights, 123, 133
Covenant on Economic, Social and Cultural Rights, 123, 133
Craig, Gordon, 48, 54
creative adjustment, 191
Crescent Moon Society (Xinyue), 36, 46–47
crimes against humanity, 132
Cruft, Rowan, 137
Cuba, 121, 228
cultural relativism, 171–73, 182–83
Cultural Revolution (1966–1976), 207
culture, right to, 224
Czechoslovakia, 122

Dalton School, 41
Danchenko, Vladimir Nemirovich, 54
Darwin, Charles, 199
Davie, Grace, 263n78
Declaration of Independence, US (1776), 131, 164, 216

Declaration of the Rights of Man and of the
  Citizen (France, 1789), 131, 164, 226
decolonization, 134
de Gaulle, Charles, 116, 129, 183
democracy, 11, 33, 71, 143; Chinese civil war
  and faded hopes for, 91–92; "democracy
  of merit," 76; democratic freedoms rooted
  in Chinese history, 146; Dewey's ideas
  on, 44; education and, 40, 42; "fake
  democracy" in Taiwan, 94, 243, 245, 249;
  promotion of, 229; suppression of, 133;
  Western ascendancy and, 39
Deng Yingchao, 17
Denmark, 45
Dewey, John, 20, 31, 64, 193, 258n26;
  Chang's doctoral dissertation and, 40;
  drafting of UN Declaration and, 101;
  influence on Chang and his brother,
  40–44, 105, 243; pragmatist philosophy
  of, 43, 203, 204, 207; views on religion
  and atheism, 203–4
dignity, human, 136, 150, 153, 164, 229,
  267n35; as core feature of UDHR, 140;
  European Enlightenment and, 210;
  respect for, 137; violations of, 194
disease epidemics, 83
diversity: ethical agreement in, 169–71;
  unity in, 188, 236
Doctors without Borders, 134
Doll's House, A (Ibsen play), 48, 49, 83, 242
Duan Maolan, 18
Dukes, Charles, 118
Dworkin, Ronald, 153, 243, 244

Eastern Bloc, 96, 119, 122, 125, 128, 144
Economic and Social Council (ECOSOC),
  UN, 83, 84, 85, 96, 97, 128, 183; drafting
  of UDHR and, 124; Malik as head of, 130;
  preference for single declaration to
  General Assembly, 122
Eden, Anthony, 90
education, 38, 45, 84, 102, 137, 155; centrality
  to realization of human rights, 168;
  Confucian ideal of learning, 35, 259n67;
  cultural identity and, 175–76; development
  of human personality and, 149; Dewey's
  ideas on, 40–44; in final years of Qing
  dynasty, 10–12, 190; full development of
  human personality and, 35, 259n67;
  implementation of human rights and, 136;
preservation of culture and, 145; right to,
  137, 149, 163, 175; role in promotion of
  human rights, 244; UDHR as tool for
  moral education, 163; universities in
  China, 64, 71–72, 178–79, 258n22
"Education for Modernization in China"
  (Chang, dissertation, 1922), 38–40, 60, 76
egoism, 44
Egypt, 124
emergency, states of, 133
Enemy of the People, An (Ibsen play), 48
Enlightenment, European, 60, 62, 131, 136,
  182, 222; civil and political rights claimed
  in, 144; commonality with Chinese
  philosophy, 158, 238; freedom conceptualized
  by, 180; French philosophers, 180, 214,
  216, 217; human dignity and, 210; human
  rights legacy and, 225–26; rights conceptualized
  in, 214–17; UDHR premised on
  Western rights traditions of, 205
Epstein, Israel, 65–66
equality, 153
Estonia, 31
European Convention on Human Rights
  (1950), 134, 136–37
European Court of Human Rights, 129
evolution, theory of, 199
extraterritoriality, 22–23, 259n39, 262n55

Fairbanks, Douglas, 54
Faisal II, King, 75
Falun Gong, 199
famine, 22, 38, 260n72
Farley, Frank, 242
fascism, 2, 4, 133
"February 28 Incident," 96
feudalism, 60, 75, 215, 226
Fists of Righteous Harmony, 9
floods, 22, 31, 51
Foreign Office, Chinese, 26, 83
Formashev, V. I., 96
Formosa. *See* Taiwan (Formosa)
France, 10, 18, 45, 141, 180; centralist state
  traditions of, 181; as colonial power, 22,
  56, 171, 182; Commission on Human
  Rights and, 119; contributions to human
  rights, 216; drafting of UDHR and, 121,
  124, 183, 184, 228; Vichy regime, 129
freedoms, four fundamental, 117, 226
Freud, Sigmund, 20

Galsworthy, John, 48, 49
General Assembly, UN, 92, 95, 122, 123, 127, 154, 187; international bill of rights and, 227; UDHR approved by, 238. *See also* Third Committee for Social Humanitarian and Cultural Affairs
Geneva Convention, Fourth, 122
genocide, 194
Germany, 45, 141; as colonial power, 22; Nazi regime, 132–33, 156, 161, 170, 172
Gibbon, Edward, 214
Gingling University (Nanking), 31
Giraud, Emile, 121
Glendon, Mary Ann, 6, 205–6
globalization, 2, 4
Goethe, Johann Wolfgang von, 214
Golden Rule, The, 27, 210, 212
Goldsmith, Oliver, 214
"Gospel in China, The" (Chang, 1914), 201
Great Neck, Long Island, 96, 98
Greece, ancient, 31
Greenpeace, 134
Guangdong Province, 11

Hall, G. Stanley, 19–20
Han dynasty, 198–99, 228
Hanping Chu, 110, 111
happiness, maximizing of, 136
Harvard University, 16
Hawaii, 57–59
Heaney, Seamus, 135
Heidegger, Martin, 130
Hinduism, 125
Hitler, Adolf, 75, 132–33
Hobbes, Thomas, 161
Hodgson, William, 116
Holcombe, Arthur N., 76
Holocaust, 2, 127, 132, 156
Hong Kong, 95, 104
Hong Xiuquan, 199
Hsia Chin Lin, 94–95
Huiyn Lin, 47
human nature, dual nature of, 157–58, 160, 197, 249
human rights, 43, 117, 144; authority of the state and, 181; broad conception of, 227; Confucian traditions and, 3, 207–10, 257n2 (Intro.); cross-cultural legitimacy of, 139; cultural relativist critique of, 171–73; definitions of, 131, 138; emphasis on human part of, 215; in European colonies, 182–83; family issues and, 235; general and academic interest in, 247; global civil community of, 134; historical precursors of, 118; international community norms for, 127; interpersonal relations and, 2; law and Western notions of, 208; moral obligations and, 132; national constitutions and, 123; rule of law and, 61; violations of, 132, 156, 168, 209, 246
Human Rights Watch, 134
Humphrey, John, 4, 5, 25, 78–79, 92, 104, 111, 241; on Chang as master of compromise, 218, 221; on Chang's attitude toward communism, 97–98; on Chang's death, 108; on Chang's interest in Lao-Tsu, 264n7; Commission on Human Rights and, 119; on conflict between Chang and Cassin, 186; on conflict between Chang and Malik, 175, 176–77; diary of, 25, 78, 97–98, 175, 246–47, 264n7; first meeting for work on UDHR and, 119–20, 121; importance in drafting team of UDHR, 128; impressions of Chang, 147–48; inventory of previous rights documents, 194; as legal expert, 129, 131, 145; on Soviet objections to Chang's position at UN, 96; in UN Declaration writing group, 115, 116; working relationship with Chang, 174
Hundred Days Reform, 47
Hung Shen, 38
Hu Shi, 9, 20, 41, 90, 258n26; Crescent Moon Society and, 36, 47; in Hawaii, 58, 105; in May Fourth Movement, 32

Ibn Battuta, 75
Ibsen, Henrik, 47, 242
ideologies, 189–90
Ignatieff, Michael, 134
"incompatibilism" (concerning Cofucianism and human rights), 208
India, 124, 192
individual, the, 43, 152, 166, 204; brotherhood (community) and, 150; dignity of, 136, 153; duties of, 151; human rights ethics and, 136; "liberal atomism" and, 144; Roman law and, 216; romantic nationalism as threat to, 161; the state and, 162; status in international law, 135; UDHR emphasis on, 3; unique value of, 202

individualism, 48, 212, 234; Dewey's criticism of, 43; as "one-man mindedness," 212; selfish, 241, 244
individuality, 39, 40, 161
industrialization, 44
information, freedom of, 86, 155
intercultural dialogue, 2, 140, 210, 219; creative changes and, 188–93; East-West cultural mediation, 239–41; UN Declaration and, 193–97
International Bank for Reconstruction and Development, 86
International Bill of Rights, 153, 184
International Conference of Pacific Nations (1933), 57
International Convention on the Elimination of All Forms of Racial Discrimination (1965), 133–34
International Labor Organization (ILO), 85, 117
International Monetary Fund, 86
Intruder, The (Chang), 27
Iran, 134
Iraq, 74, 75, 104
Islam, 75–77, 124, 125, 198, 205, 240

Japan, 10, 18, 27, 101; colonial policies and atrocities committed in World War II, 55–56, 73, 98, 118–19, 156–57, 261n27; as colonial power, 22, 183; cultural imports from the West, 24; defeat in Second World War, 54; geopolitical ambitions in China, 31; historical relationship with China, 61; importing of Western technology, 192; militarism, 138; Pearl Harbor attacked by, 74, 130; top-down command structure in, 191; wars with China, 10, 14, 19, 41
Jiangxi Province, 64

Kandel, Isaac, 41
Kant, Immanuel, 210, 216
Kapakas, F. C., 53
Katz-Suchy (Polish UN representative), 96
Keats, John, 36
Keller, Helen, 90
Kellogg, Frank, 56
Kellogg-Briand Pact, 56–57
Khan, Sir Muhammad Zafrulla, 125
Khrushchev, Nikita, 259n39

Kilpatrick, William Heard, 41, 43, 105
King, Martin Luther, Jr., 159, 217
Kipling, Rudyard, 173
Koo, Wellington, 26
Korea, North, 134
Korean War, 95, 123
Koretskij, Vladimir, 116
Krumbein, Fréderick, 163
Kung, H. H., 80
Kunming, 67–68, 72
Kuomintang (KMT), 18, 29, 101, 231, 243, 259n39; Chang's critical attitude toward, 249; civil war with Communists, 92; coalitions with Communists, 49–50, 65, 73, 90–91; flight to Taiwan (Formosa), 93; Leninist idea of the party and, 50; martial law regime of, 96; UN representation of China and, 93–94; women's rights and, 236. *See also* China, Republic of
Kuo Ping-Wen, 20, 258n26

Lady Windermere's Fan (Wilde play), 49
Lagerkvist, Johan, 271n47
Lake Success, Long Island, 115, 121, 157
language reform, 9, 20; replacement of Classical with Vernacular Chinese, 32; simplification of written language, 22
Lao-Tzu, 73, 264n7
Lary, Diana, 9
Laski, Harold, 71
Latvia, 31
law, international, 101, 131, 135, 166
League of Nations, 51, 56, 57, 129, 261n27; Cassin's involvement with, 186; failure of, 193–94; minority rights and, 117, 135
Lebanon, 119, 120, 130, 175, 176
Leibniz, Gottfried Wilhelm, 214
Lew, Timothy T. F., 203
Liang Qichao, 47
Liang Sicheng, 47
liangxin ("benevolent heart"), 212, 219
liberal atomism, 154
liberating inventiveness, 192
liberalism, 9, 21, 246; Dewey's ideas on education and, 41; "social liberalism" of Dewey, 43; student movements, 167
Li Dazhao, 32
life, right to, 182
Lindström, Ulla, 128, 138
Lithuania, 31

localization, of interests and understanding, 146
Locke, John, 216
Lodén, Torbjörn, 271n50
"Looking Back on My Five Periods of Service in Diplomacy" (Hsia Chin Lin), 94–95
Loomis School (Windsor, Conn.), 80
Lowell, Amy, 38
Lu Xun, 32
Lu Zongyu, 33
Lytton Report (1932), 57, 261n27

"Madman's Diary, A" (Lu Xun), 32
Magna Carta (1215), 134, 208, 228
Malik, Charles, 6, 98, 108, 125, 197, 225, 241; Christianity (Thomism) of, 120, 126, 130, 144, 177, 205–6; on danger of collectivism, 161; diary of, 1, 108, 164, 175, 177, 184, 187, 246–47; humanistic background of, 145; on human nature, 161; importance in drafting team of UDHR, 128; as a key author of UDHR, 155; philosophical differences with Chang, 119–20, 147, 164–65, 174–79, 248; rights of minorities and, 231; on sources of Chang's ideas, 4–5; in UN Declaration writing group, 115, 116
Malik, Habib, 108, 125–26, 164, 176, 177
Malik, Jakob, 185
Manchukuo, 56, 261n27
Manchuria, 29, 55, 73, 92, 261n27
"mandate of heaven," 132, 217
Manichaeism, 199
Man in Grey, The (Chang), 27, 28
"Man Was Made to Mourn: A Dirge" (Burns, 1784), 159
Mao Zedong, 5, 9, 17, 18, 97, 236; emergence as Communist leader, 65; increasing popularity in China, 91; measures taken against religion, 199; rise to power, 54, 82; victory in Chinese civil war, 95, 96
Ma Qianli, 12
Marco Polo Bridge Incident (1937), 65
Maritain, Jacques, 170–71
Marxism, 5, 122, 144
materialism, consumerist, 1, 39, 40, 50, 106, 176, 244
materialism, philosophical, 195
May Fourth Movement, 31–36, 232

May Thirtieth Movement, 35–36
McCarthy, Sen. Joseph, 1, 105
Mehta, Hansa, 4, 128, 231, 247
Mei Lanfang, 53–55, 57, 59, 63
Mei Lanfang in America: Reviews and Criticism (foreword by Chang), 54
Mei Yiqi, 14
Meiji restoration, 11
Mencius (Meng Tse), 61, 84, 101, 145, 237, 271n49; on human moral growth, 158; on inherent natural human qualities, 163; "problem of religion" and, 200; on revolution against unjust rulers, 209, 217; societal engagement of, 250; "two-man mindedness" (*ren*) and, 212
Meng Chih, 41
metaphysics, 161, 219; art of living preferred to, 204, 223, 226, 237; Chang's criticism of, 194–96, 229; natural rights and, 131; thin and thick, 165, 226
metaphors (used by Chang), 5, 34, 109, 192, 218
Mexico, 42, 95
Meyerhold, Vsevolod, 54
Miller, Mrs. Todd M., 80
Ming dynasty, 100
minorities, rights of, 117, 134, 135, 175, 231
Miracle Worker, The (play and film), 90
missionaries, 10, 24, 29
modernization, in China, 10, 22, 30, 62, 273n18; Chang's dissertation on, 38–40; comparison with Japan's modernization, 61, 190–91; education and, 43; in Nanking period, 50; phases in social transformation, 190–92; republican revolution and, 101; science/technology and, 55
Molière, 48, 59, 73
Monroe, Paul, 41, 258n26
Montesquieu, Baron de, 62
Morsink, Johannes, 151
Moyn, Samuel, 117, 247
Mui Tsai ("little sister") custom, 232
Mukden incident (1931), 56, 261n27
Mu Lan (Chang, 1921), 38
multiculturalism, 2, 193
music, 87, 88, 89, 106
Muslim countries, 22, 23
Mutual Friendship Treaty (1942), 75
"My View of the United Nations" (Chang, 1948), 85–86

Nankai Schools, 14–19, 27, 28, 248; alumni of, 41; China's social transformation and, 100; Chinese nationalism and, 236–37; in Chungking, 57, 68; Confucian ideal of learning and, 35; Dewey's ideas on education and, 42; expansion of, 101; fame of, 89; PCC's teaching in, 30, 47; reclaimed property of, 83
Nankai University, 16, 17, 45, 47, 53, 246; Chang as principal, 47; China's social transformation and, 100; Japanese invasion and, 65–66, 72, 262n55; at Kunming, 68; reclaimed property of, 83
Nanking, 67, 69, 71, 91
Nanking period (1928–1937), 50, 80
"National Ideals" (Chang), 21
nationalism, Chinese, 21, 236–37
nation-states, 63, 140, 166, 172, 179
natural law, 120, 153, 177
natural rights, 131, 132, 215, 238
Nazism, 132–33, 138, 156, 161
Netherlands, 144, 171, 195
New Atlantis, The (Bacon), 150
New Culture Movement, 20, 32, 33, 36, 43
New Life Movement, 50
New Order Cometh, The (Chang, 1915), 28–29, 234
New Village Head, The (Chang 1918), 31, 47
"New World, A: A New Attitude" (Chang, 1915), 201
"New Year in Princeton" (Chang poem, 1935), 59
New Youth Magazine, 32
Nine-Power Treaty (1912), 56
North China Famine (1920–1921), 260n72
Northern Expedition (1926–1927), 49
Nuremburg Trials, 75

Olympic Games, 15–16
Opium Wars, 10, 181
Orientalism (Said, 1978), 27
Origin of Species, The (Darwin), 199
Ottoman Empire, 22
overlapping consensus, 188, 219, 243
over-specialization, 146
Oxfam, 134

Paine, Thomas, 216
Pakistan, 125
Palestine, 126

Panama, 5, 121, 183
Papen, Franz von, 75
Parkhurst, Helen, 41
patriotism, 11, 21, 166, 167
Pavlov (Russian delegate), 96, 159
peace organizations, international, 194
Peking Opera, 53
Peng Chun Chang. *See* Chang, P. C.
People's Liberation Army (PLA), 93
People's Political Council, 70
Peru, 79
Peterson, Willard J., 62–63, 198, 207–8, 209, 232
Philippines, 119, 183
Phillips Academy (Andover, Mass.), 16
Pian, Ted, 111
Pickford, Mary, 54
Plautus, 159
Poland, 122
"political cultural exchange," 60
Polo, Marco, 75
pragmatism, 86, 207, 221
Princeton University, 16
"Problems of the Pacific, The" (Chang lecture, 1920), 38
Progressive Education (journal), 61
property rights, 244
Prost, Antoine, 6, 186
Pufendorf, Samuel von, 159
Puyi (last Qing emperor), 29, 56

Qian Xuantong, 32
Qing (Manchu) dynasty, 10–14, 22, 37, 258n7; decadent final years of, 100; disaffection with, 29; education system of, 10–12; foreign origins of, 100–101; Taiping Rebellion and, 199; toppled by revolution (1911), 51
Quesnay, François, 214

racial discrimination, 134
racism, 170, 172, 194
Rawls, John, 188, 219, 220, 243
"Redirecting Educational Effort in China" (Chang, 1933), 34
Red Turban Rebellion, 198, 199
Reinhardt, Max, 48
religion, 79, 203–4, 242, 262–63n78
religion, freedom of, 117, 125–26, 133, 140, 148–49, 154, 250; comparison of Europe

and China, 197–201; as freedom of conscience, 230; humanization of humanity and, 163; liberal view of, 219; metaphysics and, 194; religious plurality, 171; Saudi Arabia's criticism of Article 18 and, 125, 198. *See also* Article 1, of UDHR
religious neutrality, 2, 3, 140, 174, 223, 250
ren (Confucian concept). See "two-man mindedness"
René Cassin and Human Rights (Winters and Prost), 6
rights of claim, 137
Rights of Man, The (Wells, 1940), 132
rights of option, 137
"Rising Consciousness of Civic Responsibility Among the Students of China, The" (Chang, 1919), 33
Rogge, Jacques, 16
Romulo, Carlos, 128, 184, 247
Roosevelt, Eleanor, 4, 6, 41, 96, 112, 124, 241; on absence of norms for human rights, 127; on Article 1 of UDHR, 213–14; as chairman of Comission on Human Rights, 130, 226, 246; on culture and flourishing of individuals, 205; on first meeting for work on UDHR, 120–21; importance in drafting team of UDHR, 128; opposition to minority rights, 176; on UDHR as new Magna Carta, 134; UN Declaration writing group of, 115–16, 127; UN Economic and Social Council and, 118; as US representative to UN General Assembly, 130; women's rights and, 231; working relationship with Chang, 174
Roosevelt, Franklin D., 51, 92, 117, 130, 226
Rousseau, Jean-Jacques, 165, 212, 229
Russell, Bertrand, 42
Russia, post-Soviet, 134
Russia, Tsarist, 10, 22, 56

Said, Edward W., 27
Sandburg, Carl, 38
Santa Cruz, Hernán, 4, 128, 145, 147, 148, 180, 246
Santayana, George, 220
Saudi Arabia, 122, 125–26
Schabas, William, 247, 255
Schenck, Norman C., 59
"scholar ghost," 34

science, 21, 24, 39, 204; China's modernization and, 55, 192; religion in conflict with, 199–200; right to scientific advancement, 150; scientific revolution, 215; Western ascendancy and, 60
"Second Phase of China's Struggles, The" (Chang, 1939), 71–73
secular (and secularism), 62, 102, 180, 221, 250
self-determination, 175
self-interest, national, 169
Sen, Amartya, 244
Shaanxi Province, 93
"Shakespeare in China" (Chang, 1915), 1
Shandong Province, 29, 260n72; Boxer Rebellion origins in, 9; as German-occupied territory, 32; Japanese control of, 31, 35
Shanghai, city of, 18, 49, 57; colonial powers' control in, 56, 199; creation of CCP in (1921), 32; French zone, 74; Wu Chinese spoken in region of, 36–37
Shanxi Province, 30, 64
Shape of Things to Come, The (Wells), 58
Shelley, Percy Bysshe, 36
Shklar, Judith, 244
Sino-Japanese War, First (1894–1895), 10
Sino-Japanese War, Second, 14, 64–69, 100, 102; Chang's "propaganda trips" and, 69–73, 239–40; Japanese bombing raids, 19. *See also* World War, Second
slavery, 133, 137, 215, 232
Slavery Convention (1926), 117
Social virtues, 27, 207
Societal transformations, 190–93
Soong, Ai-ling, 80
Soong, Charlie, 80
Soong, T. V., 26, 82–83
Soong May Ling [Song Meiling] (Madam Chiang Kai-shek), 50, 51, 71, 82–83, 89; address to US Congress (1943), 79, 80; as international celebrity, 79–80
South Africa, 122, 134, 159
Southwest Associated University, 68
Soviet Union, 42, 59, 91, 119; Chang's position at UN questioned by, 93, 96; Cold War and, 105; Commission on Human Rights, and, 119; drafting of UDHR and, 121, 124, 183; position on implementation of UDHR, 174

speech, freedom of, 4, 43, 146, 147, 218, 251
Sperry Gyroscope plant (Lake Success, NY), 81, 115, 121, 184, 185
Stalin, Joseph, 91, 259n39
Stanislavski, Konstantin, 48, 54
"Statement of Essential Human Rights" (American Law Institute, 1945), 132
Stout, Jeffrey, 217
Strife (Galsworthy play), 49
Stubborn Doctor, The [An Enemy of the People] (Ibsen play), 48
Study of History, A (Toynbee), 48
Sullivan, Anne, 90
Summer School of Pacific and Oriental Affairs (Honolulu), 57
Sun Tzu, 92
Sun Yat-sen, 29, 36, 49, 50, 51, 270n10; education system and, 263n10; as founder of Chinese Republic, 209; inner circle of, 80
Sun Yat-sen University (Canton), 17
Sun Yu, 17

Tagore, Rabindranath, 36, 47
Taiping Rebellion, 29, 37, 198, 199
Tairov, Alexander, 54
Taiwan (Formosa), 4, 51, 93, 105, 249, 253
Taoism, 106, 198, 250
Tao Xingzhi (T'ao Hsing-chih), 34, 42
Tarski, Alfred, 49
"Teachings of Confucius, The" (Chang lecture, 1921), 46
theater, 26–29, 31
theism, 153, 177, 178, 195, 222
theology, 153, 195
There Is Another China anthology, 86
Third Committee for Social Humanitarian and Cultural Affairs, 124, 127, 178, 263n5; clarity as defining feature of UDHR and, 138; UDHR articles debated in, 130, 143–44; wording of Geneva text and, 196. *See also* General Assembly, UN
Third World's Christian Citizenship Conference (1919), 33
Thomas of Aquinas, 120, 130, 164, 205, 206
Tianjin (Tientsin), 12, 14, 18, 45, 57; Japanese control of, 65, 67, 262n55; Nankai Schools in, 83
tolerance, pluralistic, 2, 126, 173, 222; Chinese philosophy and, 200; freedom of religion and, 198, 250

torture, 133, 137
totalitarianism, 161
Toynbee, Arnold, 48
trade unions, 131
Treaty of Nanjing (1842), 259n39
Truman, Harry S., 130
Ts'a Sieu-Tsu [Sieu-Tsu Ts'a] (wife of PCC), 36–37, 38–39, 45–46
Tsiang Tingfu (Jiang Tingfu), 94
Tsien Hsue-shen, 20
Tsinghua School, 46, 47
Tsinghua University, 14
Turkey, 102, 134
Turkey, Chang's diplomatic post in, 4, 42, 45, 73–77, 81, 109; cultural interactions and, 118; interest in relation of Islam to Chinese culture, 240
Twenty-One Demands, 29, 32
"two-man mindedness" (*ren*), 143, 211–14, 215, 226, 238

Ukraine, 122
Uncompromising dogmatism, 172–73
United Nations (UN), 4, 22, 25, 28; Charter, 118, 135; Chinese (nationalist) delegation, 51; Conference on Freedom of Information, 86, 155, 170; Food and Agriculture Organization, 85–86; formation of, 80, 81, 82–90; question of China's representation at, 93–96; temporary premises on Long Island, 110; UNESCO, 170. *See also* Economic and Social Council; General Assembly
United States (US), 1, 10, 23, 35, 100, 109, 141; anti-communism in, 105–6; drafting of UDHR and, 124; "frontier mentality" of American society, 42, 273n10; racism in, 106; rapid pace of change in, 43–44; support for Taiwan, 95
Universal Declaration of Human Rights (UDHR), 1, 116–19, 152; Article 2 (antidiscrimination article), 224; Article 18 (freedom of religion), 125–26, 198; Article 27 ("culture and science" article), 137; Chinese philosophy as influence on, 61; Confucian philosophy and, 40, 226; "core articles" in, 148; drafting of, 2, 5, 257n2 (Intro.); drafting team, 128–31; duties in, 151; fiftieth anniversay of signing of (1998), 111;

finished declaration, 131–33; historical catalysts for, 132–33, 156; history of, 133–34; humanization of man as ethical function of, 157–63, 222, 237; human rights covenants, 264n30; implementation of, 166–69, 174; multicultural history of, 138–40; obstructive and facilitative factors for, 124–28; primary function of, 162, 194–95, 220, 237; properties of, 135–38; as result of compromise, 220–24; tenth anniversary (1958), 108; universality of, 251; vote in General Assembly on, 92. *See also* Article 1, of UDHR; Chang, P. C., drafting of UN Declaration and universalism, 3, 5
"Universities and National Reconstruction in China" (Chang, 1939), 71
University of Chicago, 55, 56, 148
University of Hawaii, 57, 105
urbanization, in China, 10, 44
Urquhart, Brian, 3
Uruguay, 124, 209
utilitarianism, 136

Vassar College, 36, 37
Versailles Peace Treaty (1919), 31–32
Vietnam, 67, 68
violence, state monopoly on, 163
Voltaire, 62, 214, 226, 238

Walzer, Michael, 84, 244
Wang Yi, 274n14
welfare, general, 151–52
welfare rights, 3, 208
Wellesley College, 16
Wells, H. G., 58, 132
Wen Jiaboa, 17
West, the, 42, 188–89, 193, 215; Chang as cultural mediator between China and, 239; China's intellectual contributions to, 75; China's material contributions to, 60, 62, 75; civilization argument and, 171–72; conflict between science and religion in, 199–200; cultural exports to China, 24; educational traditions of, 21; era of religious intolerance in, 197; imitation of, 192; period of ascendancy over China, 39; religious conflicts in, 126
Westphalia, Peace of (1648), 216

Whitehead, Alfred North, 130
White Lotus Movement, 199
"White Man's Burden, The" (Kipling), 173
White Paper on Human Rights (1991), 245
White Terror Period (Taiwan), 96
Wilde, Oscar, 48, 49
Will, Pierre Étienne, 142, 143, 210–11, 217, 253
Williams, Clifford, 58
Wilson, Geoffrey, 116
Winter, Jay, 6, 186
women's movements/rights, 131, 231
World Health Organization (WHO), 84, 86
World Made New, A (Glendon), 6
world state/world citizenship, 21, 101, 167
World War, First, 9, 31–32, 129
World War, Second, 2, 4, 10, 100, 117; Allied support to China, 80; as catalyst for UN Declaration, 132–33, 156; Chang's diplomatic service during, 77, 81; Chinese families and rituals undermined by, 233; duality of human nature and, 160; end of, 82; human rights catastrophes of, 162; as period of calm for Chang family, 77; UDHR and memories of, 127, 139. *See also* Sino-Japanese War, Second
Wright, Frank Lloyd, 89
Wu, John C. H. (Wu Jinxiong), 141, 142
Wu, K. C., 18
Wuhan, 69, 90
Wu Mi, 46

Xi'an Incident (1936), 64–65
Xin Cun Zheng [*The New Village Head*] (Chang play), 31, 47
Xinhai Revolution (1911), 9
Xu Zhimo, 36, 47

Yale University, 28
Yang Shi (mother of PCC), 13, 46
Yan Xin, 14
Yan Xishan, 30
Yellow Turban Rebellion, 198–99
Yen Jen-Ying, 107
YMCA, 23, 80
Yuan dynasty, 199
Yuan Shikai, 29, 32
Yugoslavia, 119, 122, 124
Yunnan Province, 72

Zhang Jiuan Zhang Yun Zhao (father of
  PCC), 12–13
Zhang Peng Chun. *See* Chang, P.C.
Zhang Xueliang, 64
Zhang Xun, 30
Zhang Zongxiang, 33

Zhao Yuanren. *See* Chao, Y. R.
Zheng Taoru, 18
Zhou dynasty, 217
Zhou Enlai, 17, 18, 33, 86, 98
Zhu Kezhen, 20
Zionism, 126

www.ingramcontent.com/pod-product-compliance
Lightning Source LLC
Chambersburg PA
CBHW032032300426
44117CB00009B/1028